# GENDER <u>IN</u> HISTORY

Series editors:
Lynn Abrams, Cordelia Beattie, Pam Sharpe and Penny Summerfield

The expansion of research into the history of women and gender since the 1970s has changed the face of history. Using the insights of feminist theory and of historians of women, gender historians have explored the configuration in the past of gender identities and relations between the sexes. They have also investigated the history of sexuality and family relations, and analysed ideas and ideals of masculinity and femininity. Yet gender history has not abandoned the original, inspirational project of women's history: to recover and reveal the lived experience of women in the past and the present.

The series Gender in History provides a forum for these developments. Its historical coverage extends from the medieval to the modern periods, and its geographical scope encompasses not only Europe and North America but all corners of the globe. The series aims to investigate the social and cultural constructions of gender in historical sources, as well as the gendering of historical discourse itself. It embraces both detailed case studies of specific regions or periods, and broader treatments of major themes. Gender in History titles are designed to meet the needs of both scholars and students working in this dynamic area of historical research.

*Men on trial*

## MANCHESTER
1824

Manchester University Press

# MEN ON TRIAL

## PERFORMING EMOTION, EMBODIMENT
## AND IDENTITY IN IRELAND, 1800–45

+= Katie Barclay =+

Manchester University Press

The right of Katie Barclay to be identified as the author of this work has been asserted by her in accordance with the Copyright, Designs and Patents Act 1988.

Published by Manchester University Press
Altrincham Street, Manchester M1 7JA

www.manchesteruniversitypress.co.uk

British Library Cataloguing-in-Publication Data
A catalogue record for this book is available from the British Library

ISBN 978 1 5261 3292 5 hardback

First published 2019

The publisher has no responsibility for the persistence or accuracy of URLs for any external or third-party internet websites referred to in this book, and does not guarantee that any content on such websites is, or will remain, accurate or appropriate.

Typeset by
Servis Filmsetting Ltd, Stockport, Cheshire
Printed by Lightning Source

For the men in my life
Steven, Dad, Liam, Gaius, Harry
and my many brothers-in-law

# Contents

# Figures

# Acknowledgements

The idea for this book originated when working for Professors Maria Luddy and Mary O'Dowd as a research assistant on their 'Marriage in Ireland, 1600–1925' project, funded by the Arts and Humanities Research Council. At that point – now almost a decade ago – studies of Irish masculinity were still embryonic. A small idea was developed into a coherent project with the help of some pilot funding by the Roberts Fund, University of Warwick, and that project in turn was the basis of a research fellowship at the Institute of Irish Studies, Queen's University, Belfast. I would like to thank Maria, Mary and Dominic Bryan for their support in these early stages as I conducted the core research and began to understand what was significant, as well as the institutions for their financial assistance. From there I went to work in the Australian Research Council Centre of Excellence in the History of Emotions and Department of History, University of Adelaide, where I found a cluster of colleagues interested in questions of law, emotion and gender. I would like to thank David Lemmings, Claire Walker, François Soyer, Merridee Bailey, Carly Osborn and Abaigéal Warfield for listening to early drafts and commenting on pieces of work. Amy Milka gets special mention for reading the whole manuscript, as do friends and colleagues elsewhere – Tanya Evans, Rosi Carr, Susan Broomhall and Joanne Begatio. Their feedback has been invaluable to making this a better book and me a better historian.

I would like to thank the staff at the National Library of Ireland (NLI) and National Archives of Ireland for their support with research and for tolerating my idiosyncratic pronunciation of Irish place names. The NLI, University of Adelaide Library, Board of Trinity College Dublin, Public Record Office of Northern Ireland, National Portrait Gallery, London and Mary Evans Picture Library have kindly provided permission to reproduce the images in this book. Part of Chapter 3 is developed and expanded in 'Performing emotion and reading the male body in the Irish court, c. 1800–1845', *Journal of Social History*, 51:1 (2017), 293–312. Perhaps reflecting the circle of academic life, I also thank Jean McBain for her research assistance in the last stages of this project.

Every academic book is sustained by our friends and family. I thank mine, not least Steven who has taught me so much about how manliness can be kind, patient, gentle, supportive and fun.

# Opening speeches: an introduction

A man never begins by positioning himself as an individual of a certain sex; he is a man, it goes without saying. (Simone de Beauvoir, 1949)

I am a man and I am a gentleman. (Peter Hoolihan, 1844)

Writing within a discussion of female alterity, De Beauvoir's claim located men as the norm against which women were defined. She argued that the ability of men to be 'sexless' – to never have to acknowledge or affirm their gender – was a position of power.[1] Peter Hoolihan claimed his gender and his class after being arrested by the Dublin Police for disturbing the peace due to his drunken singing.[2] His claim, 'I am a man and I am a gentleman', was an assertion of that same power De Beauvoir understood 'man' to hold. But, it was necessary because the political category of 'manhood' that Beauvoir identifies was not universally available to all in early nineteenth-century Ireland. In claiming to be a man, Hoolihan resisted the emasculation that he believed was inherent in the act of being arrested, something he associated with men lower down the social ladder – men who had fewer claims to political authority. In this, he was not alone.

The history of masculinity is now a burgeoning field with the way men created and understood their identities explored in different contexts, from marriage to the military.[3] Whilst early studies aimed to explore hegemonic, or dominant, perceptions of manhood and compared ideals to experience, it is now known that multiple masculinities can exist alongside each other, competing for control in different contexts (or not competing at all).[4] The relationship between masculinity and femininity is highlighted, where men make sense of themselves by what they are not, but, increasingly, it is recognised that it is how men made sense of each other that is key to their conception of self.[5] In the context of the late eighteenth and early nineteenth centuries, masculinity was not only central to identity, but to political rights, where gender determined access to suffrage and public office.[6]

This monograph contributes to a history of masculinity through an exploration of how men discussed and enacted manliness in the context of the Irish justice system. It has three main objectives: to explore how men from different social groups interacted in courtrooms; to highlight how they created, understood and used different resources for manliness in this process; and to think about the implications of their interactions for power relationships across class, ethnicity and in the context of political rights. This is a history of the important role that gender played in the production of social, legal and political power within courtrooms. Ultimately, it seeks to ascertain how men's performances of masculinity impacted on the justice which they received from the legal system.

Whilst Ireland's tumultuous history has ensured that the relationship between men of different social classes has not been ignored, there is very little work on Irish masculinity in any context or period.[7] Two notable exceptions are Padhraig Higgins' *A Nation of Politicians* and Joseph Valente's *The Myth of Manliness in Irish National Culture*. Higgins explores the politicisation of the Irish population through the Volunteer Movement in the 1770s and 1780s, highlighting that political participation was a gendered practice.[8] Valente situates the Irish nationalist movement of the late nineteenth century within a number of Victorian cultural motifs of masculinity, showing how the Irish used and failed to use these ideals in their claims for political rights.[9] *Men on Trial* situates itself between these works, focusing on the period after the 1798 Revolution and before the Irish famine, decades marked by agrarian unrest, the campaign for Catholic Emancipation and to repeal the 1801 Union of Britain and Ireland, increasing social control, seen in the expansion of policing and the broadening of the court system, and increased literacy, which led not only to a growing number of local newspapers but also increased reportage of Irish affairs. Whilst Higgins and Valente each look at a nationalist phenomenon and provide important insights into how they operated in gendered terms, this work focuses on men and works outwards to look at the implications arising from their behaviour in court for social class relationships and political power. It is a study of the ways that power is negotiated through social interaction, highlighting the significance of everyday gendered behaviours in the creation, maintenance and instability of the law, social class and national identity.

*Men on Trial* also contributes to a conversation about the functioning of legal systems across the United Kingdom. How courts operate, and why, and why people think they work like that, has changed over time, providing historians of the law and legal systems opportunity to discuss not only what happened, but the implications for present legal practice.[10] One of the key questions that emerges from this scholarship is whether the legal system is or was a space to determine 'truth' (whatever that may mean), or perhaps simply a consensus about what happened, and how these things relate to justice.[11] In a late eighteenth- and early nineteenth-century context, metaphysical debates aside, most people accepted that the legal system was meant to seek truth, where truth was an objective set of facts about what happened that was closely tied to normative judgements about how such facts should be interpreted. For many, this was underpinned by a belief in a deity that knew the truth of all things and would act on that knowledge in the afterlife. There was also a healthy level of scepticism around whether finding truth was achievable in practice.[12] Such attitudes were perhaps exasperated by the expansion of lawyers into the criminal courts in the eighteenth century (they had long been part of civil practice), which raised questions at the time and for historians about how their interventions shaped access to truth.[13] Yet, as has been shown, lawyers were not the only dynamic element in the courtroom, with jurors, judges, plaintiffs, defendants and others shaping the production of justice.[14]

This period also saw changes in evidentiary procedures. Whilst the credible witness remained key, and documents, clothing and other goods had always been used to support testimonies, scientists and doctors were bringing new forms of evidence to court and endowing it with the authority of their (sometimes newly) professional identities.[15] This book takes account of such developments whilst also looking seriously at men's performances of identity as part of what juries, judges and the general public used to determine both truth and justice. *Men on Trial* emphasises how wider social relationships and values were inextricably tied into the processes of justice, in a space that was made as much by the people as blackletter law.

### The Irish court as a 'performative space'

At the heart of the nineteenth-century justice system was the court, where men and women from different social backgrounds were prosecuted, sued or defended, often through middle-class, cosmopolitan male lawyers, using witnesses from all walks of life, before middle-class and elite all-male juries, and presided over by a male judge, usually from the middle or upper classes. It was a place where men, and occasionally women, told stories to men with the aim of convincing them to believe their version of events or the law. In this process, they drew on wider cultural discourses, including literature and folklore, as well as different spatial and rhetorical strategies, such as speech-making and banter, to help bring meaning to the disparate events of everyday experience.

Thinking about courts of law as spaces where performances occur is increasingly central to analyses of the law and to social histories built on legal records. The use of popular culture by lawyers and witnesses in shaping the stories that they told in court, the costumes worn by lawyers and judges within the United Kingdom court system, and that the courts provided a central form of entertainment to past societies, have been highlighted by historians and sociologists to emphasise the theatrical nature of legal practice.[16] The importance of courts as 'spectacles' designed to convey authority to a watching public, or alternatively as spaces for 'counter-theatre' where power could be contested, forms a central strand in scholarship of eighteenth-century law and order. Debate ranges from those that emphasise the legal system's judicial majesty and its importance in cowing the lower orders to those that argue that the ability of the ordinary person to intervene in courtroom dynamics acted as an effective restriction of its power.[17] The public is given heightened importance in shaping power dynamics in the nineteenth century, due to the increasing size of court audiences and because of the fixture of the court reporter, who transformed legal proceedings into copy for local or national papers.[18]

The performance of manliness was central to a legal system where men dominated as judges, juries and lawyers, and formed the majority of plaintiffs, defendants and witnesses. As Phillip Mackintosh and Clyde Forsberg argue, 'masculine behaviour in all its varied forms generates masculine identity'.[19] That the law was dominated by men was invisible in scholarly analysis for many years. As attention turned to women, their access to justice and later their ability to enter the profession, the maleness of the legal system has come into sharp relief.[20] The law is now understood as an instrument moulded by deeply held assumptions about gender. The classic historical example is the legal construction of homicide. Definitions of provocation that reduced the severity of a murder charge were built on experiences and emotions more closely associated with men than women. Women by their location in different spheres, such as the home rather than the alehouse, and because emotion is both cultural and gendered, had difficulty evidencing a performance that fulfilled the legal definition of provocation.[21] The masculine culture of the Inns of Court and the courtroom thus shaped how the law was accessed and practised.[22]

Court records have long been used by historians to reconstruct the past. The court is recognised as a site where ideas about gender and gendered behaviour were articulated, negotiated, redefined and legitimised.[23] Several important studies have demonstrated the reciprocal relationship between social constructions of gender and the law, with the courtroom a key site for enforcing and enabling gender norms.[24] Masculinity has been given some attention here. Martin Wiener, for example, argued that growing expectations that men exercise emotional self-control in the nineteenth century were initially contested by juries but ultimately led to harsher sentencing.[25] Historians have paid less attention to the *masculine culture* of the legal profession and how it shaped the practice of the law.[26] As importantly, and because historians typically access the legal system through process papers, how men negotiated masculinity in court – their use of bodies, clothes, language – has been ignored in favour of how people articulated ideas about gender or their gendered experiences. A focus on courtroom behaviours draws attention to the negotiation of competing masculinities and how they became central to justice.[27] Such performances turned the metaphorical theatre of the courtroom into an actual theatre where identity and power could be explored.

The court was more than a physical stage on which the actors involved in legal dramas played their parts for a watching community, it was a 'performative space'. As Henri Lefebvre suggests, and has since been developed by several theorists, space is both constituted by and produces social relations.[28] It is created through the interaction between physical location, landscape and architecture, the activity and bodies of people in that place, and the social norms and cultural meanings associated with all of the above. In this sense, the court is not the building, but the cultural product that results from bringing together plaintiffs, respondents, lawyers, judges, clerks, witnesses (and more) in the courtroom in the performance of legal business. The court is not a fixed entity, but inherently unstable, created in the everyday.[29]

Central to performative space is the idea that identity is constructed through performative practices. This 'dramaturgical model' was famously articulated by the anthropologist Erving Goffman, who thought that social reality was created through interaction between individuals within 'situations'. In these 'situations', individuals presented the most appropriate version of themselves required to achieve their aim in a specific social context ('a performance'). In effect, individuals had multiple 'selves'.[30] Judith Butler developed this model with her concept of 'performativity', where the repetition of culturally normative gestures generates the gendered self.[31] For Butler, the self does not pre-exist its performance, but is constituted through it. The self is therefore inherently unstable, 'becoming' through action.[32] Following Gilles Deleuze, as the self is created through interaction – through the negotiation of meaning – the self incorporates difference, so that it cannot be understood without its 'other'.[33] This model of selfhood is useful as it disrupts Western, individualised ideas of 'the self' as a stable and unified entity, which groups that are defined in terms of their alterity – that is in opposition to a norm – cannot access. It is more inclusionary, rebalancing power differentials through destabilising the 'norm', and emphasising the relational nature of self and its embeddedness within society.[34]

A performative model for self has implications for how power relationships within the court are understood, where power is defined loosely as the ability of people to influence the outcome of legal proceedings.[35] Rather than power being located in the 'institution' of the court, as a stable entity, with different actors within the legal system holding varying amounts of social, cultural and political capital, and using that capital to either enforce or resist the power of 'the court', instead both authority and resistance are created through negotiation.[36] This is not to deny that social capital exists or that people within the legal system had different levels of authority, but it relocates power from larger external institutional structures or systems on to the gendered bodies of individual actors. In doing so, it highlights how power is created, maintained and negotiated *through practice*, in the Bordieuan sense.[37]

Social power is only partially within the control of the individual. In this, 'the law' provides a useful exemplar. The law can be understood as an external regulating force that shapes social norms and which people either follow or resist. 'The law', however, has no physical being outside of its application. It only exists at the level of 'representation'; that is, the law is a 'text' that can be drawn on by people in the creation of meaning. It is only when the law is practised (and practise here can include its uses as a norm in everyday contexts) that it becomes implicated in power relationships. Resistance to the law therefore is not an actor pushing against an external entity, but contesting or negotiating what the law means. In this, the 'resistant' actor, the plaintiff or defendant, is no different from the 'dominant' actor, the judge, jury or legislature, as all are engaged in the same practice of negotiating meaning.

This model for power requires a particular understanding of agency. The self that is constituted through practice has been criticised for lacking intention or motivation.[38] Here Goffman's performances, which imply the existence of a subject, if one that is still socially constituted, appear useful, if under-developed.[39] Yet, as Karen Barad notes, such models portray a division between representation and the material world, with discourse coming to constitute a reality that is layered upon an inert physical body.[40] This has led scholars to focus on language and description in interpreting social phenomenon, which downplays the role of physical environment, material culture and human body in producing meaning.

Within the New Materialist tradition of which Barad is a part, agency is located in the generative capacities of the material world, which are constituted reciprocally with language.[41] Here the division between language and the material is collapsed as artificial, and instead phenomena (which can range from an atom to the human to the universe) are material-discursive practices, where both matter and language work together. This is not to say that language has no representational quality, but that in the production of phenomenon both language and matter are engaged, each constraining and shaping what they seek to produce. Barad's example is of wave formation. When the peak of two waves meet, they are joined to become a new larger wave; whereas a trough and a peak cancel each other out. Artificially dividing the components of phenomena (two waves) therefore risks losing sight of the fullness of its dimensions (a smaller or larger wave). This approach redirects agency from either discourse or prediscursive matter to their intersections, drawing attention to the ways that agency is distributed.[42] Like the performative self, agency is not located in one place but in relationships with others and the environment. In the context of courtrooms, agency is distributed across its actors, physical environment and discursive structures, with each contributing to the outcome of the trial and so justice itself.

A focus on phenomena as material-discursive structures also draws attention to the role of embodiment in the production of power. At its most literal, embodiment refers to 'the biological and physical presence of our body as a necessary precondition for the experience of emotion, language, thought and social interaction'.[43] It more usually is explored in terms of how the experience of being 'in body' operates as part of subjectivity.[44] The counterpart of this is that embodied subjectivity is shaped through engagement with others – how others respond to the actor's body, the value they place on that type of body, and how those valuations fold into systems of power that inform both agency and selfhood.[45] As power is negotiated by bodies and their performances, the embodied nature of humanity becomes central to analyses of power systems. Thus, this book gives attention to how power in the court is produced by physical bodies, visible behaviours, material cultures and environment, by the actor 'in body' and in the world.

This exploration of power varies significantly from Marxist interpretations, which have been prominent in Irish history, and where 'consciousness', in the sense of political self-awareness, has been key to explaining Irish nationalism, as well as political activity more broadly.[46] For many historians, for example, peasant 'resistance', such as barn-burning, could only be viewed as 'political' to the extent that peasants were aware that they were engaged in a broader political movement, not a local economic grievance. Performance theorists, however, are interested in the impact of resistances, exploring how they were received by their audience and their political effects. As a result, such activities may be viewed as political acts, regardless of the intention of the actor. Similarly, male behaviour in court may contribute to a broader social discourse on manliness, Irishness and political rights, even if that was not the intent of the men in question.

## Masculinity, power and performance

As a methodology for studying power relationships between men, performativity acts as a critique of the key model for understanding power within masculinity studies, Raewyn Connell's 'hegemonic masculinity'.[47] Connell argues that in every society there is an ideal masculinity that all men should aspire to, but few achieve, and against which all other forms of masculinity are measured. The ability to achieve the hegemonic ideal provides men with power. Men who cannot achieve the hegemonic archetype and all women, who are excluded by gender, are restricted in their exercise of power. Given that the model of performativity used here recognises the importance of cultural discourse in shaping social practice, these perspectives are not incompatible, with 'hegemonic masculinity' operating as the model for manliness that held the most cultural recognition and authority. However, in focusing on social practice, rather than representation, the concept of hegemonic masculinity is emptied of power.

When attention is directed to social practice, what becomes visible is not different 'types' of masculinity, but individual men drawing on a range of cultural resources to negotiate their identities and relationships. In doing so, the contingent, contested and distributed nature of those identities comes to fore, as does the range of resources available in the production of the self. These might include wider cultural ideals, values and models for gendered behaviour, but they equally include material resources, such as clothing and money, skills and talents including wit or charm, personality and the variable physical body. The ability of people to combine such resources, and the constraints on them doing so, allow for the production of individuals, both socially constituted and resolutely unique. Moreover, the capacity for individuals to exercise power or agency is not simply located in their relationship to a single representational mode, but is distributed across this multitude of resources and the environment with which they are interacting.[48] The intersectionality and hybridity of identity is thus better accounted for.[49]

External observers may note the prominence of particular models of masculinity in a culture and the ways that human practices correspond and thus can be generalised about. But the operation of power is not reduced to the achievement or similitude to a hegemonic model alone. Instead, it is coherence that comes to be significant, where the 'ideal' model of masculinity for a given individual (manliness) is that which reads as 'authentic', where a person's external performance is viewed as successfully conveying her or his internal 'self'. It is a model that is useful for contexts like early nineteenth-century Ireland where there is genuine contest, and even open conflict, over who holds, and who should hold, power in society.

It is also a model that may have had some resonance with a nineteenth-century Irish public, who placed authenticity at the centre of their readings of manliness. Whereas outward appearance, including biological sexual characteristics, family resemblance, accent and clothing, had since the medieval period been used to help identify a person's social class, occupation, gender, as well as piety and temperament, over the course of the early modern period, these expressions of identity became associated with an internalised and individualised personality.[50] This placed a different emphasis on the long-standing concern with the authenticity of external appearances and their relationship to 'truth', by creating a dualism between the internal and external person.[51]

From the late eighteenth century, the authentic internalised self of the individual was discussed using the vocabulary of 'character'. As Stefan Collini argues, character was a complex entity.[52] On the one hand, it was a moral code instilled during youth and which determined action in later life and so reflected an internalised set of values that could be either negative or positive (character could be bad as well as good); on the other hand, it was a set of behaviours that could be viewed and assessed by others and so references to character were allusions to an external code of behaviour that people were expected to follow. The use of the word 'character' often implied that it was synonymous with self, if an aspect of self that was formed through socialisation.[53] Character was thus performative, with men becoming of good character through their daily behaviours. Reflecting a contemporary concern that action might not display intention, however, the nineteenth-century public also worried about the deceptive nature of appearances, looking for cracks that might give insight into the internal self and so allow 'true' character to be revealed.

## Performing 'the court' in the press

A monograph exploring behaviour within the court might be expected to draw heavily on court records. Unfortunately, the destruction of the

Public Record Office in 1922 obliterated most of Ireland's historical legal records, requiring the historian to look elsewhere. This book draws mainly on newspaper reports drawn from fourteen regional newspapers, spread across the country, and accessed through a comprehensive survey of papers on microfilm or (on occasion) in original paper form; this core sample is supported by regional papers that appeared online towards the end of this project. It encompasses several thousand reports over a half century. News reports are complemented by over sixty printed pamphlets describing court cases and several trial compilations and collections of lawyers and judges' speeches.

Printed pamphlets based on legal suits were available in Ireland throughout the eighteenth century and continued in popularity well into the nineteenth, usually focusing on high-profile, politically important or scandalous cases. The earliest newspapers in Ireland date to the seventeenth century, and a provincial press flourished from the 1780s.[54] Despite this, not every town had a local paper in the early nineteenth century and many only survived for short periods. Three papers used in this study, Dublin's *Freeman's Journal*, Kilkenny's *The Leinster Journal* (renamed the *Kilkenny Journal* in 1830) and the *Belfast Newsletter*, survive across the period 1798 to 1845 with only minor gaps in their surviving runs. This is supplemented with eleven regional papers, chosen to give geographical breadth, which often had shorter runs, as well as keyword searches of digitised provincial papers.[55] Regional coverage is wider than this suggests as many papers borrowed freely from each other (the same stories appeared across the country) and, particularly in counties where local papers were scarce, many papers provided coverage over a reasonably wide geographical area. Across the period, court cases were a popular source of news. The Four Courts in Dublin provided high-profile trials all year round, and regular accounts of the assizes reflected its significance to urban life as they processed twice a year across the country. After their restructuring in the 1820s, reports from the petty sessions and police courts also became a staple in many papers.

For a study of performative space, newspaper reports are often a stronger source of information than court records. Official court stenographers did not exist in the early nineteenth century, and court records usually consist of documents of process (such as depositions or writs), minute books that provide summaries of the case written by the clerk, and occasionally the personal notes of the prosecutor, judge or other participants of a trial.[56] Evidence of what happened during the trial is therefore usually limited to brief summaries or notes with a particular focus on recording testimony and legal decisions (although judges' notes can vary enormously in quality). In contrast, court reports could offer detailed descriptions of events. As well as staples, such as transcriptions of speeches and testimony, they may include descriptions of the courtroom; of the various people in the court, their bodies, clothing and expression; the behaviour of the central cast within the courtroom drama, including how they moved across the space or whether they wept or laughed; and the behaviour of the courtroom audience and how they responded to the events they witnessed. As a result, such accounts provide greater detail on social interaction, allowing a performative reading.

As reports written primarily for public information and entertainment, there were no formal guidelines on what to record and some variety in what was considered important and worth reporting. Reports that were subsequently printed in newspapers or trial compilations were often edited to 'fit', so that different lengths of the same report can be found across newspapers, occasionally with missing information given as summaries. On the few, usually high-profile, occasions where cases were recorded by more than one reporter, there could also be variation between different reports.

As a form of entertainment, newspaper reporters were comfortable with adding editorial commentary; some reports are heavily stylised, containing a narrative structure and leading to a climatic ending, often the verdict or sentence.[57] They were frequently conducive to being read aloud, which was particularly evident in the structure of tales from the lower police courts and petty sessions. Cases that were reported (selected from the numerous that happened every day) were chosen for their newsworthiness, emphasising those of political importance, involving high-profile individuals, or which were 'sensational', ranging between the sublime, the gruesome and the ridiculous. Yet, this should not be overstated. Much court reporting was quite functional, edited down to terse lists of convicted felons and their sentences, brief summaries of the legal significance (particularly in civil cases), or restricted to the dialogue of central witnesses and speeches of lawyers and judges. Whilst brief summaries are not unimportant, often reported as the public had a vested interest in the outcomes, this monograph uses longer accounts that provide insight into social interaction in court.

Despite genre conventions, there is evidence that reports were considered to be reasonably accurate.[58] Various forms of shorthand had been available since the medieval period, and this was further refined in the 1830s.[59] Reporters were able to record events and particularly speech in some detail.[60] Many journalists sent their copy to judges and barristers to allow them to approve the copy of their speeches, and conversely judges and lawyers sometimes provided this copy directly to journal-ists.[61] Judges often recognised the value in newspaper reports in an era before formal transcriptions. Some added newspaper reports to the official record; lawyers and judges also drew on reports and the fuller printed pamphlets when making arguments about legal precedence or during appeals.[62] The journalist Thomas Shinkwin, and importantly his written notes, was even called as a witness in a perjury case, where he recounted the testimony of the perjured defendant.[63] Stylistic flourishes therefore do not appear to have been at the expense of providing an account that was felt to represent events by participants.

As this suggests, the historian's access to events in the court is medi-ated through the eyes of the reporter and through the writing and editing process. Apart from those by well-known lawyers (who were male and typically from the upper middle classes/gentry) who generally provided accounts of the higher courts, reports are anonymous. During the early nineteenth century, most were written either by lawyers and other court personnel, journalists directly employed for newspapers or freelance writers who were paid for copy. In the case of smaller papers, 'journal-ists' may have been the editors and even owners of the press, as in the case of Thomas Carroll, who at different times edited the *Carlow Sentinel* and the *Carlow Morning Post*, and who personally reported on events from Carlow's courts.[64] The social class of newspaper owners, editors and journalists appears to have varied, although the need for capital to start a newspaper tended to put owner-editors in the lower-middle and middle classes.[65] Potentially, as some provincial papers were edited by women, such as Frances Knox, proprietor of the *Clare Journal* for over thirty years from 1807 (possibly the daughter of the previous proprietor, Thomas Saunders Knox), and because women were known to be present at many court cases, some of these accounts may have been written by women.[66] If gender made a difference to the style of reporting, it is not immediately evident to the reader.

The content of many newspaper articles suggests that reporters were usually well-educated, with reports making literary allusions to novels and high literature as well as showing an awareness of broader politi-cal and cultural events. Journalists and newspapers also ranged across the political/religious spectrum. It is not surprising therefore that the social positioning of the journalist shaped their practices of observation, so, for example, some characters or events are portrayed more sympa-thetically than others. Importantly, most nineteenth-century reporting explicitly acknowledged the 'journalist as observer' function of the genre. Court reporters situated themselves as 'outsiders' to what they described, producing ethnographic accounts that denaturalised events. This external position was designed to reinforce the journalist as 'objective', without denying that it was a singular 'objectivity', the product of one perspective. In concert, these techniques emphasised the 'truthfulness' of the account for the reader by setting boundaries on its claims to 'truth'. Moreover, it permitted reporters to provide social commentary, to render accounts comic, or provide sarcastic observations without such additions undermining their legitimacy.

The court reporter provides the central access point to the court for the historian and it is her or his decisions about what to include and what to ignore that produce meaning. How the historian accesses the operation of power in court is therefore largely an effect of what the reporter thought was significant in shaping events. It is therefore risky to claim that the outcome of any particular case was the product of what the journalist described. Rather what is suggestive is that reporters across the country focused on similar things – bodies, clothes, behaviours, testimony – as central to the production of meaning and so power. What such reports provide is not unadulterated access to courtroom experience, but insight into wider cultural beliefs about how power is produced within them.

This not only informs our interpretation of these accounts as representational sources for the past, but is suggestive of their function in the nineteenth century.[67] Not only did much of the public access the court through such reporting, informing their relation to the court and justice, but the fact that the court would be reported also shaped behaviour within it. As I argue at length elsewhere, courtroom actors – from judges to audiences – recognised that events in courts could be published. For some, this enforced the need to retain a gentlemanly air; for others, it provided opportunity for publicity.[68] The lawyer and politician, Daniel O'Connell (1775–1847), used the court to give political speeches and so circumvent censorship; the Dublin ballad-singer Zozimus (Michael J. Moran) advertised his wares and his political opinions from the courtroom.[69] The court reporter was part of 'the court' as a performative space, such that these representations came to inhere in social practice.

That these cases became part of public discourse through the press is also part of their historical importance. For many theorists of the eighteenth and nineteenth centuries, the press played a leading role in creating the citizen. For Jürgen Habermas, it enabled the creation of a public sphere, separate from the state, that was essential to giving a voice to the disenfranchised and to allowing the eighteenth-century public to imagine itself as part of the polity.[70] Benedict Anderson goes further, arguing that community formed through the press created the modern nation-state.[71] In an Irish context, Padhraig Higgins demonstrates that the provincial press allowed men and women across the social ladder to 'participate imaginatively in the national community'.[72]

Court reporting similarly inserted the activities and voices of the participants in legal dramas into a wider public debate around the nature of Irishness, the Irish community and its political significance. At local and national levels, court reporters created community through regular reporting, ensuring that magistrates and judges were not just the impartial face of justice, but individual characters with particular politics, values and quirks. Lawyers, policemen and those involved in repeated anti-social behaviour became known to the regular reader. The court became a familiar space with recognisable characters even to those who used it irregularly. Readers were thus encouraged to identify with the 'leading actors' of these dramas, learning to understand why they behaved as they did. In doing so, they were asked to emotionally invest in justice, but as importantly, in identifying with these characters, to accept the models of behaviour and values they displayed.[73] Readers could reject such identifications, but the plurality of voices that appeared in the courts provided considerable variety to engage with, whilst still constraining choice. As a central source of representations, reports on court activities became implicated in a public debate around what it meant to be Irish.

This was an increasingly democratic discussion as newspaper reportage expanded over the decades, covering not only high-profile cases, typically featuring well-known and elite individuals, but also everyday events in the lower courts. Such coverage was mirrored in the expansion of the readership for the press. In a British context, from the beginning of the century, but especially from the 1830s, newspapers reached further down the social scale with a take-off in sales after 1836 with the reduction of the newspaper tax.[74] This trend also appears in Ireland, although the reduction in tax did not reduce newspaper costs. Most provincial papers cost between 4d and 7d an issue before and in the years after 1836.[75] Some of the larger papers reduced their prices, but often not significantly. The popular Dublin paper, the *Freeman's Journal*, only fell from 5d to 4d. Despite these prices, circulation figures remained strong, with the fourteen Dublin papers selling 45,000 issues a week in 1774, and even a provincial paper, like the *Belfast Newsletter*, reaching sales of 2,100 in 1789. If the British figures for readership also apply to Ireland, most individual papers were read by between twenty and fifty people.[76]

Court officials recognised that newspapers reached a broad audience, asking journalists to report particular cases to encourage further witnesses, often in instances where such witnesses could not have been expected to afford the cost.[77] Working-class biographies demonstrate the many ways such people accessed local news, from group-purchases and reading aloud to visits to coffee shops, public houses and circulating libraries, where newspapers were cheaply available to patrons.[78] Through being represented in the press and increasingly acknowledged as a potential readership, people from across the social classes in Ireland were able to participate in the construction of Irish identity, as they did in other contexts like the theatre or boxing ring.[79]

### The Irish courtroom in context

Like in much of Europe, late eighteenth- and early nineteenth-century Ireland was experiencing rapid social, economic and political change. Between 1750 and 1840, Ireland's population exploded, growing from 2.5 million to eight million.[80] In 1800, Dublin city had a population of 170,000, which had almost doubled to 318,000 by 1850. In a British context, this growth was not exceptional, but by the end of the century, Dublin had some of the worst over-crowding in the United Kingdom and a significantly higher death-rate.[81] Its expansion was mirrored in some of the larger regional towns. Belfast's population grew from 19,000 in 1800 to 70,000 by 1841.[82] Cork's growth had primarily taken place in the later eighteenth century, but it also rose from 80,000 to 85,000 people between 1820 and 1851.[83] Most Irish towns were commercial and transport centres, with some minor manufacturing concerns, notably in brewing, distilling and flour-milling. Ireland also had a successful wool and cotton trade until the 1820s when they failed to compete after the introduction of free trade across the United Kingdom.[84] The only area of Ireland to significantly industrialise was the north-east, particularly Belfast and Londonderry, which developed flourishing linen and ship-building concerns.[85]

Like elsewhere, Irish towns were home to the growing middle classes, made up of merchants, professionals and, in some areas, industrialists, as well as 'functionaries' (ministers, teachers, police, customs, etc.), tradesmen, domestic servants and similar workers (like washerwomen, messengers and taxi drivers), and a growing group of 'poor', who were sometimes itinerant and made a precarious living.[86] Some towns, especially cities like Dublin, housed the gentry and aristocracy for part of the year, although the politically active and rich tended to winter in London after 1800.[87] Throughout this period, Ireland predominantly remained a rural society. In 1841, three-quarters of people solely or principally relied on agriculture as their means of support, whilst almost 90 per cent either lived rurally or in towns of less than 2,000 people.[88]

Below the level of the aristocracy and gentry, social structure in rural Ireland was related to land, with secure farmers situated near the top of the social ladder. Farmers were typically divided into classes by farm size, with small (one to ten Irish acres), medium (ten to thirty acres) and large or strong (over thirty acres) farmers, but social class did not always correlate with the amount of land held. Wealth was shaped by farm size, but also quality of land and the types of farming conducted.[89] In the 1840s, one estimate suggests that 'strong' farmers made up around 15 per cent of all farmers with more than two acres, around 128,000 families; beneath them were the very heterogeneous group of middling farmers, whose 253,000 families formed around 30 per cent of the farming class. Finally, there were c. 410,000 smallholding and joint tenancy families, who were effectively engaged in subsistence farming with limited engagement with markets.[90] Rural society also incorporated cottiers, who usually held less than one acre and had to supplement their incomes (similar to many small farmers), and farm labourers, who were landless and waged. In the prefamine period, the latter two groups expanded dramatically to about 56 per cent of the rural population, providing ample cheap labour that kept wages low and contributed to the increasing poverty of this social group.[91]

The prefamine period was one of economic instability. This should not be exaggerated: the industrial north-east thrived, and farming outputs generally grew across the period. The end of the Napoleonic War, however, opened up European markets, driving down agricultural prices, sometimes by more than 50 per cent, whilst the introduction of free trade across the United Kingdom provided tough competition for Ireland's under-developed manufacturing industry.[92] Dublin experienced recurrent economic depressions due to the closure of the Irish Parliament and changing fashions that reduced demand for local textiles.[93] There were also periods of harvest failure, notably in the early 1820s, which led to subsistence crisis.[94] A large amount of the Irish population lived precariously and such downward fluctuations could be devastating, pushing poor families into destitution.

The economy informed and was informed by political developments. If the eighteenth century saw the entrenchment of the Protestant Ascendancy in Ireland, where protestant landowners secured their political and economic domination, it was also an era where the make-up of the political community was contested. In addition to a vocal middle-class Catholic population, Ireland's public sphere flourished, with an expanding print trade and newspaper industry, coffee houses in Belfast and Dublin, and the rise of militia and volunteer organisations.[95] Literacy improved during the period, enabling greater access to print culture. Whilst in 1841, 27.6 per cent of the population could read and write and a further 19.8 per cent read alone, just under two-thirds of men born between 1820 and 1830 could do both, largely a result of the expanding national school system.[96] Increased literacy was combined with a decline in the Irish language (although with great regional variation), with 28 per cent of children born between 1831 and 1841 speaking Irish, compared to 45 per cent of people born in the 1770s.[97]

The American Revolution heightened the debate about who formed the political community, as well as making the question of national governance more pressing.[98] As a result, there was a push for greater legislative independence for Ireland from the United Kingdom, which was finally granted in 1782 in the limited form of 'Grattan's parliament'.[99] The French Revolution rejuvenated politics in Ireland, where ideas of liberty, fraternity and equality were quickly popularised. In 1791, the United Irishmen was formed. Like many radical organisations of the era, it had an elite, university-educated leadership, heavily influenced by Thomas Paine and French Republicanism, and a large plebeian following, mainly amongst urban artisans, whose politics were more varied, often falling at the radical end of constitutional reform. They promoted civic humanism, which drew on a broadly defined 'public', with the goal of introducing 'virtue' into public life, countering the corruption and tyranny of the current government.[100] The movement was given mass support through promising the lower classes that political reform would bring resolution to local grievances, including high tithes, high taxes and high rent, and transformation of their social position, ensuring greater respect by their social betters and a system of national education.

The United Irishmen movement grew into a quickly quashed open rebellion in 1798.[101] Whilst the rebellion failed, it was a central event in the imaginary of the Irish people, featuring in numerous songs and ballads, where '1798' became a byword for political radicalism.[102] Whilst not explicitly nationalist, that much of the grievances the United Irishmen sought to address were caused or exasperated by their perceived colonial status (a status many United Irishmen rejected), and a lack of political rights for Catholics, meant that the movement came to be understood in terms of protecting the Irish 'nation'.[103]

In 1800, Ireland was granted full political union with Britain, dissolving the Irish Parliament. In 1803, there was a minor rebellion in Dublin led by the United Irishman Robert Emmet, and its failure ended the movement.[104] By this date, there was an overt nationalist movement led by Daniel O'Connell, which aimed through constitutional reform to emancipate Catholics and later to Repeal the Union of 1800.[105] Like the United Irishmen, O'Connell pointed to reform of tithes, taxes and rent to encourage popular backing.[106] Simultaneously, from the flourishing economy in the north-east emerged 'Unionism'. Growing similarly out of the United Irishmen movement, several Irish people, particularly in the north-east and Dublin, endorsed the Union with Britain, and particularly the rhetoric of British constitutionalism that provided a language of rights for a greater part of the population. In these early years, this was a cross-party movement.[107]

The prefamine period was also marked by social unrest, particularly in rural Ireland during times of poor harvest. Various secret societies, such as Rockites, Ribbonmen, Shanavests and Caravats, engaged in violent protest to enforce their idea of a moral economy. Whilst these movements were often inspired by local and regional grievances, they drew on the rhetoric of the United Irishmen and O'Connell, as well as millenarianism and even British constitutionalism, placing their complaints into a larger political framework.[108]

Political tensions in Ireland were informed by the religious context. In 1834, a Royal Commission showed that 80.9 per cent of the population was Catholic; 10.7 per cent were Church of Ireland and 8.1 per cent were Presbyterian.[109] Catholics were widely spread out and in no area were less than 20 per cent of the population. Church of Ireland members never made up more than 40 per cent of any diocese, with the largest numbers found in south Ulster and Leinster. Presbyterians commonly lived in Antrim and Down, but even there they never made up more than 60 per cent of the population.[110] Both Catholics and Protestants were found at all social levels, although Catholics were generally under-represented amongst the skilled trades, the liberal professions and landed proprietors.[111] Protestants, particularly Church of Ireland members, tended to be concentrated in towns.[112] As a result, urban areas were often religiously mixed. Dublin was a predominantly Protestant town at all social levels, but inward migration in the eighteenth and nineteenth centuries brought large numbers of Catholics to the city.[113] Similarly, Belfast was a Protestant town, with a large Presbyterian population, but it was to see its Catholic population grow from 8 per cent in 1785 to 32 per cent in the mid-1830s. Some estimates suggest that the Catholic population reached 40 per cent before the famine.[114]

During the late eighteenth century, penal restrictions on those who were not members of the established Episcopalian Church of Ireland were reduced, providing space for Catholic and Presbyterian Churches to form openly recognised (if not uncontested) institutions.[115] Many people of all denominations welcomed these developments, but some protestants were equally concerned about the implications for their traditional privileges. This led to sectarian tensions that on occasion broke into outright violence, and the rise of sectarian-political organisations, such as Peep O'Day Boys, Catholic Defenders and the Orange Order.[116] Sectarianism should not be overstated, nor understood as a simple determinant of political belief. O'Connell's movement for Catholic Emancipation was supported by people across the religious spectrum, whilst not every Catholic was a nationalist, nor every Protestant a unionist. Nonetheless, religion was a central aspect of prefamine identity that informed people's sense of self, how they interacted with others and shaped wider beliefs about Irishness and political rights.

Similarly, gender identity was central to how people interpreted the world with political conflict mapped onto the bodies of men. In a wider European context, the concept of 'independent manhood' that was central to civic humanism shaped understandings of political rights for much of the eighteenth century.[117] The social elite and increasingly the middle classes had defined 'independence' in terms of property ownership, but, from the 1790s, Thomas Paine's *The Rights of Man* transformed this political landscape by grounding political rights in human rights. Lower-class men sought political participation on the merits of the individual, emphasising the importance of 'personality, intellect and gender'.[118] Whilst gender had long limited women's political participation, it was now given increased emphasis, reinforced by the location of political culture within fraternal organisations. Amongst the elite, this included all-male learned societies, universities and clubs, whilst lower-class groups founded working-men's associations and secret societies.[119] It was also informed by a patriarchal model for family life that reinforced the position of men as head of the household and representative of their families.[120] The emphasis on gender as a basis of political rights invited increasing critique of the behaviour of individual men and of men as part of wider social groups, placing manliness and male behaviour at the heart of politics.[121]

What manliness looked like was not only refracted through class, ethnicity and sexuality, but underwent notable change over the nineteenth century in both Britain and Ireland. John Tosh identified this as the shift from 'gentlemanly politeness' to 'manly simplicity'.[122] Gentlemanly politeness, as a mode of masculinity, was not only associated with 'gentlemen' and independence, but suggestive of a specific mode of socialisation, requiring polished manners, education and knowledge of the world, a cosmopolitan outlook and a particular aesthetic of dress. It required engagement with the 'culture of sensibility' and so required the controlled display of some emotion and the restraint of others. For some men, it could incorporate a sense of honour and chivalric treatment of women.[123]

'Manly simplicity', closely tied to the middle class, was by contrast rooted in 'rugged individualism' and 'personal integrity'. It was associated with 'muscular Christianity', due to its emphasis on the virile healthy male body, militarism and team-work.[124] It could also incorporate honour and chivalric treatment of women, placing less importance on heterosociability than its predecessor.[125] Manly simplicity was stoic, not only emphasising emotional self-control, but closing down the opportunities to express manly emotion.[126] It sat alongside 'respectability', an increasingly important value amongst both the middle and upper-working classes, and, with independence, tied to political rights. Respectable men showed good taste and manners, were sober, earnest, hard-working and industrious, kind and charitable, and aspired to moral and intellectual self-improvement.[127] They were often evangelicals, rooting their respectability in Christian morality, whether Catholicism or one of the branches of Protestantism.[128]

With the benefit of hindsight, the larger shift from gentlemanly politeness to manly simplicity might be evident, but on the ground things were less clear. Particularly in the early nineteenth century, different models for male behaviour competed and were challenged through men's performances. Manly ideals were complicated by the men who could or did not conform to such values, and the tension that arose within a model of masculinity rooted in a 'rugged individualism' that simultaneously limited self-expression.[129] How the 'eccentricity' that the British prized as a symbol of their freedom fits into this context is still to be told.[130] Moreover, as Valente reminds us, masculinity was complicated in Ireland by colonialism, which not only rendered the colonised male body feminine, but limited political protest by tying it to unmanly and uncontrolled expression of emotion.[131] It is this complexity, and the implications for social power relationships, that lies at the core of this book.

### Performing manliness in the Irish court

Within this book, the courtroom is: an arena for law and justice; a microcosm of Irish society that provides a partial perspective on its wider social, economic and political power relationships; and, through the press, an agent in shaping Irish national identity. Across the book, different components of the phenomenon that is the court are explored with the goal of teasing out its nature and the way that justice was produced. Whilst many previous studies of courts have focused on particular angles – whether architecture, lawyers, passionate speech or race and gender – few have sought to explore the broad range of dynamics at play in the production of justice. This book argues for a model of power rooted in negotiated and embodied practices that better explains why certain individuals get superior outcomes than their social characteristics (race, gender, class) might suggest. It also contributes to understandings of the court's capacity to exercise power and the implications for social order.

As explored above, power in this context is produced through negotiations between men, who draw on a broad range of cultural resources in a performance that is embodied and located in place. As will become evident across this book, these performances are also emotional. Like other embodied experiences, emotion here is recognised as a temporally and spatially specific, materio-discursive practice, which is performed by individuals and groups and acts as a cultural resource to be drawn on in the production of meaning.[132] Emotion then can be compared to clothing, witty banter or education in its ability to function as a mode of communicating identity for an audience. As is explored in Chapter 3 and again in Chapters 4 and 5, reading the emotional body could provide key evidence for observers about character, guilt and innocence.

Emotion also performed other functions within courtrooms, some of which were distinctive to the nineteenth century. As is explored in Chapter 4, emotion – in this case sympathy – was understood as vital to successful communication between actors, providing important information about the truth or otherwise of somebody's words or behaviour. This was a form of emotional contagion that passed between bodies. As a mechanism for communication, emotion became implicated in a range of courtroom negotiations, whether that was the way the responses of the public gallery shaped the mood of the court (Chapter 2) or how certain types of humour and laughter inflected on how other evidence should be interpreted (Chapter 5). Whilst other studies of emotion in group dynamics have emphasised how emotional communities or regimes act to shape emotional norms and thus power, this book looks at how emotion was used as a tool within negotiations of power.[133] Broader cultural beliefs (such as shaped by communities and regimes) are of course vital to shaping how emotion was understood and experienced by people in court, but it is how emotion is put to use that is of interest in this book.

Whilst the courtroom is a distinct space with its own dynamics, it also played an important role in society. The court acted reciprocally with wider social, economic and political systems, with the latter feeding into the performance of justice and the former shaping both individual behaviour and normative actions. Thus, a study of the court can provide evidence of the nature of Irish society itself. *Men on Trial* uses this opportunity to offer a social history of men's behaviours and identities in early nineteenth-century Ireland, about which very little has been written. It provides insights not only into law and order but clothing cultures, perceptions of beauty, education, popular culture, humour and joking, character, and engagements between men across ranks. Through exploring performances in court, the daily lives of ordinary people are uncovered. Some of the examples explored resonate with the picture we have for the rest of the United Kingdom and the United States, but they also highlight how wider trends are explored and redefined within national contexts.

Men are the centre of this history, but this is not a book that seeks to produce a new set of masculinities for an Irish context. It rather interrogates the key role that gender – and particularly manliness – played in shaping power relationships in Ireland. Investment by men and women in their gendered identities, reinforced by contemporary biology and scripture, ensured that gender was a key framework through which people interpreted their experience and the world. When embedded within contemporary constructions of patriarchal and political power, gender became implicated in a broad range of social power structures.[134] What it meant to be a man or woman, however, was more open to negotiation. In focusing on how men, and occasionally women, constructed their gendered identities, this book highlights gender as a creative, dynamic force and not simply as constrictive.[135]

Part of the creativity offered by gender was its capacity – through the circulation of its performances in the national press – to construct Irish national identity. This final line of argument in *Men on Trial* takes seriously newspapers not just as evidence of past events, but as an active component in the construction of Irish society. The stories told of the court and the people who used them were given life beyond the moment; on occasion, their wide circulation extended to the rest of the United Kingdom and its colonies.[136] During a moment where a nationalist Irish identity was in production, these texts played an important role in shaping what it meant to be Irish, its boundaries and scope. Importantly, it enabled men and women from all walks of life to contribute to this conversation.

This book is structured to highlight a range of components that the nineteenth-century press identified as significant to shaping power relationships within the court. It breaks down the court into parts to provide insight into how each section of the whole was a creative, dynamic process, and thus how the whole itself was unstable. This is by necessity an artificial imagining of the court, and indeed the human, for whom these varying dynamic parts worked together in the formation of identity and meaning. It is for this reason that I have not given much consideration to the outcome of trials. It is rare that only one element of a trial can explain a verdict; rather the same trial might involve a moving speech by a top prosecutor, some vigorous and entertaining banter on cross-examination, and an attractive and compelling defendant. The jury had to weigh each of these performances, and usually many others, against each other when deciding justice. The structure of the book does not allow these competing dynamics to be held against each other. Rather in exploring several key parts of the whole, it enables a better insight into the diversity of factors involved in the operation of power.

Situated at the intersection of law and society, the court was a space where both interacted. Chapter 1 explores this dynamic, highlighting how authority situated in the law, in traditional sites of power (land), and in a newly burgeoning public, competed in that space and shaped the nature and gendering of negotiations within it. It particularly emphasises 'the lawyer' as a key figure in the imagining of the law, coming to 'embody' the law for the public. Chapter 2 continues this discussion through an exploration of courtroom architecture, the ways it acted to constrain and situate gendered legal actors and the law itself, and how some members of the court sought to disrupt its logic. Chapter 3 concentrates on men's bodies, particularly appearance, clothing and displays of emotion. The physical body acted as both a constraint on identity and an opportunity for creative play that enabled men to communicate complex messages to their brethren. All three of these chapters share a concern with the relationship between material structures, space and performance in producing the court, the law and the nation.

The next three chapters explore oral performances, recognising the emphasis placed by the law on legal speeches and oral testimonies. What people said in court has long been a staple of historical analysis; *how* people said it has been given less consideration. Chapter 4 focuses on the legal speech given by professional men in courtrooms, exploring the role of formal oratory in enabling sympathetic communication, and so the transmission of truth, between speaker and listener. Chapter 5 looks at the cross-examination, and particularly banter on the stand, as a site where legal truth was produced through confrontation between men. Chapter 6 continues this discussion in an exploration of informal story-telling and the uses of popular culture in speeches and testimony. Across these chapters, the creativity of spoken performance is brought to the fore, particularly its capacity to shape the emotions of audiences, not least through the carnivalesque, and its ability to situate class at the heart of a contested national identity.

If the first chapter moves from society to the court, the last substantive chapter moves back to society and the law. Chapter 7 explores how men's performances in the preceding chapters relate to 'character', which was so central to determining guilt or innocence. If character was one form of proof, it must be located against the physical and oral evidence that was increasingly informed by the new forensic science. Thus, this chapter explores how the claims to truth made through embodied courtroom performances became part of the logic of the legal system.

The conclusion draws together the different components of courtroom performance to argue for a justice made not in parts but in their interaction. It emphasises the important emotional dynamics of nineteenth-century courtrooms, from the sympathy that communicated truth to empathetic engagements with the embodied performance of character by individuals. It argues for a law that, whilst having its own logic and procedures, was rooted in Irish society and provided an important space for the negotiation of social power relationships. Finally, it demonstrates how these courtroom performances did not remain in court, nor even in the pages of the local paper, but moved outwards to inform the making of Irish national identity.

## Notes

1  S. de Beauvoir, 'Woman as other', *Le Deuxième Sexe*, [The Second Sex] (Paris: Galimard, 1949), trans. and extracted in D. Simonton (ed.), *Women in European Culture and Society: A Sourcebook* (London: Routledge, 2013), p. 206.

2  'Dublin Police', *Freeman's Journal* (28 December 1844) Dublin. To allow an appreciation of regional spread, I have added the county in which the court was located beside each newspaper source. Dublin is over-represented as it is home to the Four Courts, insolvency courts and several others that have national coverage; not all Dublin cases involve Dublin locals.

3  K. Harvey and A. Shepard, 'What have historians done with masculinity? Reflections on five centuries of British history, circa 1500–1950', *Journal of British Studies*, 44 (2005), 274–80; J. Tosh, 'What should historians do with masculinity? Reflections on nineteenth-century Britain', in R. Shoemaker and M. Vincent (eds), *Gender and History in Western Europe* (London: Arnold, 1998), pp. 65–84; M. Francis, 'The

domestication of the male? Recent research on nineteenth and twentieth-century masculinity', *Historical Journal*, 45 (2002), 637–52.

4   P. Carter, 'Men about town: Representations of foppery and masculinity in early-eighteenth-century urban society', in H. Barker and E. Chalus (eds), *Gender in Eighteenth-Century England: Roles, Representations and Responsibilities* (London: Longman, 1997), pp. 31–57; M. Cohen, '"Manners" make the man: Politeness, chivalry, and the construction of masculinity, 1750–1830', *Journal of British Studies*, 44 (2005), 312–29; J.E. Early, 'A new man for a new century: Dr Crippen and the principles of masculinity', in G. Robb and N. Erber (eds), *Disorder in the Court: Trials and Sexual Conflict at the Turn of the Century* (New York: New York University Press, 1999), pp. 209–30; T. Hitchcock and M. Cohen (eds), *English Masculinities 1660–1800* (London: Longman, 1999).

5   A. Ballinger, 'Masculinity in the dock: Legal responses to male violence and female retaliation in England and Wales, 1900–1965', *Social and Legal Studies*, 16:4 (2007), 459–81; H. Barker, 'Soul, purse and family: Middling and lower-class masculinity in eighteenth-century Manchester', *Social History*, 33:1 (2008), 12–35; K. Wilson, 'Nelson's women: Female masculinity and body politics in the French and Napoleonic wars', *European History Quarterly*, 37 (2007), 562–81.

6   A. Clark, *The Struggle for the Breeches: Gender and the Making of the British Working Class* (Berkeley: University of California Press, 1995); M. McCormack, *The Independent Man: Citizenship and Gender Politics in Georgian England* (Manchester: Manchester University Press, 2006); M. McCormack (ed.), *Public Men: Masculinity and Politics in Modern Britain* (Basingstoke: Palgrave Macmillan, 2007); S. Broomhall and J. Van Gent (eds), *Governing Masculinities in the Early Modern Period* (Aldershot: Ashgate, 2011); L. Carter, 'British masculinities on trial in the Queen Caroline affair of 1820', *Gender & History*, 20:2 (2008), 248–69.

7   The few examples include: C. Kennedy, '"A Gallant Nation": Chivalric masculinity and Irish nationalism in the 1790s', in McCormack, *Public Men*, pp. 73–92; M. Cohen and N.J. Curtin (eds), *Reclaiming Gender: Transgressive Identities in Modern Ireland* (New York: St Martin's Press, 1999); K. O'Donnell, 'Affect and the history of women, gender and masculinity', in M. Valiulis (ed.), *Gender and Power in Irish History* (Dublin: Irish Academic Press, 2009), pp. 183–98; P. Kelleher, 'Class and Catholic Irish masculinity in antebellum America: Young men on the make in Chicago', *Journal of American Ethnic History*, 28:4 (2009), 7–42; C. Ní Laoire, '"You're Not a Man at All!": Masculinity, responsibility and staying on the land in contemporary Ireland', *Irish Journal of Sociology*, 14:2 (2005), 94–114; C. Nash, 'Men again: Irish masculinity, nature and nationhood in the early twentieth century', *Cultural Geographies*, 3 (1996), 427–53.

8   P. Higgins, *A Nation of Politicians: Gender, Patriotism and Political Culture in Late Eighteenth-Century Ireland* (Madison: University of Wisconsin Press, 2010).

9   J. Valente, *The Myth of Manliness in Irish National Culture, 1880–1922* (Urbana: University of Illinois Press, 2011).

10   M. Gaskill, *Crime and Mentalities in Early Modern England* (Cambridge: Cambridge University Press, 2000); J.H. Langbein, *The Origins of Adversary Criminal Trial* (Oxford: Oxford University Press, 2005).

11   A. May, *The Bar & the Old Bailey, 1750–1850* (Chapel Hill: University of North Carolina Press, 2003); J.M. Beattie, 'Scales of justice: Defense counsel and the English criminal

trial in the eighteenth and nineteenth centuries', *Law and History Review*, 9:2 (1991), 221–67; D. Lemmings, 'Criminal trial procedure in eighteenth-century England: The impact of lawyers', *Journal of Legal History*, 26:1 (2005), 73–82; J. Oldham, 'Truth-telling in the eighteenth-century English courtroom', *Law and History Review*, 12:1 (1994), 95–121.

12  B. Shapiro, 'Oaths, credibility and the legal process in early modern England: Part One', *Law and Humanities*, 6:2 (2013), 145–78; B. Shapiro, 'Oaths, credibility and the legal process in early modern England: Part Two', *Law and Humanities*, 7:1 (2013), 19–54.

13  Lemmings, 'Criminal trial procedure'; Langbein, *Origins*; W.N. Osborough, 'The regulation of the admission of attorney and solicitors in Ireland, 1600–1866', in D. Hogan and W.N. Osborough (eds), *Brehons, Serjeants and Attorneys: Studies in the History of the Irish Legal Profession* (Dublin: Irish Academic Press, 1990), pp. 101–52.

14  M. Wiener, 'Judges v. jurors: Courtroom tensions in murder trials and the law of criminal responsibility in nineteenth-century England', *Law and History Review*, 17:1 (1999), 467–506; D.G. Barrie and S. Broomhall, *Police Courts in Nineteenth-Century Scotland, Volume 1: Magistrates, Media and the Masses* (Farnham: Ashgate, 2014), especially pp. 225–80; N. Howlin, 'Controlling jury composition in nineteenth-century Ireland', *Journal of Legal History*, 30:3 (2009), 227–261; D. McCabe, '"That part that laws or kings can cause or cure": Crown prosecution and jury trial at Longford assizes, 1830–45', in R. Gillespie and G. Moran (eds), *Longford: Essays in County History* (Dublin: Lilliput Press, 1991), pp. 153–72.

15  Gaskill, *Crime and Mentalities*; Shapiro, 'Oaths, credibility: Part Two'; Shapiro, 'Oaths, credibility: Part One'.

16  S. Steinbach, 'The melodramatic contract: Breach of promise and the performance of virtue', *Nineteenth-Century Studies*, 14 (2000), 1–34; D. Featherstone, 'Counter-insurgency, subalternity and spatial relations: Interrogating court-martial narratives of the Nore Mutiny of 1797', *South African Historical Journal*, 61:4 (2009), 766–87; G. Robb and N. Erber (eds), *Disorder in the Court: Trials and Sexual Conflict at the Turn of the Century* (Basingstoke: Macmillan, 1999); A. McLaren, *Trials of Masculinity: Policing Sexual Boundaries, 1870–1930* (London: University of Chicago Press, 1999); P. Carlen, *Magistrate's Justice* (London: Martin Robinson, 1976).

17  D. Hay, 'Property, authority and the criminal law', in D. Hay *et al.* (eds), *Albion's Fatal Tree: Crime and Society in Eighteenth-Century England* (London: Verso, 1975), pp. 17–64; E.P. Thomson, 'Patrician society, plebeian culture', *Journal of Social History*, 7:4 (1974), 382–45; P. King, *Crime, Justice and Discretion in England, 1740–1820* (Oxford: Oxford University Press, 2003); J.M. Beattie, *Crime and the Courts in England, 1660–1800* (Oxford: Oxford University Press, 1986); V.A.C. Gattrell, *The Hanging Tree: Execution and the English People, 1770–1868* (Oxford: Oxford University Press, 1994); Barrie and Broomhall, *Police Courts in Nineteenth-Century Scotland: Volume 1*, pp. 227–82.

18  D. Lemmings (ed.), *Crime, Courtrooms and the Public Sphere in Britain, 1700–1850* (Farnham: Ashgate, 2012).

19  P.G. Mackintosh and C.R. Forsberg, 'Performing the lodge: Masonry, masculinity, and nineteenth-century North American moral geography', *Journal of Historical Geography*, 35 (2009), 451–72.

20　For example see: R. Pepitone, 'Gender, space, and ritual: Women barristers, the Inns of Court, and the interwar press', *Journal of Women's History*, 28:1 (2016), 60–83; M.J. Mossman, 'Women lawyers and law-making in nineteenth and twentieth-century Europe', in E. Schandevyl (ed.), *Women in Law and Law-Making in Nineteenth and Twentieth-Century Europe* (Farnham: Ashgate, 2014), pp. 231–52; A. Logan, 'Professionalism and the impact of England's first women justices, 1920–1950', *Historical Journal*, 49:3 (2006), 833–50.

21　G. Walker, *Crime, Gender and Social Order in Early Modern England* (Cambridge: Cambridge University Press, 2003), pp. 113–58; for how that has changed over time see: K.J. Kesselring, 'No greater provocation? Adultery and the mitigation of murder in English law', *Law and History Review*, 34:1 (2016), 199–225.

22　For a survey of the contemporary literature see: R. Collier, 'Masculinities, law and personal life: Towards a new framework for understanding men, law and gender', *Harvard Journal of Law and Gender*, 33 (2010), 431–75; for historical discussions of the masculine culture of the law: S. McSheffrey, 'Jurors, respectable masculinity and Christian morality: A comment on Marjorie MacIntosh's controlling misbehaviour', *Journal of British Studies*, 37:3 (1998), 269–78; L. Magnusson, 'Scoff power in *Love's Labour's Lost* and the Inns of Court: Language in context', in Peter Holland (ed.), *Shakespeare Survey: An Annual Survey of Shakespeare Studies and Production* (Cambridge: Cambridge University Press, 2004), pp. 196–208.

23　This is a huge literature. Some interesting examples include: J. Bailey, *Unquiet Lives: Marriage and Marriage Breakdown in England, 1660–1800* (Cambridge: Cambridge University Press, 2003); M. O'Dowd, 'Women and the Irish chancery court in the late sixteenth and early seventeenth centuries', *Irish Historical Studies*, 31:124 (1999), 470–87; L. Gowing, *Domestic Dangers: Women, Words and Sex in Early Modern London* (New York: Oxford University Press, 1996); K.M. Phillips, 'Masculinities and the medieval English sumptuary laws', *Gender & History*, 19:1 (2007), 22–42; D. Neal, 'Suits make the man: Masculinity in two English law courts, c. 1500', *Canadian Journal of History*, 37 (2002), 1–22; V. Bates, '"Under cross-examination she fainted": Sexual crime and swooning in the Victorian courtroom', *Journal of Victorian Culture*, 21:4 (2016), 456–70; A.J. Hammerton, *Cruelty and Companionship: Conflict in Nineteenth Century Married Life* (London: Routledge, 1992).

24　McLaren, *Trials of Masculinity*; D.Y. Rabin, *Identity, Crime and Legal Responsibility in Eighteenth-Century England* (Basingstoke: Palgrave Macmillan, 2004); L. Bland, *Modern Women on Trial: Sexual Transgression in the Age of the Flapper* (Manchester: Manchester University Press, 2013); E. Gordon and G. Nair, *Murder and Morality in Victorian Britain: the Story of Madeleine Smith* (Manchester: Manchester University Press, 2009).

25　M. Wiener, *Men of Blood: Violence, Manliness and Criminal Justice in Victorian England* (Cambridge: Cambridge University Press, 2004).

26　Collier, 'Masculinities, law'.

27　McLaren, *Trials of Masculinity*; A. Schoppe, '"Losing him in a labyrinth of his own cloth": Beau Fielding's 1706 bigamy trial reprints and the politics of male fashion criticism', *Journal for Eighteenth-Century Studies*, 39:3 (2016), 413–29.

28　H. Lefebvre, *The Production of Space*, trans. D. Nicholson-Smith (London: Wiley, 1991); D. Conlan, 'Productive bodies, performative spaces: Everyday life in

Christopher Park', *Sexualities*, 7 (2004), 462–79; D. Massey, *Space, Place and Gender* (Cambridge: Polity Press, 1994).

29 M. Rose, 'The seductions of resistance: Power, politics, and a performative style of systems', *Environment and Planning D: Society and Space*, 20 (2002), 383–400; N. Gregson and G. Rose, 'Taking Butler elsewhere: Performativities, spatialities and subjectivities', *Environment and Planning D: Society and Space*, 18 (2000), 433–52.

30 E. Goffman, *The Presentation of the Self in Everyday Life* (New York: Anchor Books, 1959).

31 J. Butler, *Gender Trouble: Feminism and the Subversion of Identity* (London: Routledge, 1999).

32 J. Butler, 'Gender as performance', in P. Osborne (ed.), *A Critical Sense: Interviews with Intellectuals* (London: Routledge, 1996), pp. 111–12.

33 G. Deleuze, *Difference and Repetition* (London: Continuum, 1994); S. Renshaw, *The Subject of Love: Hélène Cixous and the Feminine Divine* (Manchester: Manchester University Press, 2009).

34 Renshaw, *Subject of Love*.

35 For an extensive discussion of my conceptualisation of power see: K. Barclay, *Love, Intimacy and Power: Marriage and Patriarchy in Scotland, 1650–1850* (Manchester: Manchester University Press, 2011), Chapter 1.

36 P. Bourdieu, *Outline of a Theory of Practice* (Cambridge: Cambridge University Press, 1972).

37 *Ibid.*

38 E.D. Ermath, 'Agency in the discursive condition', *History and Theory*, 40 (2001), 34–58.

39 C. Brickell, 'Masculinities, performativity, and subversion: A sociological reappraisal', *Men and Masculinities*, 8 (2005), 24–43.

40 K. Barad, *Meeting the Universe Halfway: Quantum Physics and the Entanglement of Matter and Meaning* (Durham, NC: Duke University Press, 2011); K. Barad, 'Posthumanist performativity: Towards an understanding of how matter comes to matter', *Signs*, 28:3 (2003), 801–31.

41 E. Grosz, *Becoming Undone: Darwinian Reflections on Life, Politics and Art* (Durham, NC: Duke University Press, 2011); A. Fausto-Sterling, '"The bare bones of sex": Part 1 – sex and gender', *Signs*, 30:2 (2005), 1491–528.

42 G. Lakoff and M. Johnson, *Philosophy in the Flesh: The Embodied Mind and its Challenge to Western Thought* (New York: Basic Books, 1999).

43 S. Gordon, 'Pyschoneurointracrinology: The embodied self', in S. Gordon (ed.), *Neurophenomenology and its Applications to Psychology* (New York: Springer, 2013), p. 122

44 D. Waskul and P. Vannini (eds), *Body/Embodiment: Symbolic Interaction and the Sociology of the Body* (Farnham: Ashgate, 2006).

45 S. Ahmed, *The Cultural Politics of Emotion* (Edinburgh: Edinburgh University Press, 2004).

46 J.S. Donnelly's introduction to *Captain Rock: The Irish Agrarian Rebellion of 1821–1824* (Madison: University of Wisconsin Press, 2009) gives a good overview of these debates.

47  R. Connell, 'Hegemonic masculinity: Rethinking the concept', *Gender & Society*, 19 (2005), 829–59; J. Tosh, 'Gentlemanly politeness and manly simplicity in Victorian England', *Transactions of the Royal Historical Society*, 12 (2002), 455–72; for a discussion of other critiques of hegemonic masculinity see: M. McCormack, 'Men, the public and political history', in McCormack, *Public Men*, pp. 17–18.

48  L. Code, *Ecological Thinking: Thinking the Politics of Epistemic Location* (Oxford: Oxford University Press, 2006).

49  L. McCall, 'The complexity of intersectionality', in D. Cooper (ed.), *Intersectionality and Beyond: Law, Power and the Politics of Location* (Oxon: Routledge-Cavendish, 2009), pp. 49–76; L.R.J. Maynard, 'Hoddin' Grey an' A' That: Robert Burn's heads, class hybridity, and the value of the ploughman's mantle', in A. Krishnamurthy (ed.), *The Working-Class Intellectual in Eighteenth- and Nineteenth-Century Britain* (Farnham: Ashgate, 2009), pp. 49–76.

50  D. Wahrman, *The Making of the Modern Self: Identity and Culture in Eighteenth-Century England* (New Haven: Yale University Press, 2006); C. Taylor, *Sources of the Self: The Making of Modern Identity* (Cambridge: Cambridge University Press, 1989).

51  T.B. Hug, *Impostures in Early Modern England: Representations and Perceptions of Fraudulent Identities* (Manchester: Manchester University Press, 2009).

52  S. Collini, 'The idea of "character" in Victorian political thought', *Transactions of the Royal Historical Society*, 35 (1985), 29–50.

53  T. Ahnert and S. Manning, 'Introduction', in T. Ahnert and S. Manning (eds), *Character, Self, and Sociability in the Scottish Enlightenment* (Basingstoke: Palgrave Macmillan, 2009), pp. 1–3.

54  Higgins, *A Nation of Politicians*, p. 37; R. Munter, *The History of the Irish Newspaper 1685–1760* (Cambridge: Cambridge University Press, 1967); B. Inglis, *The Freedom of the Press in Ireland, 1784–1841* (Westport: Greenwood Press Publishers, 1975).

55  For Leinster: *Carlow Morning Post* (1818–1835); *Carlow Sentinel* (1832–1845); *Freeman's Journal* (1800–1845); *Leinster Journal* (1800–1845). For Munster: *Ennis Chronicle and Clare Advertiser* (1800–1831); *Kerry Evening Post* (1828–1845); *Cork Examiner* (1841–1845). For Ulster: *Belfast Newsletter* (1800–1845); *Enniskillen Chronicle and Erne Packet* (1836–1845). For Connaught: *Ballina Advertiser* (1840–1843); *Ballina Impartial* (1823–1835); *Connaught Journal* (1823–1840); *Mayo Mercury* (1840–1841); *Sligo Champion* (1836–1838). Digitised papers were located on the British Newspaper Archive and the Irish Newspaper Archive.

56  J. Wallace, *The Reporters* (Philadelphia: T. and J.W. Johnson, 1855).

57  For an extended discussion see: K. Barclay, 'Narrative, law and emotion: Husband killers in early nineteenth-century Ireland', *Journal of Legal History*, 38:2 (2017), 203–27.

58  This is not to say that there were no 'fake' reports, but they are usually in a different format from standard trial reporting to indicate this. See, for example, 'Scene at the Head Police Office Dublin', *Belfast Newsletter*, (27 August 1844). This was a widely published story that also appeared (with English names) as 'A Mem. From my Notebook', in G.P Morris and N.P. Willis (eds), *The New Mirror* (New York: Fuller & Co., 1843), vol. 2, p. 296.

59  H.M. Scharf, 'The court reporter', *Journal of Legal History*, 10 (1989), 191–227.

60  The accuracy of reported speech is a topic of debate and some accounts used 'constructed dialogue'; at the same time, many articles include apologies by reporters where speech

was difficult to record which indicate that journalists were attempting to accurately capture events. Even with the best intentions, this would have been subject to human error. For discussion see: N. Goc, *Women, Infanticide, and the Press, 1822–1922: News Narratives in England and Australia* (Aldershot: Ashgate, 2013), Chapter 1.

61 N. Duxbury, *The Nature and Authority of Precedent* (Cambridge: Cambridge University Press, 2008), p. 56.

62 An example of a judge using a newspaper this way: National Archives of Ireland [hereafter NAI] CRF 1855 C8.

63 'Criminal Business', *Southern Reporter and Cork Commercial Courier* (11 August 1840) Cork.

64 *Report from Committees: Eight Volumes: VI. Carlow Borough Election* (London: House of Commons, 1839), pp. 264–6.

65 A. Aspinall, 'The social status of journalists at the beginning of the nineteenth century', *Review of English Studies*, 21:83 (1945), 216–32.

66 Frances Knox appears in numerous records, but see B.P. Arthur, *Newmarket-on-Fergus Looking Back* (Nenagh: Nenagh Guardian, s.n.). It is also notable that the correspondent for the *Irish Reporter*, a serial publication reporting on legal business, was a woman, Miss O'Connell, during the 1820s.

67 J.L. Austin, *How to Do Things with Words* (Oxford: Clarendon Press, 1962).

68 K. Barclay, 'Stereotypes as political resistance: The Irish police court columns, c. 1820–1845', *Social History*, 42:2 (2017), 257–80.

69 K. Barclay, 'Singing and lower-class masculinity in the Dublin Magistrate's Court, 1800–1845', *Journal of Social History*, 47:3 (2014), 746–68.

70 J. Habermas, *The Structural Transformation of the Public Sphere: An Inquiry into a Category of Bourgeois Society*, trans. T. Burger and F. Lawrence (Cambridge, MA: Massachusetts Institute of Technology, 1991).

71 B. Anderson, *Imagined Communities: Reflections on the Origin and Spread of Nationalism* (London: Verso, 1983), pp. 41–9.

72 Higgins, *A Nation of Politicians*, p. 37.

73 J. Cohen, 'Audience identification of media characters', in J. Bryant and P. Vorderer (eds), *Psychology of Entertainment* (London: Routledge, 2006), pp. 190–3.

74 J.D. Popkin, 'Press and the "counter-discourse" in the early July Monarchy', in D. de la Motte and J.M. Przyblyski (eds), *Making the News: Modernity and the Mass Press in Nineteenth Century France* (Boston: University of Massachusetts Press, 1999), pp. 15–42.

75 Inglis, *Freedom of the Press*, pp. 224–7.

76 J. Kelly, 'Political publishing, 1700–1800', in R. Gillespie and A. Hadfield (eds), *The Oxford History of the Irish Book, Volume III: The Irish Book in English, 1550–1800* (Oxford: Oxford University Press, 2006), p. 229.

77 For example, 'A Case of Distress', *Belfast Newsletter* (25 November 1842) Dublin; 'Dublin Police', *Freeman's Journal* (4 July 1839) Dublin. Newspapers were also used as evidence, e.g. death announcements used to prove innocence in bigamy cases. For example 'Extraordinary & Interesting Trial Commission Court, Dublin', *Belfast Newsletter* (1 May 1829) Dublin.

78 K.J. Mays, 'Domestic spaces, readerly acts: Reading(,) gender and class in working-class autobiography', *Nineteenth-Century Contexts*, 30:4 (2008), 342–68; D. Vincent,

*Bread, Knowledge and Freedom: A Study of Nineteenth-Century Working Class Autobiography* (London: Methuen, 1981), pp. 24–5.

79  J. Stiles, 'Nationalism, Patriotism and the Stage Irish on the Early Nineteenth Century Dublin Stage' (PhD thesis, Tufts University, 2002); A. Chills, 'Boundaries of Britishness: Boxing, Minorities, and Identity in Late-Georgian Britain' (PhD thesis, Boston College, 2007), p. 156.

80  S. Hood, 'The significance of the villages and small towns in rural Ireland during the eighteenth and nineteenth centuries', in P. Borsay and L. Proudfoot (eds), *Provincial Towns in Early Modern England and Ireland: Change, Convergence and Divergence* (Oxford: Oxford University Press, 2002), p. 245.

81  A. Power, *Hovels to High Rise: State Housing in Europe since 1850* (London: Routledge, 1993), p. 319.

82  P. Roebuck, 'The Donegall family and the development of Belfast 1600–1850', in P. Butel and L.M. Cullen (eds), *Cities and Merchants: French and Irish Perspectives on Urban Development, 1500–1900* (Dublin: Trinity College, 1986), p. 125.

83  M. Murphy, 'The economic and social structure of nineteenth-century Cork', in D. Harkness and M. O'Dowd (eds), *The Town in Ireland* (Belfast: Appletree Press, 1981), p. 125.

84  T.W. Freeman, *Pre-famine Ireland: A Study in Historical Geography* (Manchester: Manchester University Press, 1957).

85  P. Ollerenshaw, 'Industry, 1820–1914', in L. Kennedy and P. Ollerenshaw (eds), *An Economic History of Ulster, 1820–1939* (Manchester: Manchester University Press, 1985), pp. 62–108.

86  T. Barnard, 'The cultures of eighteenth-century Irish towns', in Borsay and Proudfoot, *Provincial Towns*, pp. 198–9.

87  J. Hill, 'Religion, trade and politics in Dublin 1798–1848', in Butel and Cullen, *Cities and Merchants*, p. 247.

88  S.J. Connelly, *Priests and People in Prefamine Ireland, 1780–1845* (Dublin: Four Courts Press, 2001), p. 15.

89  *Ibid.*, p. 17.

90  K. Miller, *Emigrants and Exiles: Ireland and the Irish Exodus to North America* (Oxford: Oxford University Press, 1985), pp. 48–9.

91  *Ibid.*, p. 52.

92  A. McKernan, 'War, gender and industrial innovation: Recruiting women weavers in early nineteenth-century Ireland', *Journal of Social History*, 28:1 (1994), 109–124.

93  Hill, 'Religion, trade', p. 247.

94  Donnelly, *Captain Rock*, p. 56–7.

95  P. McNally, 'Ireland: The making of the Protestant ascendancy, 1690–1760', in H.T. Dickinson (ed.), *A Companion to Eighteenth-Century Britain* (Oxford: Wiley-Blackwell, 2002), pp. 403–14; M. Wall, 'The rise of a Catholic middle class in eighteenth-century Ireland', *Irish Historical Studies*, 11:42 (1958), 91–115; D. Kennedy, 'The Irish opposition, parliamentary reform and public opinion, 1793–1794', *Eighteenth-Century Ireland*, 7 (1992), 95–114; Barnard, 'Cultures of eighteenth-century Irish towns', pp. 195–222; Inglis, *Freedom of the Press*.

96  H.J. Graff, *The Legacies of Literacy: Continuities and Contradictions in Western Culture and Society* (Bloomington: Indiana University Press), p. 337; *Report of the*

*Commissioners appointed to take the Census of Ireland, for the Year 1841* (Dublin: Alexander Thom, 1843), pp. xxxii–vi.

97  S. Connelly, 'Translating history: Brian Friel and the Irish past', in A. Peacock, *The Achievement of Brian Friel* (Gerrards Cross: Colin Smythe Limited, 1993), p. 150; W.J. Smyth, 'A plurality of Irelands: Regions, societies and mentalities', in B. Graham (ed.), *In Search of Ireland: A Cultural Geography* (London: Routledge, 1997), p. 36.

98  M.R. O'Connell, *Irish Politics and Social Conflict in the Age of the American Revolution* (Philadelphia: University of Pennsylvania Press, 2007).

99  M.J. Powell, 'Ireland: Radicalism, rebellion and union', in Dickinson, *Eighteenth-Century Britain*, pp. 416–17.

100  N. Curtin, *The United Irishmen: Popular Politics in Ulster and Dublin, 1791–1798* (Oxford: Clarendon Press, 1994), pp. 14–15.

101  *Ibid.*; K. Whelan, *The Tree of Liberty: Radicalism, Catholicism and the Construction of Irish Identity 1760–1830* (Cork: Cork University Press, 1996); J. Hill, *From Patriots to Unionists: Dublin Civic Politics and Irish Protestant Patriotism, 1660–1840* (Oxford: Oxford University Press, 1997).

102  M. Cronin, 'Memory, story and balladry: 1798 and its place in popular memory in pre-famine Ireland', in L. McGeary (ed.), *Rebellion and Remembrance in Modern Ireland* (Dublin: Four Courts Press, 2001), pp. 112–34; G. Beiner, *Remembering the Year of the French: Irish Folk History and Social Memory* (Madison: University Wisconsin Press, 2007).

103  Curtin, *United Irishmen*, pp. 13–37.

104  R. O'Donnell, *Robert Emmet and the Rising of 1803* (Dublin: Irish Academic Press, 2003); A. Dolan, P.M. Geoghegan and D. Jones (ed.), *Reinterpreting Emmet: Essays on the Life and Legacy of Robert Emmet* (Dublin: UCD Press, 2007).

105  P.M. Geoghegan, *King Dan: The Rise of Daniel O'Connell, 1775–1829* (Dublin: Gill & Macmillan, 2008).

106  C.C. Trench, *The Great Dan: A Biography of Daniel O'Connell* (London: Jonathan Cape, 1984); Geoghegan, *King Dan*.

107  J. Bew, *The Glory of Being Britons: Civic Unionism in Nineteenth-Century Belfast* (Dublin: Irish Academic Press, 2009); Hill, *From Patriots to Unionists*.

108  Donnelly, *Captain Rock*; C.H.E. Philpin (ed.), *Nationalism and Popular Protest in Ireland* (Cambridge: Cambridge University Press, 2002), pp. 219–43.

109  *First Report of the Commissioners of Public Instruction, Ireland* (London: William Clowes, 1835), p. 7.

110  I.N. Gregory, N.A. Cunningham, C.D. Lloyd, I.G. Shuttleworth and P.S. Ell, *Troubled Geographies: A Spatial History of Religion and Society in Ireland* (Bloomington: Indiana University Press, 2013).

111  T. Guinane, *The Vanishing Irish: Households, Migration, and the Rural Economy in Ireland, 1850–1914* (Princeton: Princeton University Press, 1997), p. 69

112  *First Report of the Commissioners of Public Instruction*, p. 7.

113  Hill, *From Patriots to Unionists*, p. 198.

114  D. Hempton and M. Hill, *Evangelical Protestantism in Ulster Society 1740–1890* (London: Routledge, 1992), p. 107.

115  K. Stanbridge, *Toleration and State Institutions: British Policy Toward Catholics in Eighteenth-Century Ireland and Quebec* (Oxford: Lexington Books, 2003), pp. 1–8.

116  Hill, *From Patriots to Unionists*; Philpin, *Nationalism and Popular Protest.*

117  McCormack, *The Independent Man*, pp. 165–9; Curtin, *The United Irishmen*, pp. 13–37.

118  Clark, *The Struggle for the Breeches*, pp. 141–7; R. Carr, *Gender and Enlightenment Culture in Eighteenth-Century Scotland* (Edinburgh: Edinburgh University Press, 2013).

119  Clark, *The Struggle for the Breeches*, pp. 141–57; Mackintosh and Forsberg, 'Performing the lodge', 451–72; S.-L. Hoffman, 'Civility, male friendship and masonic sociability in nineteenth-century Germany', *Gender & History*, 13:2 (2001), 224–48; T. Garvin, 'Defenders, Ribbonmen and others: Underground political networks in pre-famine Ireland', *Past and Present*, 96 (1982), 133–55.

120  Clark, *The Struggle for the Breeches*, pp. 141–57; M. McCormack, '"Married men and the fathers of families": Fatherhood and franchise reform in Britain', in H. Rogers and T. Broughton (eds), *Gender and Fatherhood in the Nineteenth Century* (Basingstoke: Palgrave, 2007), pp. 31–42.

121  Clark, *The Struggle for the Breeches*, pp. 141–57; A. Clark, *Scandal: The Sexual Politics of the British Constitution* (Princeton: Princeton University Press, 2004); V. Kreilkamp, 'Losing it all: The unmanned Irish landlord', in Cohen and Curtin, *Reclaiming Gender*, pp. 107–22.

122  Tosh, 'Gentlemanly politeness'; P. Carter, '"Polite" persons: Character, biography and the gentleman', *Transactions of the Royal Historical Society*, 12 (2002), 333–54; P. Carter, *Men and Emergence of Polite Society, Britain 1660–1800* (Harlow: Pearson Education, 2001); K. Glover, *Elite Women and Polite Society in Eighteenth-Century Scotland* (Woodbridge: Boydell and Brewer, 2011).

123  Kennedy, '"A Gallant Nation"', pp. 73–92; Cohen, '"Manners" make the man'; Carr, *Gender and Enlightenment.*

124  P. McDevitt, 'Muscular Catholicism: Nationalism, masculinity and Gaelic team sports, 1884–1916', *Gender & History*, 9:2 (1997), 262–84; J.A. Mangan and C. McKenzie, 'Martial and moral complexities: Changing certainties in changing imperial landscapes', *International Journal of the History of Sport*, 25:9 (2008), 1168–88.

125  L. Delap, '"Thus does man prove his fitness to be the master of things": Shipwrecks, chivalry and masculinities in nineteenth- and twentieth-century Britain', *Cultural and Social History*, 3 (2006), 45–74; Tosh, 'Gentlemanly politeness'.

126  Tosh, 'Gentlemanly politeness'.

127  G. Crossick, 'The Labour aristocracy and its values: A study of mid-Victorian Kentish London', *Victorian Studies*, 19:3 (1976), 306–28; C. Clausen, 'How to join the middle classes: With the help of Dr Smiles and Mrs Beeton', *American Scholar*, 62:3 (1993), 403–18; A.J. Hammerton, 'Pooterism and partnership? Marriage and masculine identity in the lower middle class, 1870–1920', *Journal of British Studies*, 38 (1999), 291–321; D. Wahrman, *Imagining the Middle Class: The Political Representation of Class in Britain, c. 1780–1840* (Cambridge: Cambridge University Press, 1995).

128  J. Nugent, 'The sword and the prayerbook: Ideals of authentic Irish manliness', *Victorian Studies*, 50:4 (2008), 587–613; L. Davidoff and C. Hall, *Family Fortunes: Men and Women of the English Middle Class, 1780–1850* (Chicago: Chicago University Press, 1987), p. 76; W. Barnhart, 'Evangelicalism, masculinity and the making of imperial missionaries in late Georgian Britain, 1795–1820', *The Historian*, 67:4

(2005), 712–32; J. Tosh, 'Methodist domesticity and middle class masculinity in nineteenth century England', in R.N. Swanson (ed.), *Gender and Christian Religion* (Woodbridge: Boydell Press, 1998), pp. 323–45.

129  D.S. Neff, 'Bitches, mollies and tommies: Byron, masculinity, and the history of sexualities', *Journal of the History of Sexuality*, 11 (2002), 395–438; N. Phillips, 'Parenting the profligate son: Masculinity, gentility, and juvenile delinquency in England, 1791–1814', *Gender & History*, 22:1 (2010), 92–108.

130  S. Morgan, 'Material culture and the politics of personality in early Victorian England', *Journal of Victorian Culture*, 17:2 (2012), 127–46; S. West, 'The Darly Macaroni Print and the politics of "Private Man"', *Eighteenth-Century Life*, 25:2 (2001), 170–82; D. Wahrman, *Imagining the Middle Class*, p. 276.

131  Valente, *Myth of Manliness*.

132  K. Barclay, 'The new history of the emotions', *Emotions: History, Culture, Society*, 1:1 (2017), 161–83.

133  W. Reddy, *The Navigation of Feeling* (Cambridge: Cambridge University Press, 2001); B. Rosenwein, *Emotional Communities in the Early Middle Ages* (London: Cornell University Press, 2006).

134  Barclay, *Love, Intimacy and Power*.

135  A parallel can be seen in Grosz, *Becoming Undone*.

136  See discussion in Barclay, 'Stereotypes'.

# 1

# Law and lawyers: 'the prerogative of the wig'

## THE IRISH BAR

A forensic scene of no slight piquancy is described in the Irish papers. Mr. Freeman, of the Munster Bar, was addressing a jury in Cork, when a Mr. Allen, a party in the cause, *put out his tongue at him*. It appears that Mr. Freeman has been making more than free welcome with Mr. Allen's name; and as the privilege of a *viva voce* reply to counsel in such cases is denied to the laity, the only retort left to the aggrieved party was to exhibit the weapon which he durst not use.

Such an interruption, however, appeared to the learned orator to be an invasion of the *prerogative of the wig*, and he made it the subject of a formal representation to the bench. 'My lord,' says he, 'this person has had the presumption to put out his tongue at me.'

Had such an outrage been perpetrated in the days of [George, Baron] Jeffreys, probably the offending member would have been cut out by its roots; but Mr. Sergeant Greene, who presided on this occasion, seems to have made as light of it as if it were the complaint of one overgrown schoolboy against another at a game of leapfrog. Nay, he almost justified the deed; for, without waiting to hear the self-vindication of Mr. Allen, his lordship said, 'I do think that counsel was indulging in observations which were stronger than I think the state of the case called for.'

. . .

Next morning the son of Mr. Allen saw Mr. Freeman in the street, and, as the learned gentlemen was no longer under the protecting aegis of his horse-hair curls, struck him. It was a premeditated and a gross assault, for which he deserves to be punished, and we hope he will be punished; but the gentlemen of the Munster bar have thrown an air of ridicule upon the affair, by representing it as a *contempt of court*, and claiming the interposition of the bench accordingly.

Sergeant Jackson . . . stood up now a champion for the privileges of the bar. And what are those privileges in this present case? The privilege of uttering language hurtful to the personal feelings of individuals, and not warranted, according to the impression of the presiding judge, by the facts proved in this case.

Sergeant Greene, and his assessor, Judge Ball, very properly resisted such an attempt to hedge about the licentiousness of the bar with immunities which are not accorded to those who abuse the opportunities they possess in the exercise of other callings and occupations. They decided that Mr. Freeman must seek his redress through the ordinary and constitutional channel of the law, which is quite sufficient to vindicate itself without any extraordinary interference of the court. We have no doubt that a jury will do him ample justice, and that the bench will not be wanting to its own dignity, and to what is really due to the bar in awarding the measure of punishment which the offence deserves.

*Dublin Morning Register*, 13 August 1840

When the barrister, Mr Freeman, asked the court to treat his assault as contempt of court, he made claim to the court as a space beyond society, where ordinary (insulting) words should be given a different status. In doing so, he contributed to a broader debate about what could be spoken in court; the protections, legal and otherwise, for those speaking, and the social impacts of such language.[1] On this occasion, the judge, Sergeant Green, thought Freeman had overstepped the unspoken rules of gentlemanly conduct that shaped courtroom behaviour.[2] Moreover, he, and Judge Ball, interpreted the subsequent assault as a personal dispute, not a legal one, and so subject to ordinary processes of justice. These were legal decisions that sought to locate the boundaries between society and the law, yet as historians have demonstrated, this boundary was highly contingent.

That 'the law', and certainly the legal profession, had its own procedures, rules and rituals, including specialist training and costume, has contributed to a discussion of the law's relationship to society.[3] For early historians of the law, the legal system was the manifestation of state authority.[4] More recently, acknowledgement of the significant usage of the law courts by ordinary people has complicated this analysis.[5] The nature of the connection of 'professional law', the 'artificial reason' of the trained lawyer, to what David Lemmings describes as 'affective jurisprudence', common sense ideas of natural justice, is now a topic of debate.[6]

This argument is especially significant for Ireland where the relationship between the legal system, the British administration and the Irish
is central to its political status.[7] Such discussions attempt to explain the
function, boundaries and legitimacy of 'the law' and its relationship to
the operation of power.

This chapter contributes to this discussion by exploring the ways
that, through legal practice, the law comes to embody particular social
relationships, notably those between coloniser and colonised, the social
classes, and men and women. This process of embodiment of social hierarchies by 'the law' enables both its culture and the capacity of individuals to receive justice from it. As discussed in the introduction, this
argument relies on the fact that the law is representational until it is
practised, with performances of the law giving flesh to power. It is professional men, like Freeman in the opening example, who are central to
the production of legal culture. Disputes over conduct between lawyers
are therefore not incidental to the law, but produce the law as masculine, even gentlemanly. Yet, the law is not just made by legal men, and
this chapter explores how the institutional structures of the law, as well
as other members of society, become implicated in the performance of
justice.

### Professional men embody the law

The gender and class dynamics of the legal system were personified in
the men who worked within it. The practice of the law was restricted to
men, primarily by custom, and reinforced by both training requirements
and legal culture. This group held the specialist legal knowledge and
reasoning that marked the law as a distinct institution; yet as gendered
individuals, members of families and often significant public actors, their
practice reflected the society of which they were part. In the eighteenth
century, there were between 800 and 1,000 barristers, solicitors and
attorneys in Ireland; this number grew significantly after Catholics were
permitted to practice in 1792, and the 1841 census listed 29 judges, 754
barristers and 2,572 attorneys.[8] Given prohibitions, the number of the
Catholics practising law in 1800 was low, but rapidly expanded. By 1861,
28 per cent of barristers and 35 per cent of attorneys were Catholic. It was
not until 1829 that they could hold senior judicial roles, such as King's
Counsel or judgeships.[9] By 1861, around a third of judgeships were held
by Catholics.[10]

Following the English system, legal men were divided into barristers
and solicitors or attorneys. Barristers specialised in courtroom advocacy

and legal pleadings. They were the senior members of the legal profession and were eligible to become King's Counsel (who represented the monarch) and to enter the judiciary. From 1796, some were promoted to 'Assistant Barrister', allowing them to judge minor criminal and civil suits at the quarter sessions.[11] Their role also expanded due to the growing importance of lawyers within criminal proceedings over the eighteenth century. Ireland used Crown lawyers to prosecute most criminal indictments across the nineteenth century, and, like England, defence lawyers became increasingly important to criminal practice.[12] Barristers had higher social status than solicitors, which in part reflected their social backgrounds where they were more likely to come from the gentry and established middle-class families.[13]

Solicitors performed everyday legal business, such as drawing up contracts, preparing cases and liaising with barristers on behalf of their clients. They were more numerous than barristers, less well paid and more likely to emerge from middle-class families.[14] The division in social background between the legal branches should not be overstated; the law was one place where social mobility was possible. John Philpot Curran was from a middling family, the son of a steward in the manorial court, but through patronage won a scholarship to Trinity College, and from there moved into the legal ranks, eventually becoming King's Counsel and Master of the Rolls (a judge in the high courts).[15] Daniel O'Connell was from a wealthy Catholic family dispossessed of their lands, whose education was supported by a rich uncle.[16]

Legal training in the early nineteenth century was not onerous. Irish barristers were required to 'train' (take a particular number of meals) at one of the English Inns of Court for a minimum of eight terms, or six if they acquired a master of arts or bachelor of laws degree from the Universities of Oxford, Cambridge or Dublin.[17] They were strongly encouraged to register with the equivalent Irish organisation, the King's Inn in Dublin, and to eat the requisite number of meals over nine semesters.[18] Towards the end of their studies, some students registered at both the English and Irish Inns to speed their completion.[19] On finishing, unlike in England, Irish barristers had to be called to the bar by a judge, creating a situation where qualified barristers could be refused the right to practice.[20] Solicitors undertook a five-year apprenticeship and a rather perfunctory exam that did not particularly test legal knowledge.[21]

At the Inns, there was no formal training. Students were encouraged to read in the law and more widely in preparation for practice, rooting their education in a broad liberal arts.[22] Some also underwent apprenticeships with practising attorneys and barristers.[23] Particularly through the sociable masculinity of the Inns, barristers were inculcated into a legal culture marked less by expert knowledge than shared social networks and comradery produced through drinking, eating and other bonding activities.[24] Unlike in England where restrictions on sociability separated barristers and solicitors, Dublin's King's Inn made no such distinction, with both groups registering and eating together. Moreover, Irish judiciary and law officers remained members even after promotion.[25] This produced a tight-knit profession that incorporated men across the legal ladder, formed through gendered social rituals that replicated those of other homosocial organisations of the period.

The limitations of this system were that the quality of the legal profession varied enormously and was determined more by an individual's desire for proficiency than systematic regulation. It meant that the law was not always strictly applied and, at times, custom, fairness and ideas of justice were given precedence over legal technicalities. Anxieties around the quality of legal practice led to improvements in teaching at Trinity College, Dublin, and to the establishment of the Dublin Law Institute in 1839, which promoted a more regular legal education.[26] It was a short-lived experiment, but marked a concern with improving the quality of the Irish legal profession. It can perhaps be located within a history of the growing professionalisation of the law in the eighteenth century, where, in England at least, litigation declined, costs rose, ordinary people chose lawyers over self-representation, and there were concerted efforts by the profession to raise their social status.[27] Yet, given that an interest in developing legal education only significantly occurred from the mid-nineteenth century, the rising status of the law cannot be explained by a growth in technical specialism alone.

Rather, the status of lawyers increased, at least partly, through their achievement of admirable masculine qualities (explored in later chapters), their role within a system that was located at the heart of political freedom and the British constitution, and the publicity that the courts received from the press and in popular culture more broadly.[28] Whilst barristers and the judiciary were not always members of the communities where they practised law, coming to Dublin for the legal term and moving around the country with the assizes, they were often, and increasingly, well-known figures in Irish public life. This was partly due to the important role of the higher courts in Irish community life. But, it was an effect exaggerated by the space given to legal business within the national and local press, as well as the flourishing trade in pamphlets and other ephemera reporting on high-profile trials. Through the press, the principal barristers and judiciary who worked in the higher courts became household names – names that were attached not only to legal abilities, but personalities, looks and behaviours.

Many lawyers were also well-known as politicians, political campaigners, writers and even amateur scientists. The publicity around their multiple roles acted to enhance their celebrity, leading to demand for details of their life and their legal practice by the general public. Notable examples of this include Daniel O'Connell, Richard Lalor Sheil (1791–1851), and John Philpot Curran (1750–1817), who at times appeared almost daily in the press. All three men were known campaigners for Catholic Emancipation giving them broad public support. Daniel O'Connell attracted huge crowds whenever he appeared in court or made political speeches; his face was available for sale on memorabilia, and his movements recorded by the national press.[29] Yet, it was not just their political allegiances that made these lawyers attractive. They were renowned for their oratory power, abilities on cross-examination and legal knowledge – skills they got as much from their liberal arts educations as their legal one. Over time, they gained status as folk heroes, with innumerable stories of their cunning and witty deeds feeding the popular imagination.[30]

Other legal men were not as widely known, or their fame lasted a more limited period. Yet, through their appearance in the press, the general public became familiar with their names and roles.[31] This allowed for reporters to make 'insider' jokes about individual lawyers assured that their regular readers would understand the significance. It brought the court into people's homes through the press, and so embedded it within local community life. Through its local and familiar actors, it invested people in the law and made intimate the public space of the court. In doing so, the professionalisation of law, through the formation of a distinct legal professional identity, was also a process of familiarisation for the general public, who were encouraged to invest in the law as part, if specialist, of the body politic. As a familiarisation produced through an engagement with charismatic men, the law's gendered make-up became central to its public identity; the professional lawyer was a man.

### The grammar of legal practice

If the law was manifested through its practitioners, it was also a system marked by its own reasoning. The Irish legal system was largely built upon the English that had been 'imposed or received' since the twelfth century, and which had given a broad shape to both its institutions and statutory law.[32] Over the centuries, however, the Irish system developed its own statutory and case law, as well as customs and rituals that marked it as distinct.[33] Thus, in *Bell v. Ahearne* (1849), a Chancery case, when English precedent was introduced by the plaintiff, the defence argued that 'English cases do not apply', and the judge agreed.[34] This relationship was a topic of some debate in the early nineteenth century, as barristers, the judiciary and the public attempted to determine the boundaries between English and Irish law.[35] In jury trials, barristers could be apologetic when introducing English precedence, defensive of the system's reputation as distinct and the public that took pride in it. Perhaps most famously, and certainly for rhetorical effect, Philpot Curran disparaged Irish treason law in the 1798 state trials arguing that the English law, which required two witnesses rather than one, was a superior form of justice. Yet, even he knew not to challenge the jury's investment in Ireland's discrete legal system: 'It has been insinuated, and with artful applications to your feeling of national independence, that I have advanced . . . the doctrine that you should be bound in your decisions by an English act of parliament . . . Reject the unfounded accusation; nor believe that I assail your independence'.[36] This independence should not be overstated. After 1800, Irish blackletter law was made at Westminster and courts used English case law where useful.

Whilst at particular historical moments the court system was understood to represent the imposition of British colonial rule on the Irish, in practice, perhaps like the nation itself, the court was a British-Irish hybrid.[37] Hybridity extends intersectionality in allowing people to hold identities that have historically been viewed as in conflict, such as that between classes or genders.[38] This complexity was manifested in the Main Hall of the building that hosted the Irish higher courts, where a series of murals marked significant moments in the making of 'Irish' law: William the Conqueror promulgating Norman laws; King John signing the Magna Carta; Henry II receiving the Irish Chieftains; and James I abolishing Brehon law.[39] Through such imagery, the Irish legal system was located in its English heritage, a narrative that emphasised continuity rather than disruption. Yet, it was a masterpiece designed and constructed by an Irish artist for a courthouse situated in Dublin. It was a compromise that captured the legal relationship between Ireland and its neighbour, where England was located as the primary and dominant tradition, thus with overtones of colonisation, but which was constructed by and for the Irish.

In 1801, there were six superior courts in Ireland.[40] There were three common law courts: the King's (or Queen's) Bench, Common Pleas and the Exchequer. Broadly speaking, the King's Bench dealt with serious criminal cases, 'Crown' cases and anything that did not fall under the jurisdiction of Common Pleas or the Exchequer. The latter courts presided over civil disputes and there was considerable overlap in their jurisdictions. Chancery was an equity court; Admiralty covered maritime law; and the Prerogative court was an ecclesiastical court that managed wills and testaments. Chancery and the common law courts appealed to the Court of Error; Admiralty and Prerogative appealed to Chancery; and all the superior courts could ultimately appeal to the House of Lords. From 1821, there was a court for the relief of insolvent debtors, and from 1836, a bankruptcy court. In the nineteenth century, all these courts sat in Dublin. The common law courts went on circuit as assizes twice year, visiting major towns and enabling justice in the regions.

At a local level, there were several courts available in theory and practice. Justices of the Peace (known as magistrates) held regular 'petty' sessions that enabled summary justice in minor criminal cases and oversaw local governance issues. In larger urban settlements, there were police courts that held much the same jurisdiction.[41] Serious crime was held over to the quarter sessions, typically performed at a county level and overseen by a bench of magistrates, or promoted to the higher courts for prosecution during the assizes. During periods of unrest, there were temporary special commissions authorised to try crime. In addition, most towns had places to settle minor criminal and civil disputes, including manor, borough or tholsel, mayor and sheriff courts. These reflected the overlapping seats of power in Irish society, where the appropriate authority might be the local landowner (manor), the mayor or sheriff, or the city council. Many of these courts had fallen into desuetude by the nineteenth century, and in 1840, a number were abolished to make legal jurisdiction more apparent.[42] In practice, it was the police, petty and quarter sessions that dealt with most local legal business and received the majority of coverage by the provincial press.[43]

Legal rules and procedures, as well as the logic of the law itself, were significant to the production of the court. Blackletter law defined the boundaries of legality – what was allowed and what was not, who owned what and how such property could be transmitted, etc. – and often set the parameters for proof, such as requiring a set number of witnesses to establish guilt. Judge-made law, as well as legal commentary, could expand 'the law' into a broader set of principles. This often operated on the logic of precedence – that similar decisions should be made by judges in similar circumstances. It incorporated the development of rules of evidence that shaped what information could be provided and how it should be weighed by judges and juries. As most evidence was provided parole, evidentiary rules often focused on determining *who* could speak and in what context.[44] Restrictions upon what was said were less encompassing during this period, the most significant being the hearsay rule developed during the previous century.[45] Most attention was given to how the character of an individual could be judged or weighed by observers.

All of this affected courtroom dynamics. As Derek Neal notes, the law provided a syntax and grammar for courtrooms.[46] If provocation required 'hot-blood', defence lawyers encouraged witnesses to evidence it; if an equity court needed injustice, plaintiffs and their representatives framed their narratives within a language of hurt and wrong-doing.[47] The distinction between common sense ideas of justice and the artificial grammar of the law were particularly prominent in discussions of libel law, where Irish law was designed not to restore the character of the defamed but to prevent breach of the peace (thus 'truth' was not a defence of libel). Justices repeatedly had to explain this law at length, emphasising the suit was not to 'restore character' but 'to see that the peace of society is preserved, and the passions of mankind are not to be excited'.[48] The 'truth' the juries were to determine was the imagined emotions of the reader of the libel. Given this, the law and the court system produced a 'truth' that conformed to the structures of the legal system. That this was the case was not lost on many in Ireland during a period where penal legislation that provided a differential justice was only latterly removed, and where libel law was repeatedly used to clamp down on political speech.

The logic of the law was not neutral, but shaped by wider social and political structures and values. Notably, it was shaped by common sense ideas about gender, class, religion and power. As discussed in the introduction, the classic case of the gendering of the law was the construal of the provocation defence for murder.[49] But, such gendered and classed assumptions were found in most legal jurisdictions. Restrictions on married women's property were underpinned by the same logic that had in the previous century prevented people who were not members of the Church of Ireland inheriting land; property was a source of power that could be used to undermine legitimate authority – a husband's patriarchal power or the rule of the Protestant state. Thus, good order was promoted through restricting the rights of women and Catholics and fed into a legal system that could not envision the importance of working-class women's wages, or a Catholic middle class.[50] Similarly, Irish law was often imagined as operating in an unruly environment, where the state required greater support to ensure the operation of justice. A treason conviction only required one witness as it was thought the Irish lower orders were less likely to testify against their brethren and that Irish juries were more reluctant to bring guilty verdicts than their English counterparts.

This legal grammar produced a court that operated in the interests of those who shared its assumptions; it required others to reconstruct their experiences in its vocabulary, something that counsel could aid them with. Yet, as shall be explored across this book, resistance to the court's logic was persistent and some were more successful in their challenges than others. Moreover, such resistance came not only from legal outsiders, but its own members. The restriction on the use of defence lawyers in felony cases, for example, appears to have been subject to greater critique in Ireland than in Britain.[51] Leonard MacNally (1752–1820), author of a key legal text on the rules of evidence, archly noted to a Dublin jury that 'Gentlemen, the Law does not allow me, this prosecution being for Felony, to state a case for prisoners. Their Counsel can only examine witnesses'.[52] It was a legally accurate but unnecessary statement that drew attention to the imbalance of power, a subtle request for the jury to provide remedy. Many other lawyers questioned the fairness of the law when it supported their client. If the law provided a 'grammar', it was through legal practice that the 'literature' of the law was produced. People gave the law definition, constructed meaning and occasionally tried to reinvent the rules.

### Society in the law

Professional men were the central cast of legal dramas, but they were not the only people who gave shape to the law. People from all walks of life came to court as litigants, to defend criminal charges or to testify in the cause of others, and reflected the broad array of social groups in Ireland. The public gallery, those who came to watch the court for entertainment or to support friends and family, could be diverse, although the frequency with which and the nature of the causes people attended was shaped by class, gender, age and whether they lived within easy travelling distance of the court. Audiences were likely dominated by men, the barristers and the elite who, as we shall explore, were privileged in the allocation of court space. Women were sometimes cleared from court in cases which were particularly violent or contained details of a sexual nature, although this is not regularly remarked on.[53] Lower-order women may have found it particularly challenging to get access to courtrooms, often described as standing outside waiting for verdicts.[54] This gendered composition meant that women, especially lower-order women, had less opportunity to participate in the production of the law and it reinforced the masculine culture of the court, further reducing women's access to justice. If gender was significant, however, class was even more so.

The courts remained an important site for the display and practice of hierarchical social and gender relationships. That the social elite had first right to seating seems to have gone largely unquestioned. When, during the 1848 trial of John Mitchel for sedition, the police took much of the seating and so deprived many of 'our fellow citizens, of the highest respectability' from attending, the nationalist press complained, arguing that the police overstepped their social position.[55] Conversely, the crowds that waited for verdicts outside courthouses were typically imagined as being of the lower orders, sometimes referred to as 'the mob' or described as emotionally unruly.[56] Once inside the courthouse, seating arrangements and the right to participate in proceedings reinforced traditional power structures.

Like in the rest of the United Kingdom, the social elite, particularly aristocrats and notable landowners, were privileged observers of court cases, reflecting their traditional roles as magistrates. Such men and occasionally women continued to take their seats at, or near, the judge's bench, an act that reminded the judiciary and the watching public of the overlapping sites of power within nineteenth-century Ireland.[57] The Mayor of Cork took his seat next to Judge Ball at the Cork Assizes in 1842.[58] It may have been to ensure their authority in this context that non-titled legal men were raised to the peerage on their appointment to the judiciary.[59] Some elite men also attended court as a reminder to their local communities of their presence and their continuing authority.

The treatment of grand juries was a clear example of this. The grand jury's primary role was in local governance, issuing contracts and authorising the collection of taxes to pay for municipal upkeep.[60] They also had a role in criminal trials, determining whether the prosecution brought a 'true bill' against the accused and thus authorising the trial. Members of the grand jury were selected by the local sheriff, but were primarily 'resident gentlemen, their agents, clergy and respectable tenantry'.[61] Studies of grand jury lists indicate that they were typically drawn from the community's elite and usually held multiple public roles, including as Members of Parliament, magistrates, sheriffs, deputy lord lieutenants and members of the borough council.[62] As elite men, members of the grand jury often situated themselves near the judge's bench or in key seating within the courtroom, and during trials interjected to ask witnesses' questions or to comment on proceedings, something that members of the public were restricted from doing. Through enabling the elite's participation in legal process, the institution of the grand jury not only acknowledged the social hierarchies of nineteenth-century society but built them into the practice of the law.

This incorporation of class hierarchy was also manifested in the lower courts, which were primarily overseen by magistrates. The magistracy were, historically and throughout much of the early nineteenth century, local landowners or similar notables, nominated by municipal corporations, the county governors or lord lieutenants and appointed by the 'Crown' (in practice the government). They were usually Protestant, despite Catholic landowners being entitled to hold this role. By 1834, only 10 per cent of magistrates were Catholic, and even in 1886, this had only risen to 25 per cent.[63] Once appointed, they were almost never stripped of their position, and their 'independence' from state control was of political importance.[64] Traditionally, magistrates operated relatively independently from each other, so that someone proffering information to one magistrate and not receiving the desired response could seek out a different magistrate for a more sympathetic hearing. From the early 1820s, the magistrates sat formally at weekly petty sessions, as a 'bench' (often simply whichever magistrates were available that day).[65]

Magistrates were not required to have legal training. From the seventeenth century, 'handbooks' provided guidance for working magistrates and many elite men had some legal training either from school or more formally.[66] However, most magistrates used the law flexibly to promote 'justice' within their communities. Here notions of fairness, coupled with a strong sense of custom, shaped legal outcomes. This is not to say that magistrates ignored the law; when lawyers or knowledgeable justices provided legal precedence during court business, it was often used determinatively in deciding outcomes.[67] But, the system relied on magistrates who understood the needs of their communities and operated accordingly. That the magistracy's notion of fairness was not always shared by the whole community could be cause of social disruption.

This context occasionally brought magistrates into conflict with the Dublin administration. The latter felt that law was imposed insufficiently strictly, with sectarian bias, or that magistrates allowed disorder to flourish in the provinces. Most magistrates disagreed, and saw interference as a challenge to their authority and the traditional structures of order in their communities. To help counter these problems, and to professionalise the magistracy, stipendiary or resident magistrates were introduced in the early years of the nineteenth century. In 1831, there were eleven, but by 1839, this had grown to fifty-four, and by 1860, seventy-four.[68] Like ordinary magistrates, there was no requirement for these men to have a legal education, but a number did. They were more likely to be middle-class professionals, such as doctors or ex-military, than their ordinary counterparts. Parachuted into communities, many were resented both by the ordinary magistracy and the public. Unlike ordinaries, they could be stripped of their role or, more commonly, moved to a different area if relationships broke down.[69] The intervention of resident magistrates did not fundamentally change the fact that a considerable part of the practice of law in Ireland, as in other parts of the United Kingdom, remained rooted within local community hierarchies.

'The law' was not an independent structure of external observers situated on the boundaries of the political, but an activity that reinforced and relied on traditional socio-political structures. These relationships were embedded into the law, not only through customary rules, but by the men who chose to exercise their privilege to sit near a judge, to intervene in a trial as a member of a grand jury, or in taking up the appointment of magistrate. Resident magistrates acted as a democratic challenge to this system, but, in this period at least, their presence did not significantly disrupt established structures. Rather the participation of men and women of different social classes in the legal system reflected broader norms for gendered and socio-political power. Through their participation, the law came to embody the power dynamics of Irish society.

### Judges and juries negotiate power

If the involvement of the social elite acted as one challenge to professional men's capacity to embody the law, so too did the jury. The petty jury was composed separately from the grand jury and its main purpose was to determine questions of fact and to deliver verdicts in both criminal and civil jury trials. Petty juries were slightly lower in the social hierarchy, often merchants and artisans, and were viewed as significant in ensuring the representation of 'the public' in legal process.[70] Their role within court dynamics has been a key discussion point for historians. John Langbein argued that the jury's role declined over the eighteenth century, particularly after the 'lawyerisation' of the trial. Their place was taken by the judge, whose authority expanded.[71] This was a transition, Langbein argued, which corresponded with a decline in the 'self-informing jury' in the nineteenth century, with the 'society of strangers', to use Wiener's evocative phrase, increasingly requiring the law to be exercised with an equity that prior knowledge might endanger.[72]

In an Irish context, however, Niamh Howlin found that juries continued to be active and engaged participants in trials across the century.
They interjected questions or commentary in 56 per cent of the 213 trials
in her sample, with little variation between criminal and civil suits. Most
juror interaction was in the form of sustained questioning of witnesses,
rather than single utterances, but they also interrupted counsel during
speeches, challenged the judge's remarks, provided sarcastic commentary and contributed to evidence.[73] Other examples of jury interactions
during trials appear across this volume. If juries did not always know the
people involved in a case (and they sometimes did), they were usually
members of the same communities and brought with them a broader
understanding of local power dynamics and relationships. Given this,
the lack of Catholics available for jury duty, due to property restrictions
and the socio-economic make-up of Irish communities, was a longstanding social concern, a particular issue in cases where religion was central
to interpreting events.[74]

As well as actively engaging in courtroom proceedings, Irish juries
were renowned for not guilty verdicts.[75] Neal Garnham found that before
1780, 77 per cent of cases at the assizes ended in acquittal; W.E. Vaughan
shows a conviction rate of only 13 per cent for murder trials in the 1860s.[76]
Explanations for Ireland's low conviction rate vary from a greater tolerance amongst juries for 'recreational violence' to an unwillingness to
cooperate with the British state.[77] Yet, as I explore elsewhere, the narrative structure of press reports was suggestive of a legal system that func-
tioned well, with jury verdicts explicable from the evidence presented
or the dynamics of the trial. This may have reflected a certain conserva-
tism in press reporting, but it also gave legitimacy to jury verdicts for
the public.[78] Whilst conflicts between judges and juries appear in the
record, and were occasionally high-profile, this was atypical of ordinary
legal business; if judges regularly disagreed with verdicts, they respected
juries enough not to put it on the public record. Moreover, judges did
not always push for guilty verdicts, with several examples of juries being
asked to reconsider cases where they found for the Crown.[79]

This is not to suggest that the judiciary did not play a significant
role in courtroom dynamics. As is explored across this volume, judges
were spatially and rhetorically located as the source of power within
court. Through their decisions and charges, they determined what was
legally relevant and what was not; their interpretations produced justice.
The capacity for the judiciary to thus embody the law was captured in
their generic title in the press: 'the court'. It was a label that collapsed the
dynamism of legal proceedings into their judgments, mirroring in many

respects the way those decisions closed possibilities, as well as generated new ones. Yet, if judicial power was authoritative, the jury verdict was equally vital to the law. Their continued active engagement in legal processes was not only largely tolerated by the judiciary and press but served as a key reminder of the public who the jury symbolised in the balance of legal power – a public who was increasingly envisioned as a significant feature of 'the court'.

## The public at court

Whilst it has been argued for the eighteenth century that the role of the elite in legal business enabled the law to be utilised as a form of top-down power, the early nineteenth century, perhaps especially after 1798 in Ireland, was a different environment.[80] Demands for greater political representation of the people were a core feature of United Kingdom politics during the era, as was the expectation of some freedom of the press, reasonable toleration of political speech, and a law that was transparent and equitable.[81] Such claims were the mark of an increasingly mature public during these decades and a public that saw the law as a central domain for the exercise of power.

Courtrooms had long been 'public' spaces, a fact that informed their function. Attending court as a leisure activity remained important in Ireland across the nineteenth century, reflecting the significance of the law courts to community life. The bi-annual assizes that brought judges, lawyers and their legal entourages to provincial towns were accompanied by public banquets, assemblies and balls, as well as court business. The middling sorts and elites, both men and women, were drawn to their local assize towns to socialise, whilst men came to perform their role on various juries.[82] In Dublin, attending the higher courts was an important leisure activity during term time, with the courts acting, like the theatre or ballroom, as a place to be seen, to flirt and to catch up on the local gossip.[83] Important events were often overcrowded and ticketing was introduced for high-profile cases; new courtrooms were designed with extra seating to allow for demand.[84]

The assizes also brought those lower down the social ladder to court due to the economic opportunities promoted by gatherings of people, and because they too enjoyed the entertainment courts provided. Lower-order men and women came as they were significantly more likely to be prosecuted for crime than their elite brethren, but also because the lives of individuals of all ranks in small communities were intertwined. This was reinforced by the communitarian ideals of the

Christian community in the early nineteenth century, where the sins of one had implications for the well-being of the nation, permitting a degree of surveillance between neighbours. This is not to suggest that such communities had no sense of personal or familial boundaries, nor that Ireland was unaffected by the growing emphasis on privacy, and the home as a private sphere, as elsewhere in the United Kingdom.[85] But it created an environment where attending court to observe was not an invasion into the private life of another, but participation in community life. Through the publicity of the press, the community could grow to include the nation.

If the Irish public was expected to invest in their national legal system, the jurisdiction and legal processes of each court shaped their relationship with them. Courts whose functions were performed publicly, rather than through writ, provided more opportunity for engagement and press coverage. Crime was a staple interest, drawing on broader concerns with morality, deviance and national security. But civil suits too were widely attended and reported, particularly where they gave insight into people's sexual behaviour and family lives, involved famous people, or had implications beyond the individual. The public's appetite and interest in the law, however, was expansive, capturing petty sessions, bankruptcy, Admiralty, Chancery and more. There were also specialist law publications, such as the *Irish Law Recorder*, which provided fuller coverage of legal business, particularly legal argument and precedence. Even daily papers were willing to summarise very technical suits if they were of legal importance, focusing on conveying the significance of the decision to the public.

The public's interest in the law's social and political functions was widespread and not always limited by access or legal speciality. Well-read members of the public likely had some familiarity with the types of business performed by all the Irish courts, whilst the common law (assize), criminal and magistrate courts were accessible to most of the public. Through the press, people were given the information they needed to invest in their system of justice and to own it as Irish. This process of publicity in turn contributed to the law's legitimacy through making it transparent and comprehensible; and it fed into wider democratic ideals that located the law as a mechanism for the negotiation of social power relationships.[86] In doing so, it may have offset any loss of familiarity with the legal system felt by the public as the law became increasingly specialised. Importantly, through framing the courts as public spaces and through inviting the public to observe (whether in person or through the press), they too became implicated in the production of the court.

The lawyer may have embodied the law through his practice, but it was the public who observed him and held him to account that determined whether justice was served.

## Conclusion

If Mr Freeman persisted in his prosecution of Mr Allen's son for assault, he would have been at a distinct advantage as a prosecutor. He would have made a case in a courtroom before a judge who likely knew him and may have socialised with him at the King's Inn. The gallery may have contained several of his legal brethren, perhaps providing a sympathetic audience for his grievance. As a barrister, his education and class would have enabled him to generally conform to the rules of gentlemanly conduct required within courtrooms. He may well have also had a sympathetic audience in the readership of the press, who perhaps recognised him from his previous role as Assistant-Barrister in Kerry, from earlier trials, or indeed from his involvement in election politics.[87] The justice he would have received would have reflected that the court was not only designed for men like him, but that men like him embodied the law in the public imagination. This was a process that construed the law as masculine and upper middle class. Whether it was British or Irish, Catholic or Protestant, was perhaps more contested, reflecting that these were key boundary markers in Irish society. Professional men were not the only way that the law came into being. The law was also produced by legal strictures, the other men and women who came to court, and the general public, as they engaged in and with its practice. Thus the colonial origins of the legal system, the class hierarchies of Irish society, and the democratic potential of a growing public sphere were inscribed in the law. These were not just contexts that the law operated within but became the law as they were drawn into its practice and representation.

## Notes

1  For further discussion see: K. Barclay, 'A sectarian middle ground?: Masculinity and politics in the 1820s petty session courts', Working Paper, and Chapter 5.

2  D.J.A. Cairns, *Advocacy and the Making of the Adversarial Criminal Trial 1800–1865* (Oxford: Clarendon Press, 1998).

3  C.W. Brookes, *Law, Politics and Society in Early Modern England* (Cambridge: Cambridge University Press, 2008).

4  D. Hay, 'Property, authority and the criminal law', in D. Hay *et al.* (eds), *Albion's Fatal Tree: Crime and Society in Eighteenth-Century England* (London: Verso, 1975), pp. 17–64.

5   M. Ingram, 'Law, litigants and the construction of "honour": Slander suits in early modern England', in Peter Cross (ed.), *The Moral World of the Law* (Cambridge: Cambridge University Press, 2000), pp. 134–60; E.P. Thomson, 'Patrician society, plebeian culture', *Journal of Social History*, 7:4 (1974), 382–45; P. King, *Crime, Justice and Discretion in England, 1740–1820* (Oxford: Oxford University Press, 2003).

6   D. Lemmings, 'Emotions, courtrooms and popular opinion about the administration of justice: The English experience, from Coke's "Artificial Reason" to the sensibility of "True Crime Stories"', *Emotions: History, Culture, Society*, 1:1 (2017), 59–90; P. Geng, 'Popular Jurisprudence in Early Modern England' (PhD thesis, University of Southern California, 2014).

7   S.J. Connolly, *Religion, Law and Power: The Making of Protestant Ireland, 1660–1760* (Oxford: Clarendon Press, 1992); H. Laird, *Subversive Law in Ireland, 1879–1920: From Unwritten Law to Dail Courts* (Dublin: Four Courts Press, 2005); A. Carter, *Was Ireland Conquered? International Law and the Irish Question* (London: Pluto Press, 1996).

8   J. McEntee, '"Gentlemen practisers": Solicitors as elites in mid-nineteenth-century Irish landed society', in C. O'Neill (ed.), *Irish Elites in the Nineteenth Century* (Dublin: Four Courts Press, 2013), pp. 99–112; C.E. Brett, *Court Houses and Market Houses of the Province of Ulster* (Ulster: Ulster Architectural Heritage Society, 1973), p. 12.

9   C. Kenny, 'The exclusion of Catholics from the legal profession in Ireland, 1537–1829', *Irish Historical Studies*, 25:100 (1987), 337–57.

10  E. Larkin, *The Historical Dimensions of Irish Catholicism* (Washington: Catholic University of America Press, 1976), pp. 32–3.

11  W.N. Osborough, 'The Irish legal system, 1796–1877', in C. Costello (ed.), *The Four Courts: 200 Years. Essays to Commemorate the Bicentenary of the Four Courts* (Dublin: Incorporated Council of Law Reporting for Ireland, 1996), p. 56.

12  N. Howlin, 'Nineteenth-century criminal justice: Uniquely Irish or simply "not English"', *Irish Journal of Legal Studies*, 3:1 (2013), 80; A.N. May, *The Bar & the Old Bailey, 1750–1850* (Chapel Hill: University of North Carolina Press, 2003). This is explored in more detail in later chapters.

13  R. Whan, *The Presbyterians of Ulster, 1680–1730* (Woodbridge: Boydell Press, 2013), pp. 127–36; C. O'Neill, *Catholics of Consequence: Transnational Education, Social Mobility, and the Irish Elite 1850–1900* (Oxford: Oxford University Press, 2014), pp. 115–19; T. Clancy, 'The Four Courts buildings and the development of an independent Bar of Ireland', in Costello, *Four Courts*, pp. 80–104; D. Lemmings, *Professors of the Law: Barristers and English Legal Culture in the Eighteenth Century* (Oxford: Oxford University Press, 2003), pp. 225–39.

14  D. Hogan, 'Solicitors and the Four Courts', in Costello, *Four Courts*, pp. 224–34.

15  J. Kelly, 'Curran, John Philpot (1750–1817)', *Oxford Dictionary of National Biography* (Oxford: Oxford University Press, 2004). www.oxforddnb.com/view/article/6950, accessed 8 June 2015.

16  P.M. Geoghegan, *King Dan: The Rise of Daniel O'Connell, 1775–1829* (Dublin: Gill & Macmillan, 2008).

17  D.H. Akenson, *Discovering the End of Time: Irish Evangelicals in the Age of Daniel O'Connell* (Montreal: McGill-Queen's University Press, 2016), p. 135; V.T.H. Delany,

'The history of legal education in Ireland', *Journal of Legal Education*, 12 (1959–60), 396–406; May, *The Bar & the Old Bailey*, p. 76.

18  Akenson, *Discovering the End of Time*, p. 135.

19  Geoghegan, *King Dan*, p. 38.

20  C. Kenny, *King's Inns and the Kingdom of Ireland: The Irish 'Inn of Court' 1541–1800* (Dublin: Irish Academic Press, 1992).

21  J.C. Brady, 'Legal developments, 1801–79', in W.E. Vaughan (ed.), *A New History of Ireland: V: Ireland Under the Union, 1 1801–70* (Oxford: Oxford University Press, 2010), pp. 476–80.

22  Lemmings, *Professors of the Law*, p. 146.

23  C. Kenny, *Tristram Kennedy and the Revival of Irish Legal Training, 1835–1885* (Dublin: Irish Academic Press, 1996), p. 2.

24  G. Bloom, 'Manly drunkenness: Binge drinking as disciplined play', in A. Bailey and R. Hentschell (eds), *Masculinity and the Metropolis of Vice, 1550–1650* (Basingstoke: Palgrave Macmillan, 2010), pp. 21–44; I. Davis, *Writing Masculinity in the Later Middle Ages* (Cambridge: Cambridge University Press, 2007), p. 141; L. Magnusson, 'Scoff power in *Love's Labour's Lost* and the Inns of Court: Language in context', in P. Holland (ed.), *Shakespeare Survey: An Annual Survey of Shakespeare Studies and Production* (Cambridge: Cambridge University Press, 2004), pp. 196–208.

25  Kenny, *King's Inns*; Akenson, *Discovering the End of Time*, p. 135.

26  Kenny, *Tristram Kennedy*.

27  P. Corfield, *Power and the Professions in Britain 1700–1850* (London: Routledge, 1995); J.H. Langbein, *The Origins of Adversary Criminal Trial* (Oxford: Oxford University Press, 2005); Lemmings, *Professors of the Law*; May, *The Bar & the Old Bailey*.

28  N. Lacey, 'The way we lived then: The legal profession and the nineteenth-century novel', *Sydney Law Review*, 33 (2011), 599–621.

29  B. Inglis, 'O'Connell and the Irish press 1800–42', *Irish Historical Studies*, 29 (1952), 1–27; G. Owens, 'Nationalism without words: Symbolism and ritual behaviour in the Repeal "Monster Meetings" of 1843–5', in J.S. Donnelly Jr and K.A. Miller (eds), *Irish Popular Culture 1650–1850* (Dublin: Irish Academic Press, 1998), pp. 242–70.

30  É. Hickey, *Irish Law and Lawyers in Modern Folk Tradition* (Dublin: Four Courts Press, 1999).

31  K. Barclay, 'Manly magistrates and citizenship in an Irish town: Carlow, 1820–1840', in K. Cowman, N. Koefoed and Å.K. Sjögren (eds), *Gender in Urban Europe: Sites of Political Activity and Citizenship, 1750–1900* (London: Routledge, 2014), pp. 58–72; K. Barclay, 'Singing and lower-class masculinity in the Dublin Magistrate's Court, 1800–1845', *Journal of Social History*, 47:3 (2014), 746–68.

32  M. Brown and S.P. Donlan, 'The laws in Ireland, 1689–1850: A brief introduction', in M. Brown and S.P. Donlan (eds), *The Laws and Other Legalities of Ireland, 1689–1850* (Farnham: Ashgate, 2011), p. 4.

33  See, for example, the publication, 'Mr Stewart's Law Precedents', which provided Irish precedence for lawyers. It was advertised in *Saunder's Newsletter* (19 November 1827) and discussed in 'Precedents in Conveyancing', *The Legal Observer, or Journal of Jurisprudence* (5 May 1838), p. 3.

34  'Irish Law Intelligence', *Cork Examiner* (16 March 1849) Dublin.

35 There are some entertaining discussions of this in the nationalist press: 'Irish-Made Law', *Freeman's Journal* (7 June 1844); 'The English against the Irish Judges', *Roscommon and Leitrim Gazette* (1 April 1843).

36 J.P. Curran, 'For Oliver Bond [High Treason]', in T. Davis (ed.), *The Speeches of The Right Honorable John Philpot Curran* (London: Henry G. Bohn, 1847), p. 345.

37 Barclay, 'Singing and lower-class masculinity'.

38 L.R.J. Maynard, 'Hoddin' Grey an' A' That: Robert Burn's heads, class hybridity, and the value of the ploughman's mantle', in Krishnamurthy, *The Working-Class Intellectual*, pp. 67–84; L. McCall, 'The complexity of intersectionality', in D. Cooper (ed.), *Intersectionality and Beyond: Law, Power and the Politics of Location* (Oxon: Routledge-Cavendish, 2009), pp. 49–76.

39 P.D. Hardy, *The New Picture of Dublin: Or Stranger's Guide through the Irish Metropolis* (Dublin: William Curry, Jun. and Co., 1831), p. 148.

40 R.B. McDowell, 'The Irish courts of law, 1801–1914', *Irish Historical Studies*, 10:40 (1957), 363–91.

41 G. Broeker, *Rural Disorder and Police Reform in Ireland, 1812–1836* (London: Routledge, 1970); K.P. O'Rorke, 'Dublin police', *Dublin Historical Record*, 29:4 (1976), 138–47; B. Griffin, *The Bulkies: Police and Crime in Belfast, 1800–1865* (Dublin: Irish Academic Press, 1997).

42 McDowell, 'The Irish courts of law'; T.C. Barnard, 'Local courts in later seventeenth- and eighteenth-century Ireland', in Brown and Donlan, *The Laws*, pp. 33–46.

43 There were also twenty-six ecclesiastical courts that are not part of this study.

44 L. MacNally, *The Rules of Evidence on Pleas of the Crown* (Dublin: J. Cooke, 1802); H. Roscoe, *A Digest of the Law of Evidence in Criminal Cases* (London: Saunders & Benning, 1835); R. McMahon, 'Introduction', in R. McMahon (ed.), *Crime, Law and Popular Culture in Europe, 1500–1900* (Collumpton: Willan, 2008), pp. 1–31; B. Shapiro, *Beyond Reasonable Doubt and Probable Cause: Historical Perspectives on the Anglo-American Law of Evidence* (Berkeley: University of California University Press, 1991).

45 J. Hostettler, *A History of Criminal Justice in England and Wales* (Hook: Waterside Press, 2009), pp. 225–43.

46 D. Neal, 'Suits makes the man: Masculinity in two English law courts, c. 1500', *Canadian Journal of History*, 37 (2002), 1–22.

47 For a discussion see: L. Gowing, 'Gender and the language of insult in early modern London', *History Workshop Journal*, 35 (1993), 1–21; T. Stretton, 'Social historians and the records of litigation', in S. Sogner (ed.), *Fact, Fiction and Forensic Evidence* (Oslo: Skriftserie fra Historisk Institutt, Universitetet i Oslo, 1997), pp. 15–34.

48 'Trial of Eneas McDonnell', *Waterford Chronicle* (15 December 1827) Dublin.

49 G. Walker, *Crime, Gender and Social Order in Early Modern England* (Cambridge: Cambridge University Press, 2003), pp. 113–58; for how that has changed over time whilst remaining gendered see: K.J. Kesselring, 'No greater provocation? Adultery and the mitigation of murder in English law', *Law and History Review*, 34:1 (2016), 199–225.

50 The literature on how property law constrained women is extensive. Some important examples are: A. Erickson, *Women and Property in Early Modern England* (London: Routledge, 1993); N.E. Wright, M.W. Ferguson and A.R. Buck (eds), *Women, Property*

*and the Letters of the Law in Early Modern England* (London: University of Toronto Press, 2004); M. O'Dowd, 'Women and the Irish chancery court in the late sixteenth and early seventeenth centuries', *Irish Historical Studies*, 31:124 (1999), 470–87.

51 See discussion in Chapter 4.

52 'Trim Assizes', *Dublin Evening Post* (19 August 1817) Meath.

53 Violent sexual crime cases, for example, often describe the courts being very crowded, but do not explicitly mention clearing them of women. It is therefore hard to judge whether this was common custom and did not require comment or whether women were present.

54 'Tipperary North Riding Assizes', *Tipperary Vindicator* (6 April 1844) Tipperary; 'Assize Intelligence', *Dublin Mercantile Advertiser and Weekly Price Current* (15 March 1844) King's County/Offaly.

55 'The Government Prosecutions', *Tipperary Vindicator* (31 May 1848) Dublin.

56 'Commission', *Dublin Evening Post* (1 September 1825) Dublin; 'Ennis Assizes', *Dublin Evening Post* (26 July 1825) Tipperary; 'Ennis Assizes', *Southern Reporter and Cork Commercial Courier* (26 July 1825) Tipperary; 'Dublin Commission', *Waterford Mail* (21 January 1843) Dublin.

57 C. Graham, *Ordering Law: The Architectural and Social History of the English Law Court to 1914* (Aldershot: Ashgate, 2003), pp. 82–8.

58 'Assize Intelligence', *Dublin Morning Register* (8 August 1842) Cork; see also 'Law Reports', *Tralee Mercury* (28 November 1829) Dublin.

59 For a discussion of alternative reasons for their promotion see: D. Lemmings, 'Ritual, majesty and mystery: Collective life and culture among English barristers, serjeants and judges, c. 1500–c. 1830', in D. Sugarman and W.W. Pue (eds), *Lawyers and Vampires: Cultural Histories of Legal Professions* (Oxford: Hart Publishing, 2003), pp. 25–63.

60 V. Crossman, *Local Government in Nineteenth-Century Ireland* (Belfast: Institute of Irish Studies, 1994); D. Broderick, *Local Government in Nineteenth-Century County Dublin: The Grand Jury* (Dublin: Four Courts Press, 2007).

61 K. Murphy, 'Judge, jury, magistrate and soldier: Rethinking law and authority in late eighteenth-century Ireland', *American Journal of Legal History*, 44 (2000), 231–56.

62 Barclay, 'Manly magistrates'.

63 Crossman, *Local Government*, p. 21.

64 *Ibid.*, pp. 15–24; D. McCabe, 'Open court: Law and the expansion of magisterial jurisdiction at petty sessions in nineteenth-century Ireland', in N.M Dawson (ed.), *Reflections on Law and History: Irish Legal History Society Discourses and Other Papers, 2000–2005* (Dublin: Four Courts Press, 2006), pp. 126–62.

65 D. McCabe, 'Magistrates, peasants and the Petty Sessions courts: Mayo 1823–50', *Cathair na Mart*, 5:1 (1985), 45–53.

66 McEntee, '"Gentlemen practisers"', pp. 99–112; Osborough, 'The Irish legal system', p. 57.

67 See, for example: 'Carlow Petty Session', *Carlow Sentinel* (18 August 1837) Carlow.

68 Crossman, *Local Government*, p. 22; P. Bonsall, *The Irish RMs: The Resident Magistrates of the British Administration in Ireland* (Dublin: Four Courts Press, 1997).

69 E. Malcolm, '"The reign of terror in Carlow": The politics of policing Ireland in the late 1830s', *Irish Historical Studies*, 32:125 (2000), 59–74.

70 Petty juries had to meet a property requirement see: N. Howlin, 'Controlling jury composition in nineteenth-century Ireland', *Journal of Legal History*, 30:3 (2009), 227–61.

71 Langbein, *Origins*, pp. 318–21; D. Lemmings, 'Criminal trial procedure in eighteenth-century England: The impact of lawyers', *Journal of Legal History*, 26:1 (2005), 73–82.

72 M. Wiener, *Reconstructing the Criminal: Culture, Law and Policy in England, 1830–1914* (Cambridge: Cambridge University Press, 1990). For challenges to the existence of the self-informing jury see: T.A. Green, *Verdict According to Conscience: Perspectives on the English Criminal Trial Jury, 1200–1800* (Chicago: University of Chicago Press, 1985); D. Klerman, 'Was the jury ever self-informing?', in M. Mulholland and B. Pullan (eds), *Judicial Tribunals in England and Europe, 1200–1700: The Trial in History* (Manchester: Manchester University Press, 2003), pp. 58–80.

73 N. Howlin, 'Irish jurors: Passive observers or active participants?', *Journal of Legal History*, 35:2 (2014), 143–71.

74 Howlin, 'Controlling jury composition'.

75 N. Garnham, 'The limits of English influence on the Irish criminal law, and the boundaries of discretion in the eighteenth-century Irish criminal justice system', in Brown and Donlan, *The Laws and Other Legalities*, pp. 108–9.

76 N. Garnham, *The Courts, Crime and the Criminal Law in Ireland, 1692–1760* (Dublin: Irish Academic Press, 1996), p. 284. W.E. Vaughan, *Murder Trials in Ireland, 1836–1914* (Dublin: Four Courts Press, 2009), p. 285.

77 C. Conley, *Certain Other Countries: Homicide, Gender, and National Identity in Late Nineteenth-Century England, Ireland, Scotland and Wales* (Columbus: Ohio State University Press, 2007), p. 207.

78 K. Barclay, 'Narrative, law and emotion: Husband killers in early nineteenth-century Ireland', *Journal of Legal History*, 38:2 (2017), 203–27.

79 Examples of juries being asked to reconsider verdicts: 'Record Court', *Limerick Reporter* (17 July 1849) Limerick; 'Maryborough Assizes', *Waterford Mail* (27 March 1824) Queen's County/Laois; 'Waterford Assizes', *Drogheda Journal or Meath & Louth Advertiser* (19 March 1825) Waterford; 'Kilkenny Assizes', *Dublin Evening Post* (20 August 1829), Kilkenny. For defence counsel asking juries to reconsider verdicts see: 'Court of the King's Bench', *Sligo Journal* (4 December 1835) Dublin; 'Circuit Intelligence', *Saunder's Newsletter* (9 April 1811) Cork. For discussion see: M. Wiener, 'Judges v. jurors: Courtroom tensions in murder trials and the law of criminal responsibility in nineteenth-century England', *Law and History Review*, 17:1 (1999), 467–506; R.B. Lettow, 'New trial for verdict against law: Judge–jury relations in early nineteenth-century America', *Notre Dame Law Review*, 71 (1995–1996), 505–54; E. Dale, 'Not simply black and white: Jury power and law in late nineteenth-century Chicago', *Social Science History*, 25 (2001), 7–27.

80 M. Cronin, 'Memory, story and balladry: 1798 and its place in popular memory in pre-famine Ireland', in L.M. Geary (ed.), *Rebellion and Remembrance in Modern Ireland* (Dublin: Four Courts Press, 2001), pp. 112–34; J. Hill, 'The legal profession and the defence of the *ancient regime* in Ireland, 1780–1840', in D. Hogan and W.N. Osborough (eds), *Brehons, Serjeants and Attorneys: Studies in the History of the Irish Legal Profession* (Dublin: Irish Academic Press, 1990), pp. 181–209.

81  M. Turner, *British Politics in an Age of Reform* (Manchester: Manchester University Press,1999); D. Craig and J. Thomson, *Languages of Politics in Nineteenth-Century Britain* (Basingstoke: Palgrave Macmillan, 2013).

82  'Ireland in 1834', *The Christian Examiner and Church of Ireland Magazine* (Dublin: William Curry, Jun. and Co., 1835), vol. 4, pp. 35–6; Garnham, *Courts, Crime and the Criminal Law*, p. 105.

83  C.P. Curran, 'Figures in the Hall', in Costello, *Four Courts*, pp. 171–3.

84  For examples of ticketing see: 'Special Commission', *Dublin Evening Mail* (29 September 1848) Dublin; 'State Trials', *The Nation* (25 May 1844) Dublin.

85  K. Barclay, D. Lemmings and C. Walker, *Governing Emotions: The Affective Family, the Press and the Law during the Long Eighteenth Century* (Basingstoke: Palgrave Macmillan, forthcoming), Chapter 3; L. Pollock, 'Living on the stage of the world: The concept of privacy among the elite of early modern England', in A. Wilson (ed.), *Rethinking Social History: English Society 1570–1920 and its Interpretation* (Manchester: Manchester University Press, 1993), pp. 78–96; T. Meldrum, 'Domestic service, privacy and the eighteenth-century metropolitan household', *Urban History*, 26:1 (1999), 27–39.

86  D. Lemmings (ed.), *Crime, Courtrooms and the Public Sphere in Britain, 1700–1850* (Farnham: Ashgate, 2012).

87  'Ennis Assize', *Limerick Chronicle* (6 July 1839) Tipperary; 'County Cork Record Office', *Saunder's Newsletter* (2 August 1836); 'Mr Freeman', *Waterford Mail* (30 January 1836); A Reporter, *The Late Election. Containing a Full Report. . .* (Cork: F. Jackson, 1830).

"that is he." Vide page 23

**Figure 2.1** Frontispiece of *An Authentic Report of the Trial of Thomas Lidwell, esq on an Indictment for a Rape committed on the Body of Mrs Sarah Sutton . . . at Naas, Lent Assizes* (Dublin: W. Wilson, 1800)

# 2

# The stage: 'the court presented a very imposing spectacle'

Spatial analyses of the court, and other social and political loca-
tions, emphasise the importance of physical architecture and its
uses in the creation of power. Studies of contemporary and historical courts have demonstrated how architectural decision-making
was influenced by political and cultural ideologies. These beliefs
inhered in brick informing the practice of the law, the building at
times ensuring consistency despite wider social and legal change.[1] The
physical location and use of furniture in courtroom interiors similarly
enabled different levels of participation in justice.[2] The English dock
in a twenty-first-century context has been critiqued for distancing the
defendant from legal activities. The decision by contemporary plan-
ners to place it, surrounded by unprecedented security, at the back
of the room next to the public is viewed as making defendants little
more than observers.[3] The place of the public has been restricted, evidenced not only in a reduction in seat allocation but their placement
in areas where much of the courtroom, and so the practice of the law,
is obscured.[4] Courtroom architecture is not a passive component of the
court – a stage to be acted upon – but significant to the production of
justice.

The theatre of the court has long been understood to play a vital role
in producing power, whether through enforcing 'judicial majesty' or enabling subversive 'counter-theatre'.[5] Courtrooms could be disorderly and
chaotic.[6] This chapter begins with an account of the architecture of the
various courts available in Ireland, exploring what difference the physical
structure of the court made to its operation and the production of power.
It then assesses the role of the press and the public gallery as a component of legal space. Taking seriously the relationship between physical environment and the production of social relationships, this chapter
contributes to a scholarship that highlights the importance of the spatial

materiality of our surroundings – buildings, landscapes, goods – to selves, societies and power.[7]

### Architecture, space and power

The four superior courts of Chancery and the Common Law sat for most of the year in the Four Courts in Dublin. The Four Courts was a new building in 1800, being built in the latter decades of the eighteenth century, opened in 1796 and finished in 1802. It was designed primarily by the English architect, James Gandon, in a neoclassical style, whose main and widely admired innovation was to situate the four courts off a large central dome. This main area was supported by two wings that held various legal offices. Whilst the planning and building (not least the expense) was subject to grumbling, the finished building was widely admired, a 'cathedral to secular power'.[8] Samuel Lewis described it as a 'magnificent structure' in his *Topographical Dictionary*. The author of *Dublin Delineated* thought it 'sumptuous'; in its interior, 'simplicity and magnificence are blended with a happy refinement of art'.[9] Reflecting the aesthetics of the period, it was admired for its 'simplicity', a rejection of flowery ornamentation for geometric lines suggestive of purity and truth, its neoclassical proportions ('magnificent'), and its size.[10] Many accounts detail all its dimensions, whilst one observer thought it one of the 'noblest structures in Dublin, both as to its magnitude and sublimity of design'.[11] It was widely agreed to be 'convenient', meaning fit for purpose.[12]

It was a building replete with meaning. Neoclassicism was popular in the late eighteenth century in the wake of archaeological discoveries in Greece. The association of classical art with simple lines, limited ornamentation and precise geometric divisions appealed to an age that emphasised stoic values, such as personal self-control, moral truthfulness, honesty, virtue and individual responsibility.[13] It spoke to the Empire-building pretensions of the period, whilst its simplicity, as Clare Graham notes, was suggestive of frugality, an important concern for taxpayers.[14]

Neoclassicism was used by French Revolutionaries as part of their cultural aesthetics, tying it to liberty, equality and fraternity.[15] This was a connection that some people made in Ireland. Lord Tullamore complained about the Grecian designs provided for Tullamore's new courthouse in 1833. He desired an Elizabethan or Saxon design, but noted that 'the democratic party runs so high that out of all the plans, all Grecian, we chose the plainest exterior, fearing a traverse at the assizes'. He later clarified that cost was a consideration, but that 'if an Elizabethan elevation had cost the same, the ignorant, the vicious and the radicals in these Reform times, wd say LdT [Lord Tullamore] spent public money in ornamenting his town . . . to indulge his taste regardless of the misery the poor endured in paying the tax for it'.[16] Some of the British elite rejected neoclassicism after the French Revolution, yet it remained the dominant choice for courthouses across the United Kingdom.[17] This, in part, reflected that the common law was associated with 'the people' in the balance of power between the monarch and his or her subjects. Thus, even in an age when democracy was just emerging, the law symbolised democratic potential in its preservation of the subject's rights.[18]

The neoclassical style of the Four Courts was the physical manifestation of a political ideal that was also embedded within contemporary models for elite manliness.[19] Actors entering the court quickly learned that this model shaped appropriate behaviour within it.[20] Yet, its associations with democracy and revolution provided alternative messages for the Irish public, suggestive of the law's liberatory potential.[21] The Four Courts also signified the power of the law. Its scale and 'magnificence' spoke to the Courts as a symbol of authority. The 'sublime', as an aesthetic, tied together beauty with awe and specifically created a feeling of delight combined with 'horror' or even 'despair'.[22] The architecture of the Four Courts perfectly captured how the period understood the law to be felt, an institution that should be admired and feared in similar measure. If the Four Courts situated the law as an elite and masculine institution, it also reinforced the majesty of a law that was 'for the people', giving confidence that (some form of) justice – who appeared in statue form inside – would be done.

The architecture of the Four Courts shaped people's emotional responses and performances of identity. The sublimity of the Courts was created by the spatial dynamics of the building where the public entered a great hall and encountered an extensive dome. The size was regularly noted, the scale part of the building's 'magnificence'. It was bathed in light, which reflected off the black and white marble floor.[23] Commentators frequently remarked on this, noting the 'power of light, which completely, as well as beautifully illumines the whole', the 'abundance of light', and that it was 'lofty, light and well-ventilated'.[24] When combined with the height of the dome, the light drew the eye upwards (captured in Figure 2.2), reminiscent of similar architectural techniques used within cathedrals to create awe.[25] Light was associated in Christian thought with truth and God, and its use in the Four Courts reinforced the court as a place to find truth and endowed it with the authority of the divine.

**Figure 2.2** 'Hall of the Four Courts, Dublin', *London Illustrated News* (London: William Little, 1844), vol. 4, p. 49, 27 January 1844

The main hall was renowned for always being full of people. It was 'a busy and motley scene' with 'an extraordinary air of bustle and confusion', and a 'perpetual buzz, like the growling of an incipient volcano'.[26] One author noted it was 'crowded with lawyers and loungers', so much that 'pickpockets will avail themselves of such crowded and confused assemblies'.[27] The barrister, Richard Lalor Sheil, describing it as 'the general rendezvous of the whole community', noted its importance to lawyers as a place to find business, to sprint across when attending court, to lounge and socialise, and to the general public who came to check on their suits, to flirt (if a 'fine girl from the country') with the junior bar, as the place of 'town resort' to 'drop or pick up the rumors of the day', and as site to enact vengeance for slights in the 'public disorder' of the horse-whipping. Beneath the main hall was a coffee house where the bar and public could take refreshment. It was a spatial arrangement that located 'the law' as a 'public' institution, along with other Enlightenment sites of civic production, such as the coffee house, the press and the drawing room.[28]

Sheil thought the scene 'perplexes and quickly exhausts the eye', and the 'din is tremendous'.[29] Another Irish lawyer thought this picture would be foreign to their English counterparts, noting 'the uproar would startle him, the strangeness of the scene discompose even *his* gravity'.[30] Whilst a popular site, it was confusing and overwhelming, likely heightening its sublimity for those that entered and reinforcing the power of the court at the expense of individual autonomy. As the male-dominated scene in Figure 2.2 suggests, if these were places where women were not formally excluded – and indeed sometimes present – like other Enlightenment public spaces, women were less visible within them.[31] This may have shaped their experience of moving through the court system.

From the main hall, those with legal business entered one of the four, almost identical, courtrooms, climbing five steps and pulling back a curtain to encounter a wainscot screen and doorways on either side to allow the entrance of lawyers and witnesses.[32] On each side of the court was a gallery (behind Daniel O'Connell's head in Figure 2.3), one for the petty jury and the other for sheriffs, officers and the grand jury. The judges were seated in an elevated cove, opposite the entrance, with an elliptical sounding board above them. Each court had six windows, three on each side; one observer thought they emitted too much light.[33] Level with the galleries were rooms for the jury to retire. In the centre was the main table, familiar to courtrooms across the United Kingdom, where counsel and clerks were seated. Around them were benches for additional legal counsel and interested professional men, closely fitted to

**Figure 2.3** *Daniel O'Connell, 'The Liberator' Defending the Rights of his Countrymen in the Court of Queen's Bench Dublin on the 5th of February, 1844* (Paris: Veuve Turgis, 1844)

the centre table, before the court opened up with tiered benches for the public. There were also raised galleries for the public above the entrance, entered by stairs, and curving to meet the jury galleries. During high-profile cases, such as Daniel O'Connell's 1844 state trial, the court administrators added additional seats for the public and gave the grand jury box to the press (who had no allocated seating).[34]

In criminal cases, the accused sat at the traverser's bar, the bench nearest the table and facing the jury. O'Connell was displayed standing at the main table at his trial in the King's Bench. He sat alongside his counsel, a courtesy allowed him as a practising barrister. His lawyer son, John, was similarly permitted to sit with the junior barristers, although in Figure 2.3, he appears seated at the traverser's bar marked by his legal wig.[35] In civil cases, the litigants, if present, sat at opposite sides of the table with their counsel. The location of witnesses may have changed over time. When in the courtroom, they were expected to sit in the first rows of seating opposite the judges, but this was not compulsory.

Where witnesses testified is more difficult to locate. At O'Connell's trial, the witness box was on a raised podium between the judge's bench

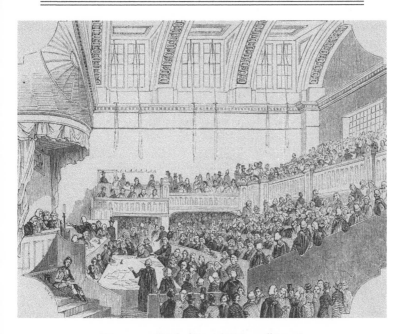

**Figure 2.4** *Trial of Daniel O'Connell* (1844)

and the jury's gallery. It is hidden by a curtain in Figure 2.3. There was a campaign by the press to have the witness box moved before the trial to allow them to better hear proceedings.[36] They asked for it to be raised level to the reporters' (grand jury) gallery. In prints, it appears level with the judge's bench. Some earlier reports describe interaction between witnesses in the box and the general public 'near the witness box', which might suggest it was originally at ground level.[37]

This layout had the dual purposes of convenience and to physically manifest the authority of different actors in the courtroom drama. Despite the importance of juries, the court was designed for the benefit of the judiciary. Their bench was raised to mark their authority and to give them a clear view of the entire room; their voices were amplified through a sounding board, and the barristers' table and witness box are close by. The courtroom 'belonged' to the judge and its architecture enabled their authority. This was counteracted by any local gentry or aristocracy that sat with them, reminding the community of alternative sites of power. Beneath them at the table, clerks, barristers, legal agents, and nearby traversers and litigants, were packed together with little room for overt dramatics. It was a layout that promoted speech as the central mode of communication. Even displaying physical evidence would have been difficult.

The use of the table was symbolic. Being invited to the table suggested some equality between parties, perhaps even communality, with table-sharing used to demarcate family and friendship networks.[38] Using different tables to delineate hierarchies remained normative in nineteenth-century Ireland, as elsewhere in Europe; elite servants (such as ladies' maids and governesses) often used their right to sit at the family table as evidence of status.[39] Nineteenth-century audiences would have been acutely aware of the significance attached to the use of the table, as O'Connell's demand that he sat at it during his trial suggested. That tables promoted familiarity perhaps also reduced the antagonism inherent in the adversarial trial by enabling comradery between members of the bar – an effect reinforced by the priority seating for professional men in the benches nearest the table.[40]

That traversers were located near to the table, but not at it, was significant. The physical spacing between the traversers' bar and the table disassociated the accused from the legal community, marking them as a distinct group. As their speaking role was generally limited, they became privileged observers of their trials. This effect was even more marked in courts that primarily dealt with criminal business. The Four Courts' courtrooms had no formal dock, but many did, particularly those that were home to quarter sessions. Dublin's Green Street Courthouse, a multipurpose court that hosted the sheriff and mayoral courts, the quarter sessions, and a number of high-profile criminal trials (such as Robert Emmet's 1803 trial for treason), had a distinct dock in the row behind the table and opposite the judges (see the location of John Mitchel standing beneath the clock in Figure 2.6). The prisoner was enclosed in a waist-height wooden box, where they could stand or sit on a stool. Some images of courtrooms, such as that which opened this chapter, depict docks that are raised and fortified with high walls and spikes.[41]

The height was for artistic effect. Ellen Byrne's portrait (Figure 2.5) during her trial at Green Street for her husband's murder placed the top of the dock at an unlikely shoulder height (even if she was sitting). Such images indicate the psychological impact of the dock to how prisoners were viewed by the public. The 'growth' of the barrier to shoulder height was suggestive of the prisoner reduced and made small by legal processes; in some cases, it may have enforced the image of the law as a restraint on danger. This can be contrasted with O'Connell in Figure 2.3 who, despite being the accused, is drawn disproportionately large at the table. The encompassing dock reinforced the limited autonomy of the

**Figure 2.5** *Mrs. Ellen Byrne, as She Appeared at the Bar on Monday 15 August 1842* (Dublin: W.H. Holbrooke, [1842–48])

prisoner, enclosed behind tall walls, powerless to act and distanced from the rest of the court, even as they remained near its heart. This has parallels with similar developments in the modern English court.[42]

In the Four Courts, the petty and grand juries were in raised galleries. This was viewed positively by reporters in providing designated seating for the jury, who, in other Irish courts, often remained amongst the general public. From their galleries, they had access to private jury rooms, but were also distanced from the primary actors in the court drama. As discussed in Chapter 1, Irish juries were notable for their volubility well into the nineteenth century.[43] Being in the gallery was not expected to reduce this. The Grand Jury that was evicted to benefit the press during O'Connell's trial were disgruntled as they believed their opportunity to ask questions would be reduced. The judges apologised, but informed them that if they wished to speak a place would be made for them.[44] This was a telling decision for its subtle rebalancing of authority from the social elites to the press.

Questioning witnesses was made easier by the witness box being placed beneath the petty jury's gallery, but their location also emphasised the jury's role as viewers of, rather than participants in, the activities below. Such placement defined the jury as a distinct category of people, but also made clear that they were not part of the body of legal men. The increased specialisation of courtroom space reinforced the growing professionalisation of the law, by demarcating individuals' roles.[45] This had its advantages in providing the public with greater opportunity to understand people's legal function, but conveyed that the law was no longer simply part of community life but a specialist domain.

The placement of the witness box emphasised the limited role of witnesses in legal proceedings. It was situated in the corner, in a location designed for the benefit of the jury and judiciary, rather than for the comfort of the witness. Most stood to testify, but in long cases witnesses were sometimes offered chairs, particularly if they were female.[46] Apart from high-profile cases, they were not generally designated seat-

**Figure 2.6** Green Street Court House, Dublin, during the trial of John Mitchel in 1848. Note the chair on the table. 'Trial of John Mitchel in Green Street Courthouse', in J. Mitchel, *Jail Journal* . . . (Dublin: M.H. Gill & Son, 1912), frontispiece

ing in the courtroom and, in some cases, were expected to remain outside until they testified. Witnesses were often raised for the benefit of an audience that watched their body language and responses carefully. The spatial dynamics of the court emphasised them as a species of evidence brought into view for a period and then removed, rather than as active participants in the trial. This effect was more marked in courtrooms like Green Street (Figure 2.6), and in many of the local courtrooms across Ireland, such as Naas in Figure 2.1, where the witness was placed on top of the table to testify. Given the absence of witness stands in descriptions and plans of Irish provincial courtrooms, this may have been the general practice.[47] At Green Street, the chair was fixed to the table into the twentieth century.[48]

Placed on the table, like other types of evidence, the witness was fully visible to the watching audience, who awaited his or her performance. This was reminiscent of the theatre. Dublin's Music Hall stage was also a raised platform surrounded on four sides by an audience on tiered benches and in the gallery above.[49] The witness had the opportunity to 'shine', like the stage actor, but not all witnesses relished this opportunity. Mrs Sarah Sutton in Figure 2.1 testified on the table after being raped. In the print, she appears exposed and vulnerable above the heads of the anonymous crowd. This sense of 'exposure' was not accidental, as shall be explored in Chapter 2. Nineteenth-century audiences understood the body to convey the truth of testimony, heightening the importance of witnesses' visibility. Some witnesses used this to great effect; either by performing for their audience or by using their displayed vulnerability to reinforce appearances of innocence and helplessness.[50] In each case, the witness remained distinct from the remainder of the court, who sat crowded beneath, or enclosed within the dock, or the well-draped judge's bench.

A final important element of the Four Courts courtroom was the public gallery. Whilst turnout varied, the expectation that large numbers would attend was reflected in the considerable room given to this group. The public were provided with tiered benches that dominated the hall, whilst additional galleries encircled three quarters of the chamber. The room was designed with the expectation that the audience wanted to see, if not always hear, proceedings. Given the limited technology for enhancing voices, the emphasis on visibility is not surprising. The nineteenth-century public was familiar with reading body language and gesture. Audiences for large political rallies, and some of the larger and noisier theatres, relied on an established set of gestures, associated with the oratory tradition, to interpret events.[51] Requests from the press to be better situated to hear witness testimony or complaints from the grand jury about being heard, act as important reminders of the significance of physical gesture and movement to allowing audiences to participate.

Whilst acknowledging auditory limitations, courtrooms were clearly designed to encourage the public to be present. When in full attendance, the audience dominated the Four Courts; in Green Street, they were pushed back from the main floor but remained a distinctive and sizable public. The galleries, situated above the judiciary and wrapping around the room, acted as constant reminders of the existence of the public, even when not there. If the prints are accurate, in both the Four Courts and Green Street, the judiciary's eye line was with the public, not the rest of the court. This can be contrasted with twenty-first-century advice for the spatial organisation of English courtrooms, where the public have only twenty-five seats, are deliberately restricted from viewing the jury, and where only the judge can be clearly seen from public seating.[52]

In comparison, nineteenth-century courtroom audiences were vested with particular significance. Like the theatre audience, they were not the 'stars', but neither were they passive observers. They were spatially situated to remind the court of the law's social and political significance within society and the place of the public in ensuring that. It was a dynamic that checked the absolute or tyrannical authority of the law, an issue of topical concern in a colonial context. Like the building it was housed in, which spoke to both the splendour of the law and its democratic potential, the situating of the public gallery in relation to the judge's bench acted as a reminder that the magnificence of the law was not vested in the judiciary alone.[53]

### On circuit and in the provinces

Throughout the early nineteenth century, when the assize entered a town they were met by its leaders, typically the mayor, sheriff, corporation and other 'gentlemen', and both groups processed to the court. Such processions attempted to replicate the majesty of the law by locating the assize as a time of festivity and carnival.[54] Edward Wakefield understood the procession as a 'grand and impressive spectacle' designed to convey the 'seriousness and solemnity' of the occasion. In the English context, these rituals are considered significant for their display of legal authority and disciplining effects on the watching public.[55] Wakefield was concerned in 1812 to find that Irish processions were full of dirty horses, old and faded liveries, and poor riders, which along with the fact that barristers did not wear their wigs and gowns on circuit, undermined the power of the court, with serious implications for the law: 'I dread any, even the smallest, diminution of that sentiment of veneration, without which laws might be contemned, and governments rendered inefficient'.[56] Similarly 'serious' and 'impressive' processions occurred after the assizes, when condemned prisoners were marched to the gallows.[57]

Wakefield was less than impressed, but hosting the assize was financially lucrative and a matter of civic pride, with towns competing for the privilege.[58] It is likely that many towns desired their processions to convey the pomp and ceremony of the event. Moreover, provincial Ireland was not unaware of their symbolism, not only using processions on other festive and political occasions but, at times, using them to challenge state authority.[59] O'Connell was often processed into town by the city elite when he came to try political cases. At his trial in 1844, the Dublin city elite, including the mayor, processed with him across the city and joined him in the prisoner's box before he entered the courtroom – an activity that displeased the judges.[60] Such displays evidenced O'Connell's remarkable popularity, but also an astute awareness of the symbolism of community support in legitimising justice. Processing O'Connell to his trial, or to his position as defence lawyer in political cases, was a direct challenge to the state's decision to prosecute.

Increasingly, urban environments attempted to display the magnificence of the law through renovating or building new courthouses. Historically in provincial areas, local courts were held in generic civic buildings with several uses.[61] In Cork and Drogheda, the court was also the tholsel, a building that hosted a range of civic activities, including the gaol, borough council meetings, and the collection of tolls and customs.[62] During an ownership dispute, Fethard's tholsel was variously called by witnesses the 'tholsel', 'court house', 'poor house' and 'market house'. Some witnesses used more than one term to refer to the same building. It was a place managed by the corporation, and where 'public petty sessions [were] held three times a week in a room of the courthouse and corporate meetings in the same room; the lower part or basement story was used by the corporation as a weighing house, with scales for public purposes'.[63] Its range of names suggest it was used more widely. In other towns, such as Ardee and Augher, the court was held above the market.[64]

Like elsewhere in the United Kingdom, the early nineteenth century saw the building and repair of provincial courthouses. This was partly informed by the Enlightenment's 'improving' drive that encouraged landowners and the urban elite to invest in civic buildings, 'beautifying' their surroundings.[65] The construction of courthouses can thus be situated alongside widening streets, laying paving stones, installing street lights and sanitation, and the building of assembly rooms, town halls, infirmaries, gaols, libraries and banks. It was encouraged by growing complaints amongst the legal profession, as well as juries and the press, that current courthouses were not fit for purpose. Legal men protested the lack of facilities to hold private meetings, to keep their clothing and papers, and to be properly fed and rested.[66] Jurymen, and even audiences, complained of cold and draughty rooms, a lack of seating and bad air.[67] The press desired better seating, asking grand juries to 'recollect the vast importance to the community of accurate Assize reports'.[68] Everybody wanted more light and better acoustics.

As a result, the government authorised grand juries to borrow money for building and repairing courthouses.[69] This allowed taxpayers to spread the cost over several years. It may have encouraged local communities to name some of their key public buildings 'courthouses', despite such buildings continuing to be multipurpose. Drogheda Borough Council rented their tholsel to the Hibernian Bank and held their meetings in the new courthouse after its construction.[70] Kilkenny Courthouse held public entertainments, including Mr Gallaher, the 'celebrated Dramatic Ventriloquist'.[71] Some courthouses contained reading rooms. Whilst designed to provide refreshment for the court, they acted as the local coffee house, where people could read the local papers and exchange gossip even when the court was not in session.[72]

As Clare Graham notes, calling such buildings courthouses, as well as decorating them with sculptures of justice, truth and similar legal symbolism, gave the magnificence and dignity of the law to all activities held within them.[73] It could also lead to complaints about the usages of 'public space'. Inhabitants of Gorey and Enniscorthy successfully campaigned for the removal of reading rooms from their courthouses, arguing it was a 'desecration' of the courts of law. Yet, their motivation was rooted in a belief that the reading rooms were sectarian 'Tory cliques', which hosted 'Orange conventicles'.[74] The Conservatives of Cork were angered about damage to the City Courthouse during a political meeting. The mayor's office defended this use, noting: 'The City Court is the City Tholsel. In default of a Town Hall it is the legitimate place for holding all public meetings at which the mayor officially presides'.[75] They also noted that the Corporation contributed £2,000 towards the building. In such cases, tensions arose due to the legitimacy that 'the law' gave to partisan or sectarian groups, rather than the principle that courthouses were available for public use. Importantly, the continuing use of courthouses for public business meant that they remained central to community life, ensuring that they remained familiar and were not exclusively the territory of 'the law'.

Like with the Four Courts and usually for the same reasons, most provincial courts adopted a neoclassical style. Local courts replicated many of the features of the higher courts interiors, particularly providing 'ample accommodation' and well-lit, well-aired rooms with better acoustics. A number created a sense of scale through situating the courts in double-height rooms with windows at the top. Where room was limited, the courtroom was placed on the second floor, allowing the roof space to provide height.[76] This had the practical function of allowing for tiered seating and galleries, but also helped to reproduce the feeling of being uplifted, which had been achieved in the Four Courts.

Whilst assuming some of the universal features of the neoclassical courthouse, grand juries were keen to locate their courthouses as Irish. 'Anxious to encourage native talent', they ran competitions with cash prizes for the best courthouse plans, so that local architects would receive some benefit even if not successful.[77] They decorated courtrooms with furnishings made by Irish artists and manufacturers. The *Cork Examiner* noted of their new courthouse that: 'all the decorations around the chair, and the different fringing are truly beautiful and have a fine effect. . . . The materials are Irish manufacture, and we believe the product of Cork artists'.[78] When combined with their various public uses, such ornamental and architectural choices signified the courts as 'Irish' and belonging to the local community. This encouraged familiarity with the court amongst locals, as well as underlining that this was 'Irish', and so legitimate, justice.

There was some variation in courtrooms across Ireland. One notable difference was that many provincial courts, particularly record courts, used a semi-circular table as their centre piece, with benches curved around. Londonderry Courthouse (see Figure 2.7) used a square configuration for the Crown Court and a semi-circular design for its Record Court. Both were tiered rooms with a public gallery above. The Record Court was a civil court with a jurisdiction over small debts and similar claims. According to Bowden's plan, the inner two rings were occupied by lawyers, the third by the jury, and the final rows by spectators. Some courts preferred this shape for all of their business. Cork City Courthouse held its assize, record court and sessions in a semi-circular room that held 400–500 people, placing witnesses on the table to testify.[79]

A semi-circular design may have provided acoustic advantages in drawing people closer together. In smaller courts, it was a choice that

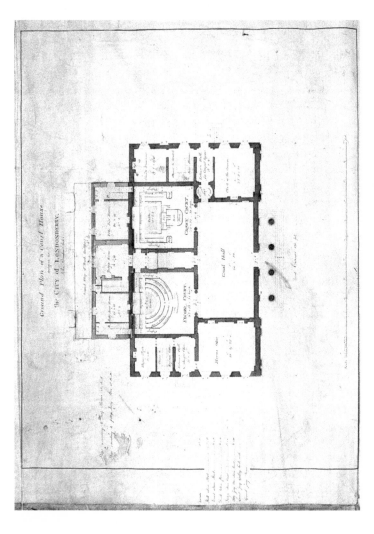

**Figure 2.7** Londonderry Court House: ground plan by John Bowden, 1813

reflected the dual use of the room for town council meetings, and the desire amongst aldermen for a design that was conducive to democratic debate whilst reinforcing the unity of the council. Not only did a semi-circular table reduce the space between parties, diminishing the sense of being on different sides, it required speakers to turn their bodies to address the room, disrupting the authority associated with 'podium' positions. Except for the judge at the front and the witness on the table, semi-circular courts enforced an equality of status through destabilising where one party (such as the prosecution) ended and the other (such as the jury) began. Sitting in proximity may have encouraged litigants in civil suits to settle, making it particularly suitable for record courts. Thus, the physical architecture of the courtroom may have offset the increasing adversarialism of the lawyerised trial and the processes of rationalisation designed for the 'society of strangers' to meet the needs of local communities, where the spaces of the law remained familiar and the actors known.[80]

Like elsewhere, the other significant difference between the high and provincial courts was greater architectural flexibility.[81] That provincial courts were used for multiple purposes required that at least some furniture was moveable. In towns without purpose-built courtrooms, this flexibility might be more marked as private houses, halls and other places were transformed into legal space.[82] Magistrates' and police courts were known for their informality, both in furnishings and ceremony. Most petty sessions appear to have a bench for magistrates and a desk for the clerk, and occasionally chairs or benches for others. But, like in Figure 2.8 of an 1853 petty session, many also provided room for litigants to stand and move.

As a result, litigants often stood taller than, or at eye level with, the sitting magistrates, reiterating the court as a place for resolution and arbitration, rather than the heavy hand of justice. Litigants typically stood near and could speak directly to each other. This could lead to physical confrontation and heated arguments. But, it also allowed them to negotiate directly, enabling settlements, compromise and speedy resolution. With room to perform, many litigants used the opportunity to tell their stories theatrically, to use props, or sing and dance.[83] It provided greater opportunity for men and women to articulate their stories than in the higher courts, allowing for cases that disrupted community life but did not sit easily within the framework of legal dispute.[84]

Like the higher courts, a controversial case in petty sessions could bring large crowds that spilled into the street, but so did the tendency for magistrates to hold them in public places where there was an available

**Figure 2.8** 'An Irish Petty Session', *London Illustrated News* (1853), vol. 22, p. 121, 12 February 1853

audience. Unlike the higher courts, where the public were directed into seating, and occasionally ticketed, the crowd in the magistrates' courts often stood in any available place.[85] Magistrates could be surrounded by the public, locating them as part of the community, if one with particular authority. Such architecture reminded litigants and magistrates that petty sessions were about rebuilding community relationships and tied people of different statuses into that project.

The physical architecture of the courtroom shaped the form that justice took. Courtroom architecture directed people into particular roles and endowed them with specific types of authority. It could be argued that the magistrates' courts did not require static furnishings due to their relative informality, but, it may be that informal furnishings allowed for justice to be flexible, responsive and more attuned to a community's needs – a conclusion that is intimated by the increasing regulation of petty session justice as they moved into more formal settings. This is suggestive of the important role of the new courtrooms of the period in the formation of a professionalised legal system, especially as so many of these new buildings predated formal reforms in legal practice.[86]

### Court theatrics: moving in court

Whilst architecture played a key role in shaping courtroom power dynamics, people could also use it creatively to articulate stories of self and to challenge hierarchies of power.[87] Physical movement could be effective in courtroom performances, the impact perhaps heightened when space was constrained. Much movement was simply to reinforce lawyers' and witnesses' performances of identity and particularly emotion. In 1824, Laurence Kilfoyle, a victim of theft, impressed the court with his 'simplicity' and with his humorous banter on cross-examination. His performance was complete, at least for the reporter of the *Dublin Morning Register*, due to his seeming comfort on the Green Street Court witness seat, 'as if he were at his own fire side'. This impression was due to his posture where 'he turned towards the Counsel, put his hands in his breeches pocket, and advanced his left leg'. When glancing at the prisoner, 'he looked as if resentment was a stranger to him'.[88] Kilfoyle presented himself as at ease in the chair. This overcame some of the destabilising impact of courtroom architecture on witnesses' self-presentations, but reinforced his truthfulness and his manly forgiveness of the defendant.

In *Bruce v. Frewen* (1790), a much-retold slander case where the plaintiff's character was not prepossessing, the jury found for the plaintiff but gave only 6d damages. The plaintiff and defendant were seated opposite each other when the verdict was given; the defendant then 'gravely' handed the plaintiff a shilling, saying, 'Take the worth of your character out of *that, and give me the change*'.[89] In front of an audience that cheered 'tremendously' at the verdict, this dismissive gesture conveyed Frewen's contempt for Bruce, reinforcing his own character. Here the table provided a platform for courtroom theatre.

Lawyers were not inured to such theatrics. Charles Kendall Bushe (1767–1843), as defence lawyer, went through a whole murder trial before asking the jury, 'Did any of you know Watt Meyer, the murdered man?' The jury cried out, 'Indeed we did; there was not a man in Wexford who did not know him'. Bushe, 'in a stentorian voice', then called: 'Walter Meyer, come and appear'. When Meyer appeared: 'the consternation was indescribable'. The *Dublin Weekly Register* noted that Bushe had 'kept [Meyer] back to produce the *stage effect* just described'.[90] O'Connell was renowned for histrionic dramatics. The barrister, Roderick O'Flanagan (1814–1900), described him 'dashing' his bag against the table in supposed irritation, and if not getting the desired effect, exclaiming that he 'would not attempt to defend his innocent client in the face of such injustice', throwing his brief at the attorney and 'swagger[ing] out of court'. O'Connell would then 'calm down' and return to his seat, muttering apologies to the bench. Displaying anger (as is explored further in Chapter 5) was designed to convey O'Connell's belief in his client's innocence for the benefit of the jury. O'Flanagan thought the technique effective.[91] For O'Connell, and lawyers like him, the courtroom table, legal briefs and even the attorney, became props in a performance of legal defence.

For others, physical movement contested the confining architecture of the court. Several defendants threw things at judges. In 1849, John Graham hurled a '2lb' rock at the judge, narrowly missing him and the registrar. The judge was initially 'dreadfully alarmed', but composed himself and had Graham searched.[92] Catherine Anderson's more accurately targeted crust of bread caused laughter under similar circumstances twenty years earlier.[93] Whilst angering the judge was not particularly strategic, throwing missiles denied the judiciary their security in the physical boundaries that the dock and bench put between them and defendants. It also provided defendants with an opportunity to express anger, even vengeance, towards the legal system. In that moment, the defendants exceeded the encompassing boundaries of the dock, challenging the power structures that courtroom architecture enforced.

Less dramatically, witnesses regularly turned their backs during questioning, particularly on cross-examination. In 1822, Denis Austin was cooperating with defence counsel, Mr Bethel, when the latter asked if he had been charged with theft. Austin denied this and turned to face the prosecution. Bethel persisted with questioning, but grew exasperated, exclaiming, 'Turn round, Sir, and answer the question – you seem to have a great eye on the Gentleman opposite'.[94] That same year, Elizabeth Sly turned her back on Mr Arabin during cross-examination.[95] Turning away was a sign of disrespect, but also made cross-examination difficult for lawyers, who used eye contact and body language to gauge how to direct their questions. That witnesses cooperated with counsel until cross-examination is also suggestive that this movement allowed them to retain dignity and control of their narrative.

Whilst the architecture of the higher courts provided opportunity for these forms of resistance to court authority, it also limited possibilities. Banging tables, striding out the door, throwing missiles or turning away provided opportunities for disruption, but they were bounded by the authority of the judiciary, furnishings and allocation of space, and by models for gendered behaviour that shaped how such actions would be interpreted. Agency was distributed between building, furnishing and legal actors, continually negotiated through practice. The police courts and petty sessions were suggestive of the performative possibilities of court space when actors had greater freedom of movement.

Magistrates' courtrooms were less orderly, hosting people who sang and told stories, and allowing at least some to move freely across the room. In 1837, Patrick O'Sullivan ran around the magistrates' bench to playfully illustrate his fear of a man he charged with assault.[96] After being fined for drunkenness in 1844, Peter Hoolihan theatrically peered out of each window in the court. When asked what he was doing, he replied that he was checking for his creditors.[97] An inebriated Jemmy Maguire in 1828 not only yelled, capered about the room, and blustered about his skills at wrestling and dancing, but grabbed a police officer and 'forced him through the movements of a most original *pas de deux*'.[98] It is not clear that all this behaviour was designed to resist judicial authority, although Maguire's behaviour was petulance at being arrested for drunkenness. But, rather through movement, such men articulated their version of manliness and tried to endow it with power.

Theatrical gesture contested hierarchies of power imposed through a legal system that assigned men to different roles and particular seats. Moving across the court claimed it as the defendant's territory, a demonstration of agency that interrupted the ideal lines of courtroom authority, without necessarily acting as an overt challenge to the magistracy. The latter often showed remarkable patience at such behaviour. At times, they found it entertaining. But their tolerance was also because they acknowledged that giving people opportunity to perform heightened the community's confidence in the legal system. Restricting theatrical behaviours threatened to limit people's ability to present their 'whole case', undermining the performance of justice. It is notable therefore that men had more leeway to behave like this, likely because liberty of movement was not associated with the ideal domestic woman.[99]

### The court gallery

If the court provided a stage on which to perform manliness, the court gallery was a rather engaged and active audience. Not all news reports mention the gallery, although their existence was implicit given that, if nothing else, the court reporter and his or her readers played that role. When they are mentioned, they are used to convey how events should be interpreted.[100] A cheering audience could signal a just verdict; weeping at a death sentence conveyed the gravity of a judicial decision. Using the public as the measure of justice enabled the press to provide important commentary on judicial authority; as David Barrie and Susan Broomhall note, the significance of the public gallery was the 'impression of justice' it created.[101] This was reinforced by the representation of the audience as a single body or large groupings, rather than as individuals.

The gallery's response to court proceedings was generally conveyed by a single word or short phrase, 'sensation', 'horror', 'laughter', noted in brackets after the event to which they are responding. 'Sensation' in nineteenth-century dictionaries was usually identified as 'perception by the senses', with no secondary definition to convey its modern meaning of 'intense public interest'.[102] It signified a reaction without conveying its exact implications. It is notable, however, that journalists did not often use words that described what the audience did (gasp, groan, clap), but those that signalled a heightened emotional response. In cases like 'horror', the meaning is clear, but what 'sensation' entailed is harder to grasp. Similarly, whilst laughter described physical behaviour, its relationship to what the audience felt is left unspoken. The reader is left to unpick the significance from the context, with emotional terminology less an account of audience feeling than their moral judgement. As is explored further in Chapter 4, this reflected that the nineteenth-century Irish public understood emotion to convey important information between actors. Through their emotional expression, the gallery could participate in the trial, disrupting their official position as silent observers.

Several reports are suggestive of the role court audiences played in influencing justice. As noted for Britain, audiences that responded with 'sensation' or 'laughter' set the tone, at times determining the value of testimonies or speeches.[103] During John Heney's 1839 trial for the murder of James Ryan, the impact of the physical evidence (mainly bloody clothing) was heightened by the audience's responses. The blood and hair on the spade produced a 'strong sensation', whilst the murdered man's clothes created a 'strong sensation of horror'.[104] The judge ended this lengthy trial at 6pm on the first day due to the 'fatigue' of the case. The court audience articulated the horror the evidence produced in this particularly violent case, conveying its seriousness for the court and public.

The most common reaction noted by the press was laughter. Many classical theories of laughter influential during the period saw it as part of social discipline, a form of mockery that acted as a shaming mechanism. Thus laughing at social superiors was sedition. Others, following Aristotle, thought that certain types of laughter, such as an expression of enjoying wit, were acceptable.[105] Contemporary philosophers, led by men like James Beattie and Frances Hutcheson, moved away from theories that relied on mockery and insult to the idea that humour was found in 'incongruity' between the ways things should be and were. Laughter was a response to absurdity.[106] More broadly, people recognised that laughter could be a reaction to emotional extremes and useful for releasing the tensions created by social hierarchies. The English barrister, Basil Montagu, believed that laughter in court was often caused by situations that disrupted the formality of proceedings. He thought the restraint placed on the public by the 'superiority' of the judiciary meant that when order was disrupted, people laughed to release tension.[107] Other authors saw laughter as a reaction to despair, alleviating pain.[108] 'You may laugh in as many ways as you talk', noted eighteenth-century wit, Samuel Johnson.[109]

Much laughter in court was in response to humorous or ludicrous situations. As explored in Chapter 4, barristers and witnesses enjoyed witty exchanges. Laughter rewarded them, affirming their manly success and reinforcing their attempts to undermine the seriousness of proceedings. Witnesses who made ludicrous remarks could face mocking laughter. In 1845, Eliza Keeffe, a 'young lady of rather doubtful reputation', was accused of theft from her drinking partner. As the victim testified, she interrupted saying: 'the like of him should not dare to associate with the like of me (laughter). Why you common fellow I would not associate with you or wipe my shoes with you ... (laughter)'.[110] The gallery's laughter undermined Keeffe's claims to respectability. Similarly, the testimonies of Belton and Lalor when accused of assaulting the publican Pat Farrell in 1827 had 'the effect of closing the appeal [they made to the bench] amid convulsions of laughter'.[111] Belton and Lalor were literally silenced by the court audience. In both these cases, the defendants were being playful, but it was the court audience that affirmed their words had little merit.

The meaning of laughter could be more ambiguous. Laughing at testimonies of victims of rape or sexual assault was common. This mirrored the humour found in the period's jokes but also reflected that the court audience was probably entirely male.[112] In many cases, laughter appeared to arise from a disjuncture between the expected image of victimised middle-class femininity, romanticised in novels, and the mundane, if not less traumatic, experiences of the lower-order women who came to court. *The Southern Reporter* attempted to capture what was humorous about Ann Farrell's 1840 testimony by rendering it phonetically: 'The witness then identified the prisoner, and stated that she accompanied him across the fields; she said he "coutcht a hoult of my apron and put his hand around my neck oh! he did (laugh)'.[113] Mary McCarthy's phonetically rendered account caused similar amusement two years later.[114] The man Farrell accused of rape was acquitted, whilst McCarthy's case was thrown out by the judge. In these cases, laughter followed closely after distressing testimonies of violence. The court's laughter challenged their claims to compassion or pity and so their right to justice. It may be such laughter reflected discomfort or distress at the violence described, but it had the effect of undermining the legitimacy of the plaintiff's claims.

Some laughter also occurred in response to conflict between the judiciary and other members of the court. After his charge to the jury in John Neill's trial for murdering James Connell, the judge's interpretation was challenged by the foreman and led to an uncomfortable, but apparently amusing, exchange:

> Mr Cahill, one of the jurors, said: My Lord, the foreman says he disagrees with your lordship (great laughter).
> Court – Is it in point of law, Sir (laughter)?
> Mr Cahill – Yes, my lord (great laughter).
> Court – Gentlemen, you had better consider what I have said to you.
> The Foreman, addressing the judge, said – I beg your pardon, my lord, but I think it is not because a man is a stranger that he should be murdered (sensation in court).[115]

The judge reiterated that the jury should not find someone guilty without evidence. The laughter at this exchange appears to have been produced by the unexpectedness of the foreman challenging the judge's legal reasoning. It was laughter founded on the 'ludicrousness' of the dispute, but it also marked anxiety at the exchange. The final confrontation caused 'sensation', as the foreman's response moved from questioning judicial authority to challenging the court's ability to provide justice. As this suggests, the public gallery's response was mediated by social norms, including those around the expected lines of authority.

This was not to say that they were fundamentally conformist. Carlow's petty sessions' gallery literally laughed Lord of the Manor, Mr Hamilton, out of court when he expressed particularly conservative political opinions before a liberal audience.[116] They did not always agree with judicial decision-making, cheering juries that found against judges' instructions, or supporting barristers or witnesses before an unsympathetic judiciary.[117] Nor did they always agree with each other, with some reporters noting that laughter or cheering was limited to certain sections, or that a response faded quickly.[118] When a wife murderer was found not guilty in a court that was 'crowded to excess', it was noted that 'a great disappointment was felt by the large crowd of females outside', a group who the reporter likely perceived to have been a similar class and gender to the victim.[119]

The expression of emotion by the court gallery played an important role in shaping power dynamics, signalling if testimonies were trustworthy, acting as public opinion on whether justice was served, and influencing how judiciaries and juries determined truth. Audience emotions acted to normatively produce the boundaries of acceptable behaviour by others in the court. Their moral judgement, signalled through their emotional response, thus played a key role in processes of justice. Like the gallery they filled, the public sat as a reminder of the law's relationship with wider Irish society, who, through the press, would use their emotional response to scrutinise judicial proceedings.

## Conclusion

In the image that opens this chapter, the viewer – the reading public – is reminded of the theatricality of the court. Separated by a partition, perhaps that bordering the gallery, and with a curtain waiting to close over the action, the courtroom becomes a stage. Mrs Sarah Sutton, the victim, is centrally placed, the light from the large windows illuminating her face and body. She looks towards Thomas Lidwell, the defendant she accuses of rape, who is enclosed within a tall dock, barely visible. The judiciary sit above her on a raised stage. They too are lit; their authority reinforced by their portly figures, large wigs and distinctive chair. Behind them are the jury, higher than the judges, but lightly sketched. Around Sutton is a mass of heads, representing barristers and attorneys, as well as the gallery. They appear predominantly male, unsurprising given the nature of the trial. The court building rises behind them, its height emphasised by long, narrow windows. Opposite the judges is a large clock, striking five.

The scene captured one of the most sensational parts of the trial where Sutton was asked to identify the prisoner: 'much embarrassed, and after some time, raising her hand, and for the first time during her examination, looked towards the dock, and pointing to the prisoner, said, "that is he"'.[120] A remarkable case from 1800 that involved a woman of the gentry class charging her husband's friend, a gentleman, with rape, it attracted a large audience that crowded to hear.[121] Sutton, a compelling witness, was accused by the defence of only 'appearing to be agitated', to which the prosecution angrily retorted: '[a]nd do you think, Sir, that we who sat round the table were acting the part, when we burst into tears at the melancholy narrative?'[122] The drama was intensified by the courtroom architecture. Sutton's 'embarrassment', her 'agitation', was visible due to her placement on the table beneath the light that would expose truth. It was her story that determined the outcome of the trial. Lidwell, enclosed in a darkened dock, played little part until after he was found guilty, when he politely thanked the court for their patience and humanity when weighing evidence.[123] His location focused attention away from him and onto the victim. The crowd of weeping men determined justice, authenticating Sutton's testimony. The distant, all-male, jury agreed, finding Lidwell guilty.

Courtroom architecture shaped the course of a trial. It not only situated people, locating them as witnesses, barristers or judges, but reinforced their relative power through physical signals, such as the height of seating or nearness to the table. Physical boundaries were not insurmountable, however, with men and women creatively adapting to their location to convey different 'truths' and identities. The extent to which they could do this was shaped by their gender, class and legal role. Not least important was the public gallery, who evaluated the truthfulness of testimony and set the 'emotional tone'. Courtrooms not only signalled the ideal order of legal proceedings, but society itself. The use of court space reinforced the law's embodiment of wider social and gender hierarchies; the gallery suggestive of a burgeoning democracy that would lead to change.

The building that housed the court was similarly suggestive. Courthouses signified the authority of the law, with new architectural styles encouraging height and light to create awe in those that entered. Neoclassical architecture embodied the masculine virtues valued during the era, self-control, truthfulness, responsibility, whilst acknowledging the law's role in producing rights and justice. Such messages tied courthouses, and the practice of law, into the wider Enlightenment project of nation and Empire-building, improvement and the expansion of the polity. This was not dissimilar from the messages conveyed by court buildings across the British Empire, but, through Irish architects, builders and furnishings, courthouses were also investments in local identities. Like the legal system itself, they reflected the multiple and diverse investments in Irish and British identity that existed in Ireland and that, as we shall see, were played out by the men who acted upon the courtroom stage before a watching public.

### Notes

1  C. Graham, *Ordering Law: The Architectural and Social History of the English Law Court to 1914* (Aldershot: Ashgate, 2003); C.E.B. Brett, *Court Houses and Market Houses of the Province of Ulster* (Belfast: Ulster Architectural Heritage Society, 1973); C. Goodsell, *The Social Meaning of Civic Space: Studying Political Authority through*

*Architecture* (Lawrence: Kansas University Press, 1988); K.F. Taylor, *In the Theater of Criminal Justice: The Palais de Justice in Second Empire Paris* (Princeton: Princeton University Press, 1993); L. Mulcahy, *Legal Architecture: Justice, Due Process and the Place of Law* (London: Routledge, 2010).

2   L. Mulcahy, 'Architectural precedent: The Manchester assize courts and monuments to law in the mid-Victorian era', *King's Law Journal*, 19:3 (2008), 525–49; P. Carlen, 'The staging of magistrates' justice', *British Journal of Criminology*, 16:1 (1978), 48–55; P. Rock, 'Witnesses and space in a crown court', *British Journal of Criminology*, 31:3 (1991), 266–79.

3   L. Mulcahy, 'Putting the defendant in their place: Why do we still use the dock in criminal proceedings', *British Journal of Criminology*, 53 (2013), 1139–56.

4   L. Mulcahy, 'Architects of justice: The politics of courtroom design', *Social and Legal Studies*, 16:3 (2007), 383–403.

5   D. Hay, 'Property, authority and the criminal law', in D. Hay *et al.* (eds), *Albion's Fatal Tree: Crime and Society in Eighteenth-Century England* (London: Verso, 1975), pp. 17–64; J.M. Beattie, *Crime and the Courts in England, 1660–1800* (Oxford: Oxford University Press, 1986); V.A.C. Gattrell, *The Hanging Tree: Execution and the English People, 1770–1868* (Oxford: Oxford University Press, 1994); D.G. Barrie and S. Broomhall, *Police Courts in Nineteenth-Century Scotland, Volume 1: Magistrates, Media and the Masses* (Farnham: Ashgate, 2014), pp. 227–82.

6   P. King, *Crime, Justice and Discretion in England, 1740–1820* (Oxford: Oxford University Press, 2003), pp. 252–3.

7   A. Flather, *Gender and Space in Early Modern England* (Woodbridge: Boydell and Brewer, 2007); K. Barclay, 'Place and power in Irish farms at the end of the nineteenth century', *Women's History Review*, 21:4 (2012), 571–88.

8   J.A. Culliton, 'The Four Courts, Dublin', *Dublin Historical Record*, 21:4 (1967), 116–26. A cathedral to secular power is used to describe equivalent legal buildings in France and England: B.S. Godfrey, 'Sentencing, theatre, audience and communication: The Victorian and Edwardian Magistrate's Courts and their message', in B. Garnot (ed.), *Les Tésmoins devant la justice. Une histoire des status et des comportements* (Rennes: Presses Universitaires de Rennes, 2003), pp. 161–71.

9   S. Lewis, *A Topographical Dictionary of Ireland* (London: S. Lewis, 1837), unpaginated 'Dublin'; *Dublin Delineated in Twenty-Eight Views of the Principle Public Buildings* (Dublin: G. Tyrrell, 1831), p. 41.

10  G. Wright, *The Gallery of Engravings* (London: Fisher, Son & Co., 1845), vol. 1, pp. 29–30; G. Wright, *An Historical Guide to the City of Dublin* (London: Baldwin, Cradock, and Joy, 1825), pp. 156–60; J. Warburton, J. Whitelaw and R. Walsh, *History of the City of Dublin: From the Earliest Accounts to the Present Time* (London: T. Cadell and W. Davies, 1818) vol. 1, pp. 523–7.

11  W. Curry, *The Picture of Dublin: Or, Stranger's Guide to the Irish Metropolis* (Dublin: William Curry, 1835), p. 103.

12  For example, Wright, *The Gallery*, p. 30.

13  R. Rosenblum, *Transformations in Late Eighteenth-Century Art* (Princeton: Princeton University Press, 1967), pp. 107–25; N. Curtin, *The United Irishmen: Popular Politics in Ulster and Dublin, 1791–1798* (Oxford: Clarendon Press, 1994).

14  Graham, *Ordering Law*, p. 145.

15   L. Hunt, *Politics, Culture and Class in the French Revolution* (Berkeley: University of California Press, 1984).

16   M. Byrne, *Legal Offaly: The County Courthouse at Tullamore and the Legal Profession in County Offaly from the 1820s to the Present Day* (Tullamore: Esker Press, 2008), pp. 33–4.

17   Graham, *Ordering Law*, pp. 328–33.

18   For discussion see: M. Lobban, 'Custom, nature and authority: The roots of English legal positivism', in D. Lemmings (ed.), *The British and their Laws in the Eighteenth Century* (Woodbridge: Boydell Press, 2005), pp. 27–58.

19   For a discussion of the ways Enlightenment was spatially located see: C.W.J. Withers, *Placing the Enlightenment: Thinking Geographically about the Age of Reason* (Chicago: Chicago University Press, 2008).

20   For a discussion of how space shapes social behaviour see: H. Lefevre, *The Production of Space* (London: Wiley, 1992).

21   D. Lemmings, 'Introduction', in D. Lemmings (ed.), *The British and their Laws in the Eighteenth Century* (Woodbridge: Boydell Press, 2005), pp. 1–26; C. Hill, *Liberty against the Law: Some Seventeenth-Century Controversies* (London: Allen Lane, 1996).

22   E. Burke, *A Philosophical Enquiry into the Origins of Our Ideas of the Sublime and Beautiful* (Basil: J.J. Tourneisen, 1792), pp. 216–18.

23   Wright, *The Gallery*, p. 29.

24   Warburton, Whitelaw and Walsh, *History of the City*, p. 525; Wright, *An Historical Guide*, p. 159; Wright, *The Gallery*, p. 30.

25   J.B. Tschen-Emmons, *Artefacts from Medieval Europe* (Santa Barbara: ABC-Clio, 2015), pp. 63–7.

26   R.L. Sheil, *Sketches of the Irish Bar*, ed. R. Shelton Mackenzie, 2 volumes (New York: Redfield, 1854), vol. 1, p. 58; Wright, *An Historical Guide*, p. 158; S. and A.M. Hall, *Ireland: Its Scenery, Character, &c* (London: How and Parsons, 1842), vol. 2, p. 303.

27   Curry, *Picture of Dublin*, p. 105.

28   B. Cowan, 'What was masculine about the public sphere? Gender and the coffeehouse milieu in post-restoration England', *History Workshop Journal*, 51 (2001), 127–58; J. Kamensky, 'Talk like a man: Speech, power and masculinity in early New England', *Gender & History*, 8:1 (1996), 22–47.

29   Sheil, *Sketches of the Irish Bar*, vol. 1, pp. 58–61.

30   'London and Dublin', *The Dublin Literary Gazette, Or Weekly Chronicle of Criticism, Belles Lettres and Fine Arts from January 2 to June 26 1830* (Dublin: John S. Folds, 1830), vol. 1, p. 290.

31   R. Carr, *Gender and Enlightenment Culture in Eighteenth-Century Edinburgh* (Edinburgh: Edinburgh University Press, 2014).

32   This description was composed through amalgamating accounts in the following sources: Curry, *Picture of Dublin*, p. 106; Wright, *An Historical Guide*, pp. 159–60; Warburton, Whitelaw and Walsh, *History of the City*, p. 526; Figures 2.3 and 2.4.

33   Curry, *Picture of Dublin*, p. 106.

34   'State Trials', *Belfast Newsletter* (4 June 1844) Dublin; 'Court of Queen's Bench', *Freeman's Journal* (12 January 1844) Dublin.

35   'The State Trials', *Monthly Critic and Magazine*, 4 (March 1844), 37.

36 'The State Trials – the Court of the Queen's Bench', *Cork Examiner* (27 December 1843) Dublin; 'The State Trials', *Southern Reporter and Cork Commercial Courier* (9 January 1844) Dublin.

37 'Trial of Eneas McDonnell', *Tipperary Free Press* (15 December 1827) Dublin.

38 Barclay, 'Place and power'; M. Drews, 'Catherine Beecher, Harriet E. Wilson, and domestic discomfort at the northern table', in M. Elbert and M. Drews (eds), *Culinary Aesthetics and Practices in Nineteenth-Century American Literature* (Basingstoke: Palgrave Macmillan, 2009), pp. 89–104.

39 'Master Litton's Office', *Freeman's Journal* (6 February 1843) Dublin; 'Record Court', *Belfast Newsletter* (29 July 1825) Antrim; R. Sarti, *Europe at Home: Family and Material Culture, 1500–1800* (New Haven: Yale University Press, 2002), pp. 155–7.

40 J.H. Langbein, *The Origins of Adversary Criminal Trial* (Oxford: Oxford University Press, 2005). For hostility in the adversarial trial see: W. Bromwich, '"Mrs Buckley you're telling a pack of lies": Cross-examination in the High Court Justiciary in Edinburgh', in C. Williams and G. Tessuto (eds), *Language in the Negotiation of Justice: Contexts, Issues and Applications* (Farnham: Ashgate, 2013), pp. 15–32.

41 See also H. Brocas, *Emmet on Trial* (1803) held by the National Library of Ireland.

42 Mulcahy, 'Putting the defendant in their place'.

43 N. Howlin, 'Irish jurors: Passive observers or active participants?', *Journal of Legal History*, 35:2 (2014), 143–71.

44 'County Grand Jury', *Dublin Evening Packet and Correspondent* (11 January 1844) Dublin.

45 M. Brown and S.P. Donlan, 'The laws in Ireland, 1689–1850: A brief introduction', in M. Brown and S.P. Donlan (eds), *The Laws and Other Legalities of Ireland, 1689–1850* (Farnham: Ashgate, 2011), pp. 1–32; D. Duman, *The Judicial Bench in England, 1727–1875: The Reshaping of Professional Elite* (London: Royal Historical Society, 1982).

46 For a discussion of the gendered treatment of women see: M. Weiner, *Men of Blood: Violence, Manliness and Criminal Justice in Victorian England* (Cambridge: Cambridge University Press, 2006).

47 See the discussion about the use of the table for witnesses, and how it distinguished Ireland from England, in: *Parliamentary Papers, House of Commons and Command, Reports from the Committees, Volume 11: Elections, Cork City* (London: House of Commons, 1852–53), p. 335; and descriptions in E. Wakefield, *An Account of Ireland, Statistical and Political* (London: Longman, Hurst, Rees, Orme and Brown, 1812), vol. 2, p. 345; 'Extraordinary Case', *Drogheda Journal, or Meath & Louth Advertiser* (25 October 1831) Dublin.

48 See photograph of Green Street in 1903 in J.J. Reynolds, *Footprints of Emmet* (Dublin: M.H. Gill & Son, 1903), p. 65; and 'The Court House, Green Street', *Weekly Irish Times* (14 April 1883).

49 See image of 'The Great Aggregate Meeting in the Music Hall, Dublin', *London Illustrated News* (20 January 1844, London: William Little), vol. 4, p. 37.

50 See Chapter 3.

51 P. Goring, *The Rhetoric of Sensibility in Eighteenth-Century Culture* (Cambridge: Cambridge University Press, 2005).

52 Mulcahy, 'Architects of justice', 396.

53 Lobban, 'Custom, nature and authority'.

54 N. Garnham, *The Courts, Crime and the Criminal Law in Ireland, 1692–1760* (Dublin: Irish Academic Press, 1996), p. 105; F. O'Gorman, 'Campaign rituals and ceremonies: The social meaning of elections in England 1780–1860', *Past and Present*, 135 (1992), 79–115; Hay, 'Property, authority'; D. Lemmings, 'Ritual, majesty and mystery: Collective life and culture among English barristers, serjeants and judges, c. 1500–c. 1830', in D. Sugarman and W.W. Pue (eds), *Lawyers and Vampires: Cultural Histories of Legal Professions* (Oxford: Hart Publishing, 2003), pp. 25–63.

55 See Mulcahy, 'Architectural precedent'; Carlen, 'The staging of magistrates' justice'; Rock, 'Witnesses and space in a crown court'.

56 Wakefield, *An Account*, 342.

57 N. Wolf, *An Irish-Speaking Island: State, Religion, Community, and the Linguistic Landscape in Ireland, 1770–1870* (Madison: University of Wisconsin Press, 2014), p. 52; Gattrell, *The Hanging Tree*.

58 Graham, *Ordering Law*, p. 100; Garnham, *The Courts*, p. 105.

59 'City Quarter Sessions', *Freeman's Journal* (16 April 1828); 'Diary of a Barrister during the Last Wexford Assizes', *The New Monthly Magazine and Literary Journal* (London: Henry Colburn, 1826) 16, p. 301.

60 'State Prosecutions', *Dublin Weekly Register* (20 January 1844) Dublin.

61 See, for example, the discussion about the uses of the Limerick Country Court House: 'County Court House', *Limerick Reporter* (23 August 1842) Limerick; Brett, *Court Houses and Market Houses*.

62 'City Court House', *Southern Reporter and Cork Commercial Courier* (11 April 1844) Cork; J. Garry, 'The Tholsel, Drogheda', *Journal of County Louth Archaeological and Historical Society*, 17:3 (1971), 154–68.

63 'Corporations Clonmel Spring Assize', *Nenagh Guardian* (6 April 1842) Tipperary.

64 P.J. Geraghty, 'Ardee and its market square, 1790–1870', *Journal of the County Louth Archaeological and Historical Society*, 22:1 (1989), 54–66; Lewis, *A Topographical Dictionary*, vol. 1, p. 95.

65 P.J. Geraghty, 'Urban improvement and the erection of municipal buildings in County Louth during the eighteenth and nineteenth centuries', *Journal of the County Louth Archaeological and Historical Society*, 23:3 (1995), 295–317; P. Borsay and L. Proudfoot, 'The English and Irish urban experience: Change, convergence and divergence', *The British Academy*, 108 (2002), 1–27; B. Harris, 'Towns, improvement and cultural change in Georgian Scotland: The evidence of the Angus burghs, c. 1760–1820', *Urban History*, 22:2 (2006), 195–212.

66 'Cork Court Houses', *Irish Examiner* (30 May 1845) Cork; 'New Court House', *Saunder's Newsletter* (27 November 1821) Dublin.

67 'Galway Assizes', *Galway Patriot* (27 March 1829) Galway; *Observations on the Grand Jury System of Ireland; with Suggestions for its Improvement* (London: James Ridgway, 1831), p. 14. Cork; 'Assizes Intelligence', *Limerick Reporter* (26 March 1844) Tipperary; 'Kerry Summer Assizes', *Tralee Chronicle* (2 August 1845) Kerry.

68 'Downpatrick Court House', *Belfast Newsletter* (5 August 1828) Down; 'The New Court House', *Waterford News* (20 July 1829) Waterford.

69 'An Act to Make Further Regulations for the Building and Repairing of Court Houses and Sessions Houses in Ireland', *The Statutes of the United Kingdom of Great Britain*

*and Ireland, 53 George III, 1813* (London: His Majesty's Statute and Law Printers, 1813), pp. 570–3; 'Court Houses – Ireland', *Tuam Herald* (17 October 1840).

70  Geraghty, 'Urban improvement', 307.

71  'Positively Only One Night', *Finns Leinster Journal* (9 May 1827) Kilkenny; 'A Scene at the Court House', *Tipperary Free Press* (3 September 1834) Kilkenny.

72  'Court House News Rooms', *Wexford Independent* (9 June 1841) Wexford.

73  Graham, *Ordering Law*, p. 93.

74  'Court-House News Rooms', *Wexford Independent* (9 June 1841) Wexford.

75  'City Court House', *Southern Reporter and Cork Commercial Courier* (11 April 1844) Cork.

76  Double height courts include Bagenalstown (built 1826); first floor courts include Cavan (1824).

77  'King's County Court-House', *Dublin Evening Post* (15 November 1832) King's County/Offaly; 'New Court House', *Dublin Evening Post* (29 December 1829) Cork.

78  'County Cork House', *Cork Examiner* (19 March 1845) Cork.

79  *Parliamentary Papers, House of Commons and Command, Reports from the Committees, Volume 11: Elections, Cork City* (London: House of Commons, 1852–53), p. 335; Lewis, *Topographical Dictionary*, vol. 1, p. 419.

80  Langbein, *Origins*; M. Wiener, *Reconstructing the Criminal: Culture, Law and Policy in England, 1830–1914* (Cambridge: Cambridge University Press, 1990).

81  Barrie and Broomhall, *Police Courts Volume 1*, p. 264; W. Miller, *Cops and Bobbies: Police Authority in New York and London, 1830–1870* (Chicago: Chicago University Press, 1977), pp. 82–3.

82  'Galway Assizes', *Galway Patriot* (27 March 1839) Galway; 'Kerry Summer Assizes', *Tralee Chronicle* (2 August 1845) Kerry.

83  K. Barclay, 'Singing and lower-class masculinity in the Dublin Magistrate's Court, 1800–1845', *Journal of Social History*, 47:3 (2014), 746–68; and Chapter 6.

84  This flexibility can be seen internationally: S. Desan and J. Merrick, *Family, Gender and the Law in Early Modern France* (University Park: Pennsylvania State University Press, 2010); E.A. Zimmerman, *Judicial Institutions in Nineteenth-Century Latin America* (London: University of London, 1999); Barrie and Broomhall, *Police Courts Volume 1*, pp. 209–10.

85  See, for example, 'Nenagh Petty Sessions', *Nenagh Guardian* (10 April 1844) Tipperary.

86  D. Hogan, *The Legal Profession in Ireland 1789–1922* (Dublin: Incorporated Law Society of Ireland, 1986).

87  For discussion see: J. Scott, 'Legal architecture re-imagined', *Law and Humanities*, 5 (2011), 415–23.

88  'Sessions Court, Green Street', *Dublin Morning Register* (1 December 1824) Dublin.

89  J.R. O'Flanagan, *The Irish Bar: Comprises Anecdotes, Bon-Mots, and Biographical Sketches of the Bench and Bar of Ireland* (London: Sampson Low, Marston, Searle, & Rivington, 1879), p. 364, Limerick.

90  'Levy's Handbook of Evidence', *Dublin Weekly Register* (16 September 1848) Wexford.

91  O'Flanagan, *The Irish Bar*, p. 234.

92  'Extraordinary Scene in the City Court House', *Waterford Chronicle* (24 March 1849) Kilkenny.

93  'Circuit Intelligence', *Freeman's Journal* (3 April 1829) Fermanagh.

94  'Carlow Assizes', *Carlow Morning Post* (1 April 1822) Carlow.

95  'Carlow Assizes', *Carlow Morning Post* (25 July 1822) Carlow.

96  'Killarney Petty Sessions', *Kerry Evening Post* (5 July 1837) Kerry.

97  'Dublin Police', *Freeman's Journal* (28 December 1844) Dublin.

98  'Dublin Police', *Belfast Newsletter* (26 December 1828) Dublin; K. Barclay, 'Stereotypes as political resistance: The Irish Police Court columns, c. 1820–1845', *Social History*, 42:2 (2017), 257–80.

99  M. McKeon, 'The secret history of domesticity: Private, public and the division of knowledge', in C. Jones and D. Wahrman (eds), *The Age of Cultural Revolutions: Britain and France, 1750–1830* (Berkeley: University of California Press, 2001), pp. 171–89; M. Legates, 'The cult of womanhood in eighteenth-century thought', *Eighteenth-Century Studies*, 1 (1976), 21–39.

100  Rosalind Crone suggests they were included to increase sales: *Violent Victorians: Popular Entertainments in Nineteenth-Century London* (Manchester: Manchester University Press, 2012), p. 235.

101  Barrie and Broomhall, *Police Courts Volume 1*, p. 268.

102  For example see: *Johnson's Dictionary, Improved by Todd* (Boston: Charles J. Hendee, 1836), p. 304; T. Sheridan, *A General Dictionary of the English Language* (London: J. Dodsley, C. Dilly and J. Wilkie, 1780), unpaginated 'sensation'.

103  K. Barclay, 'Emotions, the law and the press in Britain: Seduction and breach of promise suits, 1780–1830', *Journal of Eighteenth-Century Studies*, 39:2 (2016), 267–84; Barrie and Broomhall, *Police Courts Volume 1*, pp. 227–9; King, *Crime, Justice and Discretion*, pp. 253–7; P. Linebaugh, *The London Hanged: Crime and Civil Society in the Eighteenth Century* (Cambridge: Verso, 1992), p. 87; Beattie, *Crime and the Courts*, p. 399.

104  'Record Court', *Clonmel Herald* (20 July 1839) Tipperary. Another example of horror: 'To the editor of the Galway Vindicator', *Galway Vindicator and Connaught Advertiser* (1 April 1848) Galway.

105  M. Billig, *Laughter and Ridicule: Towards a Social Critique of Humour* (London: Sage, 2005), pp. 57–83.

106  Billig, *Laughter and Ridicule*, pp. 71–6; J. Beattie, 'An essay on laughter and ludicrous composition', in *The Works of James Beattie: Essays*, 3 volumes (Philadelphia: Hopkins and Earle, 1809), vol. 3, pp. 127–301.

107  B. Montagu, *Thoughts on Laughter by a Chancery Barrister* (London: William Pickering, 1830), especially p. 35.

108  'Laughter', *Tipperary Free Press* (26 May 1838); C. Maturin, *Melmoth the Wanderer: A Tale*, 2 volumes (New York: Harper and Bros, 1835), vol. 2, pp. 84–5; 'Mrs Heman's Poems', *The Analectic Magazine*, 1 (Philadelphia, Moses Thomas, 1820), p. 505.

109  S. Johnson (1763), quoted in J. Boswell, *The Life of Samuel Johnson*, 2 volumes (London: H. Baldwin 1791), vol. 1, p. 244.

110  'Police Cork', *Cork Examiner* (14 April 1845) Cork.

111  'Carlow Quarter Sessions', *Kerry Evening Post* (29 January 1827) Carlow.

112  S. Dickie, *Cruelty and Laughter: Forgotten Comic Literature and the Unsentimental Eighteenth Century* (Chicago: Chicago University Press, 2011).

113  'Commission of Oyer and Terminer', *Southern Reporter and Cork Commercial Courier* (27 June 1840) Dublin. See also: 'Limerick Assizes', *Southern Reporter and*

*Cork Commercial Courier* (13 March 1834) Limerick; 'Ennis Assizes', *Southern Reporter and Cork Commercial Courier* (24 July 1848) Clare.

114 'Quarter Sessions Court', *Southern Reporter and Cork Commercial Courier* (7 April 1842) Cork.

115 'Assize Intelligence', *Dublin Evening Post* (12 August 1841) Cork.

116 'Carlow Petty Session', *Carlow Morning Post* (1 October 1832) Carlow.

117 'The State Trials', *Freeman's Journal* (12 February 1844) Dublin.

118 'State Trials', *Belfast Newsletter* (4 June 1844) Dublin; 'Court of the Queen's Bench', *Southern Reporter and Cork Commercial Courier* (11 May 1841) Dublin.

119 'Assize Intelligence', *Dublin Morning Register* (21 July 1835) Limerick.

120 *An Authentic Report of the Trial of Thomas Lidwell, esq on an Indictment for a Rape committed on the Body of Mrs Sarah Sutton . . . at Naas, Lent Assizes* (Dublin: W. Wilson, 1800), p. 23.

121 *Trial of Thomas Lidwell*, pp. 76 and 87.

122 *Ibid.*, p. 76.

123 *Ibid.*, p. 90.

# 3

## Bodies in court: 'Hogarth would have admired him forever'

'By Jove,' said I, 'this man was born particularly for the office of examination' – A peculiar sober shrewdness of look, combined with an Irish sarcastic leer, characterized his clear, interesting, and well-chiselled face; and although an openness and candour of countenance invited all apparently to his heart, yet a close observer could discover in the angular lines that crossed each other every where on his large visage, that you would sooner learn the solution of a problem in Euclid than find a way to his thoughts. 'By the law,' said I, 'I shall follow this fellow to court – there is something original about him; he has certainly some talent; and instantly giving up my intention of pursuing my journey to Dublin on that day,' I followed the crowd that thronged around Costelloe, welcoming him and saluting him with multifarious expressions of gratitude for coming (as they expressed it) 'to take their part agin the yeomen.' . . . I begged of [another member of the gallery] to mention in plain language who were the other four persons whom I saw in court . . . 'there is Mr St[e]w[a]rd wud the whip and the big breeches and makin game, that the glass thing he has lookin at the people, is fastened on his eye. There agin is Mr N[e]wt[o]n wud the big hair and whiskers upon em, whatsomeuvur is the raisin iv id. Musha, shure, it would'nt cost em a pinorth o' soap in the year to cut them hairy things we his face, an not to be makin us believe that he's a Turk, or a wild Injun, wud them big things upon em—ids a shame for em, so it is, not look like a Christian any how; but id's all the fashion, I believe, in this country among the gintilmin to strive to be Turks; bee-the-power-o'kin, they'd frighten a body, so they wud, if you warn't used to em, so they wud. . . . There again,' said he (with his finger pointed) 'there is Mr W[a]ts[o]n' – 'where said I' – 'blur-an-ouns man,' said he, 'don't you see the quere lookin fellow, thats there scratchin himself, wud the cane under his chin, as if in a manner his head was spiked on id for all the world; that I may never sin, plaise your honor but you must be stupid entirely not to see that fellow the minnet you come into the court, barn a man was blind entirely the could'nt help seein that youth any how, wud his ould caubeen upon em, and his great big coat, thats ten times to big for him, wrapped round about em, for all the world like a dog in a sack. But may be I'm talkin ill o' the coat; maybe it was nuver made for em at all at all; may be the man's head does'nt ach that owned that coat afore now, and iv that be the case, the lord have marcy on the man's soul that first got it made, and also for the tailor that made it.' 'Why,' said I, 'you are an exceedingly queer fellow, cant you barely mention the name of these people without entering into so much slang and gibberish about it, such as nobody understands but yourself.' 'Hould easy, please your honner,' said he, "I have only one little fellow more to tell you about.' . . .

'Petit Session Sketch at Bagnelstown', *Carlow Morning Post*, 23 June 1831

In 1721, William Hawkins protested the use of defence lawyers, arguing that 'the very Speech, Gesture and Countenance, and Manner of Defence of those who are Guilty, when they speak for themselves, may often help to disclose the Truth'.[1] A century later, that a close observation of the body offered the viewer 'truth' remained central within European society. With modern scientific techniques, nineteenth-century observers felt confident that they had the technologies, knowledge and ability to accurately 'read' the body for evidence of character.[2] Moreover, when bodies were abstracted from the individual, they could be viewed as a synecdoche for wider society, national identity and state of civilisation.[3] The body became implicated in hierarchies of meaning that reified social class, gender, race and nationality as biological, rather than social, constructs. These 'biological' categories then informed how individuals were interpreted when they came to tell their 'truth' to the court.

How being embodied shapes people's experience of the world is an area of growing interest, with physical presentation understood as a resource in the production of identity and power.[4] The body can be read as a map of past experiences, with scars, tattoos or missing limbs evidence of a person's history and identity.[5] Creative practices that range from dress to bodily modification provide a source of agency for individuals. Beautiful bodies, those that conformed to the cultural ideal, might hold power, but could also be produced through dress, diet and exercise.[6]

Conversely material constraints, from physical disability to wealth, limited people's capacity to control their presentation.[7] This chapter explores how the body – and not just the voice – spoke within courtrooms.

It contributes to a debate in the legal literature on how lawyers shape courtroom dynamics. It has been argued that the expansion of lawyers into criminal trials reduced the role of ordinary people, and especially defendants, to actively contribute to the production of justice.[8] The early nineteenth century, marked by the passing of the Prisoners' Counsel Act in 1836 that removed prohibitions on defence counsel in felony cases, is considered a key moment in this history.[9] As Ariela Gross notes for slaves in the courtroom of the Antebellum South, however, the body could play a central role in the making of the law.[10] Moreover, it was not just the body of the criminal defendant that was subject to scrutiny by the court. This chapter looks at the display and use of the body by a range of legal actors, from judges to lawyers, witnesses, plaintiffs and defendants. It explores how clothing, physical characteristics and particularly displays of emotion were used as evidence of character, arguing that bodily performances shaped men's ability to negotiate power in the courtroom.

### Clothes make the man

> He had used the precaution to come down to the dock that morning in his best attire, for he knew that with an Irish jury, the next best thing to a general good character is a respectable suit of clothes.[11]

By 1800, the importance of clothes to personal identity was firmly established.[12] Clothing was understood not only as a reflection of economic wealth, occupation and regional or national background, but a multitude of personal traits, including sexual probity, modesty, political leaning, religion and alignment to a range of social groups.[13] Following a long-running anxiety about the relationship between luxury and national decline, clothing was also thought to shape the identity and character of the wearer.[14] Clothing reform movements, particularly after the French Revolution, saw control of sartorial choice as a method of reforming character, beliefs and values.[15] Men and women of all classes understood the importance of clothing to self-presentation, with even the very poor attempting to demarcate themselves through their apparel.[16] How the Irish dressed became implicated in their courtroom performance. Outfits were analysed as a measure of the 'truthfulness' of the wearer – did a person present an honest measure of the self or remake character through disguise? This was as true for judges as beggars.

The sartorial choices of barristers and judges when attending the higher courts in Dublin were restricted by the customary uniform. Like elsewhere in the British Empire, lawyers and judges typically wore black double-breasted suits and white shirts with stiff collars and bands. This was generally covered with a black cloak, although judges had ermine-trimmed red cloaks for special occasions (see Figure 3.1). Following fashion, early nineteenth-century lawyers wore knee breeches with black stockings and shoes. They all wore wigs, with shorter wigs for daily practice, and full wigs for ceremonial occasions. When not in court, lawyers' and judges' professional clothing was still represented as dark tailcoat suits with knee breeches and black stockings or knee boots (see Figure 3.2). The black-cloaked, white-headed image of the legal profession that this presented often formed the basis of jokes. As their gown resembled wings and drawing on lawyer's money-hungry reputations, they were compared to carrion birds, such as vultures, crows or magpies.[17] The print *The First Day of Term!* (1817, Figure 3.1) captured this avian theme with the legal profession flying in for the first day of session.

The distinct costume of the legal profession marked them out and could be a matter of pride. Richard Sheil described how, as a new barrister in the 1810s, he reflected on the 'dignity and importance' of his

**Figure 3.1** *The First Day of Term! Blessings of Ireland or A Flight of Lawyers* (Dublin: McCleary, 1817)

A VIEW of the FOUR COURTS

**Figure 3.2** This image shows lawyers in their professional dress of black knee breeches and tail coat. From left to right: John Toler, 1st Earl of Norbury and Chief Justice of the Court of Pleas; Standish O'Grady, 1st Viscount Guillamore and Chief Baron of the Exchequer; Thomas Manners-Sutton, 1st Baron Manners and Lord Chancellor; William Downes, 1st Baron Downes and Chief Justice of the King's Bench. *A View of the Four Courts* (Dublin: William McCleary, 1809).

station when heading to the chamber in the Four Courts where the Bar's gowns were kept.[18] His reverie was disturbed by a 'remarkable specimen of wretchedness', a starving man whose clothing 'served to set his destitution off'. The man had a 'coat that had once been black', but 'hung in rags', pinned tightly at the throat to conceal the lack of a neckcloth. He wore no vest, but a 'tattered yellow' shirt that 'adhered to his withered body'. The man's breeches were a 'prismatic diversity of colour' tied with twine, his stockings 'ragged worsted and accumulated mire'. Naked feet could be seen through his wet shoes. Sheil turned away with a 'mingled sentiment of disgust and horror'. He was shocked to see the same man in court dressed as a barrister, reflecting whether 'I had not a little exaggerated the importance to which I imagined that every barrister possessed an indisputable claim'.[19] In telling this story, Sheil teased his younger self for his naive pomposity, using the experience to reflect on the difficulty lawyers had making money during the period.[20] The relationship he made between clothing and professional authority, however, reflected broader cultural associations between dress and status. As *Irish March of Intellect* (1829, Figure 3.3) suggests through its insinuation that it was ridiculous for poor Catholics to access the bar, wealth, class and professional identity reinforced each other, rooting judicial authority in propertied power.[21]

For men without wealth or dress, the lawyer's wig and gown could disguise inadequacies. Legal costume, designed to display judicial majesty, came to stand for its authority. One humorous tale saw Daniel O'Connell advising his guilty client to knock the 'black cap' worn by the judge from his head during sentencing. The client does so, O'Connell declares the punishment invalid, and the prisoner is freed.[22] This incident had no legal basis. The story spoke to O'Connell's image as defender of the people, but also how judicial clothing came to symbolise the judiciary's power. The legal authority vested in the judge was collapsed into the judicial costume, tying together the man with his outfit.

Legal clothing marked judges and barristers as 'in place' within the courtroom, providing them 'home advantage'. Its success is evidenced through the general lack of commentary on the clothing of legal men in press reports. The garb of the legal profession provided a corporate identity, shrouding them in 'dignity and importance'. The removal of sartorial 'choice' ensured that this aspect of their court performance went unquestioned; their masculinity secured through uniform. As their own identities were embedded within their legal personas, the adversarial process was depersonalised (although not always successfully as explored in Chapter 5). During a period where personal slights were not taken lightly and men still duelled for honour, this corporate branding helped maintain social order.[23]

More broadly, a respectable outfit was read as evidence of character. When prosecuted for theft in 1832, William Beatty was described as a 'well dressed respectable-looking young man' by the press, a description his witnesses suggested was mirrored in his character. Whilst the prosecution used his clothing to identify him as the thief, he was found not guilty.[24] 'Respectable-looking' was a common adjective used to describe people from a wide variety of walks of life, often coupled with occupations like 'farmer' to reflect sartorial variation.[25] Respectability held common characteristics that were expected across social groups. Clothing was to be clean, unfaded and not ragged or patchwork. It should include the common items of clothing thought necessary for decency: neckerchiefs, stockings, shirt or petticoat, breeches or gown, and shoes. Most of the body should be covered, certainly those parts

**Figure 3.3** The speech bubble reads, 'Och, good luck to your honour! I've brought you my little Paddy, as bright a lad as any in Killarney – and now we've got mancipation I would <u>bind</u> the jewel 'prentice to your honor to make a Judge of him just for all the world like your Honor's Lordship'. A Sharpshooter, *Irish March of Intellect; or, The Happy Result of Emancipation* (London: S. Gans, 1829)

conventionally hidden from display. Whilst many Irishmen wore colourful clothes, colour created through mending with cloths and threads in a variety of fabrics reflected lack of access to materials and poor workmanship. Clothes were similarly expected to fit well. The loquacious local who opened this chapter condemned Mr Watson for his suit 'ten times too big for him'.[26] He hoped it was because the suit was made for someone else, at least rendering the tailor innocent of this 'sin' against fashion.

Whilst the association between poor dress and poverty was recognised, responses to sartorial deficiency were not straightforwardly sympathetic. Like their British counterparts, nineteenth-century Irish middling sorts and elites balanced a need for Christian charity and pity, with a belief in personal responsibility that located much of the poor as 'undeserving'.[27] Sheil described the 'horror' and 'disgust' he felt at the 'pitiable' barrister outside the Four Courts, but these emotions only affirmed his own social standing.[28] In 1836, Hickey, a poor farmer, was brought from his home in Waterford to the Four Courts charged with not paying his tithes. The reporter sympathised with his plight, describing the 'rack rent' of £3 an acre that 'scantily clothed' Hickey paid whilst supporting a widowed mother and family of small children.[29] He also noted that Hickey 'suffered dreadfully' on the journey, placed on the roof of a stage coach in bad weather and left to starve, but for the charity of a passenger.

Yet, whilst the reporter showed sympathy and located Hickey's poverty as beyond his control, he still used clothes as a measure of worth. The bailiff who transported the farmer was described as a 'poor-looking, ragged creature, apparently, if possible, even still worse off than his prisoner, at least in point of raiment'.[30] His cruel and unreasonable behaviour was reflected in his costume – an outfit compared directly with that of the suffering man. A sympathetic reading might suggest the bailiff also deserved pity for his poverty, his actions reflecting an unjust system, but this did not appear to be the journalist's intent. Rather, whilst poverty provoked pity, this feeling was not expected to break down social barriers. Poverty, manifested in clothing, located both men at the bottom of the social ladder; pity for the deserving poor did not restore their character any more than pity for the fallen woman restored her virginity. The line between 'respectable' and 'unrespectable' illustrated through dress was a meaningful social division, as were those between the social classes, a categorisation similarly reflected through wardrobe. Clothing became a shorthand for character, a quick measure of social value.

A coat that was 'buttoned close' intimated poverty and so lack of character. One bankrupt arrested for begging in Dublin was described by the *Connaught Journal* in 1839 as 'dressed in a black coat, which was buttoned close under his chin; his nether garment was of the same material, but more threadbare'.[31] The schoolmaster Ignatius O'Mara, brought before the bar in 1837, wore a:

> coat (once black) [which] was pedantically classic, closely buttoned round his neck, eclipsing the sight of a waistcoat or of shirt, and exhibiting a map of such dire economy, that a pin's point could scarce find entrance between the interstices of perches and fine drawings of colored worsted.[32]

The closed jacket hid what was beneath, or indeed what was not, suggestive of lack and possibly deception. It threatened longstanding manly ideals of openness and honesty, as well as social and financial credit.[33] Credit relied on sartorial honesty, allowing shopkeepers and bankers to make accurate judgements of 'worth'.[34] This conflation of social, often sexual, and financial credit tied men's consumer choices into their character. To hide poverty beneath a close-buttoned coat denied others the opportunity to judge credit and character accurately. Similarly, wearing the clothes of others, evidenced by an ill-fitting suit, raised questions about a person's identity.

How those that were unable to achieve sartorial respectability interpreted clothing is harder to access. That people of all occupations received the appellate 'respectable' when appearing in court suggests that sartorial propriety was desirable across class. But there is evidence that people were happy to work, converse and have relationships with those that reporters deemed poorly dressed. The eccentrically costumed O'Mara was sued by an irate father, a 'simple country farmer', who hired him to teach his children, but found instead he was 'sleeping by day and romancing all night'.[35] Neither O'Mara's dress, nor his 'long *o'harrig* locks which hung in neglected wilderness, nearly to his shoulders', deterred this farmer from viewing him as a suitable educator, nor, if the farmer is believed, did it prevent the village women from finding him attractive.

Not every sartorial performance in court was interpreted in the same way. All social classes appeared to appreciate, if not at all times, 'eccentric' individuals, whose clothing did not conform to social norms. Eccentricity was a full bodily performance, where clothing only played one part. Such men, and most courts were more tolerant of eccentric men than women, were portrayed as 'larger than life' characters marked by loquaciousness, quick wit, or musical or storytelling ability, and with odd clothing, haircuts or evident bodily 'difference', such as blindness or a limp.[36] Jerry, Paddy and Shamus' clothing was just one aspect of their performance when they appeared before Killarney Petty Sessions in 1837.[37] The plaintiff, Jerry, was described as a youth in 'natural galligaskins', wide-legged breeches that were fashionable in the seventeenth century, whilst the defendant, Paddy, was noted for 'his locks standing back from his brow like the quills of a porcupine'. Jerry's witness, Shamus, however, stole the show. Dressed in a coat 'like an astrologer's', 'his nether garment [was] like nothing in heaven or earth, for it must have been made when tailoring was out of fashion, no one being able to say whether [well known tailoring establishments] Kean and Turnbull, of Cork, or Tom Barry of Killarney, had the honor of designing it'. On his head, Shamus wore 'a natural hair turban wreathed in matted folds around his head'. He was also blind in one eye. As the journalist noted, 'Hogarth would have admired him for ever'. This sartorial show was accompanied by considerable posturing between the men who 'exchanged looks of mortal defiance' and winked at the bench whilst recounting their story, which was rendered phonetically to convey a strong brogue. The magistrates discouraged the men from pursuing the case and sent them on their way.

The odd clothing described here, like the threadbare rags of the poor, was understood to speak to the character and identity of these men. As fashion increasingly marketed itself to individual physiognomies, showing awareness of how clothing and accessories flattered particular bodies, individuals were provided with the opportunity for sartorial distinction.[38] Politicians, celebrities and other well-known people took advantage of this, using specific clothing or styles to allow them to be identified by the public in the flourishing print market and in person.[39] British culture also became captivated by 'odd fellows' and 'queer subjects', who came to form the subject matter of prints, books and police court columns.[40] It was an interest that has been read as a key moment in the making of British modernity, where the individual flourished at the expense of the community.[41] Such men were construed as evidence of Britain's liberty, which allowed its subjects to display individuality, personality and unique character.[42]

Few of the men who dressed distinctively in court were embracing traditional models of respectability. Rather, they questioned whether the 'respectability' conveyed through conventional clothing was a useful measure of manliness and so social authority. Through their performances of dress, such men countered conservative measures of social worth and renegotiated how clothing should be interpreted when making determinations of manliness. Moreover, many 'eccentric' men rendered themselves as manly actors, receiving little critique from others in the court or the journalists who later described them. For such men, dress was a more individualised and complex measure of character than generic trends in fashion allowed. In turn, traditional lines of authority were muddied, providing room to negotiate social hierarchies.[43]

Not all men successfully used fashion in this way. Nineteenth-century audiences were aware of the deceptive potential of dress. Seduction and breach of promise of marriage suits, where damages for harm were determined by social class (richer defendants were 'fined' larger amounts), were ridden with accusations of 'dressing for the jury'.[44] Women were as subject to this criticism as men, if not more so due to the negative association between fashionable frivolity and modesty.[45] In 1827, the *Ballina Impartial* quietly censured Anne McGarahan, the daughter of a country publican, during her seduction suit, noting 'For a person in her condition, she was superbly dressed'.[46]

McGarahan's clothing was highlighted during cross-examination when she was asked whether she had been given gifts of clothing from men, an attempt to undermine her claims to chastity. She acknowledged that the beautiful Leghorn bonnet she wore came from the defendant, Mr Maguire, which, as the quality was too good for her social class, implied she was not a social equal to the defendant and so could not have expected marriage. McGarahan also admitted that the fashionable veil she wore belonged to her mother, noting that it cost one pound two years ago. Her expensive veil was used by the defence to imply that not only she, but her family, spent their money frivolously – carelessness with money might suggest a looseness of virtue; it certainly damaged any suggestion that she would make a frugal wife.[47]

Whilst borrowing clothing for trial was commonplace amongst the lower orders, it was consistently used by lawyers to suggest that they were trying to deceive juries.[48] Sheil, when describing lower-class witnesses in the early 1820s, whose 'emaciated and discoloured countenances showed their want and their depravity', noted that: 'They generally appeared in coats and breeches, the external decency of which, as they were hired for the occasion, was ludicrously contrasted with the ragged and filthy shirt'.[49] The lawyer Henry Deane Grady (1764–1847), 'well acquainted with "the inner man" of an Irish witness', repeatedly gave the poor 'injunctions to unbutton' their suit coat, which in exposing ragged shirts also displayed 'true' character.[50] Thus even when poor men and women attempted to demonstrate their understanding of and conformity to wider codes of sartorial respectability, they were condemned. Such censorship reinforced the association between character and wealth and denied the opportunity for mobility across social groups.

Whilst men and women were accused of dressing up, accusations of dressing 'down' tended to be reserved for men. When sued by Anne Seretton for breach of promise in 1833, William McElligot, a labourer, was declaimed for trying to disguise his wealth through poor dress and thus limit the size of any award against him. During testimony, Seretton's father described how McElligot had promised to marry her 'as soon as he got clothes', but he married someone else who had 'an ass, a car and a pig'.[51] The defence asked him 'was [McElligot] not married in old clothes?', but the witness did not know. When asked whether he 'wear[s] the same clothes now as when he promised you to marry the plaintiff', the witness 'looking at the defendant and apparently excited (in a loud voice) [said] he does not'. The barrister awarded the full amount asked for: £9 4s 6d.

Whilst risky if the court suspected deception, clothing provided people with an opportunity to shape how they and their character were interpreted. Men, who in the imagination of the period were less endangered by luxurious excess and for whom fashion was not generally used as a measure of sexual probity, were freer to do this than women.[52] A sartorial misstep was less likely for men, as their fashion choices were not the focus of such significant regulation and critique. If anything, following extremes of fashion spoke poorly of manliness as measured by mainstream Irish society.

As in other parts of the United Kingdom, a subculture of 'dandies' grew up in Dublin, particularly in the 1810s and 1820s.[53] Their tight clothing, as well as the significant expenditure associated with it, was viewed as 'unmanly', endangering the nation through the uncontrolled pursuit of luxury.[54] As the Scot Thomas Carlyle noted in 1836, '[a] Dandy is a clothes-wearing Man, a Man whose trade, office and existence consists in the wearing of Clothes'.[55] Dandies were typically depicted as effeminate, physically slight and lacking vigour (with clothing that restricted their range of movement), irresponsible with money, and sly or dishonest (see Figure 3.4).[56] Many images of dandies depicted them in ragged underwear and stockings as they cleaned their fashionable outerwear, suggestive of their deceptive nature and lack of character (see Figure 3.5).

In 1819, when two 'fancy dandies', gentlemen 'not very *masculine* in their appearance', appeared before the Dublin magistrate, Alderman Darley, for defrauding a hackney coachman of his fare, the newspaper declined to publish their names, noting that it was 'not from any delicacy towards themselves, but to their families'.[57] The dandies' defence was that

**Figure 3.4** *Dandy Pickpocket's Diving* (Dublin: J. Le Petit, [n.d. c. 1820])

'the dresses they wore were so *tight*, they were unable to come to their pockets!' The magistrate humorously responded that 'if they thought proper to trammel themselves in such a manner, they should have carried sufficient money to pay their immediate demands in their hands, or in a *ridicule*'. A reticule was a small drawstring purse carried by fashionable women. It was referred to as a 'ridicule' in commentaries on female fashionable excess.[58] Alderman Darley's suggestion was a reprimand, suggesting that the dandies were 'womanly', and so should carry a female accessory, and 'ridiculous' due to the play on words. He ordered them to pay the fare and moderate compensation for the coachman's loss of time. Through refusing to name them, the paper further unmanned these youths, denying them pride in their fashionable identity. Whilst their social class spared them a harsher sentence, these fashionable young men were humiliated by the magistrate and the press for their sartorial presentation. Not all performances of male dress successfully demonstrated a recognised masculinity in the conservative space of the court.

An important medium for conveying character and identity, clothing became implicated in negotiations of power within the courtroom. Professional legal costume was endowed with authority, enveloping the wearer in judicial majesty.[59] Respectable clothing demonstrated probity. Those that could not afford to dress well, or whose sartorial choices

**Figure 3.5** *A Dandy Family Preparing for the General Mourning!* (Dublin: McCleary, 1821)

stepped beyond the boundaries of acceptable manly garb, were in a weaker position as their character was brought into question. Clothing was not a stable entity, however, allowing people to dress up or down and to express facets of identity. Some men even used clothing to rearticulate manliness and so social power, challenging the status quo. As a result, dress provided an opportunity for even voiceless defendants to convey multiple and complex messages. The detailed descriptions given to clothing by observers suggest how seriously such messages were taken.[60] Bodies played a similar role.

### Bodies on display

Whilst the close-buttoned coat potentially hid a missing neckerchief or ragged shirt, its capacity to hide the body was not as encompassing. Gwenda Morgan and Peter Rushton highlight the ways that the bodies of the early modern poor were scrutinised and described in attempts to identify them and regulate their movements and agency.[61] Ragged clothing that displayed corporal markings made the bodies of the poor more visible, whilst the full coverage and quality of the elites' clothing not only hid what lay underneath but signalled that such bodies did not require such close monitoring. By the first half of the nineteenth century, however, it was not just the bodies of the poor that were open to debate. The increasing popularity of sciences and pseudosciences that claimed to be able to measure character, disposition, criminal proclivities, religious leanings and numerous other qualities through a study of the body imbued it with new meaning.[62] These ideas were not always novel to the period, but were rejuvenated by popular science lectures and publications, where the work of physiognomists, phrenologists and medical doctors was made available to a wider public.[63]

The works of the Swiss physiognomist Johann Lavater (1741–1801) were remarkably popular, regularly advertised in the Irish press for sale from the mid-1800s into the 1830s.[64] His name was well-known enough to be dropped into news reports or literature without his identity needing explanation. When Jane Costello appeared before the Dublin magistrate in 1831, the reporter noted she was a 'mild and modest looking young woman, whom the most uncharitable, on minute examination of her physiognomy, however skilled he might be in the science of Lavater, would never think of charging with "having set the Liffey on fire"'.[65] Although phrenology was treated rather sceptically, it had a following in parts of Ireland, especially after the visit of practitioner Johann Spurzheim (1776–1832) to the non-conformist followers of Joseph Priestly in 1815.[66] Like elsewhere, these ideas became part of popular discourse in the following decades. The policeman Sergeant Reid explained in an 1847 theft case that he believed the prosecutor to be an 'honest man, if I be allowed to form an opinion based on the laws of phrenology'.[67] He entertained the court by continuing that the defendant was not an 'honest man': 'I lay my hands gently on the cranium, and by a comparative analysis of the respective organs, I arrive at a conclusion incontrovertible'.

Although the works of Lavater and his colleagues were not read uncritically, that the body should be read for knowledge of character was apparent in descriptions of those who appeared in court, from judges to the lowest criminal. Not without some contest, a healthy, attractive body and countenance was related to good character, whilst bodily deformity, ugliness or disability were evidences of weaknesses of personality or disposition. It was a science that tied personal characteristics to generic physical features, but also placed significance on the individual. 'This belief in the indispensability and individuality of all men, . . . is one of the unacknowledged, the noble fruits of physiognomy', noted Lavater.[68]

The highest members of the court were not immune to such analysis. Richard Sheil's outstanding character sketches of his fellow colleagues at the bar in the early 1820s drew heavily on the idea that physical description provided insight into them as men.[69] His text, serialised in the *New Monthly Magazine*, suggests he was heavily influenced by theorists such as Lavater, spending several paragraphs for each man on appearance and associating bodily features with dispositions. Given the vagaries of this analysis, his interpretation of his colleagues was influenced by his personal relationship with them.

Charles Kendal Bushe, Solicitor General and later Lord Chief Justice of the King's Bench, was a favourite (see Figure 3.6). He was the epitome of manliness for Sheil, not too beautiful but comely, and suggestive of strength and power. His 'complexion is too sanguineous and ruddy, but has no murkiness or impurity in its flush; it is indicative of great fullness, but at the same time of great vigour of temperament'.[70] A sanguineous nature was suggestive of passion and power, but this was not necessarily a problem, especially in men, with such people more benevolent, as well as quick to anger.[71] Sheil did not consider Bushe an 'intellectual'; his 'forehead is more lofty than expansive, and suggests itself to be the residence of an elevated rather than of a comprehensive mind'. It was 'smooth, polished and marble'. Following Lavater, the latter was a compliment where a lack of wrinkles and clear skin were 'the most indubitable signs of an excellent, a perfectly beautiful and significant, intelligent and noble forehead'.[72] Bushe's eyes were 'large, globular, and blue'. According to

**Figure 3.6** James Heath, after John Comerford, *Charles Kendal Bushe* (1809)

physiognomists, blue-eyed people were inclined to 'weakness, effeminacy, and yielding', whilst 'globular' eyes were suggestive of less control, but also greater honesty.[73] These anatomical failings were offset by his mouth, which was 'characteristic of force, firmness, and precision, and is at once affable and commanding, proud and kind, tender and impassioned, accurate and vehement, generous and sarcastic, and is capable of the most conciliating softness and the most impetuous ire'.[74]

Bushe was not 'perfect', but combined great feeling with manly firmness. He was not too 'intellectual', with its associations with bookishness and timidity, but intelligent and precise.[75] His physiological 'weakness' signified him as manly, indicative that he could be brought to honourable anger, whilst his feminine eyes spoke to openness and honesty. His general physique complemented his face. Sheil thought Bushe 'too corpulent and heavy', but that he framed it well beneath his legal gown: 'however many speakers of eminence have overcome the disadvantages of a weak and slender configuration, it cannot be doubted that we associate with dignity and wisdom an accompaniment of massiveness and power'.[76] Even Bushe's corpulence contributed to the impression of him as wise, powerful and manly.

Sheil, a key leader of the Catholic Association, was much less complimentary of the Attorney-General William Saurin (1757–1839), who was hostile to Catholic Emancipation.[77] Saurin's eyes were 'black and wily, and glitter under the mass of a rugged and shaggy eye-brow'.[78] 'Wild and perplexed' eyebrows denoted a corresponding mind, argued Lavater, an idea that Sheil reinforced with Saurin's 'thoughtful' forehead that was 'neither bold nor lofty'.[79] Saurin's physiognomy spoke to a sly, dishonest nature. He lacked an 'intellectual elevation in his aspect, but he has a cautious shrewdness and discriminating perspicacity'. Beyond the initial appearance of 'affability' about the mouth, 'a sedate and permanent vindictiveness may be readily found'. Saurin's movements intimated 'slowness and suspicion' and 'a spirit of caution', and whilst there was 'no fraud about him', 'there is a disguise of his emotions which borders upon guile'.[80] Sheil concluded that 'he looks altogether a worldly and sagacious man – sly, cunning, and considerate – not ungenerous, but by no means exalted. . . . moral, but not pious: decent but not devout: honourable, but not chivalrous: affectionate, but not tender: a man who could go far to serve a friend, and a good way to hurt a foe'.[81]

As was the nature of physiognomic science, no physical characteristic was entirely negative, but Saurin's slow, cautious and discriminating qualities were used to suggest that he was cunning and vindictive. Whilst the ability to control the expression of emotion was generally viewed as a marker of manliness, Sheil suggested that in this case it was less control than disguise: 'his passions are violent, and rather covered than suppressed'.[82] Moreover, he was not capable of deep, sociable and moral emotions, 'decent, but not devout . . . affectionate, but not tender', that enabled elite men to put aside their personal selfishness and work together for the good of the nation.[83] Saurin may have been a 'useful and estimable member of society', but he was not the model of masculinity that Bushe presented. He lacked the honesty and openness, the practical intelligence, the deep feeling, and the physical stature that signified an ideal masculinity.

Whilst men like Sheil did not expect lower social groups to conform to models of elite masculinity, nonetheless the same standards were used to measure the worth and honesty of all men that appeared in courtrooms. Sheil described several criminals using similar language. He showed a general disdain for the Irish lower classes, viewing the respectable as 'greatly superior to persons of [their] class' or 'a remarkable contrast with the ordinary class of culprits'.[84] The 'honest, industrious' farmer Mathew Hogan, when charged with manslaughter, was more like 'an English yeoman, than an Irish peasant'. His appearance at the bar was 'moving and impressive – tall, athletic, and even noble in his stature, with a face finely formed, and wholly free from any ferocity of expression'. Rather than having his 'guilt and depravity stamped upon him', his 'countenance was indicative of gentleness and humanity'. When sentenced to transportation, Hogan went pale, his hands shook, but his eyes were unable to cry. The sentence was felt 'with more deep intensity, because he is naturally a sensitive and susceptible man'.[85]

This interesting account, not atypical of what appeared in newspapers, combined physiognomic theory with assumptions around the manliness of the lower classes. Hogan's superiority over his fellow peasants was marked by his masculine, athletic body, attractive face and gentle humanity. Like Bushe and Saurin, the right combination of emotions marked Hogan as civilised and manly; this required deep and controlled feeling, but should lack violence or excess. Moreover, for Sheil, a peasant who combined an attractive body with a display of sensibility, not only exceeded his social class but his national identity, moving from Irish to English. Sheil was not an anglophile, situating the poverty of Ireland's peasantry as a product of the colonial relationship between Britain and Ireland.[86] Nonetheless, like the reporter who sympathetically described Hickey's situation whilst using it to affirm social boundaries, Sheil associated an embodied poverty with character. The colonial relationship created the unmanly Irish body.

The connection between the beautiful body and humane feeling is notable given Sheil's link between 'want' and 'depravity'. The emaciated body, whilst demanding pity, was threatening. He described John Brown, charged with murdering his master, as 'cadaverous and charnel . . . eyes in which fear and famine glared together; his wild and matted hair; his stooping and contracted form; his ragged clothes, and the union of physical meanness with cowering debasement' constituted a 'nauseating combination'.[87] Brown was sickeningly ugly, starving and fearful; he not only lacked manly courage, but hinted at violence and lack of control through his 'wild' hair and hunched physical form. For Sheil, Brown's body was a physical signifier of his inner self, not only demonstrating the unfortunate consequences of poverty, lack of food and disease, but a twisted soul.

The *Freeman's Journal* similarly described the approver Nash as 'a very ill-looking and miserable creature' in 1833; John Hickey, found guilty of conspiracy to murder in 1844, was 'a rather ill-looking man, aged about 35, low stature and robust make'; and William Lyons, indicted for criminal violation of a child in 1831, was 'of an uncommonly forbidding countenance and appearance'.[88] Body and crime here reinforced each other, affirming guilt. In many respects, the science of physiognomy gave voice to an older belief system which associated beauty and morality, where sin had the potential to corrupt the outer body.[89] Yet, perhaps more so than in the past, the ugly body was accountable for its monstrosity, allowing it to be read as lack of character.

The existence of beautiful bodies conversely acted as a reminder that individuals could overcome their backgrounds and circumstances – a belief that might have been particularly important for a middle class in a colonial context who needed to explain their achievement of civility and justify their ability to rule. Beautiful criminals were therefore challenging to interpret. When charged with assault in 1832, John Tobin was described as: 'one of the brightest specimens of an unsophisticated innocence', because of his good looks and physical size. The *Carlow Morning Post* found the contradiction between his appearance and alleged criminality humorous, a levity that made the assault appear less serious to the reader.[90] Bryan Donnelly was 'an individual of superior appearance, and of the middle-class', but nonetheless found guilty of attacking a dwelling house and sentenced to seven years transportation in 1833.[91] His respectability may have worked against him. He had been refused bail before trial as the judge noted '[a] man like you ought to be a pattern for the country. . . . Your respectability and station in life ought to have taught you better; and I am prouder to catch you than one thousand poor ignorant creatures'.[92] Sheil himself complained that many prisoners 'exhibit a set of features from which a committee of craniologists would never infer a propensity to crime' with 'honest, open, manly countenances'. He thought this was because they were 'either as guiltless as they appear to be, or their crimes have been committed under circumstances of excitation, which, in their own eyes at least, excuse the enormity', using the modern psychology of guilt, rather than the corrupting power of sin, to explain how crime impacted on physical appearance.[93]

Whilst the wretched and miserable body was associated with criminality, it could provoke compassion. When prosecuted for not paying his tithes in 1836, John Reilly was described as 'an aged, wretched, emaciated looking creature – an unfortunate, who had evidently drained the last cup of bitterness and human misery'. He was dressed 'literally in rags, sickness and want and suffering were strongly depicted in his hollow cheeks . . . poverty and oppression it was evident, had done its worst'.[94] Like other accounts of poor men, Reilly's poverty was assumed to have affected his character, 'having drained the last cup of bitterness'. This may have implied that he was twisted by malice, but in the period, it also held the more neutral quality of being full of grief.[95] In either case, his emotions had debilitated him and he was unable to provide for himself, both locating him as unmanly. When Reilly appeared in court, the 'awful spectacle' excited a 'thrill of horror', creating fear mixed with hatred in his audience.[96] The 'professional gentlemen' 'enlisted their sympathies' and paid his fine. Whilst Reilly's appearance led to a positive outcome in this case, had he been charged with a crime, the court's 'horror' may have gone against him.

The relationship between the beautiful body and innocence and its reverse at times created dilemmas, when 'wretched' men accused 'respectable' people of crimes. In 1840, a 'miserable looking cripple (an itinerant piper)', Daniel Cronin accused a 'respectable farmer', Florence McCarthy of assault in front of the Tralee Petty Sessions. Cronin's testimony was supported by his child and the 'evident marks of violence on his face', but the reporter noted that McCarthy was a 'man of excellent character, very respectable in his line of life, and of sober and peaceable habits'. To settle the dispute, McCarthy's lawyer, Mr Supple, 'feeling compassion for Cronin's deplorable condition' offered his fee for the case to Cronin to drop the complaint. Cronin 'after some hesitation' accepted.[97]

The news report, and it suggested the court, was ambivalent about how to interpret this case. A 'cripple' and itinerant man (who it was assumed was without character) accused a man with 'excellent character' of assault, evidencing his claims with visible injuries. Crippled musicians were not without cultural status in Ireland. Musical ability was prized and many notable musicians across the centuries were disabled, often blind.[98] Training disabled children as musicians gave them both an occupation and status, if one situated at the edges of respectability. The disabled musician provided an exemplar of an alternative model of masculinity for the non-conforming body. In turn, the disabled body authenticated and reinforced claims to musical talent and ability, by locating such men in a long cultural tradition. That Cronin's claim was true was also suggested by his observed hesitation, which belied a purely economic motivation for prosecution. In an era where financial recompense for injury was still a culturally valid alternative to prosecution, if a declining practice, Cronin's decision to accept did not necessarily imply greed or dishonesty.[99] Mr Supple's compromise allowed the magistrate to avoid judgment, but the 'truth' was left untold. Moreover, only Mr Supple left the court with his reputation untainted; McCarthy's 'innocence' was not established, whilst Cronin's 'guilt', even as a victim, remained intact.

The body was an important cultural signifier of guilt or innocence, a site that could be read for evidence, whether in the form of character or marks that supported personal testimony. But reading the body was not straightforward. Not only was there variation in how physiognomists interpreted it, people combined various features and traits that provided complex and mixed messages. People did not always perform the character suggested by their bodies, with beautiful men committing crimes and ugly men appearing as victims. The body also evidenced alternative stories, whether that was the emaciated body that demanded pity or the disabled body suggestive of musical talent. Nor were lawyers and judges immune from such analysis; their physical presentation contributing to their success as advocates and their ability to maintain authority within the court. Bodies interweaved with other forms of evidence, at times reinforcing character or guilt, at others destabilising assumptions.

## Moving the court

Bodily performances of emotion were equally vital to understanding character. Sheil's writing is suggestive of a wider cultural norm, where manliness required men to feel deeply and to express emotion appropriately, but also to control violence or excess. This was reinforced by the 'culture of sensibility' of the eighteenth century, that emphasised the important role of emotion in human behaviour and communication. According to eighteenth-century science, the body interpreted the world through the senses, judging experience according to the levels of pain or pleasure produced. When placed into a sophisticated moral value system, emotion became a central mechanism by which the body interpreted right or wrong.[100] The 'sensible' man who saw the emaciated body felt pity, which, if he was of good character, would encourage him to behave charitably. The decision to behave charitably required not only feeling, however, but the exercise of self-control and the application of reason. Uncontrolled pity could lead to despair; reasoned emotion ensured appropriate action. Importantly, the ability to exercise self-control was associated with elite and middle-class men; women and others who did not have access to reason were controlled by their emotions, rendering them unsuitable for public life.

On the British mainland, the nineteenth century saw a contraction in the culture of sensibility for a greater emphasis on stoicism.[101] The latter was not new and played an important part in British discourses of masculinity across the eighteenth century, but whereas previously men were expected to show controlled emotion, increasingly emotion, or perhaps specifically sentimental values, were eradicated from models of manliness. Male lovers were now expected to falter over their sweet nothings, and it became more endearing for men to be lost for words than to have a fluency in romantic language.[102] Duelling for honour, as a method of expressing manly anger, declined.[103] Lawyers in the English courts, often disingenuously, claimed that they did not have the skills to sway a jury using sentimental language, and asked juries to bear with them.[104] The legal system itself attempted to rid emotion from its processes. As Martin Wiener notes, 'instead of being a feeder of emotion *into* the trial, the judge would become a monitor *against* it'.[105]

Yet, Ireland did not follow these trends, at least in the first half of the century. Rather, Irish manliness continued to require a greater level of visible emotional engagement from men, marked through gestures and emotional display. Just as Sheil explored Bushe's portrayal of emotion as a measure of his manliness, so other Irish men were lauded for their visible emotionality. Perhaps most noticeably, weeping by Irish judges on pronouncing death sentences was a mainstay in Irish courts into the 1840s. This was not unique to Ireland, but as Thomas Dixon notes, judges' weeping was only noted rarely in English press reports, with the Irish Justice Willis, sitting on the English bench, one of the last examples of this pattern there.[106]

In contrast, overt displays of emotion in Irish courts was not only expected but viewed positively by news reporters. Upon pronouncing death on Luke Dillon for rape in 1831, Justice Torrens 'burst into a flood of tears', a response that was mirrored in the courthouse where 'there were few who appeared so unmoved as the prisoner'.[107] The judge at the Waterford assizes was 'moved even to tears as was a great proportion of the thronged crowd', when, in 1821, he sentenced James Darcy for murdering his brother. Earlier, the foreman could 'scarcely articulate the fatal word and evidently his fellow Jurors shared his emotion'.[108] Even when the judge was not recorded as weeping, the gallery was described with tears at a pronouncement of death. At the sentencing of Henry Canny for embezzlement in 1822, the jury requested mercy due to his youth and that he was 'deprived of his parents at an age when he most required their care'. The *Carlow Morning Post* noted that '[t]he tears of almost every person in the court, whether arising from the youth and condition of the prisoner, or the earnestness of the judge, speak more on the subject than any report we have attempted'.[109]

As Dixon notes, weeping during death sentences was a complex cultural phenomenon, 'an intellectual, social and religious performance', informed by the association between weeping and religious experience, medical understandings of the purpose of tears in expressing emotion, and the need to embody a particular form of pity and religious awe for the court.[110] The audience of the weeping judge, however, also read it as evidence of his elite masculinity, a marker of status – manifested through his emotional depth – and his manliness. It was a performance not only of pity, but authority, demonstrating his awareness of the power, literally over life or death, that he held. It gave gravitas to the decision, but also to the judge as its enactor. Audiences were described responding appropriately, joining in tears. As a result, not only did the judge retain his humanity but enlisted the public in his decision. Together, the gallery and the judge felt pain at the judgment and sympathised with it, reducing the potential dislocation that an execution might have on other members of the condemned party's community.

This was important in Ireland, where the relationship between the general public, but particularly the lower classes, and the legal system was not always positive. Legal decisions were not always viewed as valid or fair and, at times, the courts were seen as a method of colonial control rather than impartial governance.[111] Executions in early nineteenth-century Ireland were sometimes accompanied by riots, attempted rescues and general unrest – behaviour that signified the discomfort that such legal decisions met.[112] The ability of the weeping judge to engage the sympathy of the public and to heighten their respect for his decision gave tears a continued practical importance. This may have been less significant in Scotland and England where the court was an important signifier of justice for most social groups.[113]

It was not just elite men who displayed sensibility in court. Not only were the tearful audiences likely socially diverse, but emotional displays by witnesses, victims and defendants were described by reporters as significant to courtroom power dynamics. Mr Pescoe, a retired owner of a malt house, complained to the magistrate in 1831 that his son-in-law, Captain Hicks, had assaulted him when he rescued his daughter from her husband's dreadful treatment. Mrs Hicks appeared badly injured, supported by a thirteen-year-old daughter. She burst into tears and fainted, and her daughter and father 'hung over her crying', trying to restore her: 'This melancholy scene overpowered the feelings of the magistrates and every person present'.[114] When the coppersmith, John Dillon, was found not guilty of murdering his wife in 1835, he became 'very agitated' and 'hugged his father', which the reporter recorded was 'an affecting scene'.[115] Sentimental displays were described as producing sympathy in other members of the court, with possible effects on their legal responses.

Some men, particularly lower-order defendants, are described as refusing to emote. During the 1822 trial of William Leary, a servant boy, and Mary Stanley, for the murder of Stanley's husband, his Lordship was 'so much overcome by his feelings, as to render some parts of [the death sentence speech] inaudible'. Afterwards, Leary 'in the most hardened manner, said, he hoped God Almighty would yet give him the power to pass sentence on his Lordship'. The news reporter noted 'no two prisoners could betray less sensibility to the awful state in which they were placed'.[116] When John Delahunt was found guilty of a horrific child murder in 1842, '[a] slight sensation was perceptible in the court, but the prisoner heard the verdict without any visible emotion'.[117] More complexly, James Darcy, during his trial for fratricide in 1821 where both the judge and court openly wept, was 'one of the least moved'. The reporter noted that '[h]e shewed, however, neither obduracy nor stupidity. . . . he was attentive, calm and firm'.[118] A lack of 'visible emotion' was as significant a measure of character as sentimental displays. In some instances, it affirmed that a person was 'hardened', meaning they lacked the sensibility that enabled right judgement and moral behaviour. In Darcy's case, it was interpreted as manly stoicism, suggestive that his criminal behaviour was out of character.

There is also some evidence that refusing to emote appropriately was a form of resistance to the expected norms of the court. To pretend disinterest was to deny the court the satisfaction of its victory in punishing the guilty, a victory that should be demonstrated on the body of the prisoner in some form of emotional display. When William Lepper and his two sons, a family of stone breakers, were tried for murdering their neighbour's son in 1843:

> [t]he demeanour of William Lepper was characterised by apparent carelessness, and his son Thomas also appeared unmoved; William, the youngest seemed at times deeply affected, and frequently shed tears, for which he was reproved by his father, who touched him with his hand on his back when he saw him weeping.[119]

With 'characterised' and 'appeared', the reporter interpreted this as a *performance* of disinterest, affirmed through the father's apparently disciplining hand.[120] It was a complex reading that conveyed an underlying distress that the men suppressed, rather than a hardened lack of sensibility. Yet, for the reporter, it was not the resilient display of controlled humanity observed above in the farmer Mathew Hogan, nor Bushe's deep but disciplined feeling. Rather, the Leppers' control of their passions was 'carelessness' and so an act of disrespect towards the court. This may have been the actors' intention, denying the court a performance of regret or contrition that would have affirmed justice was done. Like the execution victims who refused to repent on the scaffold, they challenged the logic of the criminal trial, resisting the court's authority.[121]

Like other bodily performances, displays of emotion spoke to character, but they also actively shaped the dynamics of power in courtrooms. Weeping judges enlisted the public in legal decisions. Sentimental displays by victims encouraged compassion, authorising their demands for justice and encouraging the court to act their part. Alternatively, men could show a hardened face to the legal system, challenging judicial authority and raising questions over its efficacy and purpose. This was possible because, through the culture of sensibility, the capacity to emote was tied to the ability to make moral judgements, and displays of emotion were thus evidence of moral character. The emotions men displayed were interpreted through normative beliefs about the appropriate and moral response for particular situations, but this allowed for a sophisticated imaginary where many types of response could be appropriate, if conveying differing insights into character. The wronged father could similarly attract sympathy through a performance of sorrow as righteous anger. Of greater concern was those who showed no emotion, suggestive of a lack of humanity and an absence of virtue. It was an emotional logic that resisted legal rationalisation and professionalisation.[122]

## Conclusion

Performances of dress, physical appearance and emotion could all be used to judge manly behaviour and so were implicated in the construction of justice. The majesty embodied by the judiciary and displayed through their gowns reinforced their authority over legal space. Their professional and emotional responses to trial proceedings could establish the normative moral values of the courtroom. Not all lawyers or judges, however, had to dress for court, and respectable clothing, suitable to rank, gender and occupation, as well as a comely body or display of sensibility, could be used by all men to contest meaning within legal space. Men who were unable to convey respectability, either through poverty or non-conforming bodies, were disadvantaged in this process. Poverty might even provoke pity, demanding charitable consideration from others but damaging claims to character. Wealth, character and authority remained linked. The ability of individuals to use their bodies to shape courtroom dynamics ensured that even with the growing lawyerisation of the trial, defendants, witnesses and others were not 'silent'. Bodies and emotions continued to be vital to the production of justice.[123]

Moreover, the implications of these performances were not limited to the courtroom. When conveying the dynamics of Bagnelstown's Petit Session in 1831, the author of the excerpt that opened this chapter spent considerable time describing the odd characters around him.[124] Placing descriptions of clothing, gesture and bodies into the mouth of a loquacious local, Bagnelstown's magistrates – Steward, Newton and Watson – appeared eccentric, almost unrespectable, yet nonetheless held authority, determining justice for several men in a dispute with the local yeomanry. Such an account may have been intended as a critique of the justice that such courts offered.[125] But this article was not published in Britain or even Dublin, but in the *Carlow Morning Post*, Bagnelstown's local paper. Readers were invited to consider whether Mr Newton's wild beard was suggestive of a Turk and, if so, what it signified about the man and the magistrate. Written by an 'outsider' on his way to Dublin, Bagnelstown was asked to consider how they appeared to those beyond their community, perhaps to the colonising gaze and certainly to the wider Irish community. The writer thus intimated that daily proceedings in a small town could not be separated from the identities of Irish men in a global context.

Through the press, negotiations around how clothing and bodies should be interpreted became an intervention in a discussion about the nature of Irishness. Eccentric men laid claim to the 'liberty' and 'individualism' of the British constitution, challenging both the boundaries of character and the colonial status of the Irish. Conservative court officials disciplined men whose fashionable excess or hardened visages disturbed their ideals of manliness, claiming the political rights associated with respectability for at least some in Ireland. Women, restricted from political rights by their bodies, found it more challenging for their performances of identity to intervene in the making of Irishness; it was their treatment by men, rather than their own action, that mattered. In contrast, men marked by poverty provided a key challenge to Irish identity; their visceral impact – often provoking disgust and horror – disturbed any claim to a unified manly Irish identity. The poverty-ravaged Irish body may have had little authority in the courtroom but, as a cultural icon, it was a central challenge to Ireland's claims to civilisation and nation.

## Notes

1 Quoted in D. Lemmings, 'Criminal trial procedure in eighteenth-century England: The impact of lawyers', *Journal of Legal History*, 26:1 (2005), 73–82.

2 L. Hartley, *Physiognomy and the Meaning of Expression in Nineteenth-Century Culture* (Cambridge: Cambridge University Press, 2008); E. Leaney, 'Phrenology in nineteenth-century Ireland', *New Hibernia Review*, 10:3 (2006), 24–42; G. Morgan and P. Rushton, 'Visible bodies: Power, subordination and identity in the eighteenth-century Atlantic world', *Journal of Social History*, 39:1 (2005), 39–64.

3 P. Levine, 'States of undress: Nakedness and the colonial imagination', *Victorian Studies*, 50:2 (2008), 189–219; L.P. Curtis, *Apes and Angels: The Irishman in Victorian Caricature* (London: Smithsonian Institute Press, 1971); J.A. Mangan, 'Images for confident control: Stereotypes in imperial discourse', *International Journal of the History of Sport*, 27:1–2 (2010), 308–27.

4 K. Canning, 'The body as method? Reflections on the place of the body in gender history', *Gender & History*, 11 (1999), 499–513; D.T. Meyers, 'Frontiers of individuality: Embodiment and relationships in cultural context', *History and Theory*, 42 (2003), 271–85; K. Downing, 'The gentleman boxer: Boxing, manners and masculinity in eighteenth century England', *Men and Masculinities*, 12 (2010), 328–52; P. McDevitt, 'Muscular Catholicism: Nationalism, masculinity and Gaelic team sports, 1884-1916', *Gender & History*, 9:2 (1997), 262–84; L. Craton, *The Victorian Freak Show: The Significance of Disability and Physical Difference in Nineteenth-Century Fiction* (Amhurst: Cambria Press, 2009).

5 J. Putzi, *Identifying Marks: Race, Gender, and the Marked Body in Nineteenth-Century America* (Athens: University of Georgia Press, 2012).

6 A. Korhonen, 'Beauty, masculinity and love between men: Configuring emotions with Michael Drayton's *Peirs Gaveston*', in J. Liliequist (ed.), *A History of Emotions, 1200-1800* (London: Pickering and Chatto, 2012), pp. 135–51.

7 See discussion in J. Butler, *Gender Trouble: Feminism and the Subversion of Identity* (London: Routledge, 1999), Chapter 2.

8 Lemmings, 'Criminal trial procedure'; J. Beattie, 'Scales of justice: Defence counsel and the English criminal trial in the eighteenth and nineteenth centuries', *Law and History Review*, 9 (1991), 221–67; J.H. Langbein, *The Origins of Adversary Criminal Trial* (Oxford: Oxford University Press, 2005).

9 A.N. May, *The Bar & the Old Bailey, 1750-1850* (Chapel Hill: University of North Carolina Press, 2003); D. Cairns, *Advocacy and the Making of the Adversarial Criminal Trial, 1800-1864* (Oxford: Oxford University Press, 1999).

10 A. Gross, *Double Character: Slavery and Mastery in the Antebellum Southern Courtroom* (Princeton: Princeton University Press, 2000). See also: M.J. Wiener, *Men of Blood: Violence, Manliness and Criminal Justice in Victorian England* (Cambridge: Cambridge University Press, 2004); N. Lacey, *Women, Crime and Character: From Moll Flanders to Tess of the D'Urbervilles* (Oxford: Oxford University Press, 2008),

pp. 141–2; B. Walker, *Race on Trial: Black Defendants in Ontario's Criminal Courts, 1858–1958* (Toronto: University of Toronto Press, 2011).

11  R.L. Sheil, *Sketches of the Irish Bar*, ed. R. Shelton MacKenzie, 2 volumes (New York: Redfield, 1854), vol. 1, p. 34.

12  J. Styles, *The Dress of the People: Everyday in Fashion in Eighteenth-Century England* (London: Yale University Press, 2008); V. Richmond, *Clothing the Poor in Nineteenth-Century England* (Cambridge: Cambridge University Press, 2013).

13  K. Navickas, '"That sash will hang you": Political clothing and adornment in England, 1780–1840', *Journal of British Studies*, 49 (2010), 540–65; C. Huck, 'Clothes make the Irish: Irish dressing and the question of identity', *Irish Studies Review*, 11:3 (2003), 273–84.

14  R. Carr, *Gender and Enlightenment Culture in Eighteenth-Century Scotland* (Edinburgh: Edinburgh University Press, 2014).

15  C. Fairchilds, 'Fashion and freedom in the French Revolution', *Continuity and Change*, 15:3 (2000), 419–33; E.C. Cage, 'The sartorial self: Neoclassical fashion and gender identity in France, 1797–1804', *Eighteenth-Century Studies*, 42:2 (2009), 193–215; S. Gerson, 'In praise of modest men: Self-display and self-effacement in nineteenth-century France', *French History*, 20:2 (2006), 182–203.

16  P. Jones, '"I cannot keep my place without being deascent": Pauper letters, parish clothing and pragmatism in the south of England, 1750–1830', *Rural History*, 20:1 (2009), 31–49; B. Lemire, 'Second-hand beaux and 'red-armed belles': Conflict and the creation of fashions in England, c. 1660–1800', *Continuity and Change*, 15:3 (2000), 391–417.

17  É. Hickey, *Irish Law and Lawyers in Modern Folk Tradition* (Dublin: Four Courts Press, 1999), 70–4.

18  R.L. Sheil, *Sketches, Legal and Political*, 2 vols, ed. M.W. Savage (London: Henry Colburn, 1855), vol. 1, pp. 197–204.

19  *Ibid.*, vol. 1, p. 205.

20  *Ibid.*, vol. 1, pp. 205–28.

21  D. Hay, 'Property, authority and the criminal law', in D. Hay *et al.* (eds), *Albion's Fatal Tree: Crime and Society in Eighteenth-Century England* (London: Verso, 1975), pp. 17–64.

22  Hickey, *Irish Law and Lawyers*, p. 76.

23  J. Kelly, *'That Damn'd Thing Called Honour': Duelling in Ireland, 1570–1860* (Cork: Cork University Press, 1995).

24  'Recorder's Court', *Freeman's Journal* (9 October 1832) Dublin.

25  For example, 'Dublin Police', *Connaught Journal* (27 February 1840) Dublin; 'Cavan Quarter Sessions', *The Times* (23 April 1840) Cavan; 'County Armagh Assizes', *Armagh Guardian* (4 March 1845) Armagh.

26  'Petit Session Sketch at Bagnelstown', *Carlow Morning Post* (23 June 1831) Carlow.

27  R. McGowen, 'A powerful sympathy: Terror, the prison and humanitarian reform in early nineteenth-century Britain', *Journal of British Studies*, 25:3 (1986), 312–34; T. Chalmers, 'The influence of Bible Societies on the temporal necessities of the poor', in *The Works of Thomas Chalmers* (Philadelphia: J. Towar & D.M. Hogan, 1830), pp. 320–9.

28  Sheil, *Sketches, Legal and Political*, vol. 1, p. 197.

29 'Court of Exchequer', *Sligo Champion* (26 November 1836) Dublin.

30 *Ibid.*

31 'Dublin Police', *Connaught Journal* (12 August 1839) Dublin.

32 'Roscrea Petty Sessions', *Kerry Evening Post* (10 June 1837) Tipperary.

33 D. Neal, 'Suits makes the man: Masculinity in two English law courts, c. 1500', *Canadian Journal of History*, 37 (2002), 1–22.

34 C. Muldrew, 'Interpreting the market: The ethics of credit and community relations in early modern England', *Social History*, 18:2 (1993), 163–83; M. Finn, *The Character of Credit: Personal Debt in English Culture, 1740–1914* (Cambridge: Cambridge University Press, 2003), p. 21.

35 'Roscrea Petty Sessions', *Kerry Evening Post* (10 June 1837) Tipperary.

36 For an extended discussion of these representations see: K. Barclay, 'Stereotypes as political resistance: The Irish Police Court columns, c. 1820–1845', *Social History*, 42:2 (2017), 257–80.

37 'Killarney Petty Sessions', *Kerry Evening Post* (5 July 1837) Kerry.

38 M. Kwass, 'Big hair: A wig history of consumption in eighteenth-century France', *American Historical Review*, 111:3 (2006), 631–59; Lemire, 'Second-hand beaux', 402–4.

39 S. Morgan, 'Material culture and the politics of personality in early Victorian England', *Journal of Victorian Culture*, 17:2 (2012), 127–46.

40 S. West, 'The Darly macaroni prints and the politics of "Private Man"', *Eighteenth-Century Life*, 25:2 (2001), 170–82; Barclay, 'Stereotypes as political resistance'.

41 D. Wahrman, *Imagining the Middle Class: The Political Representation of Class in Britain, c. 1780–1840* (Cambridge: Cambridge University Press, 1995), p. 276.

42 West, 'The Darly macaroni prints', 176.

43 A similar possibility of eccentricity can be seen in France: M. Gill, *Eccentricity and the Cultural Imagination in Nineteenth-Century Paris* (Oxford: Oxford University Press, 2009), pp. 285–8.

44 On the performativity of breach trials see: S.L. Steinbach, 'From redress to farce: Breach of promise theatre in cultural context, 1830–1920', *Journal of Victorian Culture*, 13 (2008), 247–76; S. Staves, 'British seduced maidens', *Eighteenth-Century Studies*, 14:2 (1980–81), 109–34.

45 M. Valverde, 'The love of finery: Fashion and the fallen woman in nineteenth-century social discourse', *Victorian Studies*, 32:2 (1989), 169–18.

46 'Trial of the Rev Thomas Maguire', *Ballina Impartial* (24 December 1827) Dublin.

47 L.E. Connors and M.L. MacDonald, *National Identity in Great Britain and British North America, 1815–1851: The Role of Nineteenth-Century Periodicals* (Aldershot: Ashgate, 2011), p. 106.

48 On borrowing clothes see: Richmond, *Clothing the Poor*, pp. 73–92.

49 Sheil, *Sketches, Legal and Political*, vol. 1, p. 100.

50 *Ibid.*

51 'Love in Kerry', *Connaught Journal* (18 April 1833) Kerry.

52 Carr, *Gender and Enlightenment*, pp. 23–7.

53 C. Breward, 'Masculine pleasures: Metropolitan identities and the commercial sites of Dandyism, 1790–1840', *London Journal*, 28:1 (2003), 60–72.

54 Carr, *Gender and Enlightenment*; M. McCormack, 'Dance and drill: Polite

accomplishments and military masculinities in Georgian Britain', *Cultural and Social History*, 8:3 (2011), 315–30.

55 T. Carlyle, *Sartor Resartus: The Life and Opinions of Herr Teufelsdröckh*, 3 volumes (London: Chapman and Hall, 1831), vol. 3, p. 188.

56 For example see: *An Exquisite alias Dandy in Distress* (Dublin: J. Le Petit, [n.d.]); *The Dandy's Disaster!* (Dublin: McCleary, [n. d.]); *Dandies of 1817! . . . The Mosaic Dandy – & Pam* (London: Sidebotham, 1817); Isaac Cruickshank, *A Nice Gentleman – an Exquisite Dandy – Prodigious!!* (Dublin: McCleary, 1818); *The Dandy's Disaster* (Dublin: J. Le Petit, [1818]).

57 'Fancy Dandies', *Carlow Morning Post* (31 May 1819) Dublin.

58 A discussion of how reticule and ridicule were confused is discussed in 'Modern Grammatical Affectations', *The Christian Observer* (London: J. Hatchard and Son, 1829), p. 169; S. Hiner, *Accessories to Modernity: Fashion and the Feminine in Nineteenth-Century France* (Philadelphia: University of Pennsylvania University Press, 2010), pp. 181–4.

59 Hay, 'Property, authority'.

60 Gross, *Double Character*.

61 Morgan and Rushton, 'Visible bodies', 42.

62 Hartley, *Physiognomy*.

63 Leaney, 'Phrenology'; E. Leaney, '"Evanescent impressions": Public lectures and the popularization of science in Ireland, 1770–1860', *Éire-Ireland*, 43:3 (2008), 157–82; for the long roots of physiognomy as a measure of masculinity see: D. Neal, *The Masculine Self in Late Medieval England* (Chicago: Chicago University Press, 2008), pp. 128–40. For similar uses of physiognomy in court see: S. Devereaux, 'Arts of public performance: Barristers and actors in Georgian England', in D. Lemmings, *Crime, Courtrooms, and the Public Sphere, 1700–1850* (Farnham: Ashgate, 2012), pp. 94–117.

64 See adverts for example in *Belfast Newsletter* (17 October 1806, 25 November 1842); *Freeman's Journal* (28 April 1808, 16 December 1809, 13 January 1815, 18 November 1823, 20 November 1835); *Dublin Evening Mail* (26 November 1824).

65 'Dublin Police', *Freeman's Journal* (11 November 1831) Dublin.

66 Leaney, 'Phrenology'.

67 'Police Court', *Limerick and Clare Examiner* (22 September 1847).

68 J. Lavater, *Physiognomy* (London: Cowie, Low & Co., 1826), p. 51.

69 These were published individually in the 1820s, but compiled later in the century as single collections. See: Sheil, *Sketches, Legal and Political*; Sheil, *Sketches of the Irish Bar*.

70 Sheil, *Sketches, Legal and Political*, vol. 1, p. 28.

71 T. Cooke, *A Practical and Familiar View of the Science of Physiognomy* (London: Camberwell Press, 1819), p. 30.

72 Lavater, *Physiognomy*, p. 59.

73 *Ibid.*, p. 60–2.

74 Sheil, *Sketches, Legal and Political*, vol. 1, p. 29.

75 M. Goode, 'Dryasdust antiquarianism and soppy masculinity: The Waverley Novel and the gender of history', *Representations*, 82:1 (2003), 52–86.

76 Sheil, *Sketches, Legal and Political*, vol. 1, pp. 30–1.

77  D. Keenan, *Pre-Famine Ireland: Social Structure* (Bloomington: Xlibris, 2000), p. 39.
78  Sheil, *Sketches, Legal and Political*, vol. 1, p. 58.
79  Lavater, *Physiognomy*, p. 67; Sheil, *Sketches, Legal and Political*, vol. 1, p. 58.
80  Sheil, *Sketches, Legal and Political*, vol. 1, pp. 58–9.
81  *Ibid.*, vol. 1, p. 59.
82  *Ibid.*, vol. 1, p. 58.
83  D. Lemmings and C. Walker, *Governing Emotions: The Affective Family, the Press and the Law during the Long Eighteenth Century* (Basingstoke: Palgrave Macmillan, forthcoming), Chapter 3.
84  Sheil, *Sketches of the Irish Bar*, vol. 2, p. 53, 152.
85  Sheil, *Sketches, Legal and Political*, vol. 1, p. 272.
86  R. Sheil, *The Speeches of the Right Honourable Richard Lalor Sheil* (Dublin: James Duffy, 1865), p. 103.
87  Sheil, *Sketches, Legal and Political*, vol. 1, p. 330.
88  'Recorder's Court', *Freeman's Journal* (24 April 1833) Dublin; 'Commission Court', *Nation* (13 April 1844) Dublin; 'City Crown Court', *Freeman's Journal* (27 July 1831) Limerick. An approver is an accomplice who turned state's evidence.
89  D. Turner, 'Introduction', in D.M. Turner and K. Stagg (eds), *Social Histories of Disability and Deformity: Bodies, Images and Experiences* (London: Routledge, 2006), pp. 5–6.
90  'Carlow Petty Session', *Carlow Morning Post* (2 January 1832) Carlow.
91  'Maryboro' Assizes', *Clare Journal* (18 March 1833) Queen's County/Laois.
92  'Queen's County – Ballickmyler Petty Sessions', *Dublin Evening Packet and Correspondent* (22 September 1832) Queen's County/Laois.
93  Sheil, *Sketches of the Irish Bar*, vol. 1, p. 31.
94  'Exchequer Court', *Freeman's Journal* (10 November 1836) Longford.
95  S. Johnson, *Samuel Johnson's Dictionary*, ed. John Walker (Boston: Charles Hendee, 1836), p. 39.
96  *Ibid.*, p. 167 (horrour); p. 339 (terrour).
97  'Tralee Petty Sessions', *Kerry Evening Post* (7 November 1840) Kerry.
98  L. Davis, *Music, Postcolonialism, and Gender: The Construction of Irish National Identity, 1724–1874* (Notre Dame: University of Notre Dame Press, 2005), pp. 45–7, 188–90.
99  L.R. Wray, 'Conclusion: The credit money and state money approaches', in L.R. Wray (ed.), *Credit and State Theories of Money: The Contributions of A. Mitchell Innes* (Cheltenham: Edward Elgar, 2004), pp. 226–7.
100 G.J. Barker-Benfield, *The Culture of Sensibility: Sex and Society in Eighteenth Century Britain* (London: Chicago University Press, 1992); R. Haidt, *Embodying Enlightenment: Knowing the Body in Eighteenth-Century Spanish Literature and Culture* (Basingstoke: Palgrave Macmillan, 1998).
101 T. Dixon, 'The tears of Mr Justice Willes', *Journal of Victorian Culture*, 17:1 (2012), 1–23.
102 K. Barclay, *Love, Intimacy and Power: Marriage and Patriarchy in Scotland, 1650–1850* (Manchester: Manchester University Press, 2011), p. 118.
103 Kelly, *'That Damn'd Thing Called Honour'*.
104 K. Barclay, 'Emotions, the law and the press in Britain: Seduction and breach

of promise suits, 1780–1830', *Journal of Eighteenth-Century Studies*, 39:2 (2016), 267–84.

105 Wiener, *Reconstructing the Criminal*, p. 66.
106 Dixon, 'The tears of Mr Justice Willes'.
107 'Commission Court', *Connaught Journal* (21 April 1831) Dublin.
108 'Waterford Assizes', *Carlow Morning Post* (22 March 1821) Waterford.
109 'Ennis Assizes', *Carlow Morning Post* (1 August 1822) Clare.
110 Dixon, 'The tears of Mr Justice Willes'.
111 J.K. TeBrake, 'Irish peasant women in revolt: The land league years', *Irish Historical Studies*, 28: 109 (1992), 63–80; M. Kotsonouris, *Retreat from Revolution: The Dáil Courts, 1920-24* (Dublin: Irish Academic Press, 1994).
112 S. Kilcommins, I. O'Donnell, E. Sullivan and B. Vaughan, *Crime, Punishment and the Search for Order in Ireland* (Dublin: Institute of Public Administration, 2004), pp. 12–13.
113 J.A. Sharpe, 'The people and the law', in B. Reay (ed.), *Popular Culture in Seventeenth Century England* (London: Croom Helm, 1985), pp. 244–70.
114 'Dublin Police', *Freeman's Journal* (6 August 1831) Dublin.
115 'Commission Court', *Ballina Impartial* (21 January 1835) Dublin.
116 'Extraordinary and Horrible Case of Murder', *Carlow Morning Post* (18 April 1822) Cork.
117 'Commission Court', *Freeman's Journal* (15 January 1842) Dublin.
118 'Waterford Assizes', *Carlow Morning Post* (22 March 1821) Waterford.
119 'Country of Antrim', *Cork Examiner* (13 March 1843) Antrim.
120 A. Synnott, 'Handling children: To touch or not to touch', in C. Classen (ed.), *The Book of Touch* (Oxford: Berg, 2005), pp. 41–6.
121 P. Lake, 'Deed against nature: Cheap print, Protestantism and murder in seventeenth-century England', in K. Sharpe and P. Lake (eds), *Culture and Politics in Early Stuart England* (Stanford: Stanford University Press, 1993), pp. 275–6.
122 For discussion see: Wiener, *Reconstructing the Criminal*.
123 *Ibid.*, pp. 65–6.
124 'Petit Session Sketch at Bagnelstown', *Carlow Morning Post* (23 June 1831) Carlow.
125 D. McCabe, 'Open court: Law and the expansion of magisterial jurisdiction at petty sessions in nineteenth-century Ireland', in N.M. Dawson (ed.), *Reflections on Law and History: Irish Legal History Society Discourses and Other Papers, 2000-2005* (Dublin: Four Courts Press, 2006), pp. 126–62.

# 4

# Speech, sympathy and eloquence: 'it is a voice full of manly melody'

### Speeches of Mr Phillips in the Case of Guthrie v. Sterne, delivered in *The Court of Common Pleas*, Dublin

My Lord, and Gentlemen,

In this case I am of counsel for the Plaintiff, who has deputed me, with the kind of concession of my much more efficient colleagues, to detail to you the story of his misfortunes. In the course of a long friendship which has existed between us, originating in mutual pursuits, and cemented our mutual attachments, never, until this instant, did I feel any thing but pleasure in the claims which it created, or the duty which it imposed. In selecting me, however, from this bright array of learning and eloquence, I cannot help being pained at the kindness of a partiality which forgets its interest in the exercise of its affection, and confides the task of practised wisdom to the uncertain guidance of youth and inexperience. He has thought, perhaps, that truth needed no set phrase of speech; that misfortune should not veil the furrows which its tears had burned; or hide, under the decorations of an artful drapery, the heart-rent heavings with which its bosom throbbed. He has surely thought that, by contrasting mine with the powerful talents selected by his antagonist, he was giving you a proof that the appeal he made was to your reason, not to your feelings – to the integrity of your hearts, not the exasperation of your passions. Happily however for him, happily for you, happily for the country, happily for the profession, on subjects such as this, the experience of the oldest amongst us is but slender; deeds such as this are not indigenous to an Irish soil, or naturalized beneath an Irish climate. . . . No matter how we may have graduated in the scale of nations; . . . it has at least been universally conceded, that our hearths were the home of the domestic virtues, and that love, honour, and conjugal fidelity, were the dear and indisputable

deities of our household; around the fire-side of the Irish hovel hospitality circumscribed its sacred circle; and a provision to punish created a suspicion of the possibility of violation. But of all the ties that
bound – of all the bounties that blessed her – Ireland most obeyed,
most loved, most reverenced the nuptial contract. . . . Gentlemen, that
national sanctuary has been invaded; that venerable divinity has been
violated; and its tenderest pledges torn from their shrine, by the pol-
luted rapine of a kindless, heartless, prayerless, remorseless adulterer!
To you – religion defiled, morals insulted, law despised, public order
foully violated, and individual happiness wantonly wounded, make
their melancholy appeal. You will hear the facts with as much patience
as indignation will allow – I will, myself, ask of you to adjudge them
with as much mercy as justice will admit. . . .

> The Speeches of Charles Phillips, Esq., Delivered at the Bar, and on
> Various Public Occasions, in Ireland and England (London and Dublin:
> W. Simkin & R. Marshall, and Milliken, 1822), pp. 76–8

In 1847, the Belfast politician, Robert Tennant grumbled that the
Irish nationalists at Westminster were 'very mediocre chaps . . .
most tedious and monotonous speakers, – no variety, no force,
no tact, especially, – never attempting, indeed appearing incapable,
to feel the pulse of the house and humour it for their own purpose'.[1]
Effective oratory performances were valued because, as Tennant suggests, they allowed the speech-giver to define meaning and shape
opinion. Respected orators could gain almost cult following. In 1840,
twenty-three years after the death of the popular lawyer and Patriot
John Philpot Curran, Clifton Barrett, a Dublin house painter, told the
Insolvency Court that, besides a harp and some poetry, the only things
of value he owned were: 'two sheets of papers that had once belonged to
the immortal John Philpot Curran, and which I would not exchange for
a parchment conferring an Earldom'.[2] Speech was central to the court,
a space designed to facilitate a truth produced through argument and
debate. Formal speech-making, such as that by barristers and judges,
was particularly important for its capacity to persuade. How to reconcile a truth born of argument and the persuasive power of effective rhetoric was a source of anxiety across the United Kingdom during the early
nineteenth century, heightened by the 1836 Prisoners' Counsel Act.[3] As
this chapter argues, it was largely resolved in Ireland due to a continuing
investment in sympathy as a mechanism for transmitting an 'emotional
truth'.

The purpose of oratory had long been understood as moving the passions, a capacity that held special relevance for the culture of sensibility. Enlightenment thought, particularly in Scotland and Ireland, placed sympathy at the heart of a social order that relied on sociability. Sympathy was 'fellow-feeling', 'the quality of being affected by the affection of another'.[4] It was transferred between people like a contagion, enabling them to understand another's perspective and put aside self-interest for the greater good.[5] It was essential to communication, but potentially dangerous, with contagious passions threatening to overwhelm the will of those – particularly women and the lower orders – who could not exercise reason and self-control over their emotions.[6] Sympathy was also increasingly related to character. The influential 'common sense' school of the Scottish Enlightenment viewed character as emerging from the struggle between innate animal passions and self-control, where character was the ability to exercise self-control over the passions, including those experienced through sympathetic engagement.[7] Those who could not exercise self-control were excluded from having 'character', at least in the form that demonstrated the ability to participate in public life.

As a medium designed to transmit emotion, oratory was a key skill for elite men, particularly those that aspired to the law. Speech-making was a central courtroom activity, from the 'state of the country' proclamations by the leading justice that opened the assizes to the charge to the jury that concluded a suit. Legal speeches by barristers, or men representing themselves, had long occurred in civil suits, and cases of misdemeanor and treason.[8] By 1800, most criminal suits were prosecuted by a Crown Solicitor, paid for by the state.[9] The few private prosecutions – those that proceeded without Crown support – also used professional counsel.[10] Until 1836, defence lawyers were prohibited from speaking for clients in felony cases (although they could cross-examine and argue points of law).[11] From this date, barristers' roles formally extended to include speeches on behalf of their felonious clients, and many took this opportunity. This chapter explores how oratory was used by barristers and the judiciary to negotiate power within courtrooms. It opens with a discussion of how nineteenth-century barristers understood the relationship between rhetoric, persuasion and truth. Speech can be greater than language, being composed in performance, where not only what was said, but how it was spoken, the physical actions of the speaker and the response by the audience become part of the text.[12] The latter part of this chapter thus highlights oratory as embodied practice of character and the ways such performances constructed 'the court'.

### Learning to persuade

Oratory was a central component of the education given to elite men in early nineteenth-century Ireland, part of a curriculum designed to educate future politicians and national leaders.[13] Speaking with eloquence, which most people agreed was the definition of oratory, was essential for those who aspired to political position.[14] It was taught at the top schools in Ireland and Great Britain, where wealthy members of the bar were educated, but could also be found in less prestigious institutions. Philpot Curran was taught 'the rudiments of the classics' by his local rector, before receiving 'more than the common' classical education in the provincial town of Midleton, Cork, under a Mr Carey.[15] Several Irish hedge schools, which provided schooling for relatively poor children, offered a classical education.[16] In 1806, the Armagh lawyer, George Ensor (1769–1843), argued in his educational treatise, *The Independent Man*, that the study of 'eloquence' was vital to preparing young men for public life.[17] Such learning was encouraged by the proliferation of books of speeches, containing the works of classical and contemporary writers.[18] Young men were expected to educate themselves in rhetorical composition and to practise using exemplars. Ensor recommended that his readers read debates aloud in their 'chamber, or as they walk abroad', and then confirm or refute the speakers using their own arguments.[19] This training was designed to make oratory a natural behaviour for elite men.

Rhetorical education, instruction in speaking or writing persuasively, was shaped in the eighteenth century by the 'new rhetoric'. Whereas in the classical tradition, rhetoric had been divided into three branches: *forensic*, or judicial, which was concerned with determining truth; *deliberative*, or political, which explored what course of action should be taken; and *epideictic*, or ceremonial, which was concerned with praise or blame, eighteenth-century rhetoricians placed more emphasis on the form, rather than the function, of the discursive product.[20] Perhaps as importantly, there was a change in the stylistic conventions of writing and speaking over the century that reflected a debate amongst Enlightenment philosophers over the uses and abuses of oratory.

It was broadly agreed, following Aristotle, that the purpose of rhetoric was to persuade the listener to the orator's position, but how this should be achieved was disputed. In the seventeenth century, John Locke and other rationalist thinkers were suspicious of figurative language arguing that 'besides Order and Clearness, all the artificial and figurative application of Words Eloquence hath invented, are for nothing else but to insinuate wrong Ideas, move the Passions, and thereby mislead the Judgment; and so indeed are perfect cheat'.[21] He placed emphasis on using clear and straightforward language.[22] With the rise of the culture of sensibility, more focus was put on language being fit for purpose, and particularly in creating *pathos*, that is appealing to the audience's emotions.

Enlightenment thinkers judged rhetoric by its ability to create sympathy between the author or orator and her or his audience. The Dublin politician and philosopher, Edmund Burke, argued that 'eloquence and poetry are as capable, nay indeed much more capable of making deep and lively impressions than any other arts'. He saw this as part of human nature, where 'we take an extraordinary part in the passions of others, and that we are easily affected and brought into sympathy by any tokens which are shewn of them; and there are no tokens which can express all the circumstances of most passions so fully as words'.[23] Ensor agreed: 'Eloquence and figurative language are native effusions; they are the throes and agonies of the mind striving to inflict its sympathies and feelings'.[24] This required the orator to give particular attention to her or his choice and composition of words.

Across the eighteenth and nineteenth centuries, rhetoricians provided advice to the educated public on appropriate compositional styles and expression for moving the passions. The popular writer and minister, Hugh Blair, argued that words should be chosen for 'purity, propriety and precision', where purity was using the correct 'idiom of the language which we speak', excluding foreign, obsolete or 'new-coined' words.[25] 'Propriety' was using words with the 'best and most established usage', and precision referred to ensuring the author's ideas were communicated accurately.[26] Ensor's educational treatise, which drew heavily on Blair, noted that 'all unnecessary words, or rather each word not necessary, should be expunged', and that as the 'performance approaches the conclusion, it should be more rapid, or rather more full, because the reader's attention has been long exercised. This rule is universal'.[27]

Eloquent words alone, however, were not enough. George Campbell provided a comprehensive model for persuasion under the heading: 'The circumstances that are chiefly instrumental in operating on the passions'. The first 'circumstance' was 'probability', which 'results from evidence and begets belief. . . . Belief raised to the highest becomes certainty', and certainty arose from the 'force of the evidence that is produced . . . or the previous notoriety of the fact'.[28] Campbell's second 'circumstance' was 'plausibility', that is 'the consistency of the narration, from being what is commonly called natural and feasible'.[29] Campbell thought these the 'principal' and 'indispensible' qualities of successful oration, followed by 'Importance', which may arise from the subject's own nature or from its consequences.[30] The Irish barrister, John Finlay, similarly noted in 1836: 'The speaker who addresses the judgment alone, may be argumentative, but never can be eloquent; for argument instructs without interesting, and eloquence interests without convincing; but oratory is neither; it is the compound of both; it conjoins the feelings and opinions of men; it speaks to the passions through the mind, and to the mind through the passions'.[31]

Campbell followed up his central points with four others: 'proximity of time', 'connexion of place', 'relations to the persons concerned' and 'interest in the consequences'.[32] These elements engaged the person, as 'bringing the object very near, most enlivens the sympathy which attacheth us to the concerns of others'.[33] As he noted, '[s]elf is the centre here, which hath a similar power in the ideal world, to that of the sun in the material world, in communicating both light and heat ... in a greater or less degree, according to the nearness or remoteness'.[34] These 'circumstances', designed to create sympathy in the listener, were viewed as rhetorical techniques, but Campbell's explicit recognition of the subjective response of the audience reflected a tension where the sympathy designed to overcome selfishness was created through an engagement with the self-interest of the listener.

If effective oratory required evidence to move the listener, it also produced a truth born through a communally enabled self-control. This raised questions about the location of truth, particularly in a legal context where defence lawyers spoke passionately for guilty men.[35] A number of rhetoricians resolved this by collapsing truth into the orator's effectiveness. Oratory was most persuasive when it captured the natural voice of the speaker, flowing from him 'without effort'.[36] Blair described this as 'simplicity of style', showing 'a man's sentiments and turn of mind, laid open without disguise'. It provided a glimpse of those 'peculiarities which distinguish one man from another' and so allowed access to a man's character.[37] Here Blair drew on the classical tradition and its modern formation in Adam Smith, locating moral character in a 'discursive propriety'.[38] Simplicity helped to convey the 'truth' of the orator's position, which became aligned with the worth and character of the orator himself.

Richard Lalor Sheil recognised the problems with this argument in the 1820s noting: 'It has often been said that true eloquence could not exist in the absence of good moral qualities. In opposition to this maxim of ethical criticism, the example of some highly gifted but vicious men has been appealed to'. But, he continued, such men:

were not engaged in the discussion of private concerns, in which, generally speaking, an appeal to moral feeling is of most frequent occurrence; and . . . there can be little doubt, that although a series of vicious indulgences may have adulterated their nature, they must have been endowed with a large portion of generous instinct. . . . Nay more: I will venture to affirm, that, in their moments of oratorical enthusiasm, they must have been virtuous men.[39]

Others were more sceptical, worrying that some people 'faked' sincerity and so conveyed a truth that was not present.[40] Ensor condemned this practice: 'Truth can be but one, and he who attempts to pervert it, for himself, or for another, by innuendo, argument, testimony, or any other means, at court, at the bar, or elsewhere, as a friend or advocate, for affection or for hire, acts a base part'.[41] In doing so, like many others, he relied less on eloquence's truth than an expectation that lawyers and other orators conformed to rules of manly deportment around truth-telling. Those who lacked faith in oratory placed their faith in men.

### Moving the passions; voicing the individual

Whether truth arose from a moral faculty of eloquence or a manifestation of gentlemanly conduct, legal speech-making offered judges and barristers the opportunity to display not only their oratory talents but also character. This required not only artful prose but skilful presentation. Contemporary commentators on legal speeches, often other lawyers, paid particular attention to oratory practices as full-body performances, locating the ability to move the passions in the intersection of the gendered body, voice and rhetoric. Oratory was a masculine art, tied to traits – stamina, strength, emotional control – long-associated with men. Thus, the barrister Thomas Wallace (1765–1847) was known for 'manly sagacity rather than captious subtilty'; William Saurin's language was 'not flowing or abundant – there was no soaring in his thought, nor majesty in his elocution; but he was clear and manly: there was a plain vigour about him . . . [his oratory] was muscular and strong'.[42] Oratory character was produced through performances of a manly eloquence, reinforcing the lawyer as male and the court as a masculine institution. Like other physical performances in the courtroom, professional legal men used oratory to engage sympathetically with listeners, to persuade judges and juries of their 'truth', and to shape power relationships.

Across the United Kingdom, speech-making was associated with vigour and strength due to the physical effort required in talking loudly and at length in a crowded courtroom.[43] Whilst rhetoricians encouraged 'brevity', many speeches in the Irish courts were of significant length.[44] This was particularly evident in civil suits, which, as Sheil noted, the Irish thought suited to being expressed at length, and in political cases, where duration seemed to be used by lawyers to demonstrate its significance. Daniel O'Connell, who often took on political causes, was known for his longevity. His concluding speech at the 1813 trial for libel of John Magee, publisher of the *Dublin Evening Post*, lasted two and a half hours, but he was often described as talking 'at length' in more everyday trials.[45]

The physical exertion required in speech-making was often referred to by lawyers who asked for adjournments during long trials to prepare themselves. Upon being expected to follow speeches from O'Connell and Edward Litton in a rowdy 1833 court, Gerald Fitzgibbon, a relatively recent entrant to the bar, argued that he was 'from the great fatigue which he had undergone, unable to address the jury with any advantage to his client, or safety to himself'.[46] After conducting 'three successive cases under an amount of exertion sufficient to break down the strongest physical energies', and four hours into his 1848 speech in defence of Thomas Francis Meagher for treason, the 'manifestly exhausted' barrister Isaac Butt (1813–1879) requested a break and was refused.[47] A few years earlier in 1842, the *Cork Examiner* ran a formal complaint from the barristers practising on the summer circuit about the 'harsh, as well as unusual' refusal to give adjournments to men labouring under 'a physical inability, induced, in a great measure, by the protracted sitting during the former part of the circuit'.[48]

These barristers (or the reporters justifying their conduct) located speech-making as a physically challenging, vigorous activity, where exhaustion endangered not only the men's health but the performance of justice. It was a risky strategy given that fatigue could be rendered unmanly, damaging claims to character. Thus lawyers were careful to delineate their previous exertions, justifying their request, but also distancing themselves from accusations of weakness and even suggesting a physical prowess only latterly depleted. The judges' resistance to adjournments reflected that some requests were more for rhetorical or strategic effect, than necessity. An emphasis on exhaustion could be used as a claim to manly strength, to gain sympathy from the gallery, for more time to prepare, or even to emphasise how hard they were working for their client, reinforcing belief in the case. Whilst Fitzgibbon's exhaustion might have been real, he may have equally thought it prudent to put distance between his own speech and those of speakers with known talent.

The focus on the energy required for speech-making, through its claims to strength and fortitude, thus reinforced the character of the orator and the truth they conveyed.

Physical exertion could go too far, however. In a politically contentious dispute, the lawyer John Rea's oratory performance was used by the reporter of the conservative *Belfast Newsletter* to render him ridiculous. During his 'long, rambling speech', he was described as 'shouting with all his might', 'panting and sweating' and 'roaring'.[49] The bench eventually lost patience and left, leaving only one magistrate and the gallery who 'applauded him at intervals'. When finished, he 'appeared completely exhausted', 'hoarse and sweating profusely', but was followed by a large crowd who 'cheered lustily'. Rea was rendered unmanly through his 'shouting' and 'roaring', rather than eloquent speaking, and by his resultant panting, sweat and exhaustion. This was unmanly excess, reinforced through the connection to, as the reporter described them, 'the mob' cheering 'lustily'.[50] Associating Rea with this group implied that he too lacked self-control and discipline, something also suggested by his well-known equivocal political position, where he moved from Young Irelander to Orange Conservative via Liberalism over his life.[51] Rather than physical exertion being used to support Rea's manliness, it was used as evidence of his weakness, lack of character and the political partiality of his words.

Manly fortitude was not the only important aspect of a legal speech. Voice equally underpinned a successful performance. Charles Kendal Bushe, widely agreed to be an excellent orator, was admired for his beautiful voice. Sheil noted that he had:

> a peculiar mellowness and deep sweetness in his voice, the lower tones of which might almost without hazard of exaggeration be compared to the most delicate notes of an organ, when touched with a fine but solemn hand. It is a voice full of manly melody. There is no touch of effeminacy about it. It possesses abundance as well as harmony, and is not more remarkable for its sweetness than its sonorous depth.[52]

Bushe's voice combined deep, organ-like tones, with 'sweetness', which in the nineteenth century meant 'pleasing to any sense' and 'melodious to the ear'.[53] It held connotations of 'assuaging' and 'soothing'.[54] Its 'mellowness' implied a softness developed from a 'ripeness or maturity', whilst nineteenth-century dictionary definitions of 'delicate' placed 'attractive, . . . pleasing . . . opposed to plain, common, coarse, vulgar', before 'dainty, tender, [and] soft'.[55] 'Manly melody' suggested a deep, rich and mature voice that was pleasing to the ear.

A deep voice was associated with the ability to move the passions. The 'deep and big' voice of the 'hanging judge', Lord Norbury, was well suited to the 'awful and appalling character' of his sentences, thought Sheil.[56] Another widely praised orator and later Chief Justice, James Whiteside, was thought by barrister Roderick O'Flanagan to have a deep voice that varied from 'convulsing the Court with laughter' to 'pathetic; . . . His plaintive tones awake an echo in your soul, and a tear moistens the eye and a sob falls on the ear'.[57] The association between deep voices and sympathetic exchange reinforced oratory as a male domain, side-lining female speakers.[58] It created a hierarchy of voice, where men with deep voices were manlier, and so more convincing, than their 'shrill' counterparts.

Whilst a sonorous tone was prized, an orator's ability to adapt his voice to different circumstances was a strength. O'Flanagan noted 'the great charm of [Bushe's] full, clear, and well modulated voice. This was carefully attuned to the subject – now soft and low, when expressing some pathetic passage, now loud and resonant when denouncing wrong or asserting right'.[59] Barrister Jonathan Henn (d. 1874) was described as 'harmonious and well modulated. No harsh or discordant tones marred the effect of his speeches, and what noble speeches they were!'.[60] A well-modulated voice gave orators greater command of their audience, whilst allowing the speaker to demonstrate the discipline of his body and vocal range. Together these effects demonstrated the orator's ability to control emotion and convey it sympathetically, reinforcing a character built upon this ability.[61]

Not all Irish lawyers and judges possessed beautiful voices. Peter Burrowes (1753–1841) had a 'very husky, unpleasant voice. . . . It was not unlike the puffs of an asthmatic bellows'.[62] O'Flanagan thought Sheil's voice 'meagre, harsh and shrill'.[63] Yet both these men were respected speakers, because they conveyed emotion effectively. Mr Burrowes' 'heart was in his words, and it was impossible to listen to his earnest and impressive pleading without responding to the conviction of the inspired speaker', whilst Sheil's voice contained 'a powerful emotion [that] seems to regulate its vibrations' and 'his enthusiasm carries you away'.[64] Ultimately, it was the ability to move and persuade their audience that marked eloquence. Burrowes 'induced others to believe what he believed in himself; whatever of prejudice his manner or his voice excited in the hearer, was soon swept away in the stream of fervent eloquence'.[65]

As noted by rhetoricians, men were believed to be most persuasive when their performance appeared to be natural and so truthful. As discussed in the previous chapter, this allowed for men to show distinct personalities and individuality within some broad norms for masculine behaviour. A number of orators had particular quirks or styles that captured their character and contributed to their ability to move the passions. George Bennett was described by O'Flanagan as having 'a homely style of addressing juries – more powerful in getting verdicts than the most eloquent address that came from human lips. It was almost impossible to doubt the truth of the case he stated in such simple language'.[66] Chief Justice John Doherty (1785–1850) was 'prompt, orderly, correct, and fluent – rarely attempting to inflame the passions to their highest pitch, but always warmly and forcibly inculcating the principles of common sense and practical good feeling', noted Sheil. His area of 'striking and particular originality' was in laughing a case out of court.[67] Whether it was cultivating an air of homely simplicity, or undermining an argument with kindly wit, oratory allowed the bar to demonstrate character through rhetorical technique. Moreover, through their particular quirks, styles and abilities, legal men provided access to their 'self', giving 'authenticity' to their performances and making their claims appear sincere.

Sincerity was reinforced through gesture and expression that should correspond with the speaker's words. Sheil's gestures were 'quick, abrupt, and rather disorderly', but 'always in perfect accord with such sentiments as he has to express'.[68] A coherent performance almost became the epitome of eloquence. O'Flanagan noted that when he defended John O'Connell at his 1844 state trial, Sheil's 'voice, action, look and gesture, were all in harmony, and as the stream of eloquence poured forth, I felt – here, indeed, was the most brilliant speaker it ever was my good fortune to hear'.[69] Bushe's reputation arose from a similar coherence. He was known as the 'orator of manner – eye, hand, every gesture, aided the voice and spoke', compared by O'Flanagan to the Roman advocate Hortensius for 'his attention to dress and deportment', 'studying the most graceful action and the most striking attitudes'.[70] Sheil agreed: 'His attitude and gesture are the perfection of "easy art" – every movement of his body appears to be swayed and informed by a dignified and natural grace. His countenance ... invests him with such a semblance of sincerity as to lend to his assertion of fact, or to his vindication of good principle, an irresistible force'.[71]

In contrast, Chief Baron Henry Joy's (1766–1838) inability to match word with action, whilst prosecuting Orangemen for riot, was interpreted as evidence of his true sentiment. Although his speech was 'judicious and well arranged', his manner was 'cold and frosty-spirited; his clearness was wintry and congealed; his reasons were upon one side and all his passions upon the other. . . . It was a personification of humbug'.[72] Though his speech 'wanted neither happiness of diction nor felicity of thought', it 'left the jury at its conclusion in as undisturbed a self-complacency, as if his lips had not been opened'.[73] For Sheil, who believed it was impossible to 'fake' eloquence, Joy could not disguise his feelings and so could not perform convincingly. Without the requisite passion in the orator, the jury were not moved to perform their duty.

Whilst oratory was understood as a 'natural' art, oratory gesture was a learned behaviour. As the writer Joseph Addison argued in *The Spectator*, proper gestures 'are a kind of comment to what he utters, and enforce everything he says, with weak hearers, better than the strongest argument he can make use of. They keep the audience awake, and fix their attention to what is delivered to them, at the same time that they show the speaker is in earnest, and affected himself with what he so passionately recommends to others'.[74] Following this, there was a growth in conduct literature that taught formal oratory gesture, and it was taken up in theatre, notably by David Garrick, as the most effective method for conveying emotion on stage.[75] Gestural guides taught readers how to position their body in juxtaposition to the audience, how to hold themselves, and how to use their arms in sweeping gestures to reinforce meaning.[76]

The popularity of formal oratory gesture and its recognised ability to move the passions suggests that this was not a culture that equated 'naturalness' with realism, but with the ability to use theatrical styling with ease. Despite Sheil's belief that eloquence could not be 'faked', he described the judge, Sir Michael O'Loghlen (1789–1842), as 'apparently frank and artless, – but he merely puts on a show of candour, for few possess more suppleness and craft. No man adapts himself with more felicity to the humours and the predispositions of the judges whom he addresses'.[77] This was not a criticism, but a comment on the sophistication of his performance, where O'Loghlen was able to adapt to the needs and demands of different audiences whilst still conveying his 'frank and artless' character. He was a true orator, because he could convey his character across multiple performance contexts.

Nor did naturalness allow men to ignore general rules for manly behaviour. Not only could similar acts of physical exertion move from admirable to excessive, but the character conveyed through oratory could be 'bad', as well as 'good'. This was evidenced during the French and Irish Revolutions where, as the prosecution during Robert Emmet's 1803 treason trial argued, powerful oratory, if truthfully reflecting the sentiments of the speaker, 'deluded' the peasantry, where the 'composition of heated minds and disordered passions, . . . supersede[d] the judgement and annihilate[d] the understanding' of an audience who could not employ reason.[78] Barristers' descriptions of their fellow bar were thus at pains to highlight that they operated within a wider code of gentlemanly behaviour. Doherty was not cruelly sarcastic or dismissive, but used 'gentleman-like irony' with a 'kindliness of tone', reinforcing that he remained within the acceptable boundaries for courtroom conduct.[79] Men were expected to demonstrate respect for other men of their own class, including addressing them politely, giving them space to speak, avoiding interruptions, and not overtly challenging their masculinity, especially through ridicule or questioning their veracity. Class-bound rules for deportment further narrowed the boundaries of eloquence, reinforcing character and truth as capacities of an elite education.

Because of the connection between eloquence and character, the claims made by barristers and judges in court were given greater weight through effective oratory performances. Men who could demonstrate strength and vigour, had deep, sonorous voices, a sound knowledge of formal gesture, and followed rules for gentlemanly deportment evidenced their character before others in the court and gave weight to the claims made in their speeches. As Campbell suggests, an eloquent performance without firm proof was not enough to persuade but competing evidences could be reinforced by manly oration.[80] As a result, the performance of oratory became a contested space for observers, where arguments about the effectiveness of a performance – was it beautiful speech or roaring and stamping – were also debates about the truthfulness of what was claimed. Through such descriptions of the orator, the male body of the lawyer came to embody not only his personal character but the truth that the court sought to discover.

## Sympathetic speech

The effect of individual performance was balanced by the generic nature of legal oratory and the ability of juries and the judiciary to exercise self-control over the sympathetic exchange of emotion. The speeches made by barristers and judges during legal proceedings were often remarkable examples of rhetorical art, widely admired and printed in newspapers, trial pamphlets, and later compilation volumes of speeches. It is likely that many of the examples selected for publication were considered exceptional, either because they were well-constructed, artful forms, or because they were part of particularly high-profile trials. They may not provide a representative coverage of the more typical and mundane speeches found in most legal business (notably many speeches in criminal trials appear to be relatively short). However, particularly in newspapers, speeches were recorded as they provided useful summaries of evidence. As importantly, oratory in similar types of cases usually followed the same rhetorical structure, where the specific details were developed through a common argumentative framework. This suggests that whilst some barristers were more talented than others, speeches were likely broadly similar across suits. It may also indicate that lawyers used published speeches as a model for their own, and it had the advantage of reassuring juries, clients and the watching public that there was something akin to equality of representation across cases.

That barristers used the rhetorical skills they were taught is evident in a variety of trials. Take, for example, the barrister and politician John Philpot Curran's speech in defence of Henry Sheares for treason in 1798. Throughout, the speech was artfully written and rhetorically compelling:

> With what spirit did you leave your habitations this day? with what state of mind and heart did you come here from your families? with what sentiments did you leave your children, to do an act of great public importance, to pledge yourselves at the throne of eternal justice, by the awful and solemn obligation of an oath, to do perfect, cool, impartial and steady justice, between the accuser and the accused? . . .
> A more artful advocate might endeavour to play with you, in supposing you to possess a degree of pity and feeling beyond that of any other human being. But I, gentlemen, am not afraid of beginning by warning you against those prejudices which all must possess . . .[81]

His language and imagery were carefully chosen, drawing on popular dichotomies – reason and emotion, self and society, family and nation – to drive home the significance of the trial and to root his request for an acquittal not in his skill as a barrister, but shared values of justice. It was a model that explicitly acknowledged the speech as a dialogue with a jury, who had to be brought into sympathy with the orator.

Curran's key rhetorical technique to enable this was to personalise the jury's decision, locating them not as external observers to events but implicated in the making of justice: 'self is the centre here'. As Campbell notes, this could be done through connecting the listener in time, place, or to people, but, in courtrooms, it was usually through giving juries an 'interest in the consequences'. This method was widely used by lawyers. Curran repeatedly addressed the emotions of the jury – 'with what state of mind and heart did you come here from your families? with what sentiments did you leave your children' – which not only warned them to exercise self-control, but reminded the jury that *their* emotions mattered. This personalised the case by encouraging listeners to look to their own emotional responses, as well as to the evidence. The second part of this technique was to emphasise the larger implications of the case for justice. Notably in Ireland, this was often done by tying the case to questions of national identity.

During the 1798 and 1803 treason trials and for a decade afterwards, Curran explicitly demanded that Irish juries reflect on the justice afforded by the law in Ireland, often making comparisons with England: 'Is that the independence of an Irish jury?'[82] In Sheares' case, not only did Curran refer to the 'great public importance' of the trial, but asked the jury to consider whether the laws of treason were 'enacted in a spirit of sound policy and supported by superior reason', noting, 'In England, a jury could not pronounce conviction upon the testimony of the purest man, if he stood alone'. 'I am reasoning for your country and your children', he remarked.[83] This argument relied on the listener having nationalist sentiments that could be provoked through comparison to England. Curran coupled it with allusions to the jury's relationship to others in the nation: 'Do you not feel, my fellow-countrymen . . . Bear with me, my countrymen; I feel my heart run away with me – the worst of men only can be cool'.[84]

Addressing the jury as the nation was not just employed in cases of genuine national significance. Charles Phillips (c. 1787–1859), as seen in the speech that opened this chapter, often commented during the breach of promise, seduction and criminal conversation suits where he made his name, that such behaviour was unusual in Ireland, a country of higher morals than England.[85] In the seduction suit *Massey v. Headfort* (1804), Curran similarly argued: 'I am addressing you as fathers, husbands, brothers. I am anxious that a feeling of those high relations should enter into and give dignity to your verdict. But I confess, I feel a ten-fold solicitude when I remember that I am addressing you as my countryman, as Irishmen, whose characters as jurors, as gentlemen, must find either honour or degradation in the result of your decision'.[86] Tying even 'private' cases into national identity drove home the trial's importance, endeavouring to get juries and the public to invest in the outcome. It required that 'the nation' was a unit that juries identified with and was a claim by lawyers to its existence. This is unsurprising from nationalist lawyers, like Curran and Phillips, but it suggested a certain confidence in these highly skilled professionals that their politically diverse juries would respond as desired. It was also a technique used across the political spectrum, although Conservatives like Abraham Brewster (1796–1874) and William Saurin were more likely to refer to their 'fellow countrymen', than 'Irishmen'.[87] As a rhetorical technique, it extended the sympathy produced through directing juries to their own emotions into a network that extended to the nation. Through recognising these horizontal bonds, sympathy's sociable effects could be produced and individuals encouraged to set aside their self-interest for the public good. It was here that the value to the polity that men like Adam Smith placed on sympathy was realised.

This was not to say that barristers relied on evocative language alone. Addressing the 'probability' and 'plausibility' of evidence was vital. Curran spent considerable time questioning the evidence in the Sheares' case: 'But go back to the testimony; I may wander from it, but it is my duty to stay with it . . .'.[88] The orator who skilfully blended argument and evidence with eloquent language engaged the sympathies of his audience. By acknowledging those sympathies and redirecting them into common national bonds, juries were asked to make decisions that were based on evidence, but felt as an emotional truth. It was sophisticated emotional management, where emotion was not removed from legal processes but appropriately directed to serve justice. Moreover, as a negotiation between orator and juries or judges, it was a model of oratory that acknowledged that power was distributed across actors and that justice was produced through their interaction, rather than an exertion of will by the powerful. The truth that came to reside in the body of the eloquent orator was thus always unstable.

## Conclusion

Charles Phillips was an Irish barrister renowned for his speech-making. In England, where he spent much of his career, he was subject to teasing for his lack of legal knowledge, but in Ireland, he was celebrated as the master of the sentimental speech.[89] A popular advocate in cases of distressed virtue, whether representing the father whose daughter had been seduced, the husband whose wife had eloped, or the woman whose lover had broken a promise of marriage, his ability to make a national crisis out of personal failing was renowned.[90] As the speech that opened this chapter suggests, he not only used emotional rhetoric to persuade, but articulated the importance of emotion to judgement and justice. Whilst acknowledging that 'truth needed no set phrase of speech', he anticipated that the jury's decision-making would be an emotional process. Phillips urged 'indignation' towards the defendant who had seduced the wife of his friend, whilst, in an allusion to gentlemanly codes of conduct, asked them to judge with mercy. It was a focus on emotion that sat at odds with the law as the site of passionless reason that some during the period advocated, but which better reflected cultural understandings of the power and purpose of eloquent speech.[91]

With his artful contrast of 'reason' with 'feelings', perhaps muddied with the parallel reference 'to the integrity of your hearts, not the exasperation of your passions', Phillips neatly captured what was at stake in the period's debates about speech-making. He acknowledged the tension between rhetoric as chicanery and oratory's ability to sympathetically convey truth; between a truth that required the application of reason and a justice formed through appeals to the mind and heart. Here the role of the orator was key, with eloquence speaking to character and reinforcing the 'truth' he asserted. This was a distinctly masculine truth embodied through rhetorical practices by men and tested by the watching jury or judiciary. Phillips' sentimental approach was dramatic even for the sensibilities of an Irish court, but he was popular because his performance was understood to be sincere. The jury of middle- and upper-class men who listened were expected to have the sensibility and self-control to assess his performances and to determine justice. The implication, of course, was that women and other subalterns could not know truth, swept away on a tide of emotion that restricted their ability to act independently and to hold character. Justice could only be determined by elite men. As Phillips implies, such men became the defenders of national virtue, the last defence against the criminal hoard, and the arbitrators of 'correct' and manly behaviour. Through the press, this model for manliness was given public airing, making a claim to Irishness rooted in a polite education, the ability to speak well, and to judge with sensibility. As we shall see, not everybody agreed.

## Notes

1 Quoted in J. Bew, *The Glory of Being Britons: Civic Unionism in Nineteenth-Century Belfast* (Dublin: Irish Academic Press, 2009), p. 99.

2 'Insolvent Debtor's Court', *Freeman's Journal* (16 November 1840) Dublin.

3 A.N. May, *The Bar & the Old Bailey, 1750–1850* (Chapel Hill: North Carolina University Press, 2003), pp. 214–18; D.J.A. Cairns, *Advocacy and the Making of the Adversarial Criminal Trial 1800–1865* (Oxford: Clarendon Press, 1998), pp. 25–55; S. Devereaux, 'Arts of public performance: Barristers and actors in Georgian England', in D. Lemmings (ed.), *Crime, Courtrooms and the Public Sphere in Britain, 1700–1850* (Farnham: Ashgate, 2012), pp. 93–119; S. Landsman, 'Rise of the contentious spirit: Adversary procedure in eighteenth-century England', *Cornell Law Review*, 74:3 (1990), 497–609; J. Beattie, 'Scales of justice: Defence counsels and the English criminal trial in the eighteenth and nineteenth Centuries', *Law and History Review*, 9:2 (1991), 221–67.

4   S. Johnson, *A Dictionary of the English Language* (London: J.F. Rivington, L. Davis, T. Longman, et al., 1792), unpaginated, see 'sympathy'.

5   M. Frazer, *The Enlightenment of Sympathy: Justice and the Moral Sentiments in the Eighteenth Century and Today* (Oxford: Oxford University Press, 2010); M. Fairclough, *The Romantic Crowd: Sympathy, Controversy and Print Culture* (Cambridge: Cambridge University Press, 2013), p. 24.

6   K. Barclay, 'Sounds of sedition: Music and emotion in Ireland, 1780–1845', *Cultural History*, 3:1 (2014), 54–80.

7   J.A. Harris, 'Reid and Hume on the possibility of character', in T. Ahnert and S. Manning (eds), *Character, Self, and Sociability in the Scottish Enlightenment* (Basingstoke: Palgrave Macmillan, 2011), pp. 31–48.

8   Cairns, *Advocacy*, pp. 25–55.

9   J. McEldowney, 'Crown prosecutions in nineteenth-century Ireland', in D. Hay and F. Snyder (eds), *Policing and Prosecution in Britain 1750–1850* (Oxford: Clarendon Press, 1989), pp. 427–58.

10  See, for example, *Authenticated Report of the Trial of Thomas Reynolds for Riot and Assault* (Dublin: W. Warren, 1835).

11  Landsman, 'Rise of the contentious spirit'; Beattie, 'Scales of justice'.

12  J. Schroeder, 'Speaking volumes: Victorian feminism and the appeal of public discussion', *Nineteenth-Century Contexts*, 25:2 (2003), 97–117.

13  J.S. Meisel, *Public Speech and the Culture of Public Life in the Age of Gladstone* (New York: Columbia University Press, 2007), pp. 12–13; T.S. Smith, 'The Lady's Rhetorick (1707): The tip of the iceberg of women's rhetorical education in Enlightenment France and Britain', *Rhetorica*, 22:4 (2004), 349–73.

14  For example, G. Ensor, *The Independent Man: Or, An Essay on the Formation and Development of those Formation and Faculties of the Human Mind, which constitute Moral and Intellectual Excellence*, 2 volumes (London: R. Taylor, 1806), vol. 2, p. 370.

15  C. Phillips, *Curran and His Contemporaries* (New York: Harper & Bros, 1862), pp. 16–17.

16  A. McManus, *The Irish Hedge School and Its Books, 1695–1831* (Dublin: Four Courts Press, 2002).

17  Ensor, *The Independent Man*, vol. 1, p. 294–6.

18  Examples include: *Irish Eloquence: The Speeches of the Celebrated Irish Orators Philips, Curran and Grattan, to which is added the Powerful Appeal of Robert Emmet* (Boston: Patrick Donahoe, 1857); C. Philips, *Specimens of Irish Eloquence* (London: William Edwards, 1819); T. Macnevin, *The Speeches of the Right Honourable Richard Lalor Sheil* (Dublin: James Duffy, 1865); T. David, *The Speeches of the Right Honorable John Philpot Curran* (London: Henry G. Bohn, 1847).

19  Ensor, *The Independent Man*, vol. 2, p. 311.

20  P.G. Bator, 'Rhetoric and the novel in the eighteenth-century British university curriculum', *Eighteenth-Century Studies*, 30:2 (1996), 173–95.

21  J. Locke, *Essay Concerning Human Understanding*, 3 volumes (London: Thomas Tegg; Glasgow: R. Griffin and Co.; Dublin: J. Cumming, 1828), vol. 2, p. 288.

22  J.M. Bradbury, 'New science and the "new species of writing": Eighteenth-century prose genres', *Eighteenth-Century Life*, 27:1 (2003), 28–51.

23  E. Burke, *A Philosophical Enquiry into the Origin of Our Ideas of the Sublime and Beautiful* (London: J. Dodsley, 1767), p. 334.

24  Ensor, *The Independent Man*, vol. 2, p. 294; J. Beattie, *Essays on Poetry and Music as they Affect the Mind* (Edinburgh: Edward and Charles Dilly, 1788), p. 136; Barclay, 'Sounds of sedition'.

25  H. Blair, *Lectures on Rhetoric and Belles Lettres* (London: Charles Daly, 1839), pp. 118–19.

26  *Ibid.*, p. 119.

27  Ensor, *The Independent Man*, vol. 2, pp. 383, 397, 407.

28  G. Campbell, *The Philosophy of Rhetoric*, 2 volumes (London: W. Strahan and T. Cadell, 1776), vol. 1, p. 209–10.

29  *Ibid.*, pp. 210–17.

30  *Ibid.*, pp. 220–1.

31  J. Finlay, 'Preface', in Member of the Bar, *The Speeches of the Celebrated Irish Orators Philips, Curran and Grattan* (Philadelphia: Desilver, Thomas & Co., 1836), p. 6.

32  Campbell, *The Philosophy of Rhetoric*, pp. 221–8.

33  *Ibid.*, p. 227.

34  *Ibid.*, p. 221.

35  May, *The Bar & the Old Bailey*, pp. 214–28.

36  Blair, *Lectures*, p. 244.

37  *Ibid.*, p. 244.

38  T. Ahnert and S. Manning, 'Introduction: Character, self and sociability in the Scottish Enlightenment', in Ahnert and Manning, *Character, Self, and Sociability*, p. 16.

39  R.L. Sheil, *Sketches, Legal and Political*, ed. M.W. Savage, 2 volumes (London: Henry Colburn, 1855), vol. 1, pp. 36–7.

40  L.-L. Marker and F. Marker, 'Aaron Hill and eighteenth-century acting theory', *Quarterly Journal of Speech*, 61 (1975), 416–27.

41  Ensor, *The Independent Man*, vol. 2, p. 297.

42  R.L. Sheil, *Sketches of the Irish Bar*, ed. R. Shelton Mackenzie, 2 volumes (New York: Redfield, 1854), vol. 1, pp. 275, 49–50.

43  Meisel, *Public Speech*, pp. 138–9.

44  Ensor, *The Independent Man*, vol. 1, p. 68.

45  For example, 'King's Bench', *Belfast Newsletter* (4 December 1832) Dublin.

46  'Court of Exchequer', *Freeman's Journal* (14 December 1833) Dublin.

47  'Mr. Meagher's Trial', *Cork Examiner* (1 November 1848) Dublin.

48  'Baron Lefroy and the Munster Bar', *Cork Examiner* (8 June 1842) Cork.

49  'Ballycastle Petty Sessions', *Belfast Newsletter* (14 January 1863) Antrim.

50  K. Barclay, 'Manly magistrates and citizenship in an Irish town: Carlow, 1820–1840', in K. Cowman, N. Koefoed and Å.K. Sjögren (eds), *Gender in Urban Europe: Sites of Political Activity and Citizenship, 1750–1900* (London: Routledge, 2014), pp. 58–72; J.A. Epstein, *Radical Expression: Political Language, Ritual and Symbol in England, 1790–1850* (Oxford: Oxford University Press, 1994).

51  [John Rea Obituary; untitled]', *Weekly Northern Whig* (21 May 1881).

52  Sheil, *Sketches, Legal and Political*, vol. 1, p. 10.

53  Johnson, *Dictionary*, unpaginated, see 'sweet';

54  C. Richardson, *A New Dictionary of the English Language* (London: William Pickering, 1839), p. 779, see 'sweet'.

55  Johnson, *Dictionary*, unpaginated, see 'mellow'; Richardson, *A New Dictionary*, p. 505, see 'mellow'; p. 200, see 'delicate'.

56  Sheil, *Sketches, Legal and Political*, vol. 1, p. 93.

57  J.R. O'Flanagan, *The Irish Bar: Comprises Anecdotes, Bon-Mots, and Biographical Sketches of the Bench and Bar of Ireland* (London: Sampson Low, Marston, Searle, & Rivington, 1879), pp. 405–6.

58  Schroeder, 'Speaking volumes', p. 98.

59  O'Flanagan, *The Irish Bar*, pp. 153–4.

60  *Ibid.*, p. 255.

61  M. McCormack, *The Independent Man: Citizenship and Gender Politics in Georgian England* (Manchester: Manchester University Press, 2005), p. 180.

62  O'Flanagan, *The Irish Bar*, p. 170.

63  *Ibid.*, p. 266.

64  *Ibid.*, pp. 170, 266.

65  *Ibid.*, p. 170.

66  *Ibid.*, pp. 377–8.

67  Sheil, *Sketches of the Irish Bar*, vol. 1, p. 312.

68  O'Flanagan, *The Irish Bar*, p. 267.

69  *Ibid.*, p. 272.

70  *Ibid.*, p. 153.

71  Sheil, *Sketches, Legal and Political*, vol. 1, pp. 10–11.

72  *Ibid.*, pp. 75–6.

73  *Ibid.*, p. 77.

74  J. Addison, 'Gesture in oratory', *Spectator*, 407 (17 June 1712).

75  Marker and Marker, 'Aaron Hill'; C.A. Feilla, 'Sympathy pains: Filicide and the spectacle of the male heroic suffering on the eighteenth-century stage', in J.R. Allard and M.R. Martin (eds), *Staging Pain, 1580–1800: Violence and Trauma in British Theater* (Aldershot: Ashgate, 2010), pp. 151–67.

76  For example, G. Austin, *Chironomia: Or a Treatise on Rhetorical Delivery* (London: T. Cadell and W. Davies, 1806); for discussion see: L. Hartley, *Physiognomy and the Meaning of Expression in Nineteenth-Century Culture* (Cambridge: Cambridge University Press, 2008).

77  Sheil, *Sketches, Legal and Political*, vol. 1, pp. 162–3.

78  W. Ridgeway, *The Trial of Robert Emmet for High Treason* (Edinburgh: Peter Hill 1803), pp. 18–19; Barclay, 'Sounds of sedition'.

79  Cairns, *Advocacy*; this often resembled Parliament: J.S. Meisel, 'Humour and insult in the House of Commons: The case of Palmerston and Disraeli', *Parliamentary History*, 28:2 (2009), 228–45.

80  Campbell, *The Philosophy of Rhetoric*.

81  J.P. Curran, 'Henry Sheares [High Treason]', in T. Davis (ed.), *The Speeches of the Right Honorable John Philpot Curran* (London: Henry G. Bohn, 1847), pp. 402–3.

82  Curran, 'Henry Sheares', p. 418.

83  *Ibid.*, pp. 418–19.

84  *Ibid.*, p. 410.

85  See, for example, 'Speeches of Mr Phillips in the case of Guthrie v. Sterne, delivered in the Court of Common Pleas, Dublin', in *The Speeches of Charles Phillips, Esq., Delivered at the Bar, and on Various Public Occasions, in Ireland and England* (London and Dublin: W. Simkin & R. Marshall, and Milliken, 1822), pp. 76–8.

86  J.P. Curran, 'Massey v. Headfort [for Criminal Conversation]', in Davis, *The Speeches*, p. 537.

87  For example, Brewster in *Court of Queen's Bench. The Right Hon. The Earl of Erne, plaintiff; John Grey Vesey Porter, esq., Defendant. Report of the Trial of an Action for Libel* (Dublin: Goodwin, Son and Nethercott, 1859), pp. 8–9; and Saurin in *The Trial of John Magee, Proprietor of the Dublin Evening Post. . .* (Dublin: John Magree, 1813), pp. 60–71.

88  Curran, 'Henry Sheares', p. 413.

89  May, *The Bar & the Old Bailey*, p. 50.

90  For a discussion of such trials and national identity see: K. Barclay, 'Emotions, the law and the press in Britain: Seduction and breach of promise suits, 1780–1830', *Journal of Eighteenth-Century Studies*, 39:2 (2016), 267–84.

91  N.E. Johnson (ed.), *Impassioned Jurisprudence: Law, Literature, and Emotion, 1760–1848* (Lewisburg: Bucknell University Press, 2015).

# 5

## *The cross-examination: 'he's putting me in such a doldrum'*

**DUNGARVAN PETIT SESSIONS**

On the bench was Doctor Fitzgerald, and Robert Longan, Esq.

**A FIGHT IN IRISH**

David Curreen was charged with assaulting one Paddy Neil.

Dr. Fitzgerald asked the complainant, 'Do you speak English?'

Neil – *Dhoul fouchaul*, yer honour; there's no English in Ballinagaul only what one gentleman have.

Mr Longan – Oh, they are all Turks, swear him in Irish.

Mr Kelly (solicitor for the defence) – The Turks at your side of the coast, Mr Longan, are better versed in the languages?

Mr Longan – Yes, they have travelled more than the aborigines of Ballinagaul.

Paddy Neil then commenced his narrative – Myself and two dogs were going the road together, when Davy Curreen met us, and set a big dog of his at my little dog, when I interfered for fair play, when he gave me two blows on the chest; and I tould him to strike me again, the way I could make of the law, when he hot me in the eye and knocked me down.

Jim Brien was then called upon; the Doctor asked if his accomplishments included speaking English?

Jim – *Nene shei gum*, myself nor nobody belonging to me never had any English.

Doctor – Well, what do you know about it?

Jim – I seed them all fighting, the dogs and Paddy Neil, and Davy Curreen, all tangled in one another, but the little dog wasn't in the fore at all.

Tim Casey was next called.

The Doctor said – Perhaps you could enlighten us a little on the subject? Do you speak English?

Tim, who was a most grotesque looking animal, replied, 'the devil a taste.'

Doctor – Sure that's English, come, do your best.

Jim – *Nadie me*, I hasn't no English, nor anybody else in Ballinagaul, barring the priest and Mr. Fitzgerald.

Doctor – Come, Sir, this won't do.

Jim – Blud an agers, Sir, the fight was in *Irish*, Doctor begor may be, Doctor, now if you wor locking at a foight in English, you wouldn't put Irish upon it yourself.

Jim was obliged to get his own way, and added not a little the difficulty of developing the real merits of the case, by the peculiarly Irish manner in which he gave his Irish testimony about the Irish fight; however, the assault was clearly proved, and the Doctor asked the defendant, 'Have you any land?'

Neil – No, Doctor, bud my brother have.

Doctor – How much?

Neil – About fifteen acres.

The Doctor then paused as if making out a calculation in the rule of three, and said, 'We fine you five shillings.' . . .

*Wexford Independent*, 7 August 1841

The 'gift of the gab', 'blarney', as well as a penchant to drop into, often humorous, story or song, has long been associated with the Irish. Irish soldiers were remembered by their comrades as characters whose quick tongues raised morale or smoothed tensions; representations of the Irish in the literatures of other nations were marked by verbosity, the tongue that used more words than most.[1] Deconstructing the roots of this national stereotype and its 'veracity' has been subject to considerable research, raising questions about Ireland's typicality compared to other oral cultures and the uses of this stereotype as a trope to justify colonisation.[2] The descriptions of and space given to oral performances in the press suggests that many early nineteenth-century Irish people took pride in their linguistic prowess, whether that was as masters of quick repartee, as able storytellers, as passionate speechmakers, or as humorous joke-tellers, and they were, in turn, widely admired.

Verbal dexterity was particularly useful within a legal system where the cross-examination was a key mechanism for accessing truth. Being unprepared for the questions put by defence council, almost a disequilibrium of the self, was thought to necessitate witnesses to give an honest account. John Philpot Curran was renowned for his capacity to 'throw the witnesses off their center, and he took care they seldom should recover it'.[3] As a humorous anecdote ran:

> a peasant witness, writhing under this mental excruciation' cried out: 'I can't answer yon little gentleman, *he's putting me in such a doldrum.*' 'A doldrum! Mr Curran, what does he mean by a doldrum!' exclaimed Lord Avonmore. 'O! m lord, it's a very common complaint with persons of this description: it's merely a *confusion of the head arising from a corruption of the heart.*'[4]

Catching witnesses out, or undermining their original statements, was a form of skilful play that allowed truth to emerge. Yet, the public were also aware that lawyers could use the cross-examination to obfuscate facts and create doubt. Daniel O'Connell was admired for his abilities in this area.[5] His 'cross' was described as a 'series of attacks and retreats, which gradually clouded the minds of the judge and jury with serious doubts to the witness's credibility, even when the witness was veracious'.[6]

Such actions located the court as an adversarial space, where truth, or at least justice, arose from successful legal strategy.[7] As discussed in Chapter 1, the use of lawyers to conduct cross-examinations at the assizes and in the higher courts was commonplace across the nineteenth century.[8] In an English context, the proliferation of lawyers in his period has been viewed as producing a particularly adversarial system, where, as Stephan Landsman put it, 'the contentious spirit had triumphed'.[9] This claim is tempered by David Cairns, who emphasises that the cross-examination – vital to producing truth – was shaped by moral boundaries that limited adversarial behaviour.[10] This chapter explores the cross-examination as a vehicle for truth and a technique for negotiating legal and social power relationships. That language plays a role in the production of power is well recognised, yet how individuals use wordplay in everyday contexts to inform power dynamics has mostly been the focus of anthropologists and sociologists.[11] Press reports often devoted considerable space to courtroom dialogue, particularly if it was entertaining or amusing. Whilst some of it was contentious, it could also be playful, knowing and engaging.

As is explored below, rhetorical techniques, including banter and joke-telling, became legitimate tools in negotiations over meaning and were viewed as such by participants and the press. The ability to perform well during the cross-examination gave authority to the speaker, although this was informed by gender, class, physicality and, not least, accent or whether the speaker used Irish.[12] This chapter begins with an exploration of how Irish-language speakers and Irish-English speakers with a 'strong brogue' were represented in the press. Whilst recognising that Irish-English can be distinguished from other Englishes, in this chapter 'English' will refer to the language spoken by Irish-English speakers, and Irish will refer to Irish-Gaelic. The chapter then explores banter and joke-telling as a key strategy during cross-examination, before looking at the limits of the possibilities of humour, particularly for elite men who conformed to codes of honourable manliness.

## Accent and Irishness: speaking in court

The language of the court was formally English, a reality that disguised the multilingual context in which it was situated.[13] Between three and four million people spoke Irish in the first decades of the century, although usage was declining. By 1851, only c. 25–30 per cent of the population identified as Irish-speaking, and just 5 per cent were monoglot Irish.[14] Following a trend that emerged in the eighteenth century, elite men and women actively engaged in language and accent reconstruction, from the standardisation of English spelling and expression to the popularity of elocution classes designed to 'improve' those with strong regional or national accents.[15] Language and accent became implicated in imperial power relationships, where the colonising demands of English standardisation demarcated particular voices as more 'civilised' than others.

This was not a case of English-dominance of Irish linguistic identity, however, either in court or more widely. Elocution classes were not designed to eradicate local accents, but to tame them, allowing easier communication across the kingdoms. Richard and Maria Edgeworth's *Essay on Irish Bulls*, a text that defended the Irish use of 'figurative language' as a form of linguistic ability, not 'blunder', admired the accent of the Scottish bar whose 'manly eloquence . . . affords a singular pleasure to the candid English hearer, and gives merit and dignity to the speakers, who retain so much of their own dialect and tempered propriety of English sounds, that they may be emphatically termed *British orators*'.[16] In combining a Scottish accent with English words and grammar, Scots became more British than the English.

A range of Irish accents and Irish-language speakers could be found in courtrooms. People at all social levels spoke Irish, from judges such as Robert Day (1746–1841) and Baron William Smith (1766–1836), magistrate Edward Deane in Mayo, lawyers like Daniel O'Connell and John Philpot Curran (also Master of the Rolls), and numerous jurymen and witnesses.[17] Many more people spoke English with an Irish brogue. Whilst Irish speakers were found in all parts of Ireland, some regions had greater concentrations than others, so that at times most of the court may have had fluency in Irish. Irish language use and Irish accents became implicated in the formation of the court as a national space where, as Terry Eagleton notes, 'verbal stratagems are at once an effect of colonialism and a form of resistance to it'.[18]

In this linguistically diverse context, translators were employed to ensure proceedings ran in English, although their presence in much reporting is invisible. Early in the century, whilst dialogue was given in detail, it was edited to remove the features of spoken language. Other early accounts, such as the Irish Bar stories and popular jokes, often referred to the courts as spaces of humour and banter that emerge in newspapers and printed trials from around the 1820s. Whilst later sources try to replicate the syntax of spoken language, and to some extent its pauses and intonations, Irish testimony was often rendered into English without comment and yet still retained the features of natural spoken word, perhaps reflecting that it was the translators' speech that was recorded.

Some reportage included the name of the translator at the top of the report, along with the key barristers and judge.[19] Yet, their intervention often goes without comment. When, in 1822, Jeremiah Collins refused to answer in English on cross-examination, the *Carlow Morning Post* noted that, 'There was much difficulty in making this witness speak English', before recording his testimony in English. The reader might presume that he had been convinced to do so, except that, after his testimony, the paper reported: 'His Lordship directed this witness to be confined for a month, in consequence of not answering in English'.[20] Who translated his testimony, or how that shaped the interaction between lawyer and witness, is unknown.

Where translators, and they were almost exclusively men, are mentioned is either when one was not readily available and someone volunteered, or when somebody commented on the translation.[21] At the relatively informal proceeding of an 1833 inquest, the *Connaught Telegraph* noted that the foreman of the jury acted as interpreter, whilst another juror was clerk to the Coroner.[22] After the testimony of Johanna Crowley in an 1840 burglary case, a juryman 'acquainted with Irish, stated that she had made the answers as delivered by the interpreter'.[23] There was no other indication that her testimony had been rendered in Irish. That interpreters were so rarely mentioned and that transcriptions of the original Irish were not reported downplayed the role of Irish language within courtrooms; at least as depicted in public accounts, the court was English-speaking and those that spoke Irish out of place within it. This presumption shaped how the testimony of Irish speakers was received.

Extended commentary on the use of Irish language was focused on cases where it was suspected that Irish speakers spoke English but refused to do so. Many Irish speakers acknowledged that they spoke some English, or understood English but did not speak it, yet wished to testify in Irish. Despite giving evidence for the prosecution in English, Jeremiah Collins wished to speak Irish when cross-examined because 'he could not tell his story in English'.[24] Mary Corcoran, testifying against the man she accused of rape in 1829, used a similar expression: 'she could not tell her story in English'.[25] In both cases, the desire to speak Irish appears to have arisen because they did not have the verbal dexterity in English that they had in Irish, which they believed necessary to 'tell their story' to an aggressive barrister. As was typical, both were compelled to testify in English and Collins' refusal resulted in his imprisonment.[26]

When fluency was suspected, refusing to speak English was associated with dishonesty. Bridget McNamara, when testifying to her rape, swore on oath in 1825 that she did not speak English, but, as the journalist noted, this 'fact was of importance in shaking her testimony'. On cross-examination, rather than questioning her account of the attack, the defence tried to prove her knowledge of English; that defence witnesses heard her speak English was used to suggest that she should not be believed.[27] During John Lally's prosecution for shooting in 1832, a policeman similarly undermined an Irish-speaking defence witness by testifying that he spoke fluent English.[28] Even requesting to speak Irish could damage a witness's reputation. After being told it would hurt her case to testify in Irish, the reporter noted, 'Without one moment's hesitation, [Corcoran] then detailed very flippantly, and with peculiar circumstantial precision, the *minutiae* connected with her accusation'.[29] Corcoran's refusal to speak English, followed by her seeming fluency, was used to reinforce the reporter's reading of her evidence as untrue.

The relationship between Irish-speaking and dishonesty was built on the belief that witnesses were advantaged by having time to prepare their answers during the translation. Ellen Tanahan successfully convicted her rapist, but when he appealed, his defence attorney argued that:

> She gave her testimony in the Irish language, and their Lordships were familiar with the difficulties eliciting the truth circumstanced as she was; she was one of those persons who, although they will not give their testimony in English, perfectly well understand the questions put to them, and they always take the benefit of preparing the answer while the question goes through the form of an interpretation.[30]

Here the defence lawyer made explicit what was at stake when witnesses testified in Irish. Such reasoning located the cross-examination as an adversarial process, almost a competition of wits, and as a key point in the trial where truth was elicited.

It is notable that many of these discussions arose during rape cases.[31] This was partly because women were more likely to testify in Irish than men, perhaps because they were less likely to know English but certainly because the judiciary believed that to be the case. It was also because the central defence strategy in rape cases lay in challenging the character of the accuser. Speaking Irish became a useful shorthand for dishonesty, and whilst commentators were clear that dishonesty did not arise from being an Irish monoglot (but testifying in Irish whilst knowing English), that speaking Irish was used to imply dishonesty by defence lawyers had repercussions for all Irish-speaking witnesses.

Where honesty was not directly questioned, Irish speakers were often viewed as particularly provincial or poor. Such witnesses were described with adjectives like 'a miserable-looking creature', or 'a poor old man, who could not speak English', locating them as poverty-stricken and uncivilised.[32] Even reports defending the right to testify in Irish applied these stereotypes. The *Cork Examiner* protested when the resident magistrate overseeing the Dungarvan Petty Session refused to hear Mary Curtin's case in 1844 against her master for non-payment of wages as she could not speak English. It noted with considerable sarcasm:

> Oh, it was the duty of a magistrate certainly to sneer at the rank ignorance of a poor country rustic – and because she could not speak her speech 'trippingly' after going to the cost of a summons . . . she must either give it up for ever, or do what she cannot, what she swore she could not do. This is certainly justice. . . . there is in this country 'one law for the rich and another for the poor'.[33]

This commentary tried to address the associations between Irish-speaking, dishonesty, 'she swore she could not', and backwardness, 'poor country rustic'. Yet, as it was the author that raised the claimant's 'rustic poverty', and in viewing this as a dispute about justice for the poor, the claimant was situated in the role of uncivilised Irish peasant.

In contrast, English-speaking was associated with civilisation and intelligence. A 'man of colour', arrested for 'sedition' after speaking in favour of O'Connell (during the period where the latter was in prison for conspiracy), was brought before the Galway Petty Sessions. The *Galway Vindicator*, a paper founded to support O'Connell's campaign for Repeal, noted that: 'The man, whose name is Jos. Keys, and about twenty-four years of age, appeared very intelligent – well able to speak English – of a quiet disposition, and a good specimen of an emancipated slave'.[34] Keys' English was viewed as evidence of his 'intelligence', in a report that was originally published in a region with particularly high levels of Irish-language fluency.[35] That Keys' English-language skills were worthy of comment was informed by negative stereotypes about his race, but such remarks reinforced the association between English and civility, at the expense of the 'backward' Irish. Whilst Irish-speaking in court was often rendered invisible by reporters, when it was brought to the attention of the public, it was to reinforce that Irish speakers were dishonest, poor or uncivilised and so lacking in character.[36] This potentially had implications for how the testimony of Irish-speakers was received.

A strong Irish accent could operate similarly, and several reports, particularly those arising from the petty sessions and lower courts, rendered testimonies into phonetic English to highlight that the speaker had an Irish accent. All people in court spoke with some accent, including judges who may have had English public school accents. Many well-known lawyers had Irish accents: O'Connell was teased by a colleague, Mr Holmes, who thought his lack of refinement surprising given the time he spent at the London Parliament, 'mimicking the English pronunciation' as he spoke and causing the court to laugh.[37] Given this, who was selected by journalists to receive such treatment is telling. At times, it may have implied the speaker was a native Irish speaker and possibly speaking Irish. The account from the *Wexford Independent* that opens this chapter translated the speech of the witnesses into English with a phonetic 'Irish' twang, despite this testimony being in Irish. It may well be that the public was expected to read other examples of phonetic 'Irish' English as Irish speakers.

That men and women from all regions, as well as non-English foreigners such as the French and Scots, were given similar treatment, however, indicates that what was conveyed with an 'Irish accent' was not just how a person talked. Rather, it indicated a wealth of social characteristics that varied by context. At times, it suggested the speaker lived rurally and was likely a peasant.[38] At others, it marked social class, particularly the urban working class.[39] Given these associations, it could be used to challenge the status of the speaker. 'Jemmy' Maguire's speech was rendered phonetically in 1828, although he was a 'college-reared man' who earned 'ten shillings a day'.[40] Whilst not denying Maguire's veracity, his 'accent' complicated his assertion of a middle-class identity, hinting that status, and its associated character, required more than economic achievement. When Bernard Lamb summoned a fellow 'praty [potato] porter', John Lynch, for 'annoying him' in 1842, the *Freeman's Journal* titled the account 'Altercation between Professional Gentlemen', and proceeded to make light of Lamb's account.[41] Lamb argued that Lynch 'was in the unceasing practice of villifying his *karakter*, and blackening his fair reputation . . . for what gintleman would trust a man with his *praties* who was reputed to be a "dishonourable spalpeen"'. Not only did the testimonies of these two men cause considerable laughter, but the magistrate dismissed them with a paternalistic 'Oh, go home, both of you – be good friends, and mind your business'. For the court, and presumably the anticipated newspaper audience, potato porters were too low down the social ladder to make claims to character, let alone gentlemanly status. Rendering their dialogue phonetically reinforced the entertainment value of these poor men's claims to a character worthy of legal protection. Such cases also provide telling evidence that the lower orders disagreed with such assessments, understanding their characters as valuable assets.

Whilst strong accents situated men outside of mainstream middling and elite masculinity, it could support performances of 'Irishness' by men who positioned themselves in a different social register. Darby Toole was brought before the Athy magistrates in 1830 for obstructing the Market Jury (who ensured fair weighing and quality at markets).[42] Toole's clothing, which was in disarray and poorly mended, did not suggest he was respectable. But what he lacked in physical prowess, he made up for in wit. When the magistrate challenged him for hiding poor-quality vegetables within bundles of good cabbage, Darby replied:

> Bethershin! Sure I got enough about that afore, when'ye took them from me. (Laughter). Hadn't they hands to open them, if they wanted to buy them, and why didn't they do it? I'll be bound, if a gintleman in a fair put a few rutlins and disordered beasts in the middle ov a dthrove iv bullocks, and sowld the lot by havin the best iv them outside, you'd let him do it if he could, an say nothing about it.

Magistrate: A fair is no market, though.
Darby: Well, agrah! If it isn't, there's many a market not *fair*. (Great laughter).

Later when the magistrate, Colonel Baggot, read a written character, he observed that Darby was said to be 'very honest, but –':

Darby (slapping his thigh): Arah, didn't I know he was the sort! That gintleman wouldn't tell a lie for the Bishop. He's the rail blood, so he is.
Colonel Baggot: Listen again; it says, 'but he is very ill-tempered, and excessively saucy.'
Darby (throwing open his arms, and leaning back with an enquiring gape): Well! An isn't it true for him! (Great laughter.) Didn't I tell you he wouldn't write a lie for Priest or Minister! (Increased laughter.)

Darby appears to have deliberately played up his 'brogue', using distinctive, but well-known, colloquialisms (bethershin; arah) and sayings ('wouldn't tell a lie for the Bishop'). Accompanied with witty comebacks and a willingness to endorse a less-than-flattering 'character', he placed significance not on being polite or well-mannered but honest and entertaining. Here a strong regional accent reinforced the humour of his performance and his construction of a comic character. Moreover, by tying his treatment to questions of 'fairness' and the different standards that applied to poor cabbage salesmen than to 'gintlemen' who sold cattle, he queried whether justice was applied equally. In doing so, Darby claimed a distinctive lower-class Irish identity, marked by a strong brogue, honesty but not necessarily 'mannerly' behaviour, a sense of humour and witty tongue. The court still fined him for obstruction, but, through making the court laugh and challenging the status quo, Darby had moved from a scruffy, shuffling peasant to an articulate, even manly, Irishman.

## Wit, humour and the lower orders

As Toole's behaviour suggests, the cross-examination was a critical moment when humour could shape courtroom dynamics. Banter between lawyers, judges and witnesses was a common occurrence as men on both sides of the stand attempted to destabilise the narrative being told, avoid answering questions, or affirm masculinity through witty wordplay. That humour provides opportunity to resist power structures, to discipline and reinforce norms, or negotiate social power relationships is widely recognised.[43] In an eighteenth- and early nineteenth-century context, humorous exchange was a source of social anxiety, as writers explored whether it was compatible with polite sociability. Thinkers, such as the Earl of Shaftsbury and Joseph Addison, made distinctions between 'true' and 'false' wit, or, as George Campbell put it, the 'raillery' of the elite and the 'banter' of the poor, as they attempted to rehabilitate humour for polite conversation.[44] Whilst author John Brown disputed whether elite men were intrinsically funnier due to their class, distinctions between high and low humour remained socially significant.[45] Within this context, entertaining exchanges between men of different social classes became implicated in social power relationships. Funny lower-order men and women not only disrupted orderly proceedings but reinforced the capacity of all classes to lay claim to a social status associated with the effective use of wit. As Jim Kelly notes, 'Folk customs, in other words, become invested with social and political capital not *a priori* but through their mediated appearance before "the better sort"'.[46] This was especially the case in Ireland where banter and joke-telling were valued as a form of social currency and their use by men of all classes was widely admired.

The cross-examination was often imagined as a particularly adversarial process, with humour providing an important weapon to barristers and witnesses alike.[47] Moreover, that truth should be able to stand the test of ridicule, as Shaftesbury asserted, provided a space for humour to serve the purposes of the court.[48] The barrister, William Curran, writing in 1819, thought that a humorous cross was necessitated by the 'lower orders' who 'abound in sagacity and repartee; qualities to which, when appearing as unwilling witnesses, or when struggling under the difficulties of cross examination, they seldom fail to fly to shelter'.[49] He argued that the barrister was required to 'adopt every artifice of humour and ridicule, as more effectual than seriousness or menace, to extract the truth and expose their equivocations'. O'Connell's success on cross-examination was apparently because witnesses were 'stunned by repeated blows with the butt-end of an Irish joke'.[50]

Humour was also understood as an effective defence, with witty retorts viewed as a tool for closing down questioning. When trying to ascertain whether a particular person was drunk in 1828, Mr Burke Bethel asked witness, John Wall: 'Was he not as drunk this evening as a *Distiller's Pig*?' 'I never saw a *drunken* pig. (*Laughter.*)', replied Wall. Bethel's next question was about Wall's occupation.[51] Bethel tried to disarm Wall with amusing imagery, but was parried. It was Wall's quick-wit that created laughter, rather than the essential humour of the joke. Bethel, recognising that he was bested, moved on without receiving an answer. This was not necessary; Bethel could have repeated the question in a more direct form ('was he drunk?'). Instead, he conformed to an unspoken set of social rules around banter, which restricted men from following up certain types of questions once defeated. The cross became a rhetorical duel, a form of play, between witness and lawyer, with points to be won along the course of the testimony – points which were expected to inform the balance of justice.[52]

The truly skilled and popular cross-examiners were not those who exercised brute force in stripping away witnesses' testimony, however, but those that used the cross to negotiate meaning, allowing witnesses to rebuild identity, as well as directing them towards particular answers. Daniel O'Connell's cross-examination of the witness John Houlahan during the 1826 trial for the murder of Patrick Hennessy (who died during a general fight between a group of men) is an adroit example.

> Cross-examined by Mr O'Connell. – Tell me, Mr Houlahan, how long is it since you made away from the police? – Oh Counsellor, sure that has nothing to do with this. You must tell me nothwithstanding? – I won't tell you; you are unpleasant today. Did you get away from the police? – well if I must tell you, I did get away, because they were not able to pursue me. Now, why did the police go after you? – Why did they! Why, sure they are an active police. Had they no other reason? – They had I suppose. Tell me why they pursued you? – How can I tell you all the reasons they had for pursuing a poor boy like me. Now, Houlahan, this will not do; you must tell me, if you know, why the police were after you? – Then if you must have it, it was all about Captain Rock. Were you one of Captain Rock's men? – I was to be sure. Perhaps you are the real Captain Rock? Why then really I am not. Are you a lieutenant? No, I was a private for the honour of the thing. You went to a fair by appointment? – I did. Now, what business had you there? To fight to be sure. What other business would I have there? Why did you make the appointment on that particular day? – Because the parties had agreed, on the Sunday before, to meet in order to have a fight, and would you have me absent on such an occasion? How many fights have you been in? – For how long? For your whole life? Oh! You're not serious; how could I tell? Could you even give a guess? – I could not indeed. Could you tell how many battles you have been in for the last three years? – I could not, without taking a great deal of time to calculate. Now Houlahan, by virtue of your oath, did you ever see a fight that your teeth did not water to be in the middle of it? – (witness, after a pause) Why, sure one could not see two dogs fighting without taking part with one or the other of them. (much laughter).[53]

O'Connell's cross-examination here was gentle, providing Houlahan with space to exert his own identity and to shape the conversation.

Houlahan began by actively prevaricating ('Oh Counsellor, sure that has nothing to do with this'), before moving to humorous asides ('Why, sure they are an active police'). When pressed, he gave a few direct answers, before bantering with O'Connell about his fighting experience. The latter questions, which were only tangentially relevant, if speaking to character, seem to have been designed by O'Connell to allow Houlahan to be funny, culminating in a set up for a joke that if answered properly would cause the court to laugh. As the joke about taking sides in a dog fight was a popular expression, O'Connell could be confident that Houlahan would take the opening. Through the court's laughter, O'Connell rewarded Houlahan for his direct answers and encouraged further cooperation. At the same time, such questioning encouraged Houlahan to present himself as uncivilised and aggressive (literally like a dog), diminishing his character for a middle-class jury. His peers, other young men who valued the ability to fight, would have read Houlahan's character differently, viewing his aggressive masculinity as admirable and respecting his honesty.[54] O'Connell knew that for some men the desire to affirm their own masculinity, such as being a fighter or witty, was more important than keeping a jury on side.

This technique was used regularly by O'Connell, relying on witnesses having a basic competency in popular situational banter. In *Magarahan v. Maguire* (1827), he asked James McGourty:

> I suppose you like scalteen [an alcoholic punch]? Why, yes, I like it very well.
> How do you like it? Sometimes strong, sometimes weak.
> When do you like it weak? After I have taken a good deal of it strong.[55]

An old joke, and one that relied on both parties knowing their lines, having a shared belief that heavy drinking was manly, and being willing to cooperate to enable one man to arise victorious. In such instances, familiarity with the joke-telling tradition was prioritised over 'originality', reinforcing the sociability of the humorous exchange.

This was not without glory for the individual setting up the joke, who was required to recognise the appropriate moment to begin. O'Connell took this opportunity when defending a group of Whiteboys for being part of an illegal organization in 1829. An ex-Whiteboy, turning state's evidence, concluded his testimony '*I know, my Lord, there are some innocent.*' Without missing a beat, O'Connell commented: 'There is no doubt we have one who is not innocent', to which the witness replied: 'There would be none of this work only for yourself, Mr. O'Connell. – *(laughter.)*'[56] Unlike in the previous example, it is not clear that O'Connell deliberately set this up as a joke (perhaps instead hoping to deprecate a state witness against his clients). Yet, gags around innocence and defence lawyers were not especially innovative, so it could not have been entirely unanticipated.[57]

Rather O'Connell took this risk because such exchanges brought benefits to him on cross-examination. Providing an opportunity for witnesses to demonstrate their wit encouraged them to cooperate. It gave them confidence in their performance that could be later undermined, and it contributed to the folklore around O'Connell, and similar men, as lawyers.[58] The men who engaged O'Connell were similarly able to demonstrate their ability to banter and respond to contextual cues. On occasion, this meant that they emerged as victor from the cross; on others, it allowed them to reinforce their masculinity and so their social authority under the barrage of aggressive questioning. In all cases, their wit spoke to their character. Not all entertaining men emerged from the cross as 'respectable', particularly when they were from the lower orders, but in demonstrating their wit, they spoke to the alternative masculine cultures available in Ireland and offered alternative readings of their bodies and behaviours for the judge, jury and gallery.

### Banter, honour and anger

Whilst men of all social groups could elicit humour on cross-examination, class and gender played an important role in shaping when it was appropriate and how it would be interpreted by others.[59] As in Scotland, women were often remarkably quick-witted and many of the best examples of witnesses outdoing lawyers feature garrulous women.[60] Mr Fitzgibbon found himself outwitted by a woman during a prosecution for sending threatening letters in 1841.

Mr Fitzgibbon – I hope you are married? Witness – Why do you ask; have I got into your good graces? (Laughter). Mr Fitzgibbon – I would like to know. Witness – Well, I am married but my husband is dead. Mr Fitzgibbon – Oh what a pity we did not meet before (laughter). Witness – Why, I hope you are not married? (loud laughter.) Mr Fitzgibbon – Indeed I am. Witness – Your wife must be a very fortunate lady; but I am sorry you told me there was such a person in question (general laughter.) Mr Fitzgibbon – Why does it concern you? Witness – Because you made such a deep impression upon my heart (laughter.) Mr Fitzgibbon – Is it an agreeable impression? Of course anything connected with you must be agreeable (loud laughter.) Mr Fitzgibbon – Is the prisoner married? Yes. Mr Fitzgbbon – Perhaps

that is the reason you would have no objection to see him transported –
did he ever make a deep impression upon you. Witness – No indeed,
I would not look at a limping fellow of his kind – (loud laughter.)
When I was married I got one of the most beautiful young men in the
country, and a man of education too? Mr Fitzgibbon – And, indeed, he
could not return the compliment (laughter.) Witness – Love is blind,
you know (laughter.) Mr Fitzgibbon – Was he deaf, for love ought
to be deaf as well as blind? Witness – No; but I made him happy –
(laughter) – the Lord has given me flippancy of tongue, and all I am
sorry for is that I was not brought up to the bar – (loud laughter).
Mr Fitzgibbon – If you will only employ a person to make you a hand-
some suit of clothes there is no doubt but you will pass for a man –
(laughter) – you may go down now; but perhaps you may wish to have
the last word. Witness – If I was here until tomorrow I would.[61]

The examination began with some light, flirtatious banter, but
Fitzgibbon quickly realised he had met his match. The witness was not
embarrassed by questioning about her romantic life and was willing to
turn it back on him. In doing so, she stretched the boundaries of respectable behaviour for, particularly middle-class, women, during a period
where sexual innocence was prized and where women often displayed
discomfort when discussing personal matters. As a widow and probably lower class (her willingness to engage in banter and Fitzgibbon's
lack of respect suggests this), she was not expected to be as innocent as a
younger, unmarried woman, and her comments were carefully chosen to
show her as assertive, but not crude or rude. The court finds her funny,
not shocking.

Unable to master the witness, Fitzgibbon insulted her, perhaps
believing that her frank flirtation opened her to reprimand. Yet, this too
backfired, and he was forced to offer her the last word, a common strategy that operated as a gendered insult. By being offered the last word,
rather than allowing the witness to take it, the lawyer suggested that she
spoke too much, playing into stereotypes of the female tongue as excessive, frivolous and without substance.[62] It devalued any 'last word' by
making it an opportunity offered by an opponent, rather than a victory
won in a battle of wits. That Fitzgibbon had to resort to such strategy was
suggestive of his own poor performance.

Whilst women were often very able on the stand, how lawyers
treated them was refracted through gendered expectations for appropriate behaviour. That this, and several other accounts, are reported at
length is suggestive of the entertainment that witty women provided for
the public. Described as 'garrulous' or 'a beautiful maiden with a quick

tongue', reporters highlighted that it was 'novelty', rather than verbal ability, that made these examples of interest.[63] It was often suggested that such women would make able lawyers, misgendering the witness and reinforcing wit as a male skill. Men with quick tongues were amusing, but not described by terms that marked their linguistic ability as unusual. Garrulous women were entertaining because they engaged in what journalists and middle-class lawyers thought was a male practice.

As a result, the opportunity for women to rebalance power dynamics within court was more limited than for men. This was not to say they had no impact; Elizabeth Sly performed so well under cross in 1822 that the *Carlow Morning Post* noted that Mr Arabin was 'forced to give up the witness'.[64] Fitzgibbon's manliness was diminished by his encounter. Yet, as curiosities, these women did not seriously challenge masculine identity, nor did their gains transform the social position of women, with their verbal skills rendered unfeminine and so derisory. Their victories were marked as exceptional and limited. Moreover, witty women were generally from the lower ranks of the population. Elite women (who very rarely appeared in court) were treated with greater delicacy by lawyers and they understood that female respectability was not best served by a quick tongue, at least in this context. Humour became a weapon of the weak, the association that Curran made between the lower orders and wit played out in practice.

It was not just gender that influenced how humour was interpreted. Elite and middle-class men admired the ability to banter well, were prone to making jokes and telling funny stories to greater or lesser success. The court officers, who worked together regularly, often had 'in-jokes' and were willing to submit to some teasing from men of their own social background. Justice Johnson got a rise out of the court for an old joke during an 1820 case where the defendant had sought charity on a fraudulent basis.[65] He remarked that: 'being himself annoyed one day by beggars, he threw a tenpenny on the ground; a lame man was the first to it, but a blind man secured the prize! – (*laughter.*)'[66] As has been seen, lawyers like Curran and O'Connell were praised for their abilities to joke and banter. Codes of polite and honourable behaviour between middle-class and elite men, however, placed rules around when laughter should be deployed, who could be laughed at and why, and even how men should laugh, with excessive laughing that contorted the face and shook the body associated with 'rusticity' and 'brutish' instincts.[67] The need for conformity to such codes made elite men sensitive to the slights and ridicule that banter and laughter could imply. Humorous exchanges and barbs could quickly sour.

The relationship between honour, character, violence and masculinity across the nineteenth century is complex. Physical prowess, the capacity to fight if necessary, remained an important dimension of manliness amongst most social groups into the twentieth century, whilst the growing militarism of the latter part of the century undermines any straightforward story of declining violence in European society.[68] That the legal system was enforced through violence ensured that it was implicated in social order. Violence was situated as the weapon to use when other forms of social control and discipline failed, the last resort of the civilised. Yet, whether men, and particularly elite men, should engage in personal violence was a topic of debate, as it had been for centuries.[69] In the United Kingdom by the end of the century, challenges to manly honour were generally not dealt with through direct personal violence, at least once men had left school and university.[70] Increasingly professional organisations, such as those that managed doctors or lawyers, brought in disciplinary structures where men could arbitrate disputes.[71] The law court was similarly available as a site for conciliation.[72] In the first half of the century, however, there remained a component of elite Irish society, like many amongst the lower orders, that saw violence, and particularly the duel, as necessary to restore 'honour'.[73]

Particularly associated with gentlemen, military and professional men (categories that could overlap), 'honourable manliness' competed alongside forms of middle-class masculinity that used the language of 'character'. 'Honourable manliness' was manifested through chivalry towards women, a sensitivity to challenges to self and family, and the need and capacity to defend honour.[74] This was not very different from constructions of honour amongst some lower-order men, who fought in response to personal slights, sexual jealousy, insults to family and many other scenarios.[75] As the arguing 'praty porters' suggest, lower-order men could have a strong sense of their own honour and character and believe it worthy of protection. Nor was violence amongst the elites more highly ritualised; as Houlahan above noted, he agreed to fight at the fair in advance and travelled for that purpose. Rather, 'honourable manliness' was distinct because it was built into codes of polite behaviour that were not accessible to the lower orders.

Unlike for many elite British masculinities, violence was a dimension of polite, and particularly sentimental, manhood in Ireland. The renowned duellist, barrister and chairman of Kilmainham Manor Court, John 'Bully' Egan was 'never known to pass a severe sentence on a criminal without blubbering tears'. This led the reporter of a humorous 1843 report to conclude that, '[t]hough so tender-hearted in passing sentence on a criminal, he was remarkably firm in shooting a friend'.[76] Duelling remained a central pastime amongst some men. James Kelly identified over 80 duels in the first decade of the nineteenth century, and whilst they subsequently declined, they were regularly reported into the 1840s.[77] Amongst Kelly's sample, over 65 per cent of the principals were 'gentleman'; only seven (8 per cent) were middle class. Six were lawyers.[78]

Given the importance of honour, that banter, or more direct challenges, might lead to violence was a considered threat. It was one recognised by elite men, who expected each other to conform to unspoken rules of polite exchange, where banter was allowed but within strict boundaries.[79] Polite comportment for elite men incorporated appropriate topics of conversation, vocabulary, the use of standard English, correct tone of voice, and not being too vehement in one's opinion.[80] 'Use palliatives such as *I may be mistaken, I am not sure, but I believe, I should rather think, &c.* Finish any argument or dispute with some little good-humoured pleasantry to shew that you are neither hurt yourself not meant to hurt your antagonist', advised the Earl of Chesterfield in his conduct manual.[81] Proper recognition of the respective social position of both parties was vital.

Burke Bethal's exchange with the witness Captain Whelan in 1829 was a typical polite encounter:

> Mr. Bethel – I believe Captain Whelan, when gentlemen retire from military life, they are generally fond of the ladies? (*Laughing*). Captain Whelan – I have no doubt but they are but I do not know whether this feeling is always confined to gentlemen of the military profession – (*Much laughter*). Mr. Bethel, was happy that he afforded the gallant captain an opportunity of displaying so much of his wit at his expense – (*Laughing.*)[82]

Both men engaged in some light banter that rested on a belief that womanising was not particularly honourable behaviour. Yet neither seriously challenged the character of the other, carefully acknowledging each other's status as 'gentlemen', aware of the tightrope between politeness and insult they walked. Not all engagements were as successful.

Carlow Petty Session, which from the late 1820s had a religiously, politically and socially mixed bench, was the site of several terse exchanges.[83] In 1837, magistrate Nicholas Vigors found himself almost bested by the attorney, Thomas Crawford Butler (from 1841 the Sessional Crown Prosecutor), in a case involving stone-throwing during election riots.

Mr Vigors – the defendant (who was not sworn) says that is was a mere pebble, while Mr Butler, in his statement, describes it as a tremendous rock.

Mr Butler – with great respect, I never said one word about rock, nor did I mention the term tremendous; these words are of your own invention.

Mr Vigors started up – I will not suffer you to contradict me so often, when I used the term I smiled.

Mr Butler – With great respect, you need not be so captious, and I will take the liberty of interrupting you whenever you misrepresent me.

Mr Vigors – You have no right to speak here without my permission.

Mr Butler – I say I have, and I am not only addressing you alone, but the Bench.

Mr Vigors – I am acting in the capacity of Magistrate, and if again interrupted, I shall commit the person who does so.

Mr Butler – Then I will interrupt you when you misrepresent me, and commit me at your peril. I say you are acting more like counsel for the defendant than a judge, and I shall not proceed further in this case.

Mr Burgess rose and stated – With great respect, an attorney attends this Court not as a matter of courtesy, but as a matter of right, under the 6th and 7th of William 4, cap 114, and sec. 2.

Mr Vigors resumed his seat.[84]

Butler's irritation at Vigors' language spiralled into a dispute with both men trying to establish their authority whilst couching their comments in polite language ('With great respect'). Notably, they both drew on their public positions – as a magistrate or barrister – to reinforce their claims, whilst also attempting to ensure the dispute did not move from the professional sphere into the personal. The attorney Burgess' intervention acted as a victory for Butler, by placing the authority of the law – more powerful than both men – on his side. Vigors accepted Butler's victory. The 'gentlemanly' response to defeat was to yield with good grace.[85]

Men of status that did not engage in polite discourse marked themselves as unmanly. Moreover, if they were provoked and displayed anger in court – lost control of their self-presentation – they suffered a loss of honour. Several Roman Catholic priests found themselves subject to provoking questions aimed at undermining the status they held as men of the cloth. The Rev. Andrew Hopkins, the victim of an assault, found his character attacked on cross-examination in 1842.[86] Mr Bourke, for the defence, asked a series of questions about his drinking habits. Hopkins acknowledged that he sometimes drank 'spirituous liquors', but when asked, 'A joking, merry priest, are you not?', he emphasised his status: 'Not ungentlemanly so; I was never in my life drunk in an ungentlemanly way'. Bourke replied: 'I understand you're a metaphysician and a logician; now will you describe what it is to be drunk in a gentlemanly manner and a blackguard manner? . . . describe to the gentleman of the jury the difference between the blackguardly drunk and the gentlemanly drunk – between the parish priest who takes his drop, and the curate who does not'. Hopkins made 'no answer'. Bourke went on to suggest that he was unchaste. Hopkins remained calm, and whilst some of Bourke's questions provoked laughter from the gallery, his more virulent attacks did not. Ultimately, the jury found Hopkins' attacker guilty.

In contrast, the Rev. Thomas Tyrrell's behaviour before the Carlow bench was used by the press to undercut his gentlemanly status, whilst affirming the authority of the magistrates. Mr Watters, the magistrate, refused Tyrrell's request to speak during a trial of two men for lock-breaking in 1830.[87] Tyrrell replied: 'These men acted under my advice and my authority. You should not have interrupted me Mr Watters. . .. which of you gentleman (to the magistrates) preserves the quiet of the country better than I do myself?' Rebuking the bench explicitly contravened the rules of polite discourse. The bench's response was portrayed as a restrained, 'we only do our duty', to which Tyrrell retorted, 'in so ungracious, so rude, so ungentlemanlike a way', challenging their honour. Another magistrate, Mr Eustace, then replied: 'I am doing my duty – I have no connexion with party, and am sorry to hear these things'. It was a response that subtly placed the Reverend as politically motivated and wrong-headed. Claiming 'duty' moreover allowed the bench to receive these insults in a professional capacity, ensuring that they did not have to defend their personal honour. Tryell offered a particularly egregious response to a bench with remarkable self-control, suggestive that the *Carlow Morning Post* provided a partial account of this encounter but also of the important role anger played in social constructions of manliness.

Displays of uncontrolled, unprovoked or poorly targeted anger undermined claims to elite identity and could even be associated with 'madness'. Roman Catholic priests were often depicted as bad tempered and such stereotypes informed legal strategy, with lawyers attempting to provoke an angry response. This was motivated both by anti-Catholic bias and by the association between priests and the lower orders. Roman Catholic priests were predominantly the sons of middling farmers (with estates of more than fifteen acres).[88] This made them middle class, but not elite, whilst their rural background challenged a middle-class identity tied to urbanity and polite education. Some priests were disliked by court officials as they claimed a social authority, through their position in the

church, which challenged hierarchies of power rooted in class, landown-
ership and Protestantism. Provoking them to anger was not only designed
to undermine their personal character, but their right to social authority.

Codes of honourable manliness demanded anger from men in certain contexts; anger that should typically be channelled into the controlled emotional outlet of the duel. Several elite men appeared angry in
court, relying on their own sense of injustice to justify their emotional
response.[89] Such men were typically portrayed negatively like Tyrrell,
but they appeared frequently enough to highlight the importance of displaying honourable anger for certain groups.[90] This was not a distinct
group from the remainder of the court who looked on in disdain. The
same men appear in both roles on different occasions. Rather, anger
was necessary to honour, but popular culture lacked a model for polite
anger that allowed men to appear both manly and angry. Whilst duelling
heroes fighting in defence of vulnerable innocence or threatened family
abounded in literature, positive portrayals of duellists focus on their
emotional restraint.[91] They often made challenges by letter, encapsulat-
ing anger in polite language. Depictions of squabbles in court focused on
the angry exchange before the duel, a picture that was often unflattering.
Disputes that escalated to challenges for duels within courtrooms were
generally frowned upon.

In 1842, the Earl of Lucan charged St Clair O'Malley, Esq., with ille-
gally hunting on his land and brought him before the Castlebar Petty
Session.[92] Both men were local landowners and magistrates who sat on
the Castlebar bench. In a fascinating piece of physical theatre, the Earl
of Lucan sat just to the right of the magistrates on duty, whilst O'Malley
placed himself on the pew for 'professional gentleman'. O'Malley challenged the bench to declare whether Lord Lucan would be acting as a
magistrate, as well as a prosecutor, in this 'mean and malicious prosecution, and I entertain the most utter contempt for it and Lord Lucan, and
everything emanating from him'. Both the magistrates and Lucan replied
that he had not interfered in cases that day, and Lucan indicated that his
seating was evidence of this. O'Malley replied:

> Although you have not acted in other cases, you may in this. I wish to
> know are you going to do so?
> Lord Lucan – I shall not answer you.
> Mr O'Malley – You must answer me. I have a right to a distinct answer
> on this point.
> Lord Lucan (to the bench) – Will you suffer such language as this?
> He uses the word 'must,' because he knows there are persons here
> to take it down. I call on you to commit the miscreant to the dock.

> Mr O'Malley – Your conduct in this matter is a piece with everything else you do; it is cowardly, blackguard, and ruffianly. If it were not for where you are, I would be licking you with this stick until I would break every bone in your body.

The magistrate, Mr Barron, asked O'Malley to be silent, as 'the language used by you cannot be tolerated in any court of justice', leading to a dispute over who gave the first insult. Barron thought it was O'Malley, but several of the gallery interjected to blame Lucan's 'miscreant' as the initial offence. O'Malley asked for a postponement to hire an attorney, but Lucan's lawyer objected that he was not entitled to such a 'courtesy'.

> Mr O'Malley – I demand it as a right. I would accept no courtesy from Lord Lucan.
> Lord Lucan – No courtesy is due to such a miscreant.
> Mr O'Malley – You cowardly poltroon, you know when you use that expression, that if you were not under the protection of four magistrates, I would lay this stick across your back – (much excitement pervaded the whole court).

O'Malley was bound to keep the peace, a typical magisterial response. To O'Malley's displeasure, Lucan was not similarly bound.

Neither Lucan, nor O'Malley behaved well on this occasion, but, despite Lucan being the first to use insulting language, O'Malley was seen as the aggressor. This was partly as he escalated his insulting language quickly and threatened physical violence, but also because his opening demand for Lucan to overtly declare that he would not interfere was an insult to the bench. Rules of polite conduct were based upon an expectation that gentlemen could be trusted to do their duty and behave well. Asking elite men to make explicit declarations of such fact – in effect to take an oath – was to challenge their identity as gentlemen and so their social status. That this was done in a public space, with a reporter to 'take it down', heightened the offence.

O'Malley was aware of this when he demanded that Lucan make such a statement. He thought it merited as Lucan's prosecution of him for something so trifling, and in a petty session in front of his peers, was a similar affront to O'Malley's status. Coming to court for trivial offences was not how gentlemen were expected to reconcile. In contrast, the duel offered justice; it clarified the honour of the men, providing both a defence and justification of the gentlemanly self. The duel paralleled the truth that was expected to emerge from the cross-examination – a truth that was rooted not in fact, but character.

## Conclusion

When Jim Brien, David Curreen and Paddy Neil came before the Dungarvan Petty Session to give their 'Irish testimony about the Irish fight', they highlighted a central tension within the legal system.[93] Determining truth through adversarial verbal exchange relied on a shared language, but not everybody who came to court spoke English. This not only provided Irish speakers with a strategic disadvantage, but increasingly situated the Irish as 'other' and 'foreign'. As the magistrate Robert Longan, Esq., humorously noted: 'Oh, they are all Turks, swear him in Irish'. The alien Irish were not just of another culture, but like the Turks within the British imagination, uncivilised: the 'aborigines of Ballinagual' as defence counsel, Mr Kelly, described them. Here Irishness was tied into the global imaginaries of Empire, situated at its edges as barbarous, ignorant, lazy and, worse, incorrigible.[94] Lacking a claim to character, such men were also associated with dishonesty, testifying in Irish undermining the truth they rendered.

This encounter raises interesting questions about what nationality Robert Longan, Esq., and George Kelly claimed. Very little survives about Kelly, who in 1840 was a young lawyer making a name for himself on the 'Dungarvan circuit'.[95] Longan, however, was a 'highly popular and much respected' magistrate of long-standing, a known Liberal and supporter of O'Connell and Richard Sheil, who he nominated to represent Dungarvan in Parliament in 1847.[96] In 1829, he was recorded cheering O'Connell as he asked the 'people of Ireland' (the Waterford hustings) to support George Beresford as the man who 'has the firmness and independence enough to demand those measures from the British ministry' that would 'expose the accumulation of abuses under which Ireland labours'. He joined with the crowd in 'giving three cheers for Old Ireland' before they dispersed.[97] Longan, at least, identified as Irish.

What the knowing reader of the *Wexford Chronicle* understood was that Robert Longan was not the 'bad guy', but rather Dr Garrett Fitzgerald, a medical doctor and Tipperary man, appointed as resident magistrate. Fitzgerald was particularly unpopular. There were complaints in the local press about the way he applied justice – objections that rested less on any lack of procedure, but that his decisions did not meet local ideas of fairness – and that he was biased against the Irish poor.[98] In 1844, he faced censure in the press for not hearing testimony in Irish; in 1845, he ordered Longan off the bench in a 'furious, overbearing and intemperate manner', after which he was bound to the peace by the other magistrates; in the same year, ten complaints were placed against him at Dublin Castle; and in 1846, O'Connell complained about him in Parliament.[99] He was finally removed to a position in Ballinasloe, Galway.[100]

This was all to come, but, in 1841, Fitzgerald was already 'disliked by all classes'.[101] Longan's use of 'Turks' was intended to overcome Fitzgerald's objections to witnesses testifying in Irish, whilst avoiding directly challenging his decision-making and so honour. It was humorous banter, where the Turks of Ballinagaul's characters were exchanged for access to justice. For Longan and men like him, the character of the Irish poor was of little value, so the cost was given little consideration. As in so many cases, humour was vital to smoothing social relationships, to negotiating power and to protecting and determining character (at least of those who mattered). Had the men on trial been of a different class, the cost may have been higher, with humour threatening to provoke anger and violence, as was seen in the dispute between Longan and Fitzgerald a few years later.[102]

Violent responses to perceived disrespect was part of life for many men at all social levels, with the ability to fight and to defend honour important to manhood. Yet, violence was interpreted differently depending on the class of the actors. Brien, Curreen and Neil's 'Irish fight' was 'disrespectable'; their dispute over 'fair play' and the formal challenge to 'strike me again, the way I could make of the law', was located in a different register from their elite brethren. Yet, Brien, Curreen and Neil were not passive recipients of middle-class justice. They brought their dispute to court and demanded to testify in Irish: 'the fight was in Irish, Doctor . . . now if you wor locking at a foight in English, you wouldn't put Irish upon it yourself'. In doing so, they claimed not only the right to speak Irish, but Irishness as an identity, one that was legitimate, manly and rooted in the way of life of the lower orders.

## Notes

1  N. Dunne-Lynch, 'Humour and defiance: Irish troops and their humour in the Penisular War', *Journal of the Society for Army Historical Research*, 85 (2007), 62–78; J. Stiles, 'Nationalism, Patriotism and the Stage Irish of the Early Nineteenth-Century Dublin Stage' (PhD dissertation, Tufts University, 2002); M. Waters, *The Comic Irishman* (Albany: State University of New York Press, 1984).

2  M. Higgins, 'Imagining and addressing the nation on Irish talk radio', in R.C. Allen and S. Regan (eds), *Irelands of the Mind: Memory and Identity in Modern Irish Culture* (Cambridge: Cambridge Scholars Publishing, 2008), pp. 96–109; N. Scheper-Hughes, *Saints, Scholars, and Schizophrenics: Mental Illness in Rural Ireland* (Berkeley: University of California Press, 2001), p. 71; A. Bourke, 'Reading a woman's death:

Colonial text and oral tradition in nineteenth-century Ireland', *Feminist Studies*, 21:3 (1995), 553–86; D. Lloyd, *Irish Culture and Colonial Modernity, 1800–2000: The Transformation of Oral Space* (Cambridge: Cambridge University Press, 2011); C. O'Halloran, 'Irish recreations of the Gaelic past: The challenge of Macpherson's Ossian', *Past and Present*, 124 (1989), 69–95.

3   C. Phillips, *Curran and His Contemporaries* (New York: Harper & Brothers, 1862), p. 58.

4   *Ibid*. Some sources attribute this quote to Plunket: C. Phillips, *Curran and His Contemporaries*, 4th edition (Edinburgh: William Blackwood, 1851), p. 473.

5   É. Hickey, *Irish Law and Lawyers in Modern Folk Tradition* (Dublin: Four Courts Press, 1999), pp. 75–82.

6   M. Cusack, *The Liberator: His Life and Times, Political and Social* (Kenmare: Kenmare Publications, 1850), vol. 1, p. 249.

7   A.N. May, *The Bar & the Old Bailey, 1750–1850* (Chapel Hill: North Carolina University Press, 2003), esp. pp. 202–37; J.H. Langbein, *The Origins of Adversary Criminal Trial* (Oxford: Oxford University Press, 2005).

8   J. McEldowney, 'Crown prosecutions in nineteenth-century Ireland', in D. Hay and F. Snyder (eds), *Policing and Prosecution in Britain 1750–1850* (Oxford: Clarendon Press, 1989), pp. 427–58.

9   S. Landsman, 'Rise of the contentious spirit: Adversary procedure in eighteenth-century England', *Cornell Law Review*, 74:3 (1990), 497–609; J. Beattie, 'Scales of justice: Defence counsels and the English criminal trial in the eighteenth and nineteenth centuries', *Law and History Review*, 9:2 (1991), 221–67.

10  D. Cairns, *Advocacy and the Making of the Adversarial Criminal Trial, 1800–1865* (Oxford: Clarendon Press, 1998).

11  J.C. Scott, *Domination and the Arts of Resistance: Hidden Transcripts* (New Haven: Yale University Press, 1990); R. Bauman, *Story, Performance and Event: Contextual Studies of Oral Narrative* (Cambridge: Cambridge University Press, 1986).

12  For the Scottish context see: D. Barrie and S. Broomhall, *Police Courts in Nineteenth-Century Scotland, Volume 1: Magistrates, Media and the Masses* (Farnham: Ashgate, 2014), pp. 363–413.

13  For further discussion see: N. Wolf, 'Language Change and the Evolution of Religion, Community, and Culture Ireland, 1800–1900' (PhD dissertation, University of Wisconsin, 2008), pp. 36–9; N.M. Wolf, *An Irish-Speaking Island: State, Religion, Community, and the Linguistic Landscape in Ireland, 1770–1870* (Madison: University of Wisconsin Press, 2014), pp. 83–110.

14  Wolf, *An Irish-Speaking Island*, p. 3; R. Hindley, *The Death of the Irish Language* (London: Routledge, 1990), p. 17.

15  M. Towsey, *Reading the Scottish Enlightenment: Books and Their Readers in Provincial Scotland, 1750–1820* (Leiden: Brill, 2010), pp. 238–42; D. Harrington, 'Remembering the body: Eighteenth-century elocution and the oral tradition', *Rhetorica*, 28:1 (2010), 67–95.

16  R. and M. Edgeworth, *An Essay on Irish Bulls* (New York: J. Swaine, 1803), p. 150.

17  Wolf, *An Irish-Speaking Island*, p. 3; L.N. Mhunghaile, 'The legal system in Ireland and the Irish language 1700–c. 1843', in M. Brown and S.P. Donlan (eds), *The Laws and Other Legalities of Ireland, 1689–1850* (Farnham: Ashgate, 2011), pp. 329–39.

18  T. Eagleton, *Heathcliff and the Great Hunger: Studies in Irish Culture* (London: Verso, 1995), p. 170.

19  For example, 'Special Commission', *Freeman's Journal* (3 February 1811) Waterford.

20  'Extraordinary and Horrible Case of Murder', *Carlow Morning Post* (18 April 1822) Cork.

21  For example, the policeman Sergeant Kennedy translated for the Dublin Police Court: 'Dublin Police', *Dublin Evening Packet and Correspondent* (6 September 1849) Dublin. Women do appear as translators but generally for deaf and dumb children who speak sign language: 'Roscommon Assize', *Dublin Observer* (8 March 1834) Roscommon. In this case the daughter was deaf and her mother translated into Irish, and another translator into English: 'Crown Court', *Wexford Independent* (4 March 1843) Wexford. See also: Mhunghaile, 'The legal system'.

22  'Inquest', *Connaught Telegraph* (16 January 1833) Mayo.

23  'County Criminal Court', *Southern Reporter and Cork Commercial Courier* (11 August 1840) Cork. See also: 'Galway Assizes', *Freeman's Journal* (23 August 1847) Galway.

24  'Ordinary and Horrible Case of Murder', *Carlow Morning Post* (18 April 1822) Cork.

25  'Cork Assizes – Rape', *Freeman's Journal* (8 April 1829) Cork; see also 'Cork Assizes', *Dublin Evening Post* (23 April 1829) Cork.

26  Other cases of a witness jailed for refusing to speak English: 'List of Convictions', *Connaught Telegraph* (30 July 1834) Mayo; 'Crown Court', *Ballina Advertiser* (6 August 1841) Mayo; see also 'Waterford County Summer Assizes', *Waterford Chronicle* (21 July 1838) Waterford.

27  'Ennis Assizes', *Southern Reporter and Cork Commercial Courier* (26 July 1825) Clare.

28  'Roscommon Assizes', *Wexford Conservative* (3 October 1832) Roscommon.

29  'Cork Assizes- Rape', *Freeman's Journal* (8 April 1829) Cork; See also 'Cork Assizes', *Dublin Evening Post* (23 April 1829) Cork.

30  'Record Court', *Connaught Journal* (3 December 1835) Dublin.

31  Wolf, *An Irish-Speaking Island*, p. 160.

32  'Tralee Quarter Sessions', *Dublin Morning Post* (28 October 1841) Kerry; 'Kilkenny Assizes', *Waterford Mail* (21 March 1835) Kilkenny.

33  'Dungarvan Petty Sessions', *Cork Examiner* (24 May 1844) Waterford.

34  Reprinted in 'Galway Petty Sessions', *Freeman's Journal* (21 August 1844) Galway.

35  For discussion of the *Galway Vindicator's* politics see: M.L. Legg, 'Introduction', *Ireland: Politics and Society through the Press, 1760–1922*. http://microformguides. gale.com/Data/Introductions/10110FM.htm, accessed 10 February 2015.

36  See also D. McCabe, 'Magistrates, peasants, and the Petty Sessions courts: Mayo 1823–50', *Cathair na Mart*, 5:1 (1985), 49.

37  'Common Pleas, Dublin', *Belfast Newsletter* (2 December 1834) Dublin.

38  For example, 'Roscrea Petty Sessions', *Kerry Evening Post* (10 June 1837) Tipperary; 'Police Office, Cork', *Kerry Evening Post* (3 June 1840) Cork.

39  See a number of examples in: K. Barclay, 'Singing and lower-class masculinity in the Dublin Magistrate's Court, 1800–1845', *Journal of Social History*, 47:3 (2014), 746–68.

40  'Dublin Police', *Belfast Newsletter* (26 December 1828) Dublin.

41  'Dublin Police', *Freeman's Journal* (30 April 1842) Dublin.

42  'Athy Petty Session', *Dublin Morning Register* (26 June 1830) Kildare.

43  S. Critchley, *On Humour* (London: Routledge, 2002); J. Boskin and J. Dorinson, 'Ethnic humour: Subversion and survival', *American Quarterly*, 37:1 (1985), 81–97;

K. Cowman, '"Doing Something Silly": The uses of humour by the Women's Social and Political Union, 1903–1914', *International Review of Social History*, 52 (2007), 259–74; M. 't Hart, 'Humour and social protest: An introduction', *International Review of Social History*, 52 (2007), 1–20 (and remainder of this special issue); J.C. Scott, *Weapons of the Weak: Everyday Forms of Peasant Resistance* (New Haven: Yale University Press, 1983), pp. 20 and 41; A. Simmonds, 'Rebellious bodies and subversive sniggers? Embodying women's humour and laughter in colonial Australia', *History Australia*, 6:2 (2009), 39.1–39.16.

44 M. Billig, *Laughter and Ridicule: Towards a Social Critique of Humour* (London: Sage, 2005), pp. 76 and 80; G. Campbell, *The Philosophy of Rhetoric*, 2 volumes (London: W. Strahan and T. Cadell, 1776), vol. 1, p. 81.

45 Billig, *Laughter and Ridicule*, p. 82.

46 J. Kelly, 'The oral tradition and literature in Ireland and Scotland: Popular culture in Robert Burns and Charles Maturin', *Journal of Irish and Scottish Studies*, 1:1 (2007), 71.

47 Beattie, 'Scales of justice'; Landsman, 'Rise of the contentious spirit'.

48 Billing, *Laughter and Ridicule*, p. 75.

49 W. Curran, *The Life of the Right Honourable John Philpot Curran, Later Master of the Rolls in Ireland* (New York: William H. Creagh, 1820), p. 69; Cairns, *Advocacy*, explores the moral dimensions of the cross.

50 R. Sheil, *Sketches of the Irish Bar*, ed. R. Shelton Mackenzie, 2 volumes (New York: Redfield, 1854), vol. 1, p. 36.

51 'Recorder's Court', *Clonmel Herald* (23 January 1828) Dublin.

52 K. Barclay, 'Manly magistrates and citizenship in an Irish town: Carlow, 1820–1840', in K. Cowman, N. Koefoed and Å.K. Sjögren (eds), *Gender in Urban Europe: Sites of Political Activity and Citizenship, 1750–1900* (London: Routledge, 2014), pp. 67–9; Landsman, 'Rise of the contentious spirit', 554, 556.

53 'Kerry Assizes', *Connaught Journal* (17 April 1826) Kerry.

54 R. McMahon, *Homicide in Pre-Famine and Famine Ireland* (Liverpool: Liverpool University Press, 2013), pp. 32–58, esp. p. 36.

55 J. Mongan, *A Report of the Trial of the Action in which Bartholomew McGarahan was the Plaintiff and the Rev Thomas Maguire was the Defendant* . . . (Dublin: Westley and Tyrrell, 1827), p. 64.

56 'Cork Special Commission', *Carlow Morning Post* (5 November 1829) Cork.

57 Hickey, *Irish Law*, pp. 75–82.

58 *Ibid.*

59 Cairns describes this as part of 'forensic morality', *Advocacy*, p. 154.

60 Barrie and Broomhall, *Police Courts, Volume 1*, p. 255.

61 'Galway Assizes', *Ballina Advertiser* (26 March 1841) Galway.

62 J. Kamensky, *Governing the Tongue: The Politics of Speech in Early New England* (Oxford: Oxford University Press, 1997), pp. 20–2; D. Clarke, *The Politics of Early Modern Women's Writing* (London: Routledge, 2013), pp. 25–30.

63 'Carlow Assizes', *Carlow Morning Post* (25 July 1822) Carlow; 'Killarney Petty Session', *Kerry Evening Post* (14 June 1837) Kerry; 'Limerick Assizes', *Ballina Impartial* (19 August 1833) Limerick.

64 'Carlow Assizes', *Carlow Morning Post* (25 July 1822) Carlow.

65 'Law Intelligence', *Carlow Morning Post* (22 May 1820) Dublin.

66 'Cork Assizes', *Carlow Morning Post* (31 Aug 1829) Cork. For a history of disability jokes see: S. Dickie, *Cruelty & Laughter: Forgotten Comic Literature and the Unsentimental Eighteenth Century* (Chicago: University of Chicago Press, 2011); A. Korhonen, 'Disability humour in English jestbooks of the sixteenth and seventeenth centuries', *Cultural History*, 3:1 (2014), 27–53.

67 K. Davison, 'Occasional politeness and gentleman's laughter in eighteenth-century England', *Historical Journal*, 57:4 (2014), 921–45.

68 L. Abrams, 'The taming of Highland masculinity: Inter-personal violence and shifting codes of manhood, c. 1760–1840', *Scottish Historical Review*, 92 (2013), 100–22; K. Harvey, 'The history of masculinity, circa 1650 to 1800', *Journal of British Studies*, 44 (2005), 296–311; J.A. Mangan and C. McKenzie, '"Duty unto Death" – the sacrificial warrior: English middle class masculinity and militarism in the age of the New Imperialism', *International Journal of the History of Sport*, 25:9 (2008), 1080–105.

69 M. Peltonen, *The Duel in Early Modern England: Civility, Politeness and Honour* (Cambridge: Cambridge University Press, 2003); K. Downing, 'The gentleman boxer: Boxing, manners and masculinity in eighteenth century England', *Men and Masculinities*, 12 (2010), 328–52.

70 J. Tosh, *A Man's Place: Masculinity and the Middle-Class Home in Victorian England* (New Haven: Yale University Press, 1999), pp. 111–12; J.A. Mangan and C. McKenzie, 'Privileged education, hunting and the making of martial masculinity', *International Journal of the History of Sport*, 25:9 (2008), 1106–31.

71 R.A. Nye, 'How the duel of honour protected civility and attenuated violence in Western Europe', in C. Strange, R. Cribb, and C.E. Forth (eds), *Honour, Violence and Emotions in History* (London: Bloomsbury, 2014), pp. 183–202.

72 R. Shoemaker, 'The taming of the duel: Masculinity, honour and ritual violence in London, 1660–1800', *Historical Journal*, 45:3 (2002), 525–45.

73 J. Kelly, *That Damn'd Thing Called 'Honour': Duelling in Ireland, 1570–1860* (Cork: Cork University Press, 1995).

74 M. Cohen, '"Manners" make the man: Politeness, chivalry, and the construction of masculinity, 1750–1830', *Journal of British Studies*, 44 (2005), 312–29; C. Kennedy, '"A Gallant Nation": Chivalric masculinity and Irish nationalism in the 1790s', in M. McCormack (ed.), *Public Men: Masculinity and Politics in Modern Britain* (Basingstoke: Palgrave Macmillan, 2007), pp. 73–92.

75 McMahon, *Homicide*, pp. 36–7; for more on the similarities between elite and non-elite violence see: R. Carr, *Gender and Enlightenment Culture in Eighteenth-Century Scotland* (Edinburgh: Edinburgh University Press), pp. 142–74.

76 'Duelling', *Irish Examiner* (7 June 1843).

77 Kelly, *That Damn'd Thing*; a number of contemporary reports discuss duelling as something more prolific in a past age, see, for example: 'Extraordinary Duelling', *Dublin Evening Packet and Correspondent* (20 March 1834); 'Duelling in Ireland', *Connaught Journal* (12 May 1825).

78 Kelly, *That Damn'd Thing*, p. 213.

79 Cairns, *Advocacy*.

80 P.G. Copley, *The Rhetoric of Sensibility in Eighteenth-Century Culture* (Cambridge: Cambridge University Press, 2005).

81  Quoted in S. Fitzmaurice, 'Changes in the meanings of *politeness* in eighteenth-century England: Discourse analysis and historical evidence', in J. Culpeper and D.Z. Kádár (eds), *Historical (Im)politeness* (Bern: Peter Lang, 2010), p. 101.

82  'Carlow Assizes', *Carlow Morning Post* (30 March 1829) Carlow.

83  Barclay, 'Manly magistrates'.

84  'Carlow Petty Session', *Carlow Sentinel* (18 August 1837) Carlow.

85  S. Banks, 'Dangerous friends: The second and the later English duel', *Journal for Eighteenth-Century Studies*, 32:1 (2009), 87–106; Cohen, '"Manners" make the man'. A case where this did escalate further between Carlow's magistrates can be found at 'Court of Queen's Bench', *Carlow Sentinel* (11 November 1837) Carlow.

86  'Mayo Assizes', *Belfast Newsletter* (2 August 1842) Mayo.

87  'Petit Session Carlow Extraordinary Proceedings', *Carlow Morning Post* (15 April 1830) Carlow.

88  D.A. Kerr, *A Nation of Beggars? Priests, People, and Politics in Famine Ireland, 1846–1852* (Oxford: Clarendon Press, 1994), p. 78.

89  'College-Street Police Office', *Freemans Journal* (9 April 1832) Dublin; see also 'Important Investigation', *Carlow Sentinel* (11 November 1837) Carlow.

90  'Carlow Petty Sessions', *Carlow Morning Post* (1 October 1832) Carlow; 'Administration of Justice', *Carlow Morning Post* (26 November 1832) Carlow.

91  Most of the commentary on duelling focuses on anti-duelling: D. Andrews, *Aristocratic Vice: The Attack on Duelling, Suicide, Adultery, and Gambling in Eighteenth-Century England* (New Haven: Yale University Press, 2013); a notable exception is: Peltonen, *The Duel.*

92  'Castlebar Petty Sessions', *Freemans Journal* (2 November 1842) Mayo.

93  'Dungarvan Petty Session', *Wexford Independent* (7 August 1841) Waterford.

94  A. Çırakman, *From the 'Terror of the World' to the 'Sick Man of Europe: European Images of Ottoman Empire and Society from the Sixteenth to Nineteenth* (New York: Peter Lang, 2002), p. 190.

95  'Dungarvan Petty Sessions', *Waterford Mail* (9 December 1840) Waterford.

96  'Dungarvan Petty Sessions', *Cork Examiner* (15 October 1845) Waterford; 'Dungarvan', *Freeman's Journal* (7 August 1847) Waterford.

97  'County Waterford Election', *Waterford Chronicle* (10 October 1829) Waterford.

98  'Dungarvan Petty Sessions', *Southern Reporter and Cork Commercial Courier* (22 October 1842) Waterford; 'Dungarvan Petty Sessions', *Cork Examiner* (24 May 1844) Waterford.

99  'Dungarvan Petty Sessions', *Cork Examiner* (24 May 1844) Waterford; 'Dungarvan Petty Sessions', *Cork Examiner* (15 October 1845) Waterford; The National Archives, Kew, HO 45/1134, Ten letters relating to Dr Fitzgerald, Stipendiary Magistrate of Dungarvan, 10 June–27 October 1845; Mr O'Connell, 'Dr Fitzgerald', Hansard April 1846, Common Sittings, *House of Commons Debate 30 April 1846, vol. 85, cc1330-3.*

100 'Medical Magistrates – Dr Fitzgerald', *Cork Examiner* (11 December 1846).

101 'Dungarvan Petty Sessions', *Cork Examiner* (15 October 1845) Waterford.

102 *Ibid.*

# 6

## Storytelling: 'quoting the poet'

### LOVE BEHIND A TOMB STONE

Cork Police Office. – Judy Sullivan, an antient dame, was indicted for inflicting divers blows on the body of Miss Juliet Donnelly, tearing her bonnet, and dishevelling her auburn dresses.

Mr J.J. O'Brien, agent for the prosecutrix, requested the gentle Juliet to stand at the end of the table and take off her glove!

Judy (casting a scornful glance at her) – Cock you up with gloves, you circumwater – little your granny thought that one of her breed would leather her skin.

Juliet – Oh! Gentlemen, I'll surely faint if you let her at me.

Mr O'Brien desired the prosecutrix, after being sworn, to acquaint the bench with the facts of the case.

Juliet – On Tuesday evening, your honours, I was walking through Shandon church-yard, when Mrs Sullivan came up, and without saying 'by your leave' or any other decent apology, pulled my new Dunstable bonnet off, tore the hair out of my head, and violated me most shockingly.

Judy (shaking her clenched fist at the prosecutrix) – Tell the gentlemen, you frisky diskey, how you sawduced my child.

Juliet – Oh! horrible incinyvation! me to seduce a man? (A laugh.)

Judy – Och! *movrone* [my sorrow], 'tis you wouldn't turn your back to it. On the varty o' my oat, your reverences, she swaduced him, for they always used to be always speechaficating like play-actors.

Juliet – (curtsying) – 'Tis all foul and malicious, your honours.

Judy – Didn't I often warn you not to be coming round him.

Juliet – Take care of my karacter, ma-am.

Judy – Wisha you haven't much o' that same to take care of. Sure you're well known to be a swaducer of youth and a destroyer of ould age – (great laughter).

Juliet – I'll bring the law against you for my karacter.

Judy: Yerra, faith my dear, twasn't I stole it, for your trepanning all the *gorsoons* in the parish, you rattrap. (Shouts of laughter).

Mr O'Brien: If that's the fact, it's a mantrap she should be called. (Laughter).

Judy (to Mr. O'B.): *You're* better take care and not get into her trap. (Immoderate laughter.)

Judy (to the prosecutrix): Tell the gentlemen what you and he wer doing behind the tomb-stone?

Mr O'Brien: They were performing the parts of Romeo and Juliet at the tomb of the Capulets.

Judy (to the prosecutrix): On the varty of your oat, weren't you questering?

Juliet: No indeed, your honours, I was only humming to myself, 'Fly not yet, tis just the hour'.

Mr O'Brien: And you beat time on her head?

Judy. You may swear to that. Now, your Reverences, I'll tell you the whole of it.

Juliet: 'Tis all lies she's going to tell your honours.

Judy (making towards the prosecutrix in a fighting attitude): Pursuing to you, you vermint, why would you give the mother o'childer the lie.

Mr. O'Brien called on the police to protect his client from the enraged Judy, when one of them stood between her and the prosecutrix.

Judy: Well, your reverences, I'll be as cool as pickled cabbage. You see how it is this lady with her bonnets and boots, is always running away with the honest women's children, and amongst the rest she puts her Judas's eyes upon my poor *stramelogue* of a Bill, and whipping him off clear and clane. Oh! The deil a good I could get o' him since she stuffed his head with what she calls tragedy! Well ses I to myself, I'll watch his doxy; so well becomes me, when he went out last Tuesday night, I makes after him, and who should he meet but Mis Donnelly. Well up with her to him in a jiffy, and what does she do; but clap her under his arm, as if he was her own, and bises him up to the church yard. Well you sees as how I follows them always, and there she was deludin' him, and 'twas with a great deal ago I keeps my hands from her; but I had the patience of fifty women. Well they planks themselves down behind a tomb-stone, while I was shaking and shivering with the fright, as myself was afred o' the good people in such a place; but no matter about that; bise-by they begins to querister, and she soon begins with all the fine talk in the world; but when I heard her asking him did he love her, fegs I couldn't hould my breath any longer, and I puts my hand over the tome stone and pulls the bonnet off her –

Juliet (interrupting) – Me to ask him did he love me! – No indeed, your honours, I was only reciting Shakspear. What I said was:

> 'O, gentle Romeo!
> If thou dost love me, pronounce it faithfully.'

(a laugh).

Judy (interrupting) – There now for you, did you ever hear more for that? See, she can't deny it. Romy is a pet name she calls Bill, your honours.

Mr. O'Brien: Don't mind the name, for, 'a rose by any other name would smell as sweet,' but you acknowledge having beaten her.

Judy: Oh, then I do: I gave her two or three wherets o' my fist, and both ran away before I could catch em, and the next morning my poor child listed with the Queen and went off to Spain. [Here Judy melted into tears.]

Mr. O'Brien: How old was the child?

Judy: Nineteen, Sir.

Mr. O'Brien: A pretty nursling indeed.

Juliet (pouting): I declare, gentlemen, 'twas she was the cause of his going away.

The Bench now stopped the case, telling the forsaken Juliet that she had acted wrong in the first instance, by keeping an acquaintance with the young man which his mother forbid; but at the same time, it was *not* justification of the assault, and they would therefore fine Judy in the amount of the costs.

Judy immediately paid the money and the parties left the office.

*Connaught Journal*, 17 December 1835

In December 1835, when Juliet brought Judy before the Cork magistrates for assault, Shakespeare's *Romeo and Juliet* was being performed in Dublin for theatre audiences. Shakespeare was well known across social groups in Ireland, regularly alluded to in court cases.[1] A lawyer, Mr O'Brien, initially raised its relevance for these star-crossed lovers, but Juliet knew it well enough to (mis)quote the play, and apparently used it when murmuring sweet nothings to her lover. She made other literary allusions when making her case. 'Fly not yet, tis just the hour' was a song by the poet Thomas Moore, published in his *Irish Melodies* in 1808. It was a ribald tale about the romance of courting by moonlight: "Twas but to bless these hours of shade/ That beauty and the moon were made/ 'Tis then their soft attractions glowing/ Set the tides and goblets flowing'.[2] Whilst the glories of Shakespeare and Moore were apparently lost on Judy, she too wielded wider culture, referencing the biblical story of Judas, as well as popular folk belief around ghosts in graveyards. After the Cork magistrates made their judgment, a court journalist transformed these events into an amusing tale of its own and published it in a local paper.

An effective legal argument typically depended upon the ability of legal actors, particularly lawyers, to take disparate evidences and to construct them into a coherent narrative that demonstrated a desired outcome – whether guilt, innocence or their version of 'truth'.[3] As a form of storytelling, constructing a case was a performative act, one that required skill, drew on props and, like all forms of good literature, referenced other texts in its construction. The importance of popular culture – written literature, folktales, song or more recently radio and TV – in providing a framework for interpreting experience and a structure for narrating identity is increasingly acknowledged.[4] Within hierarchical oral cultures, storytelling has also been implicated in negotiating power relationships, offering subalterns a language to speak the unspeakable, to complain about injustice, or to discuss abuse.[5] Cultures with a strong storytelling tradition are often sensitive to the importance of analogies and tales in shaping wider social relationships. Such messages did not go unheeded.[6] This chapter explores how men used wider popular culture in constructing their narratives, asking what their choices say about identity construction. It then looks at storytelling as a tool for lower-order men to negotiate power relationships.

Thus far, this book has highlighted how men from different social groups clashed, where disjunctures in models of manliness and national identity were marked. Storytelling, with its allusions to 'high' and 'low' culture, as well as distinctions between the tales of the (implicitly rural) 'folk' and the literature of classes formed through urbanity and cosmo-politanism, has until recently been viewed as a key site where social difference can be found.[7] Accounts that explore the poor's engagement with 'high' culture have often struggled with the relationship between culture and class identity.[8] Within this context, lower-order writers were, for some historians, 'rather untypical members of the working class';[9] they suffered from the 'suspicion ... that they were working in self rather than collective interest', as if there was a single collective or class interest to work for.[10] Such histories deny the complex way that people construct identity, marked in the growing use of 'hybridity' to understand identities that cross social groups.[11] A performative reading of class identity enables that hybridity to be acknowledged. Class identity is not a static construct for individuals to step beyond, but produced through behaviour, clothing, displays of education and learning, accent and the use of the physical body. It could be fashioned against the desire of the performer, seeking to pass as something else, or could be successful and accepted as 'authentic'. The uses of literacy, orality and literature therefore do not create class, but were tools in its construction. When used in the performance of peasant identities, Shakespeare became peasant literature.

### Stories within stories: the uses of popular culture

Whilst not denying the multiple literatures that existed, storytelling was prized across social groups in Ireland, a key dimension of sociability.[12] The novelist and journalist, Gerald Griffin (1803–1840), a son of a brewer, even located storytelling in the courthouse. The collection of folktales, *Talis Qualis, or, Tales of the Jury Room* (1842), was based on the premise that a jury, unable to come to a verdict, were locked in overnight and to pass the time chose to each tell a story or forfeit a shilling.[13] As discussed in Chapter 1, whilst petty juries were socially mixed, they had to hold at least £10 of property.[14] Griffin described them as 'gentlemen' and their polite interactions supported this designation.[15] Whilst intended as an amusing scenario, Griffin clearly did not believe that it was ridiculous for such men to know a wide array of Irish tales, nor felt that this would detract from the book's value for its audience.[16] As Andy Woods has recently noted, there is no more an autonomous 'Little Tradition', than a 'Grand Tradition' that has gone untouched from below.[17]

Just as the elites engaged with traditional folk culture, so the poor had access to a wide range of literatures. Living in large towns, particularly Dublin, increased the opportunities for engagement with a wide range of material, especially with the rise of circulating and subscription libraries, and coffee houses (although, given the significant rural to urban migration of the period, it is not easy to disaggregate the impact of living rurally on engaging with popular literatures). Schools were important sites for introducing children to literature. In 1825, of the 401 books that were being used in schools in Galway, Donegal, Kerry and Kildare, 301 were 'works of entertainment, histories, tales etc', including *Roderick Random* and cheap chapbook literature.[18] Like elsewhere in Britain, the lower orders showed an affinity with 'the English classics' – Milton, Shakespeare, Byron, Dickens – a popularity that may have stemmed from their availability in abridged and cheaply available forms.[19] If commentary in court can be used as a measure of popularity, Thomas Moore was widely known.[20] Printed works in Irish were still rare, although a growing specialist and mostly middle-class market was developing.[21] Translations of Irish tales were more widely available, whilst a flourishing oral culture remained.[22] All these sources were drawn on in courtrooms in the production of legal narratives, the construction of identity and negotiations of power.

The most common references to wider literature in court reporting were not by those on the stand, but by journalists. Providing analogies from well-known tales, either 'the classics' or more ephemeral works, to juxtapose with ongoing cases, or quoting literature to describe the character or appearance of those in court, were commonplace: 'A young man, who gave his name as Edmund Burke, but whose appearance, notwithstanding, was neither "sublime nor beautiful" . . .'.[23] Whilst typically placed in quotation marks, such references were rarely explained, relying on an audience that had a broad general knowledge of mainstream literatures and authors and who commonly memorised significant passages. They were designed to influence the public's interpretation of events. Describing a case as 'A Gay Gallant Lothario' or a 'Mrs Caudle Business' signified that they should be read as humorous tales through their association with Nicolas Rowe's or Douglas Jerrold's comic writing.[24] They spoke to the character of those represented, where a vociferous wife could be transformed into the scolding nag of fiction, as well as the seriousness of the case (in the eyes of the journalist, if not the protagonists). If not informing the dynamics of the case described, such news reports contributed to the production of interpretative narratives for similar cases and characters of the period.

Lawyers and judges used wider culture to shape their accounts for the jury and gallery. Charles Phillips littered his speeches with references to literature, particularly sentimental poetry. Robert Burns' *The*

*Cotter's Saturday Night* was a particular favourite, found in *Guthrie v. Sterne* (1815), *Connaghton v. Dillon* (1816) and *Brown v. Blake* (1817). An analysis of four of his most reprinted speeches saw William Shakespeare, John Milton and Thomas Moore appear twice each, and he also referred to James Thompson, James Beattie, Oliver Goldsmith, Samuel Butler, Charles Dibden, Alexander Pope and Samuel Rogers.[25] Such quotes added dramatic emphasis to his speeches, sometimes relying on the emotional tenor of the poem to add depth to his oratory, at others providing comic relief.

Not all his quotes were accurate; on occasion, this may have been misremembering but it could be a deliberate choice, such as when he replaced the names of literary characters with those of the people at trial or when he changed words for emphasis.[26] Phillips expected others in court, but especially the jury, to be familiar with his quotations that were generally given without the source. The impact of a misquotation, for example, relied on the audience's appreciation of the 'mistake': 'I see by your smiling, Gentlemen, that you correct my error'.[27] As a result, his literary choices were highlighted and he created a sympathetic camaraderie between men of a similar background through recognition of their common education and shared appreciation of the 'joke'.

Lower-order men were not excluded from such interactions, particularly those who had access to the literary culture being referenced. Unsurprisingly given literacy patterns, references to core 'classic' texts were more common amongst artisans and tradesmen.[28] Just as middle-class men like Phillips used quotations from wider literature to speak to their social class, education and cosmopolitanism, lower-order men drew on an array of texts to speak to their identities. References to Shakespeare or Milton, and even occasionally works in Greek or Latin, demonstrated that they were literate, widely read and knowledgeable about the culture they shared with their elite brethren.[29] In 1840, Jeremiah O'Grady, a fiddler with a 'splendid round hand' (possibly a clerk), quoted Dryden's *Absalom and Achitophel:* 'Stiff in opinion, always in the wrong/ Everything by starts, and nothing long!', during a dispute with the mother of the woman he was courting.[30] More esoterically a few years later, Sub-Constable Duncan, when testifying against a drunken Anne Powers, noted: 'What man on earth has power or skill/ To change the torrent of a woman's will? For if she *will*, she *will*, you may depend on't/ And if she *won't*, she *won't*, and there's an end on't'.[31] These lines were attributed to a carving on a tree in Canterbury, commonly thought to be a medieval relic, and found within several publications of the period.[32]

Jemmy Smith, a hedge-school teacher in Clontarf, who abandoned his sweetheart Eliza for another called Honor, tried to explain his infidelity by quoting the poet Richard Lovelace: 'This inconstancy is such/ As you, too, should adore; I could not love thee, dear, so much,/ Loved I not *Honor* more'.[33] More dramatically, the actor playing *Othello* in a Dublin 'three-penny theatre' in 1838 quoted the play repeatedly when before the magistrates for being drunk and disorderly. Still in costume, including black paint, John Browne found lines within the tale that enabled him to tell his story.[34] In all these cases, the quotations demonstrated the speaker's cultural knowledge, and spoke to the narrative being told, using fiction to shape fact.[35] Quotations that insulted unruly women undermined female testimony and implied that their words were trivial and unreasonable, whilst allowing men to sidestep accusations of ungallantry. In a case of art meets life, Browne's excuse for his drunken antics was that his beloved, like Desdemona, had jilted him. Through inter-textual engagements, fiction enabled men to explain their experiences through a sympathetic lens or to complicate a narrative by suggesting alternative readings.

Careful selection of the 'right' author could similarly provide messages to a knowing public. Thomas Moore was popular as he was closely associated with Irish national identity and men used his, often quite innocent, words to make political claims without the need to risk charges of sedition.[36] Lord Byron, a close friend of Moore's, sharp critic of British foreign policy, political radical and known lady's man, was widely quoted, especially in the 1840s. The shoemaker, James Barrett, referenced *Don Juan* when humorously describing how he lost his job for admiring a lady's ankle: 'you know what Byron says about ankles'.[37] Patrick Burns, when charged with stealing an ass and car, denied his guilt and quoted Byron: 'The world is a bundle of hay,/ Mankind are the asses that pull;/ Each tugs it a different way,/ But the greatest of all is John Bull'.[38] This quote originally appeared in a letter from Byron to Thomas Moore, which the latter published in 1830 after Byron's death.[39] It was well known in Ireland, and also used by Gerald Griffin in his novel, *The Collegians* (1829, a story that was based on an Irish murder trial). The poet Timothy Casey rewrote Byron's *Maid of Athens, Ere We Part*, to immortalise the romance of Constable 184B and Bridget M.: 'Sweet policeman, ere we part,/ Give, oh! Give me back my heart;/ Soon the Inspector will be here –/ Soon he'll rob me of my dear,/ Ere upon your beat you go/ *Zoe mou sas agapo*'.[40] Casey helpfully translated the Greek for the magistrate, who grumpily replied: 'I was aware, Mr Casey, that such was the fact, before I had the honour of your acquaintance', quickly trying to restore his own cultural capital.

Like working-class men in other parts of Europe, referencing wider literature allowed speakers, in the words of an astute Italian prisoner of war, 'to identify himself with the author'.[41] Such men located themselves alongside Byron, as renowned lovers, infamous political radicals or esteemed poets. At times, they may have wished to draw on all three identifications.[42] It allowed them to make claims on the status that Byron held within Irish and British society, to shore up their reputations not only as well read and worldly, even gentlemanly, but as slightly, but not too, disrespectable, talented and worthy of admiration. By drawing on a wide range of authors, they shaped identities that were outward-looking, tying Irishness into British but also European and global identities. It was a claim to the cosmopolitanism that polite culture reified as a marker of refinement and learning and the ability of not just Irishmen, but working-class Irishmen, to participate in the 'civilisation' of the British Empire.[43]

It was also a strategy that resonated with an older Irish tradition. Identifying with poets tied men into a widely admired bardic tradition. Irish poetry and song was renowned at home and internationally, often viewed as Ireland's only redeeming feature by its colonisers.[44] Poetic and musical ability was used by men as a marker of status, as well as a source of income. Lesser poets were accused of being 'imposters', taking a rank to which they were not entitled. It was associated with 'genius', 'long-life' (like Homer surviving for generations), but also poverty and disability.[45] Ballad singers and street poets regularly appeared in court, particularly in Dublin. The more famous, such as Zozimus or Casey, were arrested disturbing the peace or blocking roads during their live performances. They performed for the watching gallery and the journalist who provided free advertising. These were often astute displays that provided poets opportunity to publicise their political opinions; at other times, they were opportunities to demonstrate creativity and play, adapting lyrics to circumstances.[46] The brogue-maker and poet Michael Mackey, also known as Pizarro, concluded proceedings after he was fined 1s, or a week in jail, for assault in 1841:

> Oh ye great Gods, on high Olympus thron'd,/ What crime of mine has been left unatoned;/ What awkward Bumpkin has my brogues misfitted;/ What Blousalinda has my talk outwitted,/ That I should be condemned without appale,/ To pay a shilling or go to jail. – (Great laughter.)[47]

It was not just professional poets that recited verse in court.[48] Several artisans gave their whole testimony in rhyme, especially in the

1840s. A harness-maker, Daniel Connor from Rathdowney, stated his case in 1845:

> Puissant sirs, I'm much in fault, I own,
> And for the same I'm willing to atone;
> But let me state my case, and then admit
> If my accusers, there, have not thought fit,
> To daub too high – 'Tis said the Old Boy's phiz
> Is painted far more hideous than it is.
> I asked my 'uncle' Moses there to 'stand
> The grin,' in tones superlatively bland,
> But he demurr'd; being anxious for a 'spree,'
> And somewhat 'in the wind,' I just made free
> To touch his 'noddle'; then his servant girl
> Rush'd in, and placed my 'peepers' in dire peril,
> I shy'd her from me – curs'd her ugly mug,
> While, all the time, she box'd by dexter lug . . ..[49]

His rhyme continued for nineteen more lines whilst he explained the context for the assault. He was fined £1 or a month's imprisonment. A few years earlier, Tipperary-man, Andrew Leary introduced himself thus:

> The name that I'm called is Andrew Leary,
> I'm thirty-first cousin to one Paddy Carey;
> That's him you so often have heard of in song,
> With great brawny shoulders and thick legs so strong.
> He was brisk as a bee, and light as a fairy.
> And he broke all the hearts of the girls in Tip'rary
> (roars of laughter).[50]

When asked if he was a poet, he replied 'No, Sir, but I'm troubled with an old rhyming devil/ And begar, he sometimes treats me mighty uncivil'. He gave every response to the magistrate's questions in rhyme, before being committed to the Bridewell for public disorder.

'Rhyming men' formed a subculture of lower-order Irish masculinity that located itself in the shadow of the bardic tradition. Their carnivalesque routines suggest they took pleasure in the opportunity to perform and the cultural capital that they gained from displaying their abilities, whilst the disruption they created acted as a form of resistance to court structures. As they typically rhymed in English and drew on English-language literatures (such as Byron or the ballad of Paddy Carey, which was reprinted across the United Kingdom), this was not an insular Irish masculinity, but one which claimed its right to compete on an international stage, something enabled by the hybrid nature of the Irish-British court and its representation in the national press.[51] Moreover, by locating such masculinities as cosmopolitan and civilised, these men resisted models of Irishness – as poor, uncivilised – that reduced their character for the watching public, and embraced the 'character' associated with the middle-class men who personified the law.

'High' culture sat alongside and overlapped with tales and allusions drawn from oral culture. Singing was often remarked on, where music could be used to complicate the meaning of sentencing or official legal narratives.[52] Jokes often drew on known patterns and schema from a shared joke-telling tradition, whilst still offering opportunity for innovation and adaption.[53] Unlike quoting verse or even passages of texts, the formal word order in oral stories could be flexible, allowing the storyteller to provide their own flourishes and emphasis.[54] References to such stories in court did not rely on rote memorisation, but familiarity with a repertoire that could be drawn on at appropriate moments. The implications of Mathew Fowlew's blithe remark in 1837 that, '"Civility costs nothing", Peter O'Sullivan, the Kerryman, said, when he walked fifteen miles in a sthrange funeral', relied on the listener knowing that this was a known epigram, not a true story.[55] The listener was expected to tie this remark to well-known tales of people that went to absurd lengths for the sake of civility and to recognise that the 'common truth' that 'civility costs nothing' was perhaps not as accurate as first seemed.

Whilst folktales could be used like other literatures as a resource to demonstrate cultural background and education, to support or complicate a story, to speak the unspeakable, or to negotiate social relationships, they also underpinned a significant part of the belief structure of some parts of the Irish community.[56] As a general rule (and there were exceptions), men with middle-class or elite educations, whilst typically having a strong faith in God, were sceptical that supernatural creatures intervened in daily life. They treated references to fairies or similar creatures as fictional tales, entertaining but not literally true, and were dismissive of those who claimed otherwise. The lower orders too did not regularly confess to believing in fairies as social actors, although fairy tales were used as metaphors to explain events and hinting that a person was a fairy was used to undermine character (the extent to which the listener should take this literally is often unclear). As today, people partook in superstitious behaviours (such as Judy's anxiety about entering a graveyard) without wholeheartedly embracing the supernatural. Ghosts, fairies and other magical beings, however, were not always imaginary, complicating how such stories were interpreted in court. Importantly, fairy stories provided a key moment of disequilibrium for courtroom power dynamics as professional legal men and journalists, who generally did not believe in fairies, engaged with people who took such beliefs seriously. The telling of tales about fairies became a site where folk culture not only intervened in legal space, but forced the legal system to work within its cultural imagination.

Across the period, cases that arose due to belief in fairy magic came before the court. Several 'fairy frauds' occurred across the 1820s to 1840s.[57] In these cases, individuals who claimed to be fairies demanded goods from people, either in exchange for a benefit or to ensure the safety of the victim, their family or property. In 1835, Ellen English, a fairy, promised two Limerick city women '2½ stone of gold' if they paid her 1s 4d a week.[58] She never paid and they complained. Ellen claimed that if given a further month, she would fulfill her promise. She also informed the bench that 'it was safer for them not to meddle with her'. 'This caution, however, was disregarded', remarked the reporter. In 1830, Mary Bourke informed the people of Castlebar that she had been abducted by fairies and held for seven years, during which time she learned several skills.[59] In return for their hospitality, she promised one family that she would return their son who had been lost in a storm, but after several weeks (during which time they ate no eggs or butter to provide a feast for the lost son), they grew suspicious and she was arrested. Whilst the court personnel treated these cases as acts of fraud, they nonetheless had to work with a community for whom such claims were meaningful. They had to make determinations of sanity in several cases where people's actions were motivated by fairy belief and come to verdicts in murder trials and inquests, where people were killed because they were believed to be fairies.[60]

Fairy belief was particularly associated with women, so that men who articulated such convictions were subject to ridicule. Asking men if they believed in fairies was regularly used to undermine character by defence lawyers.[61] Men were often grudging witnesses to fairy magic. Martin Heston testified against Mary Bourke 'with great reluctance'. When asked why he believed her, he answered, 'Faith, the people wanted to give her a fair trial', distancing himself from the situation.[62] The Pallasgrean Petty Session found its male witnesses reluctant to discuss a fairy army that was reported marching through the countryside in 1838.[63] Mr Bourke, whose title is suggestive of his class, admitted that he saw 'a great number of people and horses going from the Lenfield side of the hill towards Pallas', but when asked, 'Were they living people?', responded, 'I don't know'. Requested to elaborate, he again replied: 'I do not know; I cannot say what they were'. Bourke was unwilling to name what he saw as fairies, but equally averse to providing a more 'rational' explanation. A second witness, Morty Hayes, heard rumours: 'I believe they were – *fairies* – immense laughter'. When asked on his oath whether he believed in fairies, he answered, 'I do (renewed laughter)'. Morty was more confident, but even he did not confess to seeing fairies. The bench decided that these 'reports' were simply rumours to 'make out this district is in a disturbed state', but thought it best to 'be on the alert'. Female witnesses were presented as more gullible. Catherine Mouldowney, a victim of a fairy fraudster in 1844, 'was in a very nervous state, burst into tears' when placed on the stand. The barrister told her 'not to be frightened' as there were no 'good people' in court (a pun that amused the gallery).[64]

There were a few men who actively associated themselves with fairy magic. Edmund Curran summoned Mr Edward Kennedy for nine shillings for treating his sick horse.[65] Curran explained that as he was the 'seventh son of his father', he was endowed with a 'peculiar faculty of curing all diseases'. He was also able to tell fortunes having been granted this gift by the 'good people' after having performed a series of rituals (which he elaborated on) at a rath (ringfort). Whilst he told his tale, 'the court became convulsed with laughter, and the magistrates, not wishing to hear any more of his miraculous powers stopped him'. Kennedy's defence was that the cure had not worked. As Curran could not adequately describe his medical treatment, he was refused payment. The court was sceptical – laughing at his ridiculous explanation for his treatment plan – but the magistracy did not immediately dismiss the case. They heard from Kennedy, the farrier that took over treatment, and asked Curran to detail his remedy. Had Curran provided a 'reasonable' course of action, he may have been entitled to his payment.

The fairy stories told in court could be more than tales used to negotiate meaning or which provided a vocabulary for the subaltern to speak the unspeakable.[66] At times, they represented the meeting of two belief structures that were incompatible yet had to cooperate. Those that lived with fairies were typically aware that by bringing this world into the courtroom, they would be open to ridicule. Many men recognised that acknowledging such beliefs undermined their masculinity, character and possibly even claims to sanity.[67] Yet, as fairy belief acted as motivation for action and an explanation for things seen, some people had little choice but to tell fairy stories to an unsympathetic audience. They often showed a resilience to laughter, affirming their beliefs despite the treatment they would receive. Men like Edmund Curran built their identities and careers around fairy magic and had to perform their conviction. For such men, a belief in fairies affirmed their masculinity. Mastering a people who were notoriously cunning and dangerous suggested intelligence, wit and courage (if with a modicum of folly). The ability to use fairy magic to cure disease or bring wealth made them an asset to their communities.[68] They were a reminder not only of the multiple modes of masculinity that existed across Ireland, but that parts of the community understood the world to operate very differently from the logic of the court. Fairy belief required the court to provide a justice which both denied the 'truth' that many witnesses offered whilst acknowledging there was injustice to be righted.

The court personnel and much of the gallery laughed at such tales. In the more serious cases, news reports condemned the 'unenlightened . . . peasantry', where there was 'a body of persons so dead to every sense of religion, so sunk in the depths of the grossest superstition, so devoid of the commonest feelings of humanity'.[69] Yet, the legal system also had to provide justice to this group, attempting to find the 'rational' within them. Fairies became frauds and swindlers; people who used fairy medicine became quack doctors; and those that caused harm when performing fairy rituals became criminals, murderers or the insane. At times, lawyers even provided belief in fairies as a rationalisation for lower-order behaviours that they otherwise found inexplicable.[70] The 'reasonable' explanation of the court became the dominant and legitimate interpretation of events, but for this to happen, court officials had to engage with fairy belief and to adapt their system to the needs of the population. Whilst mainstream popular culture complemented a legal system that relied on stories, providing men opportunities to negotiate the meaning of events, fairy stories provided a point of disjuncture, which required the law to acknowledge its alterity for some parts of the Irish population. Such storytelling provided an opportunity for fairy-believing communities to be heard in their own words.

### Performing the story

> Please your worship, said Mrs. Murphy here I am, I am an Orangewoman and a Brunswicker since I was born. All belonging to me are orangemen and orangewomen, and I'll stick to the Brunswickers as long as I live.
>
> The magistrate requested her to come to the charge.
>
> Mrs. Murphy. – I'll come to it in time enough, I have a son an Orangeman and another lad of mine died in the good old cause. Now, your worship, this is Mrs. Mooney, who is quite a different sort of woman, she's an Emancipator.

Magistrate. – What has this to do with the assault.
Everything in the world, said Mrs. Murphy.
Magistrate. – Indeed.[71]

As well as using popular culture to intervene in the production of legal narratives, individuals told stories of their lives and experiences. The opportunities for ordinary people to do this was limited. In the higher courts, their speech was often restricted to answering questions on the stand, a format that encouraged short replies. Defendants in criminal cases were prohibited from testifying, although they could put questions to witnesses.[72] The lower courts, where procedure was less formal, provided more occasion for storytelling, although it required a sympathetic magistrate: 'The magistrate here reminded the vocalist of the charge brought against him and to confine himself to it.'[73] This could be difficult for those that were accustomed to articulating their experience in story form.

Several people, male and female, persisted in giving evidence as an extended narrative, despite the objections of the judiciary. Mrs Murphy provided a historical backdrop of the politico-religious differences between her family and that of Mrs Mooney, before speaking to the assault that brought her to court in 1828. For her, if not the magistrate, the conflict could not be understood without that background. Another complainant, named only as Ruan, began his tale in 1840: 'that man at the bar and myself are from the county Kerry; we lodged in the same house in town here, and I stood to him while I had a penny; but although he was a man of great learning, he is a noted drunkard and a villain, and no money could stand him', before being interrupted by the magistrate: 'We don't want the history of the man's life. Come to the present charge against him'.[74] For those accustomed to telling their lives as stories, the issue that brought them to court could not be extracted from the social context and relationships that gave it meaning. In contrast, the magistracy was interested in 'the charge', the legal complaint, from which they could determine what contextual information was needed to ensure justice. Moreover, as they repeatedly told defendants, a compelling story of misconduct by the victim 'was *not* justification' for illegal activity by those wronged.[75]

Numerous lower-order men, and particularly women, who appeared before the court were noted for their 'volubility', something also identified in the Irish petitioning style.[76] Patrick Rogers gave his testimony with 'astonishing flippancy, volubility, and rapidity of utterance' in 1828.[77] Laurence Crolly stated his 1845 case in a 'very voluble style'; Margaret McCabe gave hers in 1836 with 'a wonderful volubility of tongue and manner'.[78] It was speech described as excessive, sometimes exuberantly so. When 'Paddy', an army veteran, was charged with bigamy in 1832, he frustrated the magistrate with his verbosity.[79]

> Magistrate – This is a terrible charge against a good man.
> Paddy (bowing) – Thank your honour for doing me justice. I was faith always sure enough a good man, and as to women, though I am brought to the bar, I always did them justice (much laughter).
> Magistrate – Sir, we don't want any of your long speeches: we are tired of long speeches; therefore I shall, to see what kind of fellow you really are come to the charge at once.
> Paddy – There again, your honour is right, and my blood warms to you. Come to the charge, your honour, come to the charge, nothing an Irishman likes so much as the charge; we were the boys that at a million of [illegible] not forgetting Waterloo, made the French, English, Greeks and all other nations under the sun, feel the charge. . . . Hurrah for the Irishman's charge (laughter).
> . . . Magistrate – Sir, we are to administer justice in the proper way and we want no tricks. Peace Officers keep that man quiet.
> Peace Officers (aside) – the devil would not do it.

Paddy's volubility was carnivalesque – the devil himself could not contain his tongue – disturbing the order of court proceedings and contesting the decorum desired by the magistrate. It was a demand to be heard at length, a political challenge to a social elite that sought to determine what evidence was relevant to justice.[80]

People, like Ruan and Mrs Murphy, wove lower-order lives into court proceedings as they reconstructed their social worlds. They gave voice to their experience, putting it into the official record for posterity, and asking that their account be used to inform meaning and justice. It was a demand for recognition, an expression of agency and identity. For Paddy, volubility became a form of resistance, taking up time and frustrating the court's desire to move quickly. It was a form of creative play that not only inverted power relationships, but, through providing space for lower-order voices, claimed a more equitable power dynamic between actors in the court.[81]

This potential for equity was reinforced through the inclusive nature of some forms of Irish storytelling. This is suggested in the joke-telling rituals that lawyers, like O'Connell, used to created rapport with witnesses, but extends this through allowing individuals to build stories together. In 1843, 'Mister Dominick Finnegan of Mullinahack' brought 'Jemmy Gaffney' before the Dublin magistrates.[82] Despite Finnegan's assurance that his testimony 'comprised in half a dozen words' ('I am very glad to hear it', noted the magistrate), he told a lengthy story of him gawking at the new lamp-posts on Carlisle-bridge, when Gaffney put his hand in his open mouth, following a poor fly that was swallowed.[83] This account, which included a discussion on the fate of the fly, 'Its really affecting to think on it', was made more entertaining by the 'imperturbable mustard-pot-like gravity' with which he delivered his tale. It was followed by Gaffney's equally amusing explanation: 'I never saw a mouth so wide open . . . the temptation of ramming in my hand came with such irresistible force upon me that it would have been utterly useless to have struggled against the impulse. . . . my defence is, that I was coerced to do so by inevitable fate (laughter)'.

Following this explanation, the complainant and defendant then bantered back and forth, leading to a discussion of what the monstrosity on Carlisle-bridge was meant to be.

> Complainant – It baffles all human speculation, and I am as far now as ever from understanding what is meant by it. I lay awake all last night 'cudgelling my brains' about it; but what could be the fun of erecting such a thing in such a spot is still a mystery to my imagination.
> Prisoner – I could have told you all about it if you had asked me. It's an asylum for destitute pedestrians who are in danger of being run over and ground to powder.
> Complainant – Oh, I understand. A sort of *refugium peccatorum*.
> Prisoner – Exactly; you hit it to a cow's thumb. It's either that or *aurora borealis*, or *delirium tremens*, or *amicus curiæ*. Something that way, you may take your oath of it (laughter).

Despite being on opposite sides of the suit, two engaging storytellers found a space for collaboration, creating a humorous exchange that subverted the desired orderliness of the court and the expectation that the complainant–defendant relationship should be adversarial. It provided an opportunity for reconciliation and a demonstration of personal character. Finnegan, through his expression of outrage at the lamp-posts' aesthetics, claimed an identity as someone with artistic judgement, whilst his use of Latin evidenced his education. Gaffney provided a funny, but practical explanation that acted as a critique on poor driving in Dublin. This was a pragmatic masculinity reinforced through trivialising the use of Latin, where one phrase was interchangeable with another. The magistrate ignored this exchange and fined Gaffney 5s.

When leaving, Gaffney 'ducked his fiery head' to the magistrate, suggestive of deference, but he 'kissed hands familiarly to Mr Finnegan', blowing a kiss as he left the building. During the period, this intimate gesture was generally used between flirting men and women, between politicians or actors and their audience as a sign of respect, or as short-hand expression for the rituals of saying goodbye.[84] That Gaffney blew his kiss 'familiarly' may indicate that he was subverting its more respect-ful usages, but, whether or not this was the case, it is suggestive of the success of the storytelling encounter at creating a connection between the parties. Like the speeches told by lawyers and judges, storytelling created 'sympathy' between the orator and his audience, but rather than acting as a transfer of 'emotional truth' from one self to another, this was a sympathy created through dialogue, exchange and disruption.

Not all storytelling was humorous. The stories that came before the court could be sentimental, tragic, indignant, designed to evoke pity and anger. But all demanded time and space in their telling, and all spoke to the character of the storyteller. Unlike the lawyer's speech where oration and character were collapsed in the making of truth, for people without recognised character, storytelling was its formation.[85] It was the crea-tion of truth through the building of self and the formation of sympathy through the demand on the other to recognise that self. For social groups that were frequently stereotyped and where individuals were lost in the condemnation and critique of those like them, storytelling provided the opportunity to demand that the court take the individual and their cir-cumstances on their own merit. This was not necessarily a rejection of class, but recognition that if they wished to receive justice, lower-order men and women had to be more than their class. In the lower courts at least, and as suggested by the space given to such accounts in the press, it was possible for this to happen.

### Conclusion

When Judy and Juliet appeared before the Cork magistracy, it was the lawyer, Mr O'Brien, who introduced their case as a tale of star-crossed lovers. This idea was never directly articulated, but references to *Romeo and Juliet* act to infer this meaning on to the events under discussion. It was a technique that relied on the actors involved, particularly the magistrate and where appropriate the jury, being familiar with the story and able to make these unspoken connections as they interpreted the evidence. Popular culture provided the framework through which the trial should be understood, although it was possible for judges and juries to reject such an interpretation.

O'Brien's intention was to shift the sympathy of the court towards his client, Juliet, through construing her culturally illegitimate relationship in romantic terms. It was a narrative that she was happy to endorse, but which Judy attempted to use as evidence of Juliet's pursuit of her son, locating the latter as breaching parental permission and feminine decorum. O'Brien's rebuff, 'a rose by any other name would smell as sweet', does not directly address these assertions, but was witty and acted to remind the court of the lawyer's interpretation. *Romeo and Juliet* was not the only story being told. In the course of her testimony Juliet referred to a satirical song by Thomas Moore, which spoke of the romance of courting by moonlight, but also hinted that one of its advantages was that female beauty was enhanced by darkness and alcohol. Juliet was likely using the song simply as a justification for her behaviour, noting that moonlight walks were endorsed by a national hero and poet. Yet, that the multiple significations within literature enabled complex and even contradictory messages was often used in court, especially for individuals, like young working-class men, who valued being associated with danger or criminality as a marker of masculinity, but wished to walk free from court.[86] Juliet may have thought the humour of the poem trivialised any wrong-doing on her part and heightened the wrong of Judy's assault. Her overarching self-presentation was as a modern, literate woman, engaged in a cosmopolitan world, where she could court for love and individual choice, hire a lawyer, quote famous plays and poetry, and, like the heroine of the period's gothic horrors, enter into graveyards at night without being overly concerned about its ghostly inhabitants.

In contrast, Judy appeared less aware of the significance of the literary allusions, referring to Romeo as Romy and failing to realise that Juliet's words were referencing a famous play. Yet, through tying Juliet to Judas, she critiqued Juliet's loyalty to her son, even implying that she would be responsible for his death – a possibility opened up by her son's enlistment. Such references suggested that Juliet's declaration of love was shallow and would lead to betrayal. Through referencing folk belief around entering graveyards, Judy also suggested that Juliet was flighty, without significant care for her own well-being or that of Judy's son. Or alternatively, she hinted that Juliet was associated with the 'good people' that abducted the vulnerable, endangering the well-being of families and their immortal souls. Judy provided an alternative interpretation of Juliet's behaviour that would have had resonance for many in their community. She performed a different form of femininity to that of Juliet; a woman rooted in an oral culture of fairytales and a religious world of biblical parables. She used this identity formation to authorise her right to interfere in the romantic choices of her son, foregrounding parental consent over love and free choice.

This was not a clash of the social classes. As Judy was quick to remind Juliet, both women were members of the lower orders: 'Cock you up with gloves, you circumwater – little your granny thought that one of her breed would leather her skin'. Nor was it necessarily a generational shift; men and women of all ages drew on both 'folk' and 'high' literatures, sometimes simultaneously. Rather, the adoption of particular forms of literature, as well as the stories themselves, were useful tools in the performance of identity that could be used to reinforce legal argument. This was a strategy that was employed by men and women alike, but with higher literacy rates and greater access to literature, men often had a greater repertoire at their disposal. As importantly, the selves made through literature were gendered selves, speaking to the making of femininity and masculinity, and requiring men and women to draw on different texts, or the same texts in different ways. In this sense, literature closed down, as well as opened up, opportunities in the making of identity.

The Irish were not content to let other people's stories talk for them. The creation of a coherent narrative out of complex experiences was central to legal business. Speaking before the court provided the opportunity to compose life stories and to tie individual crimes or events into larger social structures and relationships. Storytelling could ensure that lower-order identities were not only heard, but implicated in courtroom dynamics – an act of agency that demanded that such stories and lives had value and deserved justice. It could be an opportunity for creative playfulness, where individuals displayed their oratory or literary prowess, disrupting legal proceedings and challenging traditional power structures. Certain groups of men, such as poets and balladists, were particularly talented at this, simultaneously claiming the cultural capital of the bardic tradition. Women had less opportunity to take a role that was closely associated with masculinity, and judiciaries were less tolerant of verbose women, in part due to the negative connotations of the female tongue.

Men and women created Irish identities, notable for their 'volubility', their exuberance and their willingness to engage with others. National identities could overlap with local investments, as people claimed themselves as Kerrymen or as a 'Brunswicker since I was born', marking the dividing lines within Ireland, as well as between Ireland and its neighbours. Whilst distinctly Irish, such identities were hybrids. The demarcation between different literatures as products of different nations disintegrated when they were adopted by readers, who mixed high and low, literate and oral, and different national texts in their creation of an Irish self. Moreover, in being acknowledge by the press, such hybrid identities were implicated in the making of the nation.

## Notes

1 See advert for the play in *Saunders' Newsletter* (12 November 1835).

2 T. Moore, *Irish Melodies* (London: Longman, Brown, Green, and Longman, 1856), pp. 8–9.

3 R. Wharton and D. Miller, 'New directions in law and narrative', *Law, Culture and the Humanities*, online first [5 June 2016], forthcoming in print; B.S. Jackson, *Law, Fact and Narrative Coherence* (Roby: Deborah Charles Publications, 1988).

4 D. Amigoni, 'Introduction: Victorian life writing: Genre, print, constituencies', in D. Amigoni (ed.), *Life Writing and Victorian Culture* (Aldershot: Ashgate 2006), p. 5; P. Summerfield, 'Culture and composure: Creating narratives of the gendered self in oral history interviews', *Cultural and Social History*, 1 (2004), 65–93; K. Halttunen, 'Cultural history and the challenge of narrativity', in V. Bonnell and L. Hunt (eds), *Beyond the Cultural Turn: New Directions in the Study of Society and Culture* (Berkeley: California University Press, 1999), p. 171.

5 D. Hopkin, *Voices of the People in Nineteenth-Century France* (Cambridge: Cambridge University Press, 2012), p. 29; R. Darnton, *The Poetry and the Police: Communication Networks in Eighteenth-Century Paris* (Cambridge, MA: Belknap Press, 2010).

6 See for example people using stories as threats in K. Barclay, *Love, Intimacy and Power: Marriage and Patriarchy in Scotland, 1650–1850* (Manchester: Manchester University Press, 2011), p. 184.

7 For a discussion of some of the complexities with these divisions see: P. Burke, *Popular Culture in Early Modern Europe*, 3rd edition (Farnham: Ashgate, 2009), pp. 1–21; S.J. Connolly, '"Ag Déanamh Commanding": Elite responses to popular culture, 1660–1850', in J.S. Donnelly, Jr, and K.A. Miller (eds), *Irish Popular Culture 1650–1850* (Dublin: Irish Academic Press, 1998), pp. 1–29.

8 For a critique of this see: M. Lyons, *The Writing Culture of Ordinary People in Europe, c. 1860–1920* (Cambridge: Cambridge University Press, 2013), esp. pp. 15–17.

9 R. McWilliam, *Popular Politics in Nineteenth-Century England* (New York: Routledge, 1998), p. 20; J. Humphries complicates this narrative: *Childhood and Child Labour in the British Industrial Revolution* (Cambridge: Cambridge University Press, 2010).

10 A. Krishnamurthy, 'Introduction', in A. Krishnamurthy (ed.), *The Working-Class Intellectual in Eighteenth- and Nineteenth-Century Britain* (Farnham: Ashgate, 2009), p. 5.

11 See discussion in Chapter 1.

12 H. O'Sullivan described drinking, singing and brawling in a tavern with a merchant, two medical students, a doctor, a fiddler and a gentleman: *The Diary of an Irish Countryman, 1827–1835*, trans. T. De Bhaldraithe (Dublin: Mercier Press, 1979), pp. 36–7; L. Davis, *Music, Postcolonialism, and Gender: The Construction of Irish National Identity, 1724–1874* (Notre Dame: Notre Dame University Press, 2006); J. Henigan, 'Print and oral culture in the eighteenth-century Irish ballad', *Studies in Eighteenth-Century Culture*, 41 (2012), 161–83; C. Nelson, 'Tea-table miscellanies: The development of Scotland's song culture, 1720–1800', *Early Music*, 28 (2000), 597–619.

13 G. Griffin, *Talis Qualis, or, Tales of the Jury Room*, 3 volumes (London: Maxwell and Co., 1842).

14 K. Murphy, 'Judge, jury, magistrate and soldier: Rethinking law and authority in late eighteenth-century Ireland', *American Journal of Legal History*, 44 (2000), 231–56.

15 Griffin, *Talis Qualis*, vol. 1, p. 24.

16 The press complimented him on this literary device: 'Tales of the Jury Room', *Waterford Chronicle* (11 September 1842).

17 A. Wood, *The Memory of the People: Custom and Popular Senses of the Past in Early Modern England* (Cambridge: Cambridge University Press, 2013), p. 29.

18 N. Ó Ciosáin, 'Oral culture, literacy and the growth of a popular readership, 1800–1850', in J.H. Murphy (ed.), *The Oxford History of the Irish Book* (Oxford: Oxford University Press 2011), vol. 4, pp. 178–9; D. Raftery, 'Colonizing the mind: The use of English writers in the education of the Irish poor, c. 1750–1850', in M. Hilton and J. Shefrin (eds), *Educating the Child in Enlightenment Britain: Beliefs, Cultures Practices* (Farnham: Ashgate, 2009), pp. 147–61; J.R.R. Adams, 'Swine-tax and Eat-Him-All-Magee: The hedge schools and popular education in Ireland', in Donnelly and Miller, *Irish Popular Culture*, pp. 97–117; A. McManus, *The Irish Hedge School and its Books, 1695–1831* (Dublin: Four Courts Press, 2004).

19 A. Murphy, *Shakespeare for the People: Working-Class Readers, 1800–1900* (Cambridge: Cambridge University Press, 2008); P.T. Murphy, *Towards a Working-Class Canon: Literary Criticism in British Working-Class Periodicals, 1816–1858* (Columbus: Ohio State University Press, 1994).

20 For example: 'Charge of Leveling', *Connaught Journal* (27 August 1829) Dublin.

21 Frank Ferguson, 'The industrialization of Irish book production, 1790–1900', in Murphy, *The Oxford History of the Irish Book*, vol. 4, pp. 20–1.

22 Henigan, 'Print and oral culture'; M. Cronin, 'Claiming the landscape: Popular balladry in pre-famine Ireland', in Ú. Ní Bhroiméil and G. Hopper, *Land and Landscape in Nineteenth-Century Ireland* (Dublin: Four Courts Press, 2008), pp. 25–39.

23 'Dublin Police', *Freeman's Journal* (19 February 1845) Dublin; see also 'Dublin Police', *Kerry Evening Post* (21 October 1837) Dublin.

24 'Dublin Police, *Freeman's Journal* (9 July 1845) Dublin; 'Dublin Office College Street', *Kerry Evening Post* (18 March 1840) Dublin.

25 *The Speeches of Charles Phillips, Esq., Delivered at the Bar, and on Various Public Occasions* (London and Dublin: W. Simpkin and R. Marshall, and Milliken, 1822): pp. 76–101, *Guthrie v. Sterne* (1815), Dublin; pp. 128–143, *Connaghton v. Dillon* (1816), Roscommon; pp. 161–81, *Blake v. Wilkins* (1817), Galway; pp. 202–24, *Brown v. Blake* (1817), Dublin.

26 For example, *The Speeches of Charles Phillips*, p. 177.

27 *Ibid.*

28 Ó Ciosáin, 'Oral culture', pp. 175–6.

29 For a poet using Latin see: 'Dublin Police', *Freeman's Journal* (13 July 1838) Dublin.

30 'Kilrush Petty Session', *Dublin Morning Register* (23 September 1840) Clare; see also *Kerry Evening Post* (26 September 1840).

31 'Parsontown Petty Session', *Leinster Express* (21 September 1844) King's County/Offaly.

32 See Elizabeth M. Knowles, *The Oxford Dictionary of Quotations* (Oxford: Oxford University Press, 1999), p. 19; amongst others, it appears in Della, *The Rambles of Captain Bolio* (London: W. Strange, 1838), p. 297.

33  'Dublin Police', *Freeman's Journal* (28 May 1842) Dublin.

34  'Dublin Police', *Freeman's Journal* (2 September 1838) Dublin.

35  N. Lacey, *Women, Crime and Character: From Moll Flanders to Tess of the D'Urbervilles* (Oxford: Oxford University Press, 2008), p. 43.

36  K. Barclay, 'Singing and lower-class masculinity in the Dublin Magistrate's Court, 1800–1845', *Journal of Social History*, 47:3 (2014), 746–68.

37  'Dublin Police', *Freeman's Journal* (30 May 1845) Dublin; 'A cure for grief – for what can ever rankle, Before a petticoat and peeping ankle?': G. Byron, 'Don Juan', in *The Works of Lord Byron in Five Volumes* (Leipzig: Bernhard Tauchnitz, 1866), vol. 1, p. 447.

38  'City of Limerick Petty Sessions', *Limerick and Clare Examiner* (22 January 1848) Limerick.

39  G. Byron, *Life, Letters and Journals of Lord Byron*, ed. Thomas Moore (London: John Murray, 1839), p. 514.

40  'Henry St Police Office', *Kerry Examiner* (1 November 1844) Dublin.

41  Lyons, *Writing Culture*, p. 64

42  Barclay, 'Singing and lower-class masculinity'.

43  F. Forman-Barzilai, *Adam Smith and the Circles of Sympathy: Cosmopolitanism and Moral Theory* (Cambridge: Cambridge University Press, 2009); K. Glover, *Elite Women and Polite Society in Eighteenth-Century Scotland* (Woodbridge: Boydell and Brewer, 2011), pp. 159–60.

44  Davis, *Music, Postcolonialism, and Gender*, pp. 3–4; C. O'Halloran, 'Irish recreations of the Gaelic past: The challenge of Macpherson's Ossian', *Past and Present*, 124 (1989), 69–95.

45  'Henry-Street Police Office', *Kerry Examiner* (1 November 1844) Dublin.

46  'Dublin Police', *Freeman's Journal* (27 September 1844) Dublin; 'Dublin Police', *Freeman's Journal* (31 October 1828) Dublin; 'Dublin Police', *Freeman's Journal* (12 September 1840) Dublin; 'Dublin Police', *Freeman's Journal* (24 October 1840) Dublin; 'Dublin Police', *Freeman's Journal* (7 September 1844) Dublin.

47  'Nenagh Petty Sessions', *Nenagh Guardian* (10 April 1841) Tipperary.

48  'Athy Petty Sessions', *The Athlone Sentinel* (5 December 1849) Kildare; 'Shinrone Petty Sessions', *Cork Examiner* (16 October 1848) King's County/Offaly; 'Dublin Police', *Freeman's Journal* (30 May 1845) Dublin.

49  'Maryborough Petty Sessions', *Wexford Independent* (8 November 1845) Queen's County/Laois.

50  'Police Intelligence', *Dublin Morning Register* (9 June 1842) Dublin.

51  See Chapter 1 for discussion.

52  Barclay, 'Singing and lower-class masculinity'; 'Crown Court', *Nenagh Guardian* (25 March 1843) Tipperary; 'Carlow Petty Session', *Carlow Morning Post* (7 February 1831) Carlow; 'Tralee Petty Session', *Kerry Examiner* (14 September 1840) Kerry; 'Dublin Police', *Freeman's Journal* (20 November 1840) Dublin.

53  See Chapter 5.

54  Hopkin, *Voices of the People*, p. 39; K. Barclay, 'Composing the self: Gender and subjectivity within Scottish balladry', *Cultural and Social History*, 7:3 (2010), 337–53

55  'Kilrush Petty Sessions', *Freeman's Journal* (12 January 1837) Clare.

56  A. Bourke, *The Burning of Bridget Cleary: A True Story* (London: Pimlico, 1999), pp. 24–38; D. Purkiss, 'Women's stories of witchcraft in early modern England:

The house, the body, the child', *Gender & History*, 7:3 (1995), 408–32; L. Roper, *Oedipus and the Devil: Witchcraft, Sexuality and Religion in Early Modern Europe* (London: Routledge, 1994); 'Tuam Petty Sessions', *Galway Patriot* (27 September 1837) Galway.

57 'Longford Quarter Sessions', *Dublin Evening Mail* (1 January 1849) Longford; 'Castlebar Petty Sessions', *Dublin Morning Register* (23 August 1828) Mayo; 'Parsonstown Quarter Session', *Leinster Express* (9 July 1842) King's County/Offaly.

58 'A Fairy', *Freeman's Journal* (19 February 1835) Limerick.

59 'Castlebar Sessions', *Westmeath Journal* (21 October 1830) Mayo.

60 See also Bourke, *The Burning*, p. 33; 'County of Armagh Assizes', *Belfast Newsletter* (11 August 1840) Armagh; 'Consistorial Court', *Cork Examiner* (26 September 1845) Cork; 'Most Extraordinary Case of Gross Superstition – A Fairy!!!', *Nenagh Guardian* (15 April 1840) Tipperary; 'Ennis Assizes', *Southern Reporter and Cork Commercial Courier* (6 March 1838) Clare.

61 'Galway Assizes', *Freeman's Journal* (1 August 1837) Galway; 'Crown Court', *Nenagh Guardian* (25 March 1843) Tipperary.

62 'Castlebar Sessions', *Westmeath Journal* (21 October 1830) Mayo.

63 'Darby O'Grady and the Fairies!', *Sligo Champion* (20 January 1838) Limerick.

64 'The Queen of the Fairies!', *Tralee Chronicle and Killarney Echo* (28 April 1844) Kilkenny.

65 'Athy Petty Sessions', *Freeman's Journal* (23 November 1835) Kildare.

66 Purkis, 'Women's stories'; Roper, *Oedipus*.

67 'Galway Assizes', *Freeman's Journal* (1 August 1837) Galway; 'Crown Court', *Nenagh Guardian* (25 March 1843) Tipperary; 'Most Extraordinary Case of Gross Superstition – A Fairy!!!', *Nenagh Guardian* (15 April 1840) Tipperary.

68 B.A. Tlusty, 'Invincible blades and invulnerable bodies: Weapons magic in early modern Germany', *European History Review*, 22:4 (2015), 658–79.

69 'Most Extraordinary Case of Gross Superstition – A Fairy!!!', *Nenagh Guardian* (15 April 1840) Tipperary.

70 See Elizabeth Rainey's testimony: 'County of Armagh Assizes', *Belfast Newsletter* (11 August 1840) Armagh.

71 'Dublin Police', *Freeman's Journal* (3 December 1828) Dublin.

72 J.H. Langbein, *The Origins of Adversary Criminal Trials* (Oxford: Oxford University Press, 2005).

73 'Dublin Police', *Freeman's Journal* (31 October 1828) Dublin.

74 'Police Intelligence', *Limerick Reporter* (11 February 1840) Dublin.

75 'Love Behind a Tomb Stone', *Connaught Journal* (17 December 1835) Cork.

76 R.A. Houston, *Peasant Petitions: Social Relations and Economic Life on Landed Estates, 1600–1850* (Basingstoke: Palgrave Macmillan, 2014), p. 135.

77 'Assizes', *Southern Reporter and Cork Commercial Courier* (10 April 1828) Cork.

78 'Drogheda Petty Sessions', *Drogheda Conservative Journal* (18 January 1845) Louth; 'Dublin Police', *Freeman's Journal* (7 December 1836) Dublin.

79 'Dublin Police', *Connaught Journal* (15 October 1832) Dublin.

80 M. Crichlow and P. Armstrong, 'Introduction: Carnival praxis, carnivalesque strategies, and Atlantic interstices', in M. Crichlow, *Carnival Art, Culture and Politics: Performing Life* (London: Routledge, 2013), pp. 1–16.

81 K.V. Mortensen and L. Grünbaum (eds), *Play and Power* (London: Karnac Books, 2010).

82 'Dublin Police', *Freeman's Journal* (3 April 1843) Dublin.

83 For another example of promising to tell short stories see: 'Kilrush Petty Sessions', *Freeman's Journal* (12 January 1837) Clare.

84 For examples of the usage of this phrase see: 'Seduction-Extraordinary Case', *Tralee Mercury* (1 June 1831) Dublin; 'The Theatre', *Freeman's Journal* (10 December 1825); 'O'Connell in Limerick', *Kerry Examiner* (11 September 1840); 'The Hedge School', *Connaught Telegraph* (6 August 1834).

85 See Chapter 4.

86 For more on this see Chapter 7.

# 7

# *On character and truth: 'you see McDonnell the value of a good character'*

**INSOLVENT DEBTORS' COURT – YESTERDAY**

(Before Mr. Commissioner Farrell.)

The Case of Thomas Steele having been called on, Mr. James Dwyer said he appeared to oppose the discharge of Mr. Steele on behalf of three creditors, namely Martha McCarthy, widow of Jeremiah McCarthy, late of Dawson-st, for 307l.; Elizabeth Carmody, of Ennis, county Clare, hotel-keeper, 480l.; and O'Gorman Mahon for the sums of 250l. and 170l. The debts to the two first-named creditors were peculiarly circumstanced and with respect to O'Gorman Mahon, there was a note entered by the insolvent at number 10 in the schedule, to the debt of 170l., of which he complained, and upon which it would be necessary for him to go into some statement. . . .

Mr. Dwyer read the note, which was to the effect that O'Gorman Mahon, Colonel Dickson, and himself, had got the bill for that sum discounted by one Charles King, for their mutual interest, and that when the bill became due O'Gorman Mahon said he had got no value for it; but law proceedings having been taken, O'Gorman Mahon was obliged to pay the 170l. for which he (Mr. Steele) had put himself down on the schedule as his debtor. Now he (Mr. Dwyer) objected to that, as he could show that O'Gorman Mahon had no mutual interest whatever in that transaction and therefore it was that he objected to such a note being placed on the schedule.

The Commissioner could not collect from the note that it bore any thing whatever on the face of it at all disparaging to O'Gorman Mahon. He had read over the schedule and he found that two country gentlemen and a military gentleman had dealings with an old usurer – he would correct himself, and say a money lender. These gentlemen having need of such accommodation, were, it appeared, at the time on the terms of closest intimacy with each other. They resolved, as persons of the highest station in the land frequently did, rather than trouble a friend, to resort to one for accommodation whose dealings in such cases were well known. In the course of such transaction accounts frequently became so complicated that if the parties were even put upon their oath they might not be able to tell exactly how they stood. For his (the Commissioner's) part, he repeated it, that he did not see any disparagement conveyed by that note as regarded O'Gorman Mahon.

Mr. Dwyer proceeded to object that Colonel Dickson was not returned on the face of the schedule as being indebted to Mr. Steele, although the latter stated that he had accepted bills to the amount of 2,400l. for him. The party in question was styled Major and Colonel Dickson by Mr. Steele, and spoken of in the most eulogistic terms by him, but he (Mr. D.) was instructed to state that he was not either a major or a colonel, and that he had never been an officer in the British service.

Commissioner – But these titles may be of courtesy, and by which the party may be more familiarly known, and better identified.

Mr. Creighton – They found that this gentleman, Colonel Dickson, an officer in the Spanish army, had, by an act of the most chivalrous generosity, made a present of 3000l. to Mr. Steele; the latter obliged him, it was true, to take his bond for the amount, but subsequently that was consigned by him to the flames. Colonel Dickson did take accommodation acceptances from Mr. Steele, but he would not, under all the circumstancee [sic], be entitled to return him (Colonel D.) as his debtor. . . . Mr. Steele was then called to the witness-box. . . .

In reply to Mr. Dwyer, Mr. Steele then proceeded to depose that he originally became acquainted with Major Dickson in the year 1823; [met in the army in Spain]; on witness's return to London, he introduced Colonel Dickson to O'Gorman Mahon; that was in the year 1829; in the year 1827 O'Gorman Mahon lent witness 250l.; witness entertained for him the most sincere friendship at the time; O'Gorman Mahon was in the habit of lending him small sums of money; he never refused doing so when he had the means; witness told him that he expected to have the means of paying him; he knew that in a case where Colonel Dickson expected an outfit of 6,000l. on his marriage, he (Mr. S.) could calculate on him, if he got it, as surely as he could upon the service of his own right hand; he and Colonel Dickson formed the closest friendship with each other – they were bound to each other by a friendship, the result of a community of danger; witness had also the most fervent friendship at the time for O'Gorman Mahon; in the year 1829 they all wanted money, and they drew or accepted a bill for 300l.; . . . The three hundred pound bill led to a five hundred pound bill, and to take up the latter King [the money lender] proposed the purchase of a picture then in the market, which he said would sell for eight hundred pounds, and for which he proposed that they should pass a bill for that amount, the surplus between the five hundred pounds and the eight hundred pounds to be divided between them. All the bills were signed by them all. . . .

Commissioner – What was got for the 800l. bill?

Witness did not know; he got nothing out of it.

O'Gorman Mahon – I denounce that 800l. bill for a forgery.

Commissioner – I am sure that O'Gorman Mahon must have suffered as a victim in this transaction; but it is equally clear that the gentleman before the court is not implicated in it.

Mr. Dwyer – Mr. Steele, I must now ask you whether did you ever put the name of O'Gorman Mahon to any bill without his knowledge or consent?

Mr. Creighton – I object to your putting that question, Mr. Dwyer. You need not answer it, Mr. Steele.

Mr. Steele – You are my counsel here, Mr. Creighton; but I must entreat of you, Sir, not to attempt to prevent my answering this as well as every other question that can possibly be put to me by the counsel at the other side. In fact, so far from wishing to avail myself of any legal privilege authorising me to decline answering, it delights me beyond all measure, I may most conscientiously say, that the question has been put to me, and I shall now answer it.

Commissioner – It is my duty, Mr. Steele, to apprise you that you are not bound to answer the question if you do not wish to do so.

Mr. Steele – My wish is to answer in the most candid manner every question that may be put to me, notwithstanding any shield that the law might throw over me to enable me to decline doing so, if such were my desire; and I now state that, in a certain public and political transaction in Limerick, in which O'Gorman Mahon and myself were engaged, I did, without his knowledge, in the pressure of the moment, sign his name to a bill; but I wrote to him immediately by the same night's post to Dublin where he was, notifying him that I had done so; in signing his name to that bill I did not feign his handwriting; I signed it in my own handwriting; my own large characters; I felt morally conscious that in what I did I committed no forgery whatever; that bill had no relation whatever to any of the transactions with King; I put no money in my pocket by it; the matter was one of public business soley . . .

Mr. Dwyer – Did you ever attend with Dickson at a London police-office on a charge of swindling about the Viago Bay?

Commissioner – Pray what has the Viago Bay to do with the business now before this court? I cannot now listen to illegal evidence not at all touching the matter before the court.

Mr. Dwyer – But this occurred in London.

Mr. Steel – I beg and entreat of your lordship that you will permit me to answer that and every other question put to me. . . . Major Dickson and myself attend at the police office in London, not I perhaps need not say, upon a charge of swindling, but for the purpose of giving securities against the peace, as Major Dickson had challenged the proprietor of the *Morning Herald* for publishing libels about him, and we were arrested while I was engaged in measuring the ground that morning [i.e. preparing for the duel]. . . .

Mr. Dwyer – You stated that you contracted these large debts for the public?

Witness – And on my private account.

Mr. Dwyer – And do you not think that the public is not in justice bound to pay for those services, which in contracting these debts you rendered them?

Mr. Steele – I trust, and have every hope, that this lady will be paid out of the residue of my property; but I have laid down a rule – an unalterable one – that the public shall never pay anything for me. In the course that I have marked out for myself, and adhered to as a public man, I have abandoned no profession. There is one, a most illustrious man [Daniel O'Connell] – he has abandoned a most lucrative and honourable profession for the sake of advocating the great cause of his country, and he, not me, who never gave up any profession in my efforts to serve my country, has a right to compensation. I never contracted any debt whatever, but solely dependant on the resources of my private property.

Mr. Dwyer – I should think, Mr. Steele, that your public services should be paid for by the public.

Commissioner – This, Mr. Dwyer, is not the proper place to discuss such a subject. . . .

Mr. Creighton – And Mr. Steele is most fully entitled to an immediate and free discharge by the court. Although Mr. Steele and myself may differ as widely as possible from each other in politics, yet I will say that for many years that I have known the character of that gentleman in private life he has ever commanded my most unqualified respect and esteem.

Commissioner – I shall not go beyond the business before the court, and I must say that nothing has occurred here to-day calculated, in my mind, to alter your opinion, Mr. Creighton, of this gentleman.

On the book being handed to Mr. Steele to take the usual oath on his being discharged, O'Gorman Mahon, who had sat by his counsel during the proceedings, addressed the court, saying that he had come there on learning by the papers that the insolvent was to come up that day to be discharged. He (O'Gorman Mahon) did not attend there for the purpose of being paid back the moneys he had lent him, but in order to prove that his statement, which appeared in the papers some time ago, was perfectly true, namely, that he had been made the victim of a gang of swindlers.

Commissioner – Do you mean to impugn the character of the gentleman before the court as such?

O'Gorman Mahon – My Lord, you misunderstand me if you think I do not. Mr. Steele is the first.

Commissioner – Sir, if you repeat one word more such as that you shall thereby impose upon me the performance of a most painful duty towards you. I can make allowances for the irritation natural under such circumstances, but I must say that after the examination I have this day heard, as far as my conscience, my judgment, and my experience go, this gentleman has come out of the trial with his character perfectly pure, and his honour perfectly unstained. [A general burst of popular applause throughout the court followed.]

*Freeman's Journal*, 24 February 1842.

The role of the court was to determine a truth that enabled justice to be served.[1] It evaluated different types of proof and tested them against each other, guided by legal principles around the nature of evidence and the boundaries of the law.[2] For most criminal procedure (with a few exceptions), a conviction only required the testimony of a single 'credible' witness or the 'voluntarily made and regularly proved' confession of the guilty.[3] Where a witness was not credible, oral testimony must be supported by significant circumstantial evidence. Civil suits operated similarly, but typically required multiple witnesses. Credibility was distinguished from 'competency', where witnesses were required to be of sufficient age, of sound mind, and to not have an interest in the case that would bias testimony. Credibility, instead, spoke to character. As the barrister and legal writer Leonard MacNally noted in 1802, 'it is not a term of art appropriated to legal notions, but has a signification universally received'.[4]

As has been demonstrated across this book, credibility or character was determined by people's performances, including their bodies, emotional displays, clothing, behaviour, wit, storytelling, and uses of wider culture. It was reinforced by a belief that the body and its behaviours provided evidence of character for the viewer and that an individual's truth could be transmitted as a sympathetic exchange between performer and audience. As noted elsewhere, character was also informed by age, education, social status and religious belief.[5] When these qualities were combined in the production of masculine identity, the court read character as a proxy for truth. Truth, however, was also produced through an adversarial system where characters and other evidences were weighed against each other. This was especially the case in civil suits, where juries were to have 'struck a fair balance' when making decisions. 'Balance' was more problematic for criminal trials, where juries were 'not to *weigh* the evidence, but in cases of *doubt* to acquit the prisoner'.[6] In practice, all forms of evidentiary assessment required some calculation of credit and value, and so courtrooms were places where the tensions between truth and justice were highlighted.

Character was not the only source of legal evidence. By the nineteenth century, written evidence was often viewed as preferable to witness testimony as 'the most certain and deliberate acts of the mind', when compared to the 'imperfections of memory; [where] as the remembrance of things fail and go off, men are apt to entertain opinions in their stead'.[7] Physical evidence was also admissible, although it was not yet treated as a category with its own evidentiary rules. The largest discussion of physical evidence in legal texts related to its use in proving specific crimes, so, for example, whether a door was open or locked was used to differentiate between types of theft. Other forms of physical evidence were associated with the 'experts' that contextualised it. Professional knowledge had been used in court for centuries, but the evolution of science expanded the meanings of physical evidence and the authority of those who testified about it.[8] The largest category of experts were medical doctors or midwives, who commented on cause of death, marks of violence or likelihood of insanity. They were increasingly accompanied by early forensic scientists. As is explored below, as such evidence was typically provided by professional men, the character of the scientist, as well as the science, was open to scrutiny.

Good character did not over-ride other forms of evidence. As MacNally argued: '*Character* is of great weight in every case, and requires particular attention when the charge is grounded on circumstantial evidence: it creates a greater degree of *doubt* than where the prosecution is supported by direct evidence'.[9] Whilst earlier chapters have explored how character was produced, this chapter turns to how character was used in courtrooms to determine truth. It begins with a discussion of how social characteristics – such as age and region – informed character, before reading men's bodies for truth and lies. The oath remained important in giving weight to truth, whilst forensic science offered a critique of common sense readings of evidence. This chapter argues that despite the growing significance of experts, character remained a key measure of truth, ensuring that the manly Irishman remained at the heart of the legal system. It thus contributes to a larger debate about shifts in the meanings and use of character over the nineteenth century, where, for the English legal context, it has been argued that generic concepts of character were replaced by individualised assessments of a person's psychology, *mens rea* and capacity to commit crime.[10]

### Weighing character

James Patrick Mahon (1800–1891), known as 'O'Gorman Mahon', and Thomas Steele (1788–1848) were both well-known proponents of Catholic Emancipation. Mahon was from a prominent Catholic family in Clare, attended Trinity College, trained as a barrister but did not practice, and held numerous civic and political roles, including MP, magistrate, deputy-lieutenant, and a captain in the local militia. His reputation was not entirely upstanding. He was unseated as an MP in 1831 for bribery, although later acquitted. He made a living as a journalist and mercenary, fighting, he claimed, for the Ottoman and Austrian Empires, as well as in South America. Mahon maintained that he fought between thirteen and eighteen duels. Money troubles plagued him. He was frequently involved in 'speculative ventures'; by the 1850s, he was forced to sell his Clare estates, and by the 1870s, on the verge of bankruptcy, he was tried for embezzlement, but again acquitted.[11] This was still to come in 1842. 'Honest Tom Steele' inherited a sizeable estate in Clare from his father and attended Trinity College and Cambridge. Although Protestant, he supported Catholic Emancipation and was tried with O'Connell in 1843 for conspiracy. He was also an adventurer, impoverishing his estates to supply the Patriot Army whilst fighting during the Spanish War, and supplementing his income through writing. He committed suicide in 1848, bankrupt and crushed by the death of O'Connell.[12]

Despite their questionable financial dealings, when Steele and Mahon appeared before Dublin's Insolvent Debtors' Court, the Commissioner, lawyers and even gallery went to great lengths to interpret their behaviour as upright and honest, if unfortunate. In the years before 1842, Mahon, Steele and a Colonel Dickson regularly borrowed from each other to maintain their lifestyles and their 'public cause', Catholic Emancipation. In 1829, they borrowed from a London moneylender and involved themselves in the speculative purchase of a painting, with the aim of selling it for profit. Mahon denied giving permission for this transaction, believing they intended to 'swindle' him. Steele also owed money to other debtors for goods and services. Rather than reading Steele, Mahon and Dickson's web of lending and borrowing as a deception designed to establish a credit that had no economic foundation, most of the court emphasised the legitimacy of financial interconnections between men 'bound to each other by friendship'. The lower-order men castigated for borrowing each other's clothing may well have looked on in askance. Instead, the Commissioner redirected the blame onto the London 'usurer' Charles King, whilst lawyers on both sides testified to the 'public' nature of the debts and Steele's honesty. The gallery cheered on his release. Only Mahon was left to complain that Steele's credit was not all it appeared.

Character was a key ideal that affirmed men's virtue and the weight that should be given to their testimony. Its importance was epitomised in the character testimony provided at most trials to affirm men and women's standing in the community. In England, it is argued that character was individualised in the nineteenth century – an 'inner virtue', 'no longer based on the perception of others', but that was nonetheless 'possessed and enjoyed in public view'.[13] It was also 'self-serving' and tied closely to 'independence', a value that operated differently across social class.[14] Superseding an older tradition of credit rooted in the wider family, status and community, character still acknowledged the centrality of the nuclear family, and particularly children, to manly identity.[15]

As has been demonstrated, character in Ireland could be highly individualised, even eccentric, but that character was rooted in family, community and status remained significant.[16] Family remained a key marker of masculinity.[17] Elite men benefited from well-known family names, associated with social authority as well as networks of patronage and obligation.[18] For them, the ideal of 'independence' was refracted through long-standing models of civic virtue for the landed classes that emphasised their paternal obligations and political freedoms.[19] Expectations that they would be treated with deference, as well as their continuing social power, impacted on their treatment in court. Poorer men too drew on familial reputation to reinforce character. When Denis Keily, 'a young lad', was charged with theft in 1844, his character witness noted, 'He is, my Lord, from the neighbourhood of Rathvilly, and his family bear a very good character'.[20] An older man, Kenna, charged with attacking the police in 1849, was similarly described as: 'a quiet, sober, industrious man; ... He is in good circumstances; his family is very large; can read and write; has children and grand-children'.[21] As patriarch, Kenna shaped the character of his family – it could not be 'good' without him – but his large family also signalled his social authority over that network and embedded him in community life.

Character was similarly tied to locality and community. Keily was described as from 'Rathvilly', locating him in a specific 'knowing' community.[22] Being known allowed the community to vouch for character, but, even where it was poor, it promoted the perception of honesty by establishing its boundaries. Being transitory could act as a risk to character. When two of his officers were accused of being drunk on duty in 1845, Ballina's police sub-inspector testified of Kennedy, 'I consider him to be a sober man', but Shelrick was 'only a few months here, and I do not like to give a character of any one until after a longer experience of him'.[23] This created anxieties around the possibilities of justice for 'strangers'. The court reporter at Nenagh Petty Session in 1835 joined with Lawrence McDonnell's attorney in criticising the police for arresting McDonnell for nothing more than being a 'Connaughtman with a suspicious countenance'.[24] Transitory men were sometimes offered space to perform character in courtrooms, but not all men could demonstrate good character, especially if they were poor. Vagrancy itself not only suggested poor character, but criminality, a transportable offence throughout the period.[25]

Social class remained a key determinant of character, particularly in Ireland where political protest was less associated with expanding the polity than threatening social order.[26] Elite men were assumed to hold character by virtue of their upbringing, background and the codes of honourable manliness on which their political and social system relied.[27] The presumption that character and status were tied together was acknowledged explicitly as late as 1848 in *Ffrench v. Ffrench*, where two brothers fought over the validity of the will of a third brother. Ffrench was an Irish baronetcy. During the trial, the brothers challenged the right of the court to judge their testimony. Lord Keatinge replied at length:

> it had been argued that in the present case, in which persons of high station were connected, the Court was not at liberty to presume that anything like fraud, perjury, or conspiracy could exist. Many learned advocates had gone further, and said that the character, and position, and station of the promovant and his family were sufficient of them-selves to repel any imputations. Now he (Judge Keatinge) begged leave to say that he knew of no character so pure, no rank so exalted, no station so elevated, as to protect parties from having their acts and their conduct made the subject of strict examination.... That was the opinion of Lord Thurlew in a case which came before him, and reported in 1 Cox7, and to which the Court cordially subscribed.[28]

That Keatinge found that social status was not enough to determine truth was not a new legal decision in 1848, but that this case was made to him and that he replied at length with (relatively recent) precedent, is suggestive of the continued cultural power of this connection within Irish society.

Credit also remained significant in Ireland. Margot Finn demonstrates that the complex entity of credit, which simultaneously situated people within social, sexual, moral and financial hierarchies, remained significant well into the nineteenth century.[29] The close relationship between financial and moral credit implicated bankruptcy or insolvency in character, as well as financial acumen. As Steele's suicide might suggest, being brought before the insolvency and bankruptcy courts was shameful.[30] It challenged men's political independence, not only by undermining its economic basis, but through placing them under the control of an 'assignee' who managed their financial affairs. Dependency was associated with dishonesty, with men not free to choose their words when embedded within networks of obligation.[31] The insolvency and bankruptcy courts provided men opportunity to restore their characters, through demonstrating that their financial circumstances were caused by misfortune, the actions of others, or that the situation arose despite their honesty and best efforts.[32]

Debtors, lawyers and the court's Commissioner (judge) cooperated with this performance to different degrees. Men whose financial dealings appeared dubious, who hid assets or otherwise behaved badly could be chastised, even being returned to gaol.[33] On other occasions, the Commissioner restored character, remarking, as for Steele, that 'this gentleman has come out of the trial with his character perfectly pure, and his honour perfectly unstained'.[34] What led the Commissioners to read such men as 'honest' was not simple accounting. How men dressed, spoke, emoted and otherwise performed character was central to this judgement. So was social background. And it is here one of the key tensions of understanding character in the early nineteenth-century court comes to the fore.

On the one hand, the court was acutely sensitive to men's performances of self; on the other, how those performances were judged was tied into a hierarchical structure where elite men's characters were given greater weight – held a greater truth value – than those of men of lower rank. To convict an elite man required more proof, as their previous 'good character' held substantially more weight. Thus, despite both Mahon and Steele having a questionable credit history, their social background acted to counterbalance their behaviour, allowing it to be judged in a different register from that of men further down the social ladder. Claiming status became an important strategy in gaining credit. Thus, the Rev. Georgius Darcy Marcus Irvine argued in 1838 that that the bills he gave his creditors were not fraudulent as he was heir to his father's estate: 'Due to his station in life, he was obliged to contract debts to support that station with the intention of paying them when he came into property'.[35] His father was currently refusing him an allowance as he married without permission, but he believed they would soon be reconciled. His lawyer noted that, 'It was to his credit that he had not left the butcher, the baker or the poorer class of merchants unpaid'.

This can be contrasted with the similar, but distinct, claim of the 'wealthy solicitor' Henry Murphy in 1842. He argued that his debts were incurred as he was 'obliged to entertain his more respectable clients occasionally, and others of equal rank whom he hoped would become clients to him, but that he never considered he incurred greater expenses that his means would justify'. He believed that given time he could pay his debtors.[36] Both men rooted their claims to credit not in their immediate financial liquidity, but in the reasonableness of such expenditure by men of their social class and the wealth, earned or inherited, that would ensure future repayment. This was not simply a request for more time to pay, but a socio-moral explanation for why that request was legitimate. Social status acted as the 'character' (which must be maintained) on which they based their demands for financial credit, disrupting the logic of independence that emphasised freedom from obligation, particularly financial, to others. When such extensions of credit were granted, the connection between status, character and financial credit was legitimised; that lower-order men did not have access to such leniency indicated the limits of their character. The latter found new models on which to base character and independence, pointing to honesty and fairness, wage-earning and hard work, and the virile male body, to name a few.[37] Character in such forms could reinforce the appearance of honesty and fair-dealing for the bankruptcy court, but were less likely to authorise extensions of credit.

It was not only regional and class identities that informed readings of personal character. Different ideals of manly behaviour competed in Ireland, shaping men's actions and how they were subsequently judged. Some were widespread. Men were expected to show concern and care towards respectable women; poor women found it difficult to achieve 'respectability'.[38] As Steele's case indicates, the ability to form strong homosocial bonds with men of a similar class was prized across social groups.[39] What signified an attractive male body, wit, humour and good storytelling spanned class boundaries. There were also areas that were considered legitimate sites of manly difference, most notably politics and religion.

The existence of conflict, including rioting, that arose from sectarian and party-political conflict, especially in the 1820s, is well evidenced.[40] Recent literature, however, argues that the first half of the century was a time of negotiation on how religious-political groups should co-exist, rather than a defining moment in modern sectarianism.[41] The courtroom was a key location where such debates were engaged. Whether Catholics received justice was subject to ongoing discussion, particularly as Protestants dominated juries and the judiciary.[42] From the 1820s, Catholic political organisations and newspapers complained about 'jury-packing', where the sheriffs who invited men to jury duty excluded Catholics or placed them at the end of long lists.[43] These concerns were not unwarranted, but it is also notable that this public debate forced the court into a performance of impartiality.[44]

The ability to put aside 'party feeling' was an essential quality in the prized 'independent' man and a legal requirement for 'competent' witnesses.[45] Those influenced by 'faction' were thought to be 'credulous': 'The feelings and opinions of men in a gregarious state, are not their own; they borrow them, by a sort of electric impulse, suddenly, and in spite of themselves'.[46] When defending Thomas Kirwan in 1812, Charles Kendall Bushe observed: 'It is the pitiable condition of faction to be credulous, there is something about it which distorts the judgment and perverts the mind; it is less distinguished by its passion for misrepresentation, than by the voracious credulity with which it swallows every thing which is false'.[47] Party or religious bias corrupted the independent man's ability to apply reason to emotion.

Whether in the role of magistrate, judge or jury, men were expected to exercise control over their politico-religious emotions and to demonstrate their impartial decision-making.[48] When praising Bushe in the 1820s, Richard Sheil noted, 'The rank or the religion of parties, has no sort of weight with him; and to every case, whatever may be the circumstances attending it, he gives an equal and unbiased hearing'.[49] Lawyers demanded this of juries. Daniel O'Connell asked the jury in *McGarahan v. Maguire* (1827), where a Protestant woman accused a Catholic priest of seduction, not to 'lend yourselves to such prejudices, you will devote to this case that cool and considered judgement which it requires'.[50] With less temperance in the 1813 prosecution of John Magee, he asked the jury: 'Has Party Feeling extinguished in your breasts every glow of virtue, every spark of manhood?'[51] As noted in Chapter 4, men were not expected to put aside prejudices created by gender or class. They were encouraged to look upon women from their position as fathers, brothers and husbands, and to imaginatively engage with men of different classes, uncovering truth through sympathetic engagement.[52] Religious and political belief operated differently, as a mantle that was worn and could be displaced for a time, not an ethnicity that defined the person.

Impartiality was a demand that most middling and elite men took seriously. Judges and magistrates went to lengths to declare their impartiality and distance themselves from accusations of bias.[53] Unless pertinent, witnesses were not typically asked to state their religion.[54] Overt declarations of impartiality cannot be read as a straightforward measure of courtroom practice. That their protests were so loud was itself a sign of anxiety, as was the practice of respectable Catholics using ministers from both the Catholic and Established Church as character witnesses.[55] However, it produced a context where religious belief did not impact straightforwardly on character. People were encouraged not to judge those of the mainstream Irish sects on their belief, but rather on accent, education, social class and other signals of respectability. As many of the poorest Irish were also Catholic, it seems likely that where Catholic bias existed, it would have reinforced readings of such men as unmanly. Such unspoken biases and judgements are difficult to prove. It is evident that middle-class and elite Catholics in non-political cases were treated with a performance of respect by their Protestant brethren; social class trumped religious belief.

This is not to say religion could not be used to measure manliness. As discussed in Chapter 5, Catholic priests were subject to particular scrutiny, even ridicule, in the courts. Quakers, Jews, Methodists and other religious 'outsiders' were unmanned by their beliefs, often viewed as eccentric curiosities.[56] Anti-Semitism, whilst rarely overtly expressed, was often not far from the surface. Given that the King family were famous Jewish moneylenders, the Commissioner's choice during Steele's trial to refer to Charles King as an 'usurer' could be read in that light. Men from minority religions and sects sometimes held to a different standard of masculinity, placing greater value on religious performance as a marker of identity.[57] The religious male body could feed wider anxieties of the era where excessive devotion was tied to femininity – a connection that all the major Christian sects attempted to reverse through their investments in muscular Christianity.[58] When contrasted with the moderation and self-control of the independent man, religious enthusiasm became a mark of effeminacy both in and outside the courtroom. What is notable about Ireland is that Catholicism avoided that signification for the laity.

The extent to which the lower-order Irish invested in impartiality is more open to question. The more mundane examples of sectarianism in everyday life arose from fights and disputes that were contextualised by wider religious divisions. As the case of Mrs Murphy in Chapter 6 suggested, the fight with her neighbour could not be properly understood without an appreciation of its sectarian environment. Several disputes arose from different sects infringing on the, often customary, territory of another.[59] Yet, when in court, it appears that all groups held that impartial justice was a social good.[60] A loudly proclaimed performance of impartial justice by the elite and the press helped to invest divided communities in legal decisions. The audience to Steele's case approved of the elaborate compliments shared between the key legal actors, where they acknowledged their political differences but also each other's character.

Character was not only constructed through individual performances, but in their intersection with wider value structures and community hierarchies. Credibility was assessed by locating individuals within varying models of masculinity and larger networks of family, community and class. Where social groupings, such as religious belief, were areas of social conflict and so their relationship to credibility disputed, justice was determined by a broad social agreement to ignore the relevance of such categories. The truth and justice produced through character were highly contingent.

### Truth affirming oaths

Theoretically at least, truth was enforced by the oath. All witnesses, juries and officers of the court were required to swear that justice would be served. Court officers were bound to uphold the law and duties of their office; juries to give verdicts based on evidence and without prejudice; and witnesses to tell the truth. In law, the oath was a sacred vow between the oath-taker and God, authorised by the state.[61] The expanding number of public offices of the era required men, especially of the middling and elite classes, to swear multiple oaths across their lives, with no clear account of how competing interests should be balanced. Illegal oaths were a concern for the authorities, who linked them to the formation of seditious societies.[62] The latter could conflict with oaths of allegiance to the Crown, oaths to magistrates to ensure good order, and oaths given by those in military service. How seriously people took oaths therefore was a topic of contemporary and now historiographical interest.[63]

The purpose of the legal oath was to impart the seriousness of the duty undertaken and to hold the doer to account in the afterlife. It required a basic knowledge of scripture, belief in God, and recognition that lying led to damnation. This was articulated explicitly when children testified and had to prove their understanding of the oath to prove legal competency. Fourteen-year-old John Donoghue claimed he did not know the nature of an oath in 1848. He was then quizzed on his religious upbringing:

> Court – Were you ever at a church or chapel?
> Witness – No, Sir.
> Court – Was your mother ever there?
> Witness – She was.
> Court – Did she never take you there?
> Witness – No, Sir.
> Court – Did you ever hear of heaven or hell?
> Witness – No, Sir.
> Court – Did you ever hear of God?
> Witness – No, Sir.
> Mr Coppinger – Do you know what would become of you, if you told a lie?
> Witness replied that he did not.[64]

He was not permitted to testify. Seven-year-old Susan Chawtor gave 'very satisfactory' answers a few years earlier, explicitly noting: 'Was told I would go to hell after I would die if I took a false oath. . . . Thinks there would be no means of salvation for her if she took a false oath'.[65] She kissed the Bible and was asked what she had done, but gave no reply.

The Court prompted, 'That book you took is the Bible you have been told about. You have sworn on it; and what will be the case if you swore wrong? A. Go to hell'. She was allowed to proceed.

The religious foundation of oath-taking was complicated by the diversity of beliefs in Ireland. Whilst Catholics and members of the Established Church were happy to swear on the Bible, many Presbyterians, Quakers and other sects were not. Presbyterians swore without the Bible and, from 1839, a number preferred the 'Scottish custom' of raising their right hand.[66] Quakers affirmed their testimony, although there was some debate as to its validity and defence lawyers pointed to its lesser value; by the mid-century, most legal writers agreed that those of any religion, provided they believed in a Supreme Being, could swear.[67] This excluded those that could not refer to God in their oaths or affirmations. Dr William Harty, Dublin city gaol's physician, could not testify in an 1828 sanity case as he refused to use the words 'So help me God'.[68]

Those with no religious belief were excluded from court. Whilst atheists were scarce, several witnesses claimed to have no understanding of religion to avoid testifying.[69] Despite living within two miles of a chapel, nineteen-year-old John Hestin claimed to have never been to church, nor to understand the consequences of false swearing. His twenty-one-year-old brother, Austin, did not know the nature of an oath, nor how many gods there were. When asked (three times) the consequences of false swearing, he persisted in saying 'he'd go to heaven'.[70] The magistrate, Lord Sligo, was left to 'severely and very justly reprimand' their parent for his 'neglect in not having his children better instructed in the principles of religion'. Other men's 'ignorance' was treated with greater scepticism, as could their 'conscientious objections'.[71]

Despite being reinforced by divine power, the value of an oath was directly related to the perceived character of the swearer. Oaths of those of little character were considered worthless. '[F]rom the general character of Gillier, he believed him not to be entitled to credit on his oath in a court of justice', argued a defence witness, Boyle, in an 1829 perjury case.[72] In the same year, John H. Barry, Esq., testified of a former employee that 'from his general character, he does not think him worthy of credit on his oath'.[73] Criminal convictions were particularly damning. Pat Liddy noted a year earlier that James Reilly 'was arrested for stealing hay; James Reilly is not worthy of belief on his oath'.[74] When Elizabeth and Helen Richards, Elizabeth Kavanaugh, and John and Catherine Lynch, all described by their lawyers as 'respectable' and 'highly-connected', were prosecuted for marrying Helen Richards to the wealthy minor, John Grady, without parental permission, the women's lawyer reflected on their characters: 'Conviction in such a case would degrade them so much in point of law, that their oaths would not be received in a Court of Justice. . . . she would become a miserable outcast from every society where character and conduct were held in estimation'.[75] As articulated by lawyers, having an oath received as credible in a court of justice was the baseline for character.

The oaths of those with good character held more weight. Men of known-standing were not always required to provide an oath. When acting in defence in 1838, Mr Creighton invited a member of the prosecuting party to speak on the availability of a witness, noting, 'His word will be deemed sufficient. I am sure no one would call upon him by his oath to verify that which he would state upon his word'.[76] When Michael Angelo was accused by a witness he was cross-examining in 1844 of 'living and drinking together' with his married client, he 'with a look of scorn and contempt' said, 'Give me the book and swear me', to which the bench responded, 'Oh, no; don't mind'. After a bit of theatrical posturing, Angelo observed, 'Then upon my sacred honour 'tis a foul calumny'.[77] Not swearing could be used to preserve honour. One duellist asked magistrates to intervene in his forthcoming engagement in 1840, but refused to make the formal oath that would allow the court to issue an arrest warrant.[78] Swearing against another elite man tarnished an 'honourable' encounter.

That honour provided a sufficient basis for truth encouraged men further down the social ladder to claim it. In 1833, the writer Francis West, 'a low, smart, gentlemanly-looking man' with 'a large pair of whiskers' proclaimed: "'Sir, my honour is sufficient; but here I'll satisfy you (taking the book). I shall tell the truth, the whole truth, and nothing but the truth – so help me God.'".[79] Mr Barlow refused in 1842 to allow his wife to swear to an assault by the police. He frequently interrupted the police witnesses' sworn testimony and accused the magistrate of 'leaning to the side of poor people'.[80] The magistrate and the reporter thought Barlow was unreasonable, but his offence is understandable within a model where being taken on honour, rather than oath, was a marker of status. Had he cooperated, Barlow's testimony would likely have been weighed more heavily than the officers. Instead, his interruptions and refusal to swear undermined his 'truthfulness'.

Requests from the lower orders to be taken on 'honour' were rare and typically part of playful engagement with the court officers. However, several poor women took exception to being sworn. Both Eliza Sly and Molly Wilson initially refused to take the oath in the 1820s, claiming they had reach old age without ever having done so.[81] Wilson noted she had 'never taken one, though past 70 years of age'. Nancy Casey, a shopkeeper, asked in 1840 whether the 'Gintlemen o'the bench wouldn't ax a lone woman to take her oath'.[82] These women claimed an honour associated with vulnerable femininity, where oath-swearing was a risk, endangering the soul, that a 'lone' or 'elderly' woman should not be asked to take. It suggested that these women needed protection by the court, itself a claim to modesty and respectability, perhaps even social status.

This was how Casey's request was heard by Dan Dempsey, who she sued for assault and robbery. He immediately responded: "'Oh! – dear me (he said) what delicacy it is. Eh, then, how do you do, Mrs Casey, this shinin' morning?" and he bowed very low. "Eh! Nelly, *a cushla*, how is every breath o' you, my 'lone woman'? Not to take the book indeed'". By ridiculing Nancy Casey's request – referring to her 'delicacy', providing her with the title 'Mrs' and bowing in respect – he did not challenge the principle that respectable women might be entitled to testify without swearing, but Casey's claim to vulnerable femininity. Despite Dempsey's interpretation, these women were not claiming to be of higher status but to be treated as 'respectable', a category they believed should encompass women from the lower orders. The narrowness of the category of respectable femininity, which had far less space than masculinity for class difference, provided lower-order women with a claim to 'honour' that their husbands could not access.

That the oath was meant to provide an assurance of truthfulness worried some commentators, who thought that it gave merit to the testimonies of those of little worth. The increasing use of 'approvers', accomplices who turned state's evidence, was subject to critique in the press.[83] 'The Swearing System', as it was described, saw men executed on the word of those with 'no character'.[84] The *Tipperary Vindicator* ranted against, '[t]he monster, Shanahan . . . glibly swearing away the life of a third victim' in the 1844 trial arising from Ryan Morgan's murder. His lies were marked by his 'imperturbable coolness' coupled with 'demoniacal savagery'. With each trial, he grew more 'hardened', 'a darker scowl was on his brow – a more mocking leer on his lip; and in his heart there was a more dogged determination to earn the gold of his paymasters – the Government'.[85] It was exactly this 'character evidence' that the jury was expected to use to weigh Shanahan's testimony, but not everybody was confident this would happen.

Such commentaries were evidence of how seriously oath-taking was to perceptions of justice. Some reporters thought that oath-taking was not done with enough formality; one account of an 1834 petty session described the 'revolting scene' of the magistracy administering oaths whilst wearing their hats and hurrying. The oath-takers 'view it more as a proscribed form than a solemn undertaking to disclose the truth'.[86] Parliamentary bills to regularise the legality of affirmations for non-conformists countered resistance from a community that saw them as an essential assurance of truth. One commentator asked if witnesses were to be given a simple choice between an oath or affirmation, why any man would take an oath: 'is there any man of honour who would so slur his own testimony as (it being itself sufficient) to prop it up with an uncalled for oath? . . . is there any jury who would give one particle of extra credit to the witness who felt so insecure of his own credibility as to varnish his testimony with superfluous averments?'[87] The man who chose to swear an oath when he did not need to, in effect, suggested that his 'word' was without merit.

Despite the lack of weight given to the voices of the poor and anti-Catholic propaganda which suggested priests absolved the sins of those that lied on the stand, it was not just wealthy men that took swearing an oath seriously.[88] The elaborate lengths some people went to avoid swearing 'valid' oaths indicates the significance placed on the exact performance of the ritual and that it tied the oath-giver into a relationship with the divine. Kissing the thumb instead of the book was the most commonly reported way that people avoided the formation of the oath's sacred bond. Martin Malley kissed his thumb three times, so was not allowed to testify in 1833.[89] A man named Donovan was caught kissing his thumb by the Douglas magistrates in 1847 and was turned out of court.[90] Some commentators thought such activity widespread amongst the poor, feeding into the general distrust of this social group.[91] Both that anxiety and that the poor performed such actions highlights the continuing significance of the oath as evidence of the truthfulness of the testimony that followed. Character was vital to determining the value of an oath, but was not the only consideration.

### Lying on the stand

As has been explored, the early nineteenth-century public were confident they could use the body and delivery of evidence, in conjunction with broader character, to determine honesty. If manly performances spoke to general character, there were also markers that evidenced a truthful, and particularly a false, testimony, allowing the public to judge whether a person of good character was being truthful on this occasion. Truth was known not only by the general demeanour of the witness, but by 'simplicity', 'firmness', 'clearness' and consistency.[92] This was evidenced not only by what was said, but by the manner in which it was said. One description of an 1817 Belfast criminal noted that after he confessed his voice 'became firm and clear'.[93] Ten-year-old Edward Walsh, when testifying against his uncle for his father's murder in 1808: 'evidenced a powerful sensibility, shedding tears profusely, and appeared perfectly conscious of the situation of the prisoners, but without shewing the slightest meditation to prevaricate'.[94] Walsh's distress was viewed as evidence of his awareness of the gravity of his words and so their credibility.

Evidences of lying were just as obvious for observers and broadly followed the signs of falsehood agreed in the United Kingdom since at least the seventeenth century: 'an overforward and hasty zeal on the part of the witness, . . . his exaggeration of circumstances, his reluctance in giving adverse evidence, his slowness in answering, his evasive replies, his affection of not hearing or not understanding the question . . . precipitancy in answering . . . his inability to detail any circumstances wherein, if his testimony were untrue, he would be open to contradiction'.[95] The *Irish Penny Journal* added 'blushing' in men, but not women, to this list, although thought it a weak proof.[96] Prevaricating and hesitation were particularly strong evidences of dishonesty in the Irish court, as elsewhere in the Empire.[97] John Mitchell refused to answer a question in 1831; when the court insisted he 'still hesitated and became confused', to which the judge noted: 'I do not know what the jury will say, but I am certain that I will not believe your evidence'.[98] Several newspaper accounts simply dismissed such testimony. 'The two approvers (Owen and Warring) prevaricated and completely contradicted each other', noted the *Saunder's Newsletter* in 1817.[99]

Courts were therefore sensitive to how testimony was given, particularly when there was a disjunction between 'general character' and how evidence was recounted. When Ellen Doran, a prostitute, testified in 1841, the magistrate, Alderman Tyrrell, noted: 'Although this girl's evidence must be received with caution, I cannot reject it. She tells her story clear enough'.[100] He affirmed this decision after it was challenged, noting: '[a] woman may be a prostitute and yet tell a correct and true story on her oath'.[101] Approvers exemplified this contradiction, as criminals required to recount their own lack of character to convict accomplices. Their testimonies presented difficulties for courts, particularly where they had long criminal records or committed horrendous crimes. James Darmody's 1846 testimony against his fellow Whiteboys included detailed descriptions of a murder he committed. It was preceded in the press by a note that 'the following frightful disclosures were elicited on the cross-examination'.[102]

Darmody's account was accompanied by 'sensation', 'murmurs', and at one point 'an audible thrill ran through the court, and there was a pause of a moment'. He was described as 'hesitating' on occasion, but if anything, his account was marked by its shocking frankness and his lack of contrition. When asked, 'Did you you [sic] blush when you saw the face of the man you went to murder?', he replied, 'No, I did not blush'. The Counsel replied, 'I believe you'. In giving a full account of his crimes, his testimony was difficult to undermine; he had nothing to hide. The news report ended: 'There was other corroborating evidence, and the prisoners were found guilty'. Corroborating evidence was legally necessary, but ultimately the trial rested on his word, his apparent honesty of greater weight than the value of his character.

As interesting in such testimony is the pleasure, perhaps even glorification, of infamy, both by the witness and the newspaper reporting it. Darmody's tale was told with little emotion and great clearness, and caused strong responses from the court, an effect reinforced for the reader through the reporting of the gallery's emotions. When giving an account of the murder, the paper redacted the testimony to: '[Here he coolly detailed the particulars of Shanahan's murder, amid great sensation.]' Refusing to print testimony, and placing a journalist's brief explanation in square brackets, was typically only used for details that were not suitable for publication, normally of a sexual nature. Doing so during a murder trial indicated there was something unusually violent or disturbing about this testimony, reinforcing Darmody's infamous character. Most approvers' stories were more mundane, but the requirement that such men 'confess' and do so with an air of frankness was challenging to understandings of character that associated honesty with morality, and likely contributed to the anxiety that this group caused for legal commentators.[103]

Approvers sometimes revelled in their infamy, finding benefit in creating an identity based on poor character. Such men placed themselves within a popular tradition of the heroic outlaw or gentlemanly highwayman.[104] Such imagined villains were notable for committing crime, whilst holding to honourable codes of gentlemanly masculinity. Sheil noted of the approver Fitzgerald during the 1826 Holycross murder trial that 'the life which he led was singular as it was atrocious', and that 'far from manifesting any anxiety to conceal or to excuse his own guilt, he on the contrary set it forth in the blackest colours. He made himself a prominent actor in the business of blood'.[105] Whilst waiting for him to appear, Sheil had imagined that he would 'be some fierce-looking, savage wretch, with baseness and perfidy, intermingled with atrocity, in his brow, and whose meanness would bespeak the informer, as his ferocity would proclaim the assassin'. He was wrong; instead Sheil encountered 'a tall athletic young man' with 'an air of easy indifference and manly familiarity', and a 'countenance as intelligent in expression and symmetrical in feature, as his limbs were vigorous and well-proportioned'. Sheil had 'never seen a cooler, more precise, methodical, and consistent witness', whose 'openness and candour' ensured he was not shaken on cross. Whilst generally tyrannising the countryside in which he lived, he was nonetheless 'a favourite with the populace', due to his willingness to revenge their injuries.

The reader suspects that Fitzgerald was also a favourite with Sheil; his beautiful body, manly familiarity and openness disrupted Sheil's moral universe and incited admiration, rather than his anticipated disgust. Such readings of this 'supervillain' were enabled due to a wider popular culture that provided a model of masculinity for explaining the contradiction such men presented. These men reinterpreted their behaviours into this alternative masculinity, giving them a foundation on which to build a character that was infamous and criminal, but still manly. Notably it was a form of character-building that, perhaps unlike in England, the press and public were willing to be complicit in, providing the sensations, murmurs and thrills that authenticated their identities.[106] As one newspaper lamented in 1843: 'a sentimental admiration of criminals, in direct proportion to the enormity of their crime, has become fashionable, and that neither the bench nor the jury-room have preserved their independence from its sickly influence'.[107]

Playing 'the villain' was a risky courtroom strategy, left to those for whom a guilty verdict was inevitable. A more everyday example of a group willing to adopt less than well-behaved personas were the young working-class men who performed a playful 'naughtiness' in the lower courts where the consequences were smaller. They revelled in their drunken antics, their low-level violence and irreverence for court proceedings.[108] Such men sought to show themselves as 'independent' of the law, a claim to the privileges of the status of the elite, and as members of a world where such behaviours were markers of homosocial bonding and belonging.[109] Their performances situated them within a particular working-class community and displaying manliness to that audience was as significant as being read as respectable by the judge.

There were also men who found it useful to actively perform dishonesty for the court. James Morgan, when he appeared before the Insolvent Debtors' Court in 1838, playfully prevaricated, swearing that

Margaret Henderson was not his wife and that all property belonged to her: 'Court – had you any children by her? Insolvent – Why, she had children. Court – But, I ask you again, had you any children by her? Insolvent – I don't know what you mean. Court – Do you mean to swear that? Insolvent – why, she fathered children on me to be sure'.[110] Nobody, not even the defendant, took this testimony particularly seriously. John Leary, a servant, was considered to be lying when accused of assaulting his wife in 1834. His neighbour testified to hearing cries of murder and found Leary's wife bleeding. Leary claimed that they were acting out a play and his wife was accidentally elbowed in the face. Leary's wife confirmed his story. The magistrate observed, 'I think it natural she would endeavor to protect her husband. At the same time, she does it at the expense of truth'.[111]

At times these stories exceeded the reasonable, stretching to remarkable 'tall tales'. A Tipperary approver named Smith accused his six neighbours of assault in 1848, but the court 'did not believe this incredulous story'.[112] Patrick Doyle claimed in 1831 he had not stolen an ass, but 'merely *borrowed* the ass in a *friendly* way'. The journalist, with his own share of irony, noted: 'notwithstanding the visible and extreme innocence of the prisoner, he was committed to the *friendly* care of Mr McDowell for 12 months'.[113] At the same assizes, James Murphy, charged with concealing himself with intent to rob, argued that he 'was pursued by dogs and was so terrified as to render it necessary for him to get on the roof of the house'. When asked why he climbed *into* the roof, he replied: 'I was so much in dread of the dogs, my lord, that I feared making the least noise and I lay down quietly'.[114] Lying was here motivated by self-preservation, something the court found explicable, but it seems unlikely that anybody was expected to find these tales true. Rather these men engaged in playful storytelling, where they hoped to engage the sympathies of the court and bind them in a collusive agreement to ignore the truth. The lower courts were more amenable to this than the higher courts, but even there it depended on the severity and nature of the case.

In other cases, lying by witnesses was designed to undermine their own testimony. This is notable in several approving cases, but also elsewhere. James Laughlin and Arthur Lennon prevaricated so considerably on cross-examination in 1829 that the journalist observed it 'evidently went to show that they did not wish to tell the truth'.[115] Mathew Hilton's prevarication in 1817 saw him gaoled, and several approvers found themselves on trial for their original crimes for not cooperating.[116] These men were not simply 'caught out' by rigorous cross-examination, but rather deliberately engaged in a performance of lying. The motivations for such behaviour were not always clear, but it appeared in some cases to be a mechanism for avoiding testifying. For some, it may be that within their own communities the penalties for testifying were too high; for others, it was an attempt to build or reinforce a reputation for infamy, the risk to salvation adding a dimension of danger.

Counteracting the effect of lying was not easy. Juries, audiences and court officers were expected to read the body and weigh evidence, and, as seen above, barristers and judges often commented on whether they felt the testimony should be given weight. On occasion, even respectable witnesses could provide testimony that contradicted each other, causing consternation.[117] In such cases, corroborating testimony or evidence could be used to determine truth, often presented to witnesses to provoke a 'truthful' response through throwing them off guard. One of the most marked examples of this was to make witnesses repeat their evidence whilst looking on the witness whose story they challenged. When Hugh Kelly testified in 1828 that he had 'criminal intercourse' with Anne McGarahan, Anne 'and the witness were placed side by side on the table, and on Mr. Bennett asking her if she ever had criminal intercourse with Kelly, she replied – So help me God! Never – I declare it in the sight of Heaven, and this honourable Court, and then turning and shaking her hand at Mr. Kelly, she said, "Oh! You are a perjured villain and a rascal."'[118] Mary Maclean had to 'confront' two defence witnesses during her 1837 rape suit; she affirmed her account and denied their testimony was true.[119] Martin Burke when confronted by evidence in 1845 that a man (Glynn) he accused of assault was working many miles away, 'with much excitement', not only prevaricated, but admitted that Glynn had previously testified against Burke.[120] Like a strong cross-examination, confrontations were designed to expose the truth of testimony through legal ritual. Only the most hardened characters should be able to lie whilst looking truth in the eye.

### Forensic evidence

It was not only other witnesses that liars were confronted with, but physical evidence and the lay and scientific accounts that gave it meaning. Like in the past, most physical evidence did not require specialist analysis. Items found on the dead or around bodies, particularly infants, that provided evidence of identity or the commission of a crime were commonly brought to court. In 1820, Ellen Bedford testified that she saw the deceased, Bridget Kelly, struck on the head with a stool and the 'stool was produced in Court, and the blood on it'.[121] A constable at the 1829 trial of James Mulvaney and James Cosgrove for the murder of James Mulvaney, the elder, noted he found: 'a quantity of bed clothes, stained with blood, and a large hammer, like a sledge, all of which were produced in court, and excited an indescribable thrill of horror'.[122] The bloody bed clothes and hammer, like the stool, were suggestive of violence, but they were not scientifically analysed or even closely described. Rather their import was to corroborate oral testimony and to engage the emotions, the 'horror', of the gallery and jury.

Those who introduced physical evidence to the court were placed in the position of experts. Witnesses sometimes described goods in detail, demonstrating not only their familiarity and ownership, but a sophisticated knowledge of quality, finishing and wear.[123] In 1844, Johanna Donovan described the clothing that her deceased sister was last seen in: 'a blue cloak, a brown gown, black and red shawl, and a Quaker check apron, with a thick cap having a "cross bar" bit behind it; . . . the cloak was an old one; knew it at Castlemartyr, as it had a sewing up the back; it had a plain hood; the women in that part of the country wore brown gowns; check aprons are going out of fashion'.[124] When found, the clothes were wet and full of maggots. Donovan's knowledge identified her sister's decomposed and dismembered body, but it also situated her as an expert in women's fashion. This formed the foundation for establishing the identity of the deceased and was supported by the physical clothing itself. The prosecuting lawyer noted that 'we have them here; they are in that bad state; but we will show them notwithstanding'.

This was not dissimilar to the evidence provided by police and scientific experts. Most testimony by medical doctors was not by men unknown to the deceased, but those that had cared for them during their last illness or after injury. In insanity and suicide cases, doctors often had lengthy relationships with those being assessed. The Commission of Lunacy in 1845 into the state of mind of Thomas Carpenter, Esq., called on the medical practitioners who had treated him for twenty years.[125] At the inquest into the suicide of Mr Robert Barber in 1841, Luke Smyth, Esq., a surgeon, testified that he had treated him for inflammation of the eye; that on their last appointment, the deceased thought 'his head very full', believed he was going to die shortly, and that he regularly drank too much alcohol.[126] He was the doctor called to the scene when Barber's body was found. A second doctor, a surgeon, performed the autopsy.

Most bodies, even in murder cases, were not given a post-mortem, mainly due to the expense but possibly also due to a lack of expertise in rural areas.[127] Where the cause of death was evident, because it was witnessed or there was visible marks, such as a bullet wound, it was not considered necessary.[128] Post-mortems were more likely when the cause of death was unclear, where poisoning was suspected, or where a correlation between the injury and death had to be proved.[129] As a result, much medical testimony was not dissimilar from other witness testimony, providing evidence not simply of the state of the corpse and the cause of the death, but familiarity with the lifestyle, behaviours and relationships of the deceased. Given that many lay witnesses also testified to injuries they witnessed and even treated, as well as the extended care they gave to victims, the line between expert and non-expert was narrow.

Rather such evidence spoke to its history in a 'knowing' legal system, where jurors and judges, as well as expert witnesses, were expected to draw on their previous knowledge of the plaintiffs, victims, defendants and witnesses.[130] It was a system that reinforced that the law was rooted within the local community, rather than beyond it. Yet, the early nineteenth century was also a period where such knowledge could no longer be guaranteed and whether it was desirable also came under debate. This provided a space for the 'expert', a term that was not used in this context during the period. Such men brought knowledge from external sources to enable them to interpret evidence.

Experts rooted their evidence in scientific knowledge and particularly experimental data. During the West wife-murder trial in 1844, Mr E.G. Leeson, M.D. and surgeon, described how, 'I have had occasion to make experiment with blood stains', before arguing that it was unlikely that it was 'blood' on the defendant's jacket, as 'if it were a stain of blood, if it was scraped it would become brighter in colour'.[131] He went on in cross-examination to describe his experimental practice, noting that it required a microscope and that for best results, the larger the quantity and the fresher the evidence the better. He observed that chemical tests would be unsuccessful in this case, and they could not determine whether the blood was human.

During Mrs Ellen Byrne's 1842 trial for poisoning her husband, medical experts grounded their arguments in their previous experience. The apothecary Arthur Harvey testified he thought Mr Byrne was dead for four to five days; when challenged, he argued: 'My experience or reading would not enable me to say that a body under certain circumstances would run into decomposition in 37 hours. . . . My experience does not enable me to say whether blood could flow from the mouth or nose of a person who was five or six day's dead'.[132] The surgeon, J.J. Fox, tied his evidence to previous bodies: 'In some cases the fluidity [of blood] is a mark of a particular death, but I have known the blood to coagulate in a case of strangulation', whilst Andrew Ellis, the surgeon who carried out the post-mortem, noted that, 'I am a member of the College of Surgeons – one of the examiners, and have been for years connected with anatomical schools'. Surgeon Geoghegan supported his case by describing his experiments with putrefying bodies: 'The subject upon which he experimentalised was the body of a child'.

Expertise here was authorised by medical training, familiarity with medical literature, and personal experimentation and experience with dead bodies. It was a claim to truth tied to 'empirical' data and personal knowledge. This is not to say that such claims had no connection with wider character. Scientific knowledge was authorised through complex social networks, where gentlemanly capital went some way to supporting scientific claims, as well as determining who was included within the scientific world.[133] The treatment of experts on the stand was related to their social status, with men of higher status holding greater authority. There was a hierarchy of expertise, particularly in the medical community. At the top were surgeons, who generally conducted autopsies and provided advice on complex causes of death; beneath them were physicians or general practitioners who had lesser qualifications but were still knowledgeable. Apothecaries and chemists were generally considered less qualified again, except when identifying poisons and chemical compounds. Professional hierarchies were closely tied to wider social status, with surgeons likelier to be better educated, wealthier and so more respectable than general physicians and apothecaries. Like the distinction between barristers and solicitors, professional boundaries overlapped with and reinforced social position. The evidence given by surgeons was thus given greater weight than other medical experts.

This growing specialisation of knowledge was a direct challenge to the community-rooted evidence that relied on contextual familiarity, allowing lawyers to question the ability of ordinary people to testify on specialised domains. During John Coghlan's trial for the manslaughter of Michael Ryan in 1828, Henry St John Brownrigg testified to seeing the deceased's fractured skull.[134] On cross, Daniel O'Connell asked him, 'Are you a medical man? Witness – No, I am a Chief Constable. Mr O'Connell – Oh, then you are a Doctor. Do you know the *occiput* from the *siucipat*, or the *parietal bone*? – No'. Whilst describing wounds was a typical component of police testimony, the emphasis on using medical experts allowed O'Connell to challenge its legitimacy. In doing so, certain forms of truth became associated with particular types of witness.

That scientific evidence could be learned opened this form of evidence to legal challenge. Not only could both sides in a suit present scientific experts, but jurors, judges and lawyers could use their reading and experience to form questions and challenges. During the Byrne trial, the barrister Mr Fitzgibbon quizzed Andrew Ellis on his interpretation, reading case studies from Dr Oxtone's treatise and asking him to guess the cause of death.[135] Testimony could also be challenged by legal definitions around evidence. Defence counsel Mr Blacker quoted *Sir Gregory Lewin's Reports*, a popular legal text, to suggest that Dr Colvan's description of the signs of strangulation in an 1840 child murder were incorrect.[136] Dr Colvan responded by explaining the medical difference between strangulation, suffocation and choking. At this, the prosecution lawyers, Sir T. Staples and Mr Hanna, each quoted from different sections of *Roscoe on Evidence* to confirm that Dr Colvan's definitions were legally permissible. These lawyers were using legal precedent to question submissions of medical evidence, challenging one form of knowledge (medical) with another (legal). In such cases, elite men engaged in rigorous debate without fundamentally challenging the 'truth' of testimony or character of the witness. Character played a smaller role in authorising these testimonies than was typical.

Scientific evidence reformed the nature of truth in court. In creating specialised domains of knowledge, it suggested that certain forms of truth were only accessible through educated men, dismissing similar testimony given by lay witnesses. In reducing the value of character, it provided a challenge to knowledge that was legitimated through social status alone. That, in the early nineteenth century, scientific education typically required significant social capital ensured that this shift was not a dramatic democratisation of the courts. Moreover, at least at this date, the use of such experts in the typical trial remained small. Yet, it was a movement towards an alternative model for determining truth that was to become increasingly significant in subsequent decades.

## Conclusion

When placed on the stand 'Honest' Tom Steele actively displayed his honesty, declaring his wish to answer 'in the most candid manner'. It was a performance that spoke to his character by suggesting he had nothing to hide. It papered over some of the more problematic financial transactions that brought him to court, and was secured by his membership of the social elite. It was a performance that illustrated several of the key markers that helped determine truth within the court. Truth was discovered through evidence given either as oral testimony, in writing or in physical goods. The weight that should be placed on all forms of evidence was supported by the people who provided an explanation of their meaning.

As most evidence continued to be in oral form, reading the character of the witness determined its value. This was not only informed by individualised performances, but how they located people within wider social networks, from family to community to class. A greater emphasis on the individual was not at the expense of a socially produced character.[137] Witness testimony was framed through wider power relationships, so that the words of those of higher status held greater truth value. This was intrinsically connected to constructions of 'independent manhood', where independence provided the opportunity for men to speak and act honestly – something that lower-order men, tied into relationships of dependency and credit, were restricted from doing. The importance of independence to a wider system of social and political order meant that at times the court was even willing to extend credit to elite men so as not to disrupt its logic.

Yet, court audiences and juries were not naïve to social complexities. Elite men, like their lower-order brethren, could and did lie. At times, such performances of dishonesty could disrupt the core belief in the relationship between manliness and character, with manly heroic outlaws challenging normative models for reading truth. Rather, men were required to be astute readers of the body, looking for evidence of truth-telling or lies that might contradict the character suggested by their looks, emotions, clothing or social status. 'Party feeling' could disrupt the lines of sympathetic engagement that enabled men to see another's truth. Physical evidence could aid it, drawing in the testimony of experts, whose knowledge was reinforced by scientific training and experimentation. Expertise provided a new method for determining the value and truthfulness of testimony, destabilising the words of lay witnesses that infringed on professional territory. As importantly, it suggested that justice was no longer something determined at a local level, through an appreciation of a person in their place in the world by a jury that was part of it. Justice could become something determined by experts who assessed empirical facts, perhaps provided to a jury that knew nothing but those facts. Yet, the latter, at least, was still to come to Ireland. Men remained at the heart of justice, drawing their legal performances of character into the production of the law, the court and the nation.

## Notes

1   For discussion see: A.N. May, *The Bar & the Old Bailey, 1750–1850* (Chapel Hill: University of North Carolina Press, 2003), pp. 178–80.

2   B. Shapiro, *Beyond Reasonable Doubt and Probable Cause: Historical Perspectives on the Anglo-American Law of Evidence* (Berkeley: University of California University Press, 1991); P. King, *Crime, Justice and Discretion in England 1740–1820* (Oxford: Oxford University Press, 2000), pp. 226–8; J. Beattie, *Crime and the Courts in England, 1660–1800* (Princeton: Princeton University Press, 1986), pp. 362–76.

3   L. MacNally, *The Rules of Evidence on Pleas of the Crown* (Dublin: J. Cooke, 1802), p. 51; H. Roscoe, *A Digest of the Law of Evidence in Criminal Cases* (London: Saunders and Benning, 1835); R. McMahon, 'Introduction', in R. McMahon (ed.), *Crime, Law and Popular Culture in Europe, 1500–1900* (Collumpton: Willan, 2008), pp. 1–31. In Ireland, unlike England, treason only required one witness for conviction.

4   MacNally, *Rules of Evidence*, pp. 15–16.

5   Beattie, *Crime and the Courts*, pp. 442–3; King, *Crime, Justice and Discretion*, pp. 33, 327–8; M. Wiener, *Reconstructing the Criminal: Culture, Law and Policy in England, 1830–1914* (Cambridge: Cambridge University Press, 1990); A. Gross, *Double Character: Slavery and Mastery in the Antebellum Southern Courtroom* (Princeton: Princeton University Press, 2008).

6   MacNally, *Rules of Evidence*, p. 578.

7   *Ibid.*, p. 394.

8   B. Shapiro, *A Culture of Fact: England, 1550–1720* (Ithaca: Cornell University Press, 2000); T. Golan, 'The history of scientific expert testimony in the English courtroom', *Science in Context*, 12:1 (1999), 7–32; C. Hamlin, 'Forensic cultures in historical perspective: Technologies of witness, testimony, judgment (and justice?)', *Studies in History and Philosophy of Biological and Biomedical Sciences*, 44 (2013), 4–15.

9   MacNally, *Rules of Evidence*, p. 579.

10  N. Lacey, *Women, Crime and Character: From Moll Flanders to Tess of the D'Urbervilles* (Oxford: Oxford University Press, 2008); D.Y. Rabin, *Identity, Crime and Legal Responsibility in Eighteenth-Century England* (Basingstoke: Palgrave Macmillan, 2004).

11  F.W. Whyte, 'Mahon, James Patrick (1800–1891)', rev. A. O'Day, *Oxford Dictionary of National Biography* (Oxford University Press, 2004; online edn, May 2009). www. oxforddnb.com/view/article/17798, accessed 6 July 2015.

12  C.L. Falkiner, 'Steele, Thomas (1788–1848)', rev. G. McCoy, *Oxford Dictionary of National Biography* (Oxford University Press, 2004; online edn, Oct 2007). www. oxforddnb.com/view/article/26348, accessed 6 July 2015.

13  S. Collini, 'The idea of "character" in Victorian political thought', *Transactions of the Royal Historical Society*, 35 (1985), 29–50; P. Langford, *Englishness Identified: Manners and Character, 1650–1850* (Oxford: Oxford University Press, 2000), especially pp. 298–300.

14  J. Tosh, 'The Old Adam and the New Man: Emerging themes in the history of masculinities, 1750–1850', in T. Hitchcock and M. Cohen (eds), *English Masculinities, 1660–1800* (London: Longman, 1999), pp. 217–28; A. Clark, *The Struggle for the Breeches: Gender and the Making of the British Working-Class* (Berkeley: University of California Press, 1995).

15  A. Shepard, *Meanings of Manhood in Early Modern England* (Oxford: Oxford University Press, 2003); J. Tosh, *A Man's Place: Masculinity and the Middle Class Home in Victorian England* (New Haven: Yale University Press, 1999); J. Bailey, '"A very sensible man": Imagining fatherhood in England, c. 1750–1830', *History*, 95 (2010), 267–92.

16  D. Hay, 'Property, authority and the Criminal Law', in D. Hay *et al.* (eds), *Albion's Fatal Tree: Crime and Society in Eighteenth-Century England* (London: Verso, 1975), p. 42.

17  E. Foyster, *Manhood in Early Modern England: Honour, Sex and Marriage* (Harlow: Longman, 1999); K. Harvey, 'Men making home: Masculinity and domesticity in eighteenth-century Britain', *Gender & History*, 21:3 (2009), 520–40.

18  See Chapter 1.

19  N.J. Curtin, *The United Irishmen: Popular Politics in Ulster and Dublin, 1791–1798* (Oxford: Clarendon Press, 1994); K. Barclay, 'Negotiating independence: Manliness and begging letters in late eighteenth and early nineteenth-century Scotland', in L. Abrams and E. Ewan (eds), *Nine Centuries of Man: Manhood and Masculinity in Scottish History* (Edinburgh: Edinburgh University Press, 2016) pp. 142–59.

20  'County of Carlow', *Dublin Evening Post* (26 March 1844) Carlow.

21  'Waterford Assizes', *Dublin Evening Mail* (20 July 1849) Waterford.

22  K. Barclay, 'Marginal households and their emotions: The 'Kept Mistress' in enlightenment Edinburgh', in S. Broomhall (ed.), *Spaces for Feeling: Emotions and Sociabilities in Britain, 1650–1850* (London: Routledge, 2015), pp. 95–111.

23  'Ballina Petty Sessions', *Freeman's Journal* (17 December 1845) Mayo.

24  'Nenagh Petty Session', *Freeman's Journal* (22 April 1835) Tipperary.

25  M.J.D. Roberts, 'Public and private in early nineteenth-century London: The Vagrant Act of 1822 and its enforcement', *Social History*, 13:3 (1988), 273–94.

26  C. Barry, 'The police and protest in Dublin: 1786–1840', in J.F. McEldowney and P. O'Higgins, *The Common Law Tradition: Essays in Irish Legal History* (Dublin: Irish Academic Press, 1990), pp. 157–84; C.H.E. Philpin, *Nationalism and Popular Protest in Ireland* (Cambridge: Cambridge University Press, 2002).

27  F. Dabhoiwala, 'The construction of honour, reputation and status in later seventeenth and early eighteenth century England', *Transactions of the Royal Historical Society*, ser. 6, 6 (1996), 201–24; M. McCormack, *The Independent Man: Citizenship and Gender Politics in Georgian England* (Manchester: Manchester University Press, 2005).

28  'Prerogative Court', *Roscommon Messenger* (29 November 1848) Dublin.

29  M. Finn, *The Character of Credit: Personal Debt in English Culture, 1740–1914* (Cambridge: Cambridge University Press, 2003); M.J. Powell, 'Credit, debt and patriot politics in Dublin, 1763–1784', *Eighteenth-Century Ireland*, 25 (2010), 118–48; B.P. Cooper, '"A Not Unreasonable Panic": Character, confidence, and credit in Harriet Martineau's "Berkeley the Banker"', *Nineteenth-Century Contexts: an Interdisciplinary Journal*, 32:4 (2010), 363–84.

30  Finn, *Character of Credit*, pp. 69–70; S. Hindle, 'Dependency, shame and belonging: Badging the deserving poor, c. 1550–1750', *Cultural and Social History*, 1 (2004), 6–35; Barclay, 'Marginal households'.

31  Powell, 'Credit, debt and patriot politics', p. 126; S.M. Pearsall, *Atlantic Families: Lives and Letters in the Later Eighteenth Century* (Oxford: Oxford University Press, 2008), pp. 171–5.

32  For a discussion of the importance of 'misfortune' in restoring economic credit see: Finn, *Character of Credit*, p. 128.

33  'Insolvent Debtor's Court', *Carlow Morning* Post (1 March 1832) Dublin; 'Insolvent Debtor's Court', *Freeman's Journal* (12 September 1821) Dublin; 'Insolvent Debtor's Court', *Freeman's Journal* (26 May 1841) Dublin; 'Insolvent Debtor's Court', *Connaught Journal* (1 March 1832) Dublin; 'Insolvent Debtor's Court', *Freeman's Journal* (3 April 1843) Dublin; 'Insolvent Debtor's Court', *Cork Examiner* (26 July 1844) Dublin.

34  See also 'Insolvent Debtor's Court', *Freeman's Journal* (9 March 1838) Dublin; 'Insolvent Debtor's Court', *Freeman's Journal* (21 December 1843) Dublin.

35  'Insolvent Debtor's Court', *Freeman's Journal* (30 July 1838) Dublin.

36  'Insolvent Debtor's Court', *Freeman's Journal* (27 December 1842) Dublin.

37  Clark, *Struggle for the Breeches*; L. Abrams, 'The taming of Highland masculinity: Inter-personal violence and shifting codes of manhood, c. 1760–1840', *Scottish Historical Review*, 92 (2013), 100–22.

38  'Dublin Police', *Freeman's Journal* (9 November 1832) Dublin; 'Dublin Police Court', *Ballina Advertiser* (10 September 1841) Dublin; 'Seduction', *Carlow Morning Post* (1 March 1832) Antrim; 'Court of Exchequer', *Freeman's Journal* (18 May 1843) Dublin.

39  'Very Remarkable Execution', *Carlow Morning Post* (19 April 1821) King's County/Offaly; 'Carlow Petty Session', *Carlow Morning Post* (2 January 1831) Carlow; 'Carlow Quarter Sessions', *Connaught Journal* (29 January 1827) Carlow; 'Sessions Court', *Freeman's Journal* (25 January 1843) Dublin.

40  D. Bowen, *The Protestant Crusade in Ireland, 1800–70: A Study of Protestant-Catholic Relations between the Act of Union and Disestablishment* (Dublin: Gill & Macmillan, 1978); I. Whelan, *The Bible War in Ireland: "The Second Reformation" and the Polarization of Protestant-Catholic Relations 1800–1840* (Madison: University of Wisconsin Press, 2005).

41  J.R. Hill, 'Artisans, sectarianism and politics in Dublin, 1829–48', *Saothar*, 7 (1981), 12–27; J.S. Donnelly, *Captain Rock: The Irish Agrarian Rebellion of 1821–1824* (Cork: Collins Press, 2009).

42  See discussion in Chapter 1.

43  'Catholic Jury', *Dublin Morning Register* (19 August 1828); 'Jury-packing – Catholic Exclusion', *Freeman's Journal* (1 December 1848); 'The Commission', *Limerick Reporter* (8 July 1842); 'The Trial of the Persons at the Cavan Assizes...', *Dublin Morning Register* (14 August 1829).

44  N. Howlin, 'Controlling jury composition in nineteenth-century Ireland', *Journal of Legal History*, 30:3 (2009), 227–61; N. Howlin, 'Fenians, foreigners and jury trials in Ireland, 1865–70', *Irish Jurist*, 46 (2011), 51–81.

45  McCormack, *The Independent Man*, pp. 187–200; K. Sennefelt, 'Masculinity, sociability and citizenship in Stockholm in the Age of Liberty', in P. Ihalainen, M. Bregnsbo, K. Sennefelt and P. Winton (eds), *Scandinavia in the Age of Revolution: Nordic Political Cultures, 1740–1820* (Aldershot: Ashgate, 2011), p. 318.

46  W. Preston, 'An essay on credulity', *Transactions of the Royal Irish Academy*, 9 (1803), 47–81.

47 *A Report of the Speeches of Charles Kendal Bushe, esq, in the Cases of Edward Sheriden, M.D., and Mr Thomas Kirwan, Merchant for Misdemeanours* (Dublin: M.N. Mahon, 1812), p. 52

48 'Assizes Intelligence', *Freeman's Journal* (28 February 1842) Down; 'The Judges', *Dublin Evening Mail* (26 July 1824); 'Judges and their Charges', *Freeman's Journal* (24 February 1843); 'The Irish Judges', *Freeman's Journal* (25 March 1841).

49 R.L. Sheil, *Sketches, Legal and Political*, ed. M.W. Savage, 2 volumes (London: Henry Colburn, 1855), vol. 1, p. 242.

50 J. Mongan, *A Report of the Trial of the Action in which Bartholomew McGarahan . . . Rev. Thomas Maguire* (Dublin: Westley and Tyrrell, 1827), p. 35.

51 *The Trial of John Magee, Proprietor of the Dublin Evening Post, for publishing an Historical Review* (Dublin: John Magee, 1813), p. 130; See also 'Record Court', *Newry Commercial Telegraph* (21 March 1828) Louth.

52 K. Barclay, 'Emotions, the law and the press in Britain: Seduction and breach of promise suits, 1780–1830', *Journal of Eighteenth-Century Studies*, 39:2 (2016), 267–84.

53 'County of Westmeath Assizes', *Belfast Newsletter* (29 July 1831) Westmeath; 'Sligo Assizes', *Freeman's Journal* (26 March 1828) Sligo; 'Assizes Intelligence', *Freeman's Journal* (28 February 1842) Down.

54 'Alleged Suicide – Mysterious Death', *Dublin Evening Mail* (2 June 1841) Dublin.

55 'Waterford Assizes', *Dublin Evening Mail* (20 July 1849) Waterford.

56 'Kilrush Petty Session', *Kerry Evening Post* (22 December 1824) Clare; 'Dublin Police', *Freeman's Journal* (1 November 1843) Dublin; 'Insolvent Debtor's Court', *Freeman's Journal* (15 January 1838) Dublin; 'Police Court', *Cork Examiner* (2 October 1844) Cork.

57 See note 56 for examples.

58 P. McDevitt, 'Muscular catholicism: Nationalism, masculinity and Gaelic team sports, 1884–1916', *Gender & History*, 9:2 (1997), 262–84; Y.M. Werner (ed.), *Christian Masculinity: Men and Religion in Northern Europe in the Nineteenth and Twentieth Centuries* (Leuven: Leuven University Press, 2011).

59 'Dublin Police', *Freeman's Journal* (28 January 1842) Dublin; 'County of Antrim Assizes', *Belfast Newsletter* (9 August 1814) Antrim; M. Duggan, 'United Irishmen, Orangemen and the 1798 rebellion in County Carlow', in T. McGrath and W. Nolan (eds), *Carlow History and Society: Interdisciplinary Essays on the History of an Irish County* (Dublin: Geography Publications, 2008), pp. 535–86; G. Curtin, 'Religion and social conflict during the Protestant Crusade in West Limerick, 1822–49', *Old Limerick Journal* (Winter 2003), 43–54.

60 K. Barclay, 'A sectarian middle ground? Masculinity and politics in the 1820s petty session courts', Working Paper.

61 B. Shapiro, 'Oaths, credibility and the legal process in early modern England: Part two', *Law and Humanities*, 7:1 (2013), 19–54; B. Shapiro, 'Oaths, credibility and the legal process in early modern England: Part one', *Law and Humanities*, 6:2 (2013), 145–78.

62 P. Mirala, 'Lawful and unlawful oaths in late-eighteenth and early-nineteenth-century Ireland', 1760–1835', in A. Blackstock and E. Magennis (eds), *Politics and Political Culture in Britain and Ireland, 1750–1850* (Belfast: Ulster Historical Foundation, 2007), pp. 209–22; E.P. Thompson, *The Making of the English Working-Class* (Harmondsworth: Penguin, 1968), p. 650.

63 Shapiro, 'Oaths', Part 1 and 2; C. Condren, *Argument and Authority in Early Modern England: The Presupposition of Oaths and Offices* (Cambridge: Cambridge University Press, 2006).

64 'Most Extraordinary Trial for Murder', *Freeman's Journal* (7 April 1848) Cork; see also 'Assizes Intelligence', *Wexford Conservative* (19 March 1842) Kerry.

65 'Tullamore Assizes', *Athlone Sentinel* (21 March 1845) King's County/Offaly; see also 'Commission Intelligence', *Saunder's Newsletter* (14 July 1803) Dublin; 'Limerick Petty Sessions', *Freeman's Journal* (21 October 1834) Limerick.

66 'The New Oath Validity Bill', *Belfast Newsletter* (8 August 1838); 'Londonderry Assizes', *Freeman's Journal* (1 August 1839) Londonderry.

67 'Recorder's Court', *Dublin Morning Register* (18 October 1830) Dublin; MacNally, *Rules of Evidence*, p. 76.

68 'Court of Inquiry-Dublin', *Kilkenny Independent* (28 May 1828) Dublin.

69 An interesting discussion of the value of an atheist's word is found in Curran's speech for the defence during the trial of Harry Shears for treason, T. Davis (ed.), *The Speeches of the Right Honourable John Philpot Curran* (London: Henry Bohn, 1847), p. 409.

70 'Westport Petty Sessions', *Kerry Evening* Post (9 September 1840) Mayo; see also 'Investigation at the Castle – Shinrone Police', *Nation* (12 October 1844) King's County/Offaly.

71 'Police Intelligence', *Dublin Morning Register* (5 May 1837) Dublin.

72 'Commission of Oyer and Terminer', *Drogheda Journal; or Meath and Louth Advertiser* (7 May 1829) Dublin.

73 'Cork Special Commission', *Belfast Newsletter* (30 October 1829) Cork.

74 'Cavan Sessions', *Newry Commercial Telegraph* (25 January 1828) Cavan.

75 'Interesting Trial', *Newry Commercial Telegraph* (4 March 1828) Dublin.

76 'City Sessions', *Freeman's Journal* (17 July 1838) Dublin.

77 'Police Court', *Cork Examiner* (2 October 1844) Cork.

78 '[No Title]', *Kerry Evening Post* (18 March 1840) Dublin. See also Chapter 5.

79 'Dublin Police', *Freeman's Journal* (5 August 1833) Dublin.

80 'College-Street Police Office', *Freeman's Journal* (9 April 1842) Dublin.

81 'Carlow Assizes', *Carlow Morning Post* (25 July 1822) Carlow; 'Cavan Assizes', *The Times* (2 August 1820) Cavan.

82 'Kilrush Petty Sessions', *Kerry Evening Post* (25 May 1840) Kerry.

83 A similar concern existed in England: King, *Crime, Justice and Discretion*, pp. 226–7.

84 'Imperial Parliament', *Leinster Express* (27 July 1844); 'Kilkenny Assizes', *Wexford Conservative* (31 July 1833) Kilkenny; 'The Assizes', *Tipperary Vindicator* (6 April 1844).

85 'The Swearing System', *Tipperary Vindicator* (31 July 1844) Tipperary.

86 'Petit Sessions', *Connaught Telegraph* (24 December 1834).

87 'Judicial Oaths', *Statesmen and Dublin Christian Record* (1 July 1842); see also 'The Irish Judge and Jury Society. A Farce', *Wexford Conservative* (11 November 1843).

88 'Parliamentary Committee', *Freeman's Journal* (17 March 1825); 'Swords Petty Sessions', *Dublin Morning Register* (9 June 1842) Dublin. Others thought that priests discouraged perjury, telling them that kissing the thumb still counted as an oath: 'Committee on the State of Crime in Ireland', *Clonmel Herald* (31 July 1839).

89 'Mayo Assizes', *Ballina Impartial* (5 August 1833) Mayo.

90 'Douglas Petty Sessions', *Southern Reporter and Cork Commercial Courier* (10 July 1847) Cork.

91 'Committee on the State of Crime in Ireland', *Clonmel Herald* (31 July 1839).

92 'Carlow Petty Session', *Carlow Morning* Post (13 February 1832) Carlow; 'Assize Intelligence', *Dublin Weekly Register* (18 March 1837) King's County/Offaly.

93 'Belfast Execution', *Glasgow Journal* (9 April 1817) Antrim.

94 'Kilkenny Assizes', *Belfast Newsletter* (2 September 1808) Kilkenny.

95 Shapiro, *A Culture of Fact*, p. 17.

96 'Blushing', *Irish Penny Journal*, 1:31 (1841), 248.

97 W.E. Schneider, '"Enfeebling the Arm of Justice": Perjury and prevarication in British India', in M.D. Dubber and L. Farmer (eds), *Modern Histories of Crime and Punishment* (Stanford: Stanford University Press 2007), 299–328.

98 'Carlow Assize', *Carlow Morning Post* (4 April 1831) Carlow.

99 'Assize Intelligence', *Saunder's Newsletter* (7 August 1817) Meath.

100 'Dublin Police', *Freeman's Journal* (18 October 1841) Dublin.

101 'Dublin Police', *Cork Examiner* (20 October 1841) Dublin.

102 'Tipperary Assizes', *Freeman's Journal* (1 April 1846) Tipperary.

103 'Carlow Assizes', *Carlow Morning Post* (29 July 1822) Carlow; 'Cork Assizes', *Freeman's Journal* (21 March 1840) Cork.

104 N. Ó Ciosáin, 'Oral culture, literacy and reading, 1800–1850', in J.H. Murphy (ed.), *The Oxford History of the Irish Book IV: The Irish Book I English, 1800–1891* (Oxford: Oxford University Press, 2011), pp. 182–3; R. Cashman, 'The heroic outlaw in Irish folklore and popular literature', *Folklore*, 111:2 (2000), 191–215; B. White, 'The criminal confessions of Newgate's Irishmen', *Irish Studies Review*, 14:3 (2006), 303–24.

105 Sheil, *Sketches, Legal and Political*, vol. 1, pp. 304–5.

106 R. Shoemaker, 'The street robber and the gentleman highwayman: Changing representations and perceptions of robbery in London, 1690–1800', *Cultural and Social History*, 3 (2006), 381–405.

107 'Trial of McNaughten – Acquittal on the Ground of Insanity', *Belfast Newsletter* (10 March 1843).

108 K. Barclay, 'Singing and lower-class masculinity in the Dublin Magistrate's Court, 1800–1845', *Journal of Social History*, 47:3 (2014), 746–68

109 Clark, *Struggle for the Breeches*, pp. 141–57; I.J. Prothero, *Radical Artisans in England and France, 1830–1870* (Cambridge: Cambridge University Press, 1997).

110 'Insolvent Debtor's Court', *Freeman's Journal* (19 January 1838) Dublin.

111 'Dublin Police', *Ballina Impartial* (28 July 1834) Dublin.

112 'An Approver', *Tipperary Vindicator* (21 June 1848) Tipperary.

113 'Carlow Assizes', *Carlow Morning Post* (28 March 1831) Carlow.

114 *Ibid.*.

115 'Assize Intelligence', *Freeman's Journal* (5 August 1829) Louth.

116 'County of Antrim Assizes', *Belfast Newsletter* (28 March 1817) Antrim; 'County of Antrim Assizes', *Belfast Newsletter* (4 August 1820) Antrim; 'Country of Donegal Assizes', *Belfast Newsletter* (29 March 1833) Donegal.

117 'Waterford Assizes', *Saunder's Newsletter* (19 August 1823) Waterford; 'Court of Queen's Bench', *Freeman's Journal* (28 June 1845) Dublin.

118 'Court of Exchequer', *The Law Recorder* (Dublin: The Proprietor, 1828), vol. 1, p. 96.

119 'Tipperary Assizes', *Clonmel Herald* (12 March 1837) Tipperary.

120 'Kingstown Police Office', *Freeman's Journal* (2 August 1845) King's County/Offaly.

121 'Tipperary Assizes', *Saunder's Newsletter* (2 August 1820) Tipperary.

122 'Assize Intelligence', *Freeman's Journal* (16 July 1829) Longford.

123 Vanessa McMahon, 'Reading the body: Dissection and the "murder" of Sarah Stout, Hertfordshire, 1699', *Social History of Medicine*, 19:1 (2006), 19–35.

124 'Cork Spring Assizes', *Cork Examiner* (27 March 1844) Cork.

125 'Commission of Lunacy', *Freeman's Journal* (5 July 1845) Dublin.

126 'Alleged Suicide – Mysterious Death', *Dublin Evening Mail* (2 June 1841) Dublin.

127 'The Practice of Secret Poisoning', *Dublin Medical Press* (27 September 1828); 'Assize Intelligence', *Belfast Newsletter* (5 May 1840) Antrim. It is notable that trials held in Dublin were more likely to use experts than those on circuit.

128 'Assize Intelligence', *Belfast Newsletter* (25 March 1844) Cork.

129 'County of Tyrone Assizes', *Belfast Newsletter* (28 July 1840) Tyrone; 'Waterford Assizes', *Freeman's Journal* (16 July 1839) Waterford; 'County of Antrim Assizes', *Belfast Newsletter* (7 March 1843) Antrim.

130 D. Klerman, 'Was the jury ever self-informing?' *Southern Californian Law Review*, 77 (2003): 123; J.H. Langbein, 'Historical foundations of the law of evidence: A view from the Ryder sources', *Columbia Law Review*, 96 (1996), 1168–202; J.Q. Whitman, *The Origins of Reasonable Doubt: Theological Roots of the Criminal Trial* (New Haven: Yale University Press, 2008), pp. 150–3.

131 'Dublin Commission', *Irish Examiner* (17 April 1844) Dublin.

132 'The Commission', *Wexford Conservative* (20 August 1842) Dublin.

133 S. Shapin, *A Social History of Truth: Civility and Science in Seventeenth-Century England* (Chicago: Chicago University Press, 1994); J. Rudolph, 'Gender and the development of forensic science: A case study', *English Historical Review*, 123:503 (2008), 924–46; H. Ellis, 'Knowledge, character and professionalisation in nineteenth-century British science', *History of Education*, 43:6 (2014), 777–92.

134 'County Criminal Court', *Southern Reporter and Cork Commercial Courier* (1 April 1828) Cork.

135 'The Commission', *Wexford Conservative* (20 August 1842) Dublin.

136 'County of Armagh', *Belfast Newsletter* (11 August 1840) Armagh.

137 Lacey, *Women, Crime and Character*; Rabin, *Identity, Crime*; Wiener, *Reconstructing the Criminal*.

# Closing arguments: a conclusion

## Dublin Police Intelligence

A LOVER IN SPITE OF HIMSELF. – A middle-aged gentleman (Mr. Ferdinand McF—y) appeared to answer the complaint of Mrs. Isabella C—s. The complainant was a little pale-faced woman, approaching to that period of life when age becomes respected. The defendant was a tall thin man; his hair seemed as dishevelled as if it were quite unacquainted with a comb; his face might accuse of his illiberality with regard to soap, and his beard darkened his chin, perfectly unmolested by a razor. A young and sentimental-looking lady stood near the complainant – she was her daughter.

Mrs. C—s – The defendant, your worship, lives next door to me in Phibsborough, and I am out of my life completely plagued by the continual indiscriminations of his nightly reconnoitres up and down his garden. He sometimes, under my daughter's window, plays most inordinately the most indiscreet music, and otherwise misconducts himself by the misapplication of quotations from several antiquated authors (laughter). He fires love-letters out of a pop-gun into my daughter's apartment, and sends kittens over into my garden with profane compositions tied round their necks with red tape (laughter). On one occasion he had the impetuosity to send a monkey up a ladder into her room with another of his combustible expositions (laughter).

Mr. F. – I deny the soft impeachment – I never had a monkey; I confess that I had a black cat – a cat remember, not a monkey; I wish that to be particularly noted in the press, for I hate monkeys and squirrels (laughter).

Mrs. C. – I think he's crased, your worship; but that's not reason that I should be extirpated from my habitation by his incompetency (laughter).

Mr. Duffy [the magistrate] – Certainly not, ma'am.

Mr. F. – Hear me explain. If you will strike, first hear me. Her daughter has encouraged me to this; she sent me, sir, a bag of puffs, and as my teeth are bad, grateful for her consideration, I loved my 'ministering angel.'

Miss C. – I deny all that he is saying; upon my word, mama, I never sent him puffs (laughter).

Mr. F. – Not puffs, not 'bull's eyes?' Come, now, do you deny the bull's eyes?

Miss C. – I protest, your worship, I never sent him any eyes (laughter).

Mr. F. – But were they not my eyes that first entranced you?

Mr. Duffy. – That is a very foolish question, sir.

Mr. F. – If I have erred in this transaction, sir, it was not my fault; I am a lover from necessity; I can't help myself; it is all in my eye, sir (laughter). A peculiar property – a loadstone power – a gluey adhesive attribute – it is all in my eye, sir. Do you know that snake, sir, that encompassed its victim in the light of its eyes, and then pounces on it; I am such a person. I'd lay you a wager, sir, if you place me in a room where there are ladies, that is, provided the females are desirable objects, in five minutes or a quarter of an hour at least, my eyes will do great execution upon them; a cannon ball amongst an enemy never did more.

Mr. Duffy – (to the complainant) – This man is evidently deranged; it is much wiser for you to let the matter drop.

Mrs. C. – But what shall I do if he annoys me again, your worship.

Mr. F. – I pity you, my good woman; but I can't help you; many a sorrowful tear I caused fathers and mothers, but I can't help it; it is all in my eye (laughter). Did you ever read Burke on the 'Sublime and Beautiful?' There he lays down that the eye next to the nose is the most expressive feature; and Shakespeare says, talking of eyes,

Would they were basilisks to strike thee dead.

And again –

The poet's eye is a fine frenzy rolling (laughter).

Mr. Duffy – Your eye is certainly very fine, and your forehead appears to be a –

Mr. F. – Oh, yes, I see you have discernment. My chin, people say, is like Shakespeare's, but it is rather too pointed, and the dimple destroys the resemblance. My forehead is like Napoleon's. See those two lines running down towards the bridge of my nose; there the likeness is astonishing. The back of my head, I've heard, is like Caesar's, but of this I am not quite certain. – My bumps, I'm told partake more of the intellectual and less of the animal than his skull.

Mr. Duffy – I think you had better leave your lodgings, if you cannot cease annoying this good woman.

Mr. F. – Oh, that I'll do. Between ourselves (and don't tell anyone), I got notice 'to quit' from my landlady, who is beginning to feel the effects of my eyes (laughter). So you see I must fly out of civilised society; I must turn hermit.

The parties shortly afterwards retired, Mr. F. promising to discontinue his annoyance to the complainant.

*Dublin Evening Post*, 4 July 1839; *Dublin Mercantile Advertiser and Weekly Price Current*, 5 July 1839; *Southern Reporter and Cork Commercial Courier*, 6 July 1839; *Connaught Telegraph*, 10 July 1839.

M r Ferdinand McF—y's appearance before the Dublin magistrates quickly made news across the country, travelling from Dublin to Cork and Galway. His was a knowing performance, actively engaging with the court reporter, 'I wish that to be particularly noted in the press', followed by his theatrical request before an open court 'not to tell anyone'. Accused of harassing the daughter of his neighbour with love songs and notes, McF—y first attempted to deflect criticism by suggesting it was wanted attention and then tried to turn the case into a farce. His demand that the press note that he disliked monkeys and squirrels was bizarre, but it also distracted from the seriousness of Mrs C—'s tale. His suggestion that Miss C— had sent bull's eyes, boiled sweets, played into a popular joke of the period. As James Bruton recorded in his song, 'Love and Lollipops', the protagonist, Sammy, was advised that if he wished to win his beloved, he should look at her with sheep's eyes and murmur sweet nothings.[1] To look at someone with 'sheep's eyes' was to look adoringly. Sammy, not finding sheep's eyes, settled for 'bull's eyes' and presented them to his love, with some rather insulting poetry. Fortunately, his love liked sweets and him into the bargain. Miss C—'s protest that she 'never sent him any eyes' caused laughter because of its dual meaning.

McF—y then suggested the problem arose because of his eyes and their ability to seduce all attractive women. As a defence for sexual harassment, it was not perhaps the most effective, but it was a display of an important form of humour where men carried a topic – in this case 'eyes' – as far as they logically could, drawing in wider literatures that displayed their reading and worldliness.[2] For McF—y demonstrating comic genius was more significant than a display of innocence. At this point, Mr Duffy, the magistrate, recognised what he was doing and encouraged him by drawing attention to his other features. This allowed

McF—y to display his knowledge of phrenology and to locate himself, in physiognomic terms, amongst the great men of history – Shakespeare, Napoleon, Caesar. His genius could not be in doubt if his body spoke to such truth. Duffy ended the performance by suggesting he move house. Not to be bested, McF—y replied that he was already moving because of his landlady's attraction to him. He thus complied with the magistrate's request but refused the reduction of status that such submission required. His public standing was also maintained by the anonymisation of his name in the press, a privilege likely offered due to his social class.

McF—y's appearance before the Dublin Police Court was a remarkable feat of carnivalesque masculinity. Through his performance he claimed to be irresistibly sexually attractive, funny, well read, cosmopolitan and, through his physiognomy, amongst the ranks of the great. Yet, it was also ridiculous, destabilising all these claims. Where truth lay in this performance was ambiguous. Importantly, this ambiguity expanded to encompass Mrs C—'s story. Her claims on justice were almost lost behind his display. A serious case of harassment was dissolved into an analysis of McF—y's behaviour. It was a performance of self that encompassed not only others in court, but the nation as it spread across the country through the press. As a demand for recognition, to be heard and acknowledged within the Irish justice system, it was hugely successful.

Duffy was a seasoned magistrate. He knew better than to lose sight of the core facts, whilst also providing space for McF—y's routine. He warned McF—y that his behaviour might seem 'deranged', directing him to be careful, before encouraging his activities. Duffy also knew the appropriate moment to shut it down and negotiate a compromise. By allowing McF—y to display his 'genius', he encouraged him to conform to his request to move house, something that may have been difficult to legally enforce. Here was a justice enabled through a sympathetic engagement, forced through carnivalesque performance, between the magistrate and defendant.

### Feeling truth

Establishing connection was particularly important in the early nineteenth-century Irish court where sympathy remained vital to determinations of truth. A sympathetic model for social relationships placed emotion at the heart of human communication, where judgement should be based not only on a rational assessment of evidence but on its ability to enliven sympathy within the listener. A truthful performance was one that moved its audience; it was a mode of persuasion that produced appropriate feeling in the listener. Truth was felt. Some social groups, notably women, the poor and non-white peoples, were more amenable to sympathy than others, likely to be overwhelmed by another's performance. Judgement required the ability to exercise self-control over the emotions of others as they acted on the self, ensuring that truth was not lost to another's self-interest. 'Party feeling' was a notable concern as an emotion that reduced the ability to sympathetically engage with others. In a context where truth was created through connection, performances that not only supported, but demanded, engagement from the audience were the more likely to receive justice. As a connection created through sympathy, emotion was an active force in shaping social power and justice.

The production of sympathy required men to be given opportunity to create emotional connections within court. A central way this was achieved was by allowing men to give a performance of self that enabled their character to be revealed and so the truth they offered to be felt. That sympathetic performances were central to the formation of justice has been highlighted throughout this volume as men used an array of strategies, from clothing and the body, to speech acts, to oath-taking, to enable an engagement between men. The courtroom was understood to be a place where truth could be discovered, but it relied on a close reading of those who brought evidence – and so the possibility of truth – before it. Court audiences, including juries and judges, drew on wider cultural norms and values around class, manliness and identity to aid them to read the men who came before them. Such wider value systems were essential in enabling people to make common sense assessments about the value of testimony, but in their reliance on norms of what respectability looked like, opportunities for sympathetic exchange could be reduced as well as enabled.

The testimonies of men who appeared respectable, and had that respectability supported through their social class, character witnesses, and a coherent bodily performance, were given greater weight than that of those for whom this was not achievable. Men who challenged social norms, either through displays of lying or criminality when respectable or who displayed honesty without markers of character, could be conceptually challenging, disrupting everyday understandings of how truth should be determined. Here an achievement of widely admired masculine traits could become more important than character, with men who displayed beautiful bodies, frank openness and talent providing an alternative ground for sympathetic connection. At times, as McF—y's case suggests, sympathy arose not from a comforting familiarity with how to interpret what was on display, but disruption, the demand of the characterless to be viewed on their own terms and not simply as an anonymous member of their class. For the poor, as a group who could not demonstrate character and who threatened the security of the middling sorts, this was vitally important. 'Larger than life' characters exceeded normative expectations and demanded to be heard; carnivalesque performances might also establish a character associated with theatrical talent or eccentricity. Lower-order stories forced themselves into the legal process.

That truth could emerge through disruption and confrontation was a key ideal of the period, perhaps especially evident in the cross-examination. The cross was designed to throw witnesses off-centre, to destabilise and test the narrative of their earlier testimony. Similarly, the act of confronting witnesses with others whose accounts differed was designed to compel truth to emerge. Truth was marked here by consistency and coherence, by the witness who remained 'true' to their account, and by the opportunity for character to be tested when placed under stress. Disruptive masculinities similarly challenged the value judgements made in courtrooms, enabling truth to become visible for those of unrespectable character. The truth transmitted through sympathetic exchange was a form of recognition of 'the other' and the character and identity they claimed for themselves. It placed performances of character at the heart of the legal system and emotion – sympathy – as central to the production of truth.

### Performing manliness; embodying the law

Performances of masculinity became implicated in the making of justice, as it was through recognition of the multiple possibilities for manly identity that sympathetic exchange was enabled. This was a process that enabled the law to be embodied by the men who practiced it. The professional men – lawyers and judges – that signified 'the court' through their costumes and roles, personified the law for the watching public; through the press, their behaviours and personalities became the central representation of legal practice for the public. If other men did not embody 'the law', through performances of character they produced embodied truths, their faces, bodies, emotional displays and physical behaviours contributing to justice as a social practice. The law was produced not in abstract, but as a relationship between men where physical performance – from virility and strength to speech-making and banter – was key to the negotiation of power. If this is not a history of men's subjective experience of embodiment, it is a story of how being embodied shaped men's reception and ability to hold power.

This was not a system that relied, or could function, with a single or dominant ideal for masculinity, as it needed to allow for manly men from all social backgrounds. Ireland was a hierarchical society, a structure that was reinforced through the legal system in its privileging of elite men. Whilst respectability was a key requirement of character, it was displayed differently across social groups. Sartorial respectability was influenced by class, occupation and wealth. Politeness was essential to elite manliness, but it not only had less resonance amongst the poor, but men of this group who affected gentlemanly identities were ridiculed. Manliness required an awareness and performance of social class, stepping beyond its boundaries was fraught with difficulty, as was failing to perform manliness at all.

More complex were men who chose to perform eccentric masculinities that rejected the norms of their class or society more broadly, and not only achieved manliness but shaped broader social power relationships. Such performances were viewed as successful because they were coherent, suggestive of a truthful rendering of character, and because they were assertive claims to identity. Not all such performances were happily received, as the dandies that appeared before the Dublin magistrates found to their dismay. Nor did every performance make a coherent claim, as the uncertainty that arose around McF—y suggests. But a focus on individual performance highlights the difficulties of talking about hierarchies of masculinity, as distinct from those of social class. If elite men held more power than their lower-class brethren, it did not mean that they all successfully achieved manliness, nor that poor men were excluded from its achievement. And when placed in competition, the manly poor man might be more compelling than an unmanly elite.

Rather, power relationships between men were contextually negotiated. Men brought with them different levels of social capital, reinforced by their role and court architecture, that made it easier for some to claim or shape power than others, but all men brought an array of tools to a negotiation of power that was determined in the everyday. In such negotiations, the distinction between authority and resistance was blurred. As a negotiation, the outcome might be predictable but it was ultimately unstable, with men and women able to disrupt normative power structures. As the existence of the gallery suggests, this was not simply a negotiation between individuals. Rather it was a complex, multi-faceted conversation, where an array of men and women communicated, drew on wider social discourse, and created meaning, judged by an audience that affirmed or denied the validity, the truth, of their performances.

As their performances were given meaning through social discourse, the individual could not be understood outside of the wider value structures through which coherence was judged. This placed limits on the boundaries of masculinity and femininity, and the tools for negotiating power, that people could draw on. Notably in the Irish context, men appeared to have a wider array of options for articulating a manly self. Women had a more restricted space in which to perform, with a smaller range of 'respectable' behaviours to access, greater critique of their dress and sexuality, and less tolerance for their playful banter, wit and even authoritative voice. Women who actively challenged lawyers on cross or the judiciary were not just playfully contesting authority, but overstepping the respectable boundaries of femininity. Whilst men could play the criminal and still endow respect for their openness and daring feats, criminal women were condemned as losing their sex. Female character was considerably more fragile.

In contrast, badly behaved men were more widely tolerated. This was a privilege that was afforded to men across the social ladder. Young men of all groups were not expected to always be well behaved, with the high-jinks associated with homosocial bonding, drunkenness, casual violence, womanising, and mischievous banter and wordplay, viewed as normative youthful behaviour – perhaps requiring discipline but not reformulation. As men aged, they were expected to put aside such childish concerns, but many did not. For lower-class men, this might feed into manly performances of criminality or identities as fighters or eccentrics. At times, such displays may have lessened criminal culpability; at other times heightened it, but all were claims to manliness. Middling and elite men might find it more difficult to reconcile such behaviours with the respectable masculine norms required of their social class, but here the willingness of courts to overlook elite bad behaviour came to their aid. Gender and class had its privileges. Performative masculinities reinscribed and destabilised social power relationships, enabling a dynamic system with space for the individual as well as the group, for personal choice alongside social structure.

### The verdict, ensuring justice

If power is the ability to influence the outcome of court proceedings then perhaps a key question within this study is, what difference did such performances make? A fraught question, not least in a context where there is continuing debate around the conviction rate. Whilst most studies are small-scale, it appears that Irish juries were less likely to convict than their

English counterparts. Typically around 30 per cent of cases that came to trial resulted in conviction compared to 60 to 70 per cent in England.[3] The low conviction rate was sometimes a topic of contemporary anxiety, followed by demands to reform the Irish jury system.[4] Yet, the few studies of jury behaviour have suggested that their decision-making was not typically against evidence.[5] This study supports this conclusion, but highlights men's performances as an explanatory factor in how juries made decisions. No single part of a performance – one man's exuberant rhyming for example – can explain an outcome, but when taken alongside other evidence, gendered performances help to explain otherwise ambiguous jury verdicts and judicial judgments. Such determinations are complicated by the narrative structure of court-reporting that usually supported jury decision-making, so that, for example, an acquittal followed a description of a prevaricating or hesitant witness. Such accounts emphasised that justice was served and perhaps reflected a wider investment in the successful functioning of the system that required reporters to explain, as well as describe, jury decisions for their readers.

This is not to say that manly men were always acquitted or that men with poor characters found guilty. But, it is a claim that, at least as reported in the press, the decisions of juries were generally explicable in light of the evidence, including performances of character, presented to them. Where juries went against evidence, the reasons for these decisions were often equally apparent and sometimes viewed sympathetically by the judiciary. It was agreed by everybody that Thomas Bayley killed Philip Turpin in a duel, but after a moving speech by the defence and ambivalent instructions by the judiciary, the not guilty verdict was hardly surprising, nor was the 'evident joy throughout the court'.[6] At least in part, such decisions were informed by the continuance of 'knowing' juries and courtrooms tied closely to their local communities. Where direct evidence was uncertain, juries took character seriously, drawing on the testimonies of witnesses as well as their own contextual knowledge of events. Decision-making was rooted within relationships, identities and sympathetic engagements between men.

This is not to say that justice was always served. As has been demonstrated across this book, that the poor did not have character, as a result of their poverty, whilst the social elite had character as a right of their class, ensured that the court was far from impartial. It was a system that reflected Ireland's hierarchical society and which most people, both rich and poor, broadly accepted as normative. Fairness and justice within this context were not determined by an external set of judgements applied equally to all, but to the contextualised positioning of individuals within their gender, community and nation. During a period of growing demo-cratic ideals, the court's bias against the poor or the lower-class Irish was sometimes open to critique, but such commentary tended to be limited to examples where people were viewed as not having been given a space to perform – the Irish speaker denied the right to testify in Irish or the poor man who was not permitted, or could not afford, to contest the claims of a wealthier antagonist. Within this context, providing room to perform, sometimes at length, was understood by the community as justice in action; that testimonies were weighted differently due to class or accent was acknowledged but received much less critique. The embodiment of social power differentials by Irish men and women natu-ralised these judgements as biological, rather than social, constructs.[7]

### The court in the nation

As a place that brought men, and occasionally women, from across soci-ety together, the activities of which were then broadcast across the nation through the press, the courtroom was significant in the making of the Irish nation. That the court building was the site within local communi-ties to meet and be seen, to host a range of legal and non-legal activities, and, in many places, was the prominent public edifice of the town, acted as a constant reminder of the importance of the law within Irish society; its architecture promoted the significance of truth, justice, and democ-racy to the Irish polity. It was a space that enforced, and recreated, long-standing social hierarchies, producing relationships through the physical placement of actors and the role played in the legal system. The increased space given to the public and to the press in the production of the court is notable then as a key evidence of changing social norms. If much of the history of courtroom performances is a story of continuity, the press's growing confidence in reporting on legal affairs and in representing the wide range of voices and personalities that appeared in court is signifi-cant. Through legal dispute and discussion, the courtroom was a place to explore and rearticulate social relationships. Through the press, the court shaped society itself.

As widely publicised events, court performances were implicated in the making of Irish identity and the Irish nation. Press reports of men in court were one of the longest-running and consistent representations of Irishness available to the public. Moreover, the Irish identity displayed in such reports was progressively marked by its diversity, as not only men from different social classes, but those of different religions, races, cultures, tastes and personalities were depicted. The press provided those that appeared in court with the opportunity to assert the value of their identities to world. Editorial gloss often reinforced prominent social hierarchies and norms of respectability, but the continued willingness of reporters to represent remarkable and sometimes carnivalesque identities provided opportunities for alternative readings. That journalists were situated as external observers and social commentators reinforced their own 'otherness', inviting audiences to engage directly with the men described. Court reporters provided readers with a range of models to accept or reject in the making of their own identities. As a result, courtroom performances helped produce the manly Irishman, turning men's assertions of personal identity into politicised acts of nation-building.

The nation that was being built through the court and its press representations was, perhaps like the law itself, distinctly Irish, but outward-looking, acknowledging its placement within the United Kingdom and the wider world. Local communities used Irish architects and builders when constructing court buildings and furnished them with Irish cloth and materials. Yet, in performing identities, men drew on a range of representations and popular cultures from across the United Kingdom, an important assertion of the cosmopolitanism and civilisation ranked so highly during the period. Individuals weighted such resources in the making of their identities differently, depending on whether they presented themselves as rural and Irish-speaking within a world of folklore and fairytales, or whether they claimed themselves as well-travelled elite men, with polite educations and a code of honourable manliness. Irish identity, depending on the individual, could be complex, multi-faceted and formed through relationships both within and without the nation.

At times, such identity-making could cause the court anxiety; notably poor men's performances remained a consistent challenge to an Irish elites' claim to civility and equality within the political union of the United Kingdom. Generally, however, representations of men in the courtroom were a form of resistance to the Irish identity propagated by a colonial press that located Ireland as parochial, stupid, poor and without character.[8] 'Larger than life', 'crazed', 'voluble' perhaps, but manly nonetheless and so entitled to the associated political and social rights. Manly courtroom performances did not just produce character, truth and justice, but the Irish nation.

### Notes

1 J. Bruton, 'Love and Lollipops', in *The Melodist and Mirthful Olio: An Elegant Collection of the Most Popular Songs . . .* (London: H. Arliss, 1828), vol. 1, pp. 244–6;

see also: S. Moodie, *Life in the Clearing Versus the Bush* (London: Richard Bentley, 1853), pp. 96–7.

2  See also: 'Dublin Police', *Belfast Newsletter* (26 December 1828) Dublin.

3  S.J. Connolly, *Religion, Law and Power: The Making of Protestant Ireland 1660–1760* (Oxford: Clarendon Press, 1992), p. 224; D. Johnson, 'Trial by jury in Ireland 1860–1914', *Legal History*, 17:270 (1996), 273–7.

4  N. Howlin, 'Controlling jury composition in nineteenth-century Ireland', *Journal of Legal History*, 30:3 (2009), 227–61.

5  D. McCabe, '"That part that laws or kings can cause or cure": Crown prosecution and jury trial at Longford assizes, 1830–45', in R. Gillespie and G. Moran (eds), *Longford: Essays in County History* (Dublin: Lilliput Press, 1991), pp. 153–72.

6  'Assize Intelligence', *Dublin Evening Packet and Correspondent* (16 March 1839) King's County/Offaly.

7  A similar point is made for late-nineteenth-century England, M. Wiener, *Reconstructing the Criminal: Culture, Law and Policy in England, 1830–1914* (Cambridge: Cambridge University Press, 1990).

8  P. Curtis, *Apes and Angels: The Irishman in Victorian Caricature* (London: Smithsonian, 1971); M. de Nie, *The Eternal Paddy: Irish Identity and the British Press, 1798–1882* (Madison: University of Wisconsin Press, 2004).

# Select bibliography

**Primary sources**

*Archives*
National Archives of Ireland
CRF Convict Reference Files

*The National Archives, Kew*
HO 45 Home Office Correspondence

*Newspapers*
Armagh Guardian
Ballina Advertiser
Ballina Impartial
Belfast Newsletter
Carlow Morning Post
Carlow Sentinel
Clare Journal
Clonmel Herald
Connaught Journal
Connaught Telegraph
Cork Examiner
Drogheda Conservative Journal
Drogheda Journal or Meath & Louth Advertiser
Dublin Evening Mail
Dublin Evening Packet and Correspondent
Dublin Evening Post
Dublin Medical Press
Dublin Mercantile Advertiser and Weekly Price Current
Dublin Morning Register
Dublin Observer
Dublin Weekly Register
Ennis Chronicle and Clare Advertiser
Enniskillen Chronicle and Erne Packet
Finns Leinster Journal
Freeman's Journal
Galway Patriot
Galway Vindicator and Connaught Advertiser
Glasgow Journal
Irish Examiner
Irish Penny Journal
Kerry Evening Post

*Kerry Examiner*
*Kilkenny Independent*
*Leinster Express*
*Leinster Journal*
*Limerick and Clare Examiner*
*Limerick Chronicle*
*Limerick Reporter*
*London Illustrated News*
*Mayo Mercury*
*Monthly Critic and Magazine*
*Nenagh Guardian*
*Newry Commercial Telegraph*
*Roscommon and Leitrim Gazette*
*Roscommon Messenger*
*Saunder's Newsletter*
*Sligo Champion*
*Sligo Journal*
*Southern Reporter and Cork Commercial Courier*
*Statesmen and Dublin Christian Record*
*The Athlone Sentinel*
*The Law Recorder*
*The Legal Observer, or Journal of Jurisprudence*
*The Nation*
*The Times*
*Tipperary Free Press*
*Tipperary Vindicator*
*Tralee Chronicle*
*Tralee Chronicle and Killarney Echo*
*Tralee Mercury*
*Tuam Herald*
*Waterford Chronicle*
*Waterford Mail*
*Waterford News*
*Weekly Irish Times*
*Weekly Northern Whig*
*Westmeath Journal*
*Wexford Conservative*
*Wexford Independent*

Prints

A Dandy Family Preparing for the General Mourning! (Dublin: McCleary, 1821)
An Exquisite alias Dandy in Distress (Dublin: J. Le Petit, [n.d.])
A Sharpshooter, *Irish March of Intellect; or, The Happy Result of Emancipation*
    (London: S. Gans, 1829)

*A View of the Four Courts* (Dublin: William McCleary, 1809)

Brocas, H., *Emmet on Trial* (1803)

Cruickshank, I., *A Nice Gentleman – an Exquisite Dandy – Prodigious!!* (Dublin: McCleary, 1818)

*Dandies of 1817! . . . The Mosaic Dandy – & Pam* (London: Sidebotham, 1817)

*Dandy Pickpocket's Diving* (Dublin: J. Le Petit, [n.d. c. 1820])

*Daniel O'Connell, 'The Liberator' Defending the Rights of his Countrymen in the Court of Queen's Bench Dublin on the 5th of February, 1844* (Paris: Veuve Turgis, 1844)

Heath, J. after John Comerford, *Charles Kendal Bushe* (1809)

*Mrs. Ellen Byrne, as she appeared at the bar on Monday 15 August 1842* (Dublin: W.H. Holbrooke, [1842–48])

*The Dandy's Disaster* (Dublin: J. Le Petit, [1818])

*The Dandy's Disaster!* (Dublin: McCleary, [n. d.])

*The First Day of Term! Blessings of Ireland or A Flight of Lawyers* (Dublin: McCleary, 1817)

*Trial of Daniel O'Connell* (1844)


## Select printed primary sources

*An Authentic Report of the Trial of Thomas Lidwell, esq on an Indictment for a Rape committed on the Body of Mrs Sarah Sutton . . . at Naas, Lent Assizes* (Dublin: W. Wilson, 1800)

*A Report of the Speeches of Charles Kendal Bushe, esq, in the Cases of Edward Sheriden, M.D., and Mr Thomas Kirwan, Merchant for Misdemeanours* (Dublin: M.N. Mahon, 1812)

*Authenticated Report of the Trial of Thomas Reynolds for Riot and Assault* (Dublin: W. Warren, 1835)

*Dublin Delineated in Twenty-Eight Views of the Principle Public Buildings* (Dublin: G. Tyrrell, 1831)

*Irish Eloquence: The Speeches of the Celebrated Irish Orators Philips, Curran and Grattan, to which is added the Powerful Appeal of Robert Emmet* (Boston: Patrick Donahoe, 1857)

*John Grey Vesey Porter, esq., Defendant. Report of the Trial of an Action for Libel* (Dublin: Goodwin, Son and Nethercott, 1859)

*The Speeches of Charles Phillips, Esq., Delivered at the Bar, and on Various Public Occasions* (London and Dublin: W. Simpkin and R. Marshall, and Milliken, 1822).

*The Trial of John Magee, Proprietor of the Dublin Evening Post, for publishing an Historical Review* (Dublin: John Magee, 1813).

*The Trial of John Magee, Proprietor of the Dublin Evening Post . . .* (Dublin: John Magee, 1813)

Austin, G., *Chironomia: Or a Treatise on Rhetorical Delivery* (London: T. Cadell and W. Davies, 1806)

Beattie, J., *Essays on Poetry and Music as they Affect the Mind* (Edinburgh: Edward and Charles Dilly, 1788)

Blair, H., *Lectures on Rhetoric and Belles Lettres* (London: Charles Daly, 1839)

Burke, E., *A Philosophical Enquiry into the Origin of Our Ideas of the Sublime and Beautiful* (London: J. Dodsley, 1767)

Campbell, G., *The Philosophy of Rhetoric*, 2 volumes (London: W. Strahan and T. Cadell, 1776)

Carlyle, T., *Sartor Resartus: The Life and Opinions of Herr Teufelsdröckh*, 3 volumes (London: Chapman and Hall, 1831)

Cooke, T., *A Practical and Familiar View of the Science of Physiognomy* (London: Camberwell Press, 1819)

Curran, W., *The Life of the Right Honourable John Philpot Curran, Later Master of the Rolls in Ireland* (New York: William H. Creagh, 1820)

Curry, W., *The Picture of Dublin: Or, Stranger's Guide to the Irish Metropolis* (Dublin: William Curry, 1835)

Cusack, M., *The Liberator: His Life and Times, Political and Social* (Kenmare: Kenmare Publications, 1850)

David, T., *The Speeches of the Right Honorable John Philpot Curran* (London: Henry G. Bohn, 1847)

Davis, T. (ed.), *The Speeches of the Right Honourable John Philpot Curran* (London: Henry Bohn, 1847)

Edgeworth, R. and M. Edgeworth, *An Essay on Irish Bulls* (New York: J. Swaine, 1803)

Ensor, G., *The Independent Man: Or, An Essay on the Formation and Development of those Formation and Faculties of the Human Mind, which constitute Moral and Intellectual Excellence*, 2 volumes (London: R. Taylor, 1806)

Finlay, J., *Member of the Bar, The Speeches of the Celebrated Irish Orators Philips, Curran and Grattan* (Philadelphia: Desilver, Thomas & Co., 1836)

Griffin, G., *Talis Qualis, or, Tales of the Jury Room*, 3 volumes (London: Maxwell and Co., 1842)

Hall, S. and A.M. Hall, *Ireland: Its Scenery, Character, &c* (London: How and Parsons, 1842)

Hardy, P.D., *The New Picture of Dublin: Or Stranger's Guide through the Irish Metropolis* (Dublin: William Curry, Jun. and Co., 1831)

Lavater, J., *Physiognomy* (London: Cowie, Low & Co., 1826)

Lewis, S., *A Topographical Dictionary of Ireland* (London: S. Lewis, 1837)

Locke, J., *Essay Concerning Human Understanding*, 3 volumes (London: Thomas Tegg, R. Griffin and Co., Glasgow and J. Cumming, Dublin, 1828)

MacNally, L., *The Rules of Evidence on Pleas of the Crown* (Dublin: J. Cooke, 1802)

Macnevin, T., *The Speeches of the Right Honourable Richard Lalor Sheil* (Dublin: James Duffy, 1865)

Mongan, J., *A Report of the Trial of the Action in which Bartholomew McGarahan was the Plaintiff and the Rev Thomas Maguire was the Defendant . . .* (Dublin: Westley and Tyrrell, 1827)

Montagu, B., *Thoughts on Laughter by a Chancery Barrister* (London: William Pickering, 1830)

O'Flanagan, J.R., *The Irish Bar: Comprises Anecdotes, Bon-Mots, and Biographical Sketches of the Bench and Bar of Ireland* (London: Sampson Low, Marston, Searle, & Rivington, 1879)

Phillips, C., *Curran and His Contemporaries*, 4th edition (Edinburgh: William Blackwood, 1851)

Phillips, C., *Specimens of Irish Eloquence* (London: William Edwards, 1819)

Ridgeway, W., *The Trial of Robert Emmet for High Treason* (Edinburgh: Peter Hill 1803)

Sheil, R., *The Speeches of the Right Honourable Richard Lalor Sheil* (Dublin: James Duffy, 1865)

Sheil, R.L., *Sketches, Legal and Political*, ed. M.W. Savage, 2 volumes (London: Henry Colburn, 1855)

Sheil, R.L., *Sketches of the Irish Bar*, ed. R. Shelton Mackenzie, 2 volumes (New York: Redfield, 1854)

Warburton, J., J. Whitelaw and R. Walsh, *History of the City of Dublin: From the Earliest Accounts to the Present Time* (London: T. Cadell and W. Davies, 1818)

Wright, G., *An Historical Guide to the City of Dublin* (London: Baldwin, Cradock, and Joy, 1825)

## Select secondary sources

Ahmed, S., *The Cultural Politics of Emotion* (Edinburgh: Edinburgh University Press, 2004)

Ahnert, T. and S. Manning (eds), *Character, Self, and Sociability in the Scottish Enlightenment* (Basingstoke: Palgrave Macmillan, 2009)

Anderson, B., *Imagined Communities: Reflections on the Origin and Spread of Nationalism* (London: Verso, 1983)

Andrews, D., *Aristocratic Vice: The Attack on Duelling, Suicide, Adultery, and Gambling in Eighteenth-Century England* (New Haven: Yale University Press, 2013)

Bailey, J., '"A very sensible man": Imagining fatherhood in England, c. 1750–1830', *History*, 95 (2010)

Ballinger, A., 'Masculinity in the dock: Legal responses to male violence and female retaliation in England and Wales, 1900–1965', *Social and Legal Studies*, 16:4 (2007)

Barad, K., *Meeting the Universe Halfway: Quantum Physics and the Entanglement of Matter and Meaning* (Durham, NC: Duke University Press, 2011)

Barclay, K., 'Narrative, law and emotion: Husband killers in early nineteenth-century Ireland', *Journal of Legal History*, 38:2 (2017)

Barclay, K., 'Stereotypes as political resistance: The Irish police court columns, c. 1820–1845', *Social History*, 42:2 (2017)

Barclay, K., 'Emotions, the law and the press in Britain: Seduction and breach of promise suits, 1780–1830', *Journal of Eighteenth-Century Studies*, 39:2 (2016)

Barclay, K., 'Manly magistrates and citizenship in an Irish town: Carlow, 1820–1840', in K. Cowman, N. Koefoed and Å.K. Sjögren (eds), *Gender in Urban Europe: Sites of Political Activity and Citizenship, 1750–1900* (London: Routledge, 2014)

Barclay, K., 'Singing and lower-class masculinity in the Dublin Magistrate's Court, 1800–1845', *Journal of Social History*, 47:3 (2014)

Barker, H., 'Soul, purse and family: Middling and lower-class masculinity in eighteenth-century Manchester', *Social History*, 33:1 (2008)

Barker-Benfield, G.J., *The Culture of Sensibility: Sex and Society in Eighteenth Century Britain* (London: Chicago University Press, 1992)

Barrie, D.G. and S. Broomhall, *Police Courts in Nineteenth-Century Scotland, Volume 1: Magistrates, Media and the Masses* (Farnham: Ashgate, 2014)

Bates, V., '"Under cross-examination she fainted": Sexual crime and swooning in the Victorian courtroom', *Journal of Victorian Culture*, 21:4 (2016)

Beattie, J.M., 'Scales of justice: Defense counsel and the English criminal trial in the eighteenth and nineteenth centuries', *Law and History Review*, 9:2 (1991)

Beattie, J.M., *Crime and the Courts in England, 1660–1800* (Oxford: Oxford University Press, 1986)

Beiner, G., *Remembering the Year of the French: Irish Folk History and Social Memory* (Madison: University Wisconsin Press, 2007)

Bew, J., *The Glory of Being Britons: Civic Unionism in Nineteenth-Century Belfast* (Dublin: Irish Academic Press, 2009)

Bland, L., *Modern Women on Trial: Sexual Transgression in the Age of the Flapper* (Manchester: Manchester University Press, 2013)

Bloom, G., 'Manly drunkenness: Binge drinking as disciplined play', in A. Bailey and R. Hentschell (eds), *Masculinity and the Metropolis of Vice, 1550–1650* (Basingstoke: Palgrave Macmillan, 2010)

Bonsall, P., *The Irish RMs: The Resident Magistrates of the British Administration in Ireland* (Dublin: Four Courts Press, 1997)

Bourdieu, P., *Outline of a Theory of Practice* (Cambridge: Cambridge University Press, 1972)

Bourke, A., *The Burning of Bridget Cleary: A True Story* (London: Pimlico, 1999)

Bourke, A., 'Reading a woman's death: Colonial text and oral tradition in nineteenth-century Ireland', *Feminist Studies*, 21:3 (1995)

Brady, J.C., 'Legal developments, 1801–79', in W.E. Vaughan (ed.), *A New History of Ireland: V: Ireland Under the Union, 1 1801–70* (Oxford: Oxford University Press, 2010)

Brett, C.E.B., *Court Houses and Market Houses of the Province of Ulster* (Belfast: Ulster Architectural Heritage Society, 1973)

Breward, C., 'Masculine pleasures: Metropolitan identities and the commercial sites of Dandyism, 1790–1840', *London Journal*, 28:1 (2003)

Brickell, C., 'Masculinities, performativity, and subversion: A sociological reappraisal', *Men and Masculinities*, 8 (2005)

Broderick, D., *Local Government in Nineteenth-Century County Dublin: The Grand Jury* (Dublin: Four Courts Press, 2007)

Broeker, G., *Rural Disorder and Police Reform in Ireland, 1812–1836* (London: Routledge, 1970)

Bromwich, W., '"Mrs Buckley you're telling a pack of lies": Cross-examination in the High Court Justiciary in Edinburgh', in C. Williams and G. Tessuto (eds), *Language in the Negotiation of Justice: Contexts, Issues and Applications* (Farnham: Ashgate, 2013)

Brookes, C.W., *Law, Politics and Society in Early Modern England* (Cambridge: Cambridge University Press, 2008)

Broomhall, S. and J. Van Gent (eds), *Governing Masculinities in the Early Modern Period* (Aldershot: Ashgate, 2011)

Brown, M. and S.P. Donlan (eds), *The Laws and Other Legalities of Ireland, 1689–1850* (Farnham: Ashgate, 2011)

Butler, J., *Gender Trouble: Feminism and the Subversion of Identity* (London: Routledge, 1999)

Cairns, D., *Advocacy and the Making of the Adversarial Criminal Trial, 1800–1864* (Oxford: Oxford University Press, 1999)

Carlen, P., *Magistrate's Justice* (London: Martin Robinson, 1976)

Carr, R., *Gender and Enlightenment Culture in Eighteenth-Century Edinburgh* (Edinburgh: Edinburgh University Press, 2014)

Carter, L., 'British masculinities on trial in the Queen Caroline affair of 1820', *Gender & History*, 20:2 (2008)

Carter, P., *Men and the Emergence of Polite Society, Britain 1660–1800* (Harlow: Pearson Education, 2001)

Cashman, R., 'The heroic outlaw in Irish folklore and popular literature', *Folklore*, 111:2 (2000)

Clark, A., *Scandal: The Sexual Politics of the British Constitution* (Princeton: Princeton University Press, 2004)

Clark, A., *The Struggle for the Breeches: Gender and the Making of the British Working Class* (Berkeley: University of California Press, 1995)

Cohen, M., '"Manners" make the man: Politeness, chivalry, and the construction of masculinity, 1750–1830', *Journal of British Studies*, 44 (2005)

Cohen, M. and N.J. Curtin (eds), *Reclaiming Gender: Transgressive Identities in Modern Ireland* (New York: St Martin's Press, 1999)

Collini, S., 'The idea of "character" in Victorian political thought', *Transactions of the Royal Historical Society*, 35 (1985)

Conley, C., *Certain Other Countries: Homicide, Gender, and National Identity in Late Nineteenth-Century England, Ireland, Scotland and Wales* (Columbus: Ohio State University Press, 2007)

Connell, R., 'Hegemonic masculinity: Rethinking the concept', *Gender & Society*, 19 (2005)

Connelly, S.J., *Priests and People in Pre-Famine Ireland, 1780–1845* (Dublin: Four Courts Press, 2001)

Connolly, S.J., *Religion, Law and Power: The Making of Protestant Ireland 1660–1760* (Oxford: Clarendon Press, 1992)

Copley, P.G., *The Rhetoric of Sensibility in Eighteenth-Century Culture* (Cambridge: Cambridge University Press, 2005)

Corfield, P., *Power and the Professions in Britain 1700–1850* (London: Routledge, 1995)

Costello, C. (ed.), *The Four Courts: 200 Years. Essays to Commemorate the Bicentenary of the Four Courts* (Dublin: Incorporated Council of Law Reporting for Ireland, 1996)

Crossman, V., *Local Government in Nineteenth-Century Ireland* (Belfast: Institute of Irish Studies, 1994)

Curtin, N., *The United Irishmen: Popular Politics in Ulster and Dublin, 1791–1798* (Oxford: Clarendon Press, 1994)

Davis, L., *Music, Postcolonialism, and Gender: The Construction of Irish National Identity, 1724–1874* (Notre Dame: Notre Dame University Press, 2006)

de Nie, M., *The Eternal Paddy: Irish Identity and the British Press, 1798–1882* (Madison: University of Wisconsin Press, 2004)

Desan, S. and J. Merrick, *Family, Gender and the Law in Early Modern France* (University Park: Pennsylvania State University Press, 2010)

Dickie, S., *Cruelty & Laughter: Forgotten Comic Literature and the Unsentimental Eighteenth Century* (Chicago: University of Chicago Press, 2011)

Dixon, T., 'The tears of Mr Justice Willes', *Journal of Victorian Culture*, 17:1 (2012)

Dolan, A., P.M. Geoghegan and D. Jones (eds), *Reinterpreting Emmet: Essays on the Life and Legacy of Robert Emmet* (Dublin: UCD Press, 2007)

Donnelly, J.S., *Captain Rock: The Irish Agrarian Rebellion of 1821–1824* (Madison: University of Wisconsin Press, 2009)

Donnelly, J.S. and K.A. Miller (eds), *Irish Popular Culture 1650–1850* (Dublin: Irish Academic Press, 1998)

Downing, K., 'The gentleman boxer: Boxing, manners and masculinity in eighteenth century England', *Men and Masculinities*, 12 (2010)

Duman, D., *The Judicial Bench in England, 1727–1875: The Reshaping of Professional Elite* (London: Royal Historical Society, 1982)

Epstein, J.A., *Radical Expression: Political Language, Ritual and Symbol in England, 1790–1850* (Oxford: Oxford University Press, 1994)

Fairclough, M., *The Romantic Crowd: Sympathy, Controversy and Print Culture* (Cambridge: Cambridge University Press, 2013)

Finn, M., *The Character of Credit: Personal Debt in English Culture, 1740–1914* (Cambridge: Cambridge University Press, 2003)

Flather, A., *Gender and Space in Early Modern England* (Woodbridge: Boydell and Brewer, 2007)

Foyster, E., *Manhood in Early Modern England: Honour, Sex and Marriage* (Harlow: Longman, 1999)

Frazer, M., *The Enlightenment of Sympathy: Justice and the Moral Sentiments in the Eighteenth Century and Today* (Oxford: Oxford University Press, 2010)

Garnham, N., *The Courts, Crime and the Criminal Law in Ireland, 1692–1760* (Dublin: Irish Academic Press, 1996)

Gaskill, M., *Crime and Mentalities in Early Modern England* (Cambridge: Cambridge University Press, 2000)

Gattrell, V.A.C., *The Hanging Tree: Execution and the English People, 1770–1868* (Oxford: Oxford University Press, 1994)

Goffman, E., *The Presentation of the Self in Everyday Life* (New York: Anchor Books, 1959)

Gowing, L., *Domestic Dangers: Women, Words and Sex in Early Modern London* (New York: Oxford University Press, 1996)

Graham, C., *Ordering Law: The Architectural and Social History of the English Law Court to 1914* (Aldershot: Ashgate, 2003)

Green, T.A., *Verdict According to Conscience: Perspectives on the English Criminal Trial Jury, 1200–1800* (Chicago: University of Chicago Press, 1985)

Gregson, N. and G. Rose, 'Taking Butler elsewhere: Performativities, spatialities and subjectivities', *Environment and Planning D: Society and Space*, 18 (2000)

Hamlin, C., 'Forensic cultures in historical perspective: Technologies of witness, testimony, judgment (and justice?)', *Studies in History and Philosophy of Biological and Biomedical Sciences*, 44 (2013)

Hammerton, A.J., *Cruelty and Companionship: Conflict in Nineteenth Century Married Life* (London: Routledge, 1992)

Harvey, K., 'Men making home: Masculinity and domesticity in eighteenth-century Britain', *Gender & History*, 21:3 (2009)

Harvey, K. and A. Shepard, 'What have historians done with masculinity? Reflections on five centuries of British history, circa 1500–1950', *Journal of British Studies*, 44 (2005)

Hay, D., 'Property, authority and the criminal law', in D. Hay, P. Linebaugh, J.G. Rule, E.P. Thompson and C. Winslow (eds), *Albion's Fatal Tree: Crime and Society in Eighteenth-Century England* (London: Verso, 1975)

Hickey, É., *Irish Law and Lawyers in Modern Folk Tradition* (Dublin: Four Courts Press, 1999)

Higgins, P., *A Nation of Politicians: Gender, Patriotism and Political Culture in Late Eighteenth-Century Ireland* (Madison: University of Wisconsin Press, 2010)

Hill, J., *From Patriots to Unionists: Dublin Civic Politics and Irish Protestant Patriotism, 1660–1840* (Oxford: Oxford University Press, 1997)

Hindley, R., *The Death of the Irish Language* (London: Routledge, 1990)

Hitchcock, T. and M. Cohen (eds), *English Masculinities 1660–1800* (London: Longman, 1999)

Hogan, D., *The Legal Profession in Ireland 1789–1922* (Dublin: Incorporated Law Society of Ireland, 1986)

Hogan, D. and W.N. Osborough (eds), *Brehons, Serjeants and Attorneys: Studies in the History of the Irish Legal Profession* (Dublin: Irish Academic Press, 1990)

Hostettler, J., *A History of Criminal Justice in England and Wales* (Hook: Waterside Press, 2009)

Houston, R.A., *Peasant Petitions: Social Relations and Economic Life on Landed Estates, 1600–1850* (Basingstoke: Palgrave Macmillan, 2014)

Howlin, N., 'Irish jurors: Passive observers or active participants?', *Journal of Legal History*, 35:2 (2014)

Howlin, N., 'Nineteenth-century criminal justice: Uniquely Irish or simply "not English"', *Irish Journal of Legal Studies*, 3:1 (2013)

Howlin, N., 'Fenians, foreigners and jury trials in Ireland, 1865–70', *Irish Jurist*, 46 (2011)

Howlin, N., 'Controlling jury composition in nineteenth-century Ireland', *Journal of Legal History*, 30:3 (2009)

Huck, C., 'Clothes make the Irish: Irish dressing and the question of identity', *Irish Studies Review*, 11:3 (2003)

Hug, T.B., *Impostures in Early Modern England: Representations and Perceptions of Fraudulent Identities* (Manchester: Manchester University Press, 2009)

Inglis, B., *The Freedom of the Press in Ireland, 1784–1841* (Westport: Greenwood Press Publishers, 1975)

Johnson, D., 'Trial by jury in Ireland 1860–1914', *Legal History*, 17:270 (1996)

Johnson, N.E. (ed.), *Impassioned Jurisprudence: Law, Literature, and Emotion, 1760–1848* (Lewisburg: Bucknell University Press, 2015).

Kamensky, J., *Governing the Tongue: The Politics of Speech in Early New England* (Oxford: Oxford University Press, 1997)

Kelly, J., *'That Damn'd Thing Called Honour': Duelling in Ireland, 1570–1860* (Cork: Cork University Press, 1995)

Kennedy, C., '"A Gallant Nation": Chivalric masculinity and Irish nationalism in the 1790s', in M. McCormack (ed.), *Public Men: Masculinity and Politics in Modern Britain* (Basingstoke: Palgrave Macmillan, 2007)

Kenny, C., *Tristram Kennedy and the Revival of Irish Legal Training, 1835–1885* (Dublin: Irish Academic Press, 1996)

Kerr, D.A., *A Nation of Beggars? Priests, People, and Politics in Famine Ireland, 1846–1852* (Oxford: Clarendon Press, 1994)

Kesselring, K.J., 'No greater provocation? Adultery and the mitigation of murder in English law', *Law and History Review*, 34:1 (2016)

Kilcommins, S., I. O'Donnell, E. Sullivan and B. Vaughan, *Crime, Punishment and the Search for Order in Ireland* (Dublin: Institute of Public Administration, 2004)

King, P., *Crime, Justice and Discretion in England, 1740–1820* (Oxford: Oxford University Press, 2003)

Klerman, D., 'Was the jury ever self-informing?' *Southern Californian Law Review*, 77 (2003)

Kreilkamp, V., 'Losing it all: The unmanned Irish landlord', in M. Cohen and N.J. Curtin (eds), *Reclaiming Gender: Transgressive Identities in Modern Ireland* (New York: St Martin's Press, 1999)

Lacey, N., *Women, Crime and Character: From Moll Flanders to Tess of the D'Urbervilles* (Oxford: Oxford University Press, 2008)

Laird, H., *Subversive Law in Ireland, 1879–1920: From Unwritten Law to Dail Courts* (Dublin: Four Courts Press, 2005)

Landsman, S., 'Rise of the contentious spirit: Adversary procedure in eighteenth-century England', *Cornell Law Review*, 74:3 (1990)

Langbein, J.H., *The Origins of Adversary Criminal Trial* (Oxford: Oxford University Press, 2005)

Langford, P., *Englishness Identified: Manners and Character, 1650–1850* (Oxford: Oxford University Press, 2000)

Lefebvre, H., *The Production of Space*, trans. D. Nicholson-Smith (London: Wiley, 1991)

Lemmings, D., 'Emotions, courtrooms and popular opinion about the administration of justice: The English experience, from Coke's "Artificial Reason" to the sensibility of "True Crime Stories"', *Emotions: History, Culture, Society*, 1:1 (2017)

Lemmings, D., 'Criminal trial procedure in eighteenth-century England: The impact of lawyers', *Journal of Legal History*, 26:1 (2005)

Lemmings, D., *Professors of the Law: Barristers and English Legal Culture in the Eighteenth Century* (Oxford: Oxford University Press, 2003)

Lemmings, D. (ed.), *Crime, Courtrooms and the Public Sphere in Britain, 1700–1850* (Farnham: Ashgate, 2012)

Lemmings, D. (ed.), *The British and their Laws in the Eighteenth Century* (Woodbridge: Boydell Press, 2005)

Linebaugh, P., *The London Hanged: Crime and Civil Society in the Eighteenth Century* (Cambridge: Verso, 1992)

Lloyd, D., *Irish Culture and Colonial Modernity, 1800–2000: The Transformation of Oral Space* (Cambridge: Cambridge University Press, 2011)

Lyons, M., *The Writing Culture of Ordinary People in Europe, c. 1860–1920* (Cambridge: Cambridge University Press, 2013)

Malcolm, E., '"The reign of terror in Carlow": The politics of policing Ireland in the late 1830s', *Irish Historical Studies*, 32:125 (2000)

Mangan, J.A., 'Images for confident control: Stereotypes in imperial discourse', *International Journal of the History of Sport*, 27:1–2 (2010)

May, A., *The Bar & the Old Bailey, 1750–1850* (Chapel Hill: University of North Carolina Press, 2003)

McCabe, D., 'Open court: Law and the expansion of magisterial jurisdiction at petty sessions in nineteenth-century Ireland', in N.M Dawson (ed.), *Reflections on Law and History: Irish Legal History Society Discourses and Other Papers, 2000–2005* (Dublin: Four Courts Press, 2006)

McCabe, D., '"That part that laws or kings can cause or cure": Crown prosecution and jury trial at Longford assizes, 1830–45', in R. Gillespie and G. Moran (eds), *Longford: Essays in County History* (Dublin: Lilliput Press, 1991)

McCabe, D., 'Magistrates, peasants, and the Petty Sessions courts: Mayo 1823–50', *Cathair na Mart*, 5:1 (1985)

McCormack, M., *The Independent Man: Citizenship and Gender Politics in Georgian England* (Manchester: Manchester University Press, 2006)

McCormack, M. (ed.), *Public Men: Masculinity and Politics in Modern Britain* (Basingstoke: Palgrave Macmillan, 2007)

McDevitt, P., 'Muscular Catholicism: Nationalism, masculinity and Gaelic team sports, 1884–1916', *Gender & History*, 9:2 (1997)

McDowell, R.B., 'The Irish courts of law, 1801–1914', *Irish Historical Studies*, 10:40 (1957)

McEldowney, J., 'Crown prosecutions in nineteenth-century Ireland', in D. Hay and F. Snyder (eds), *Policing and Prosecution in Britain 1750–1850* (Oxford: Clarendon Press, 1989)

McEldowney, J.F. and P. O'Higgins, *The Common Law Tradition: Essays in Irish Legal History* (Dublin: Irish Academic Press, 1990)

McEntee, J., '"Gentlemen practisers": Solicitors as elites in mid-nineteenth-century Irish landed society', in C. O'Neill (ed.), *Irish Elites in the Nineteenth Century* (Dublin: Four Courts Press, 2013)

McGowen, R., 'A powerful sympathy: Terror, the prison and humanitarian reform in early nineteenth-century Britain', *Journal of British Studies*, 25:3 (1986)

McLaren, A., *Trials of Masculinity: Policing Sexual Boundaries, 1870–1930* (London: University of Chicago Press, 1999)

McMahon, R., *Homicide in Pre-Famine and Famine Ireland* (Liverpool: Liverpool University Press, 2013)

McMahon, R. (ed.), *Crime, Law and Popular Culture in Europe, 1500–1900* (Collumpton: Willan, 2008)

McMahon, V., 'Reading the body: Dissection and the "murder" of Sarah Stout, Hertfordshire, 1699', *Social History of Medicine*, 19:1 (2006)

Meisel, J.S., *Public Speech and the Culture of Public Life in the Age of Gladstone* (New York: Columbia University Press, 2007)

Mirala, P., 'Lawful and unlawful oaths in late-eighteenth and early-nineteenth-century Ireland', 1760–1835', in A. Blackstock and E. Magennis (eds), *Politics and Political Culture in Britain and Ireland, 1750–1850* (Belfast: Ulster Historical Foundation, 2007)

Mulcahy, L., *Legal Architecture: Justice, Due Process and the Place of Law* (London: Routledge, 2010)

Mulcahy, L., 'Architectural precedent: The Manchester assize courts and monuments to law in the mid-Victorian era', *King's Law Journal*, 19:3 (2008)

Munter, R., *The History of the Irish Newspaper 1685–1760* (Cambridge: Cambridge, University Press, 1967)

Murphy, K., 'Judge, jury, magistrate and soldier: Rethinking law and authority in late eighteenth-century Ireland', *American Journal of Legal History*, 44 (2000)

Nash, C., 'Men again: Irish masculinity, nature and nationhood in the early twentieth century', *Cultural Geographies*, 3 (1996)

Neal, D., 'Suits make the man: Masculinity in two English law courts, c. 1500', *Canadian Journal of History*, 37 (2002)

Ní Laoire, C., '"You're Not a Man at All!": Masculinity, responsibility and staying on the land in contemporary Ireland', *Irish Journal of Sociology*, 14:2 (2005)

Nugent, J., 'The sword and the prayerbook: Ideals of authentic Irish manliness', *Victorian Studies*, 50:4 (2008)

Ó Ciosáin, N., 'Oral culture, literacy and the growth of a popular readership, 1800–1850', in J.H. Murphy (ed.), *The Oxford History of the Irish Book* (Oxford: Oxford University Press 2011)

O'Donnell, K., 'Affect and the history of women, gender and masculinity', in M. Valiulis (ed.), *Gender and Power in Irish History* (Dublin: Irish Academic Press, 2009)

O'Dowd, M., 'Women and the Irish chancery court in the late sixteenth and early seventeenth centuries', *Irish Historical Studies*, 31:124 (1999)

O'Gorman, F., 'Campaign rituals and ceremonies: The social meaning of elections in England 1780–1860', *Past and Present*, 135 (1992)

Oldham, J., 'Truth-telling in the eighteenth-century English courtroom', *Law and History Review*, 12:1 (1994)

Phillips, N., 'Parenting the profligate son: Masculinity, gentility, and juvenile delinquency in England, 1791–1814', *Gender & History*, 22:1 (2010)

Philpin, C.H.E. (ed.), *Nationalism and Popular Protest in Ireland* (Cambridge: Cambridge University Press, 2002)

Powell, M.J., 'Credit, debt and patriot politics in Dublin, 1763–1784', *Eighteenth-Century Ireland*, 25 (2010)

Powell, M.J., 'Ireland: Radicalism, rebellion and union', in H.T. Dickinson (ed.), *A Companion to Eighteenth-Century Britain* (Oxford: Wiley-Blackwell, 2002)

Prothero, I.J., *Radical Artisans in England and France, 1830–1870* (Cambridge: Cambridge University Press, 1997)

Rabin, D.Y., *Identity, Crime and Legal Responsibility in Eighteenth-Century England* (Basingstoke: Palgrave Macmillan, 2004)

Richmond, V., *Clothing the Poor in Nineteenth-Century England* (Cambridge: Cambridge University Press, 2013)

Robb, G. and N. Erber (eds), *Disorder in the Court: Trials and Sexual Conflict at the Turn of the Century* (Basingstoke: Macmillan, 1999)

Roberts, M.J.D., 'Public and private in early nineteenth-century London: The Vagrant Act of 1822 and its enforcement', *Social History*, 13:3 (1988)

Rock, P., 'Witnesses and space in a crown court', *British Journal of Criminology*, 31:3 (1991)

Rose M., 'The seductions of resistance: Power, politics, and a performative style of systems', *Environment and Planning D: Society and Space*, 20 (2002)

Rudolph, J., 'Gender and the development of forensic science: A case study', *English Historical Review*, 123:503 (2008)

Scott, J.C., *Domination and the Arts of Resistance: Hidden Transcripts* (New Haven: Yale University Press, 1990)

Scott, J.C., *Weapons of the Weak: Everyday Forms of Peasant Resistance* (New Haven: Yale University Press, 1983)

Shapin, S., *A Social History of Truth: Civility and Science in Seventeenth-Century England* (Chicago: Chicago University Press, 1994)

Shapiro, B., *A Culture of Fact: England, 1550–1720* (Ithaca: Cornell University Press, 2000)

Shapiro, B., *Beyond Reasonable Doubt and Probable Cause: Historical Perspectives on the Anglo-American Law of Evidence* (Berkeley: University of California University Press, 1991)

Sharpe, J.A., 'The people and the law', in B. Reay (ed.), *Popular Culture in Seventeenth Century England* (London: Croom Helm, 1985)

Shepard, A., *Meanings of Manhood in Early Modern England* (Oxford: Oxford University Press, 2003)

Shoemaker, R., 'The street robber and the gentleman highwayman: Changing representations and perceptions of robbery in London, 1690–1800', *Cultural and Social History*, 3 (2006)

Smyth, W.J., 'A plurality of Irelands: Regions, societies and mentalities', in B. Graham (ed.), *In Search of Ireland: A Cultural Geography* (London: Routledge, 1997)

Staves, S., 'British seduced maidens', *Eighteenth-Century Studies*, 14:2 (1980–81)

Steinbach, S., 'From redress to farce: Breach of promise theatre in cultural context, 1830–1920', *Journal of Victorian Culture*, 13 (2008)

Steinbach, S., 'The melodramatic contract: Breach of promise and the performance of virtue', *Nineteenth-Century Studies*, 14 (2000)

Styles, J., *The Dress of the People: Everyday in Fashion in Eighteenth-Century England* (London: Yale University Press, 2008)

Tosh, J., *A Man's Place: Masculinity and the Middle-Class Home in Victorian England* (New Haven: Yale University Press, 1999)

Valente, J., *The Myth of Manliness in Irish National Culture, 1880–1922* (Urbana: University of Illinois Press, 2011)

Wahrman, D., *Imagining the Middle Class: The Political Representation of Class in Britain, c. 1780–1840* (Cambridge: Cambridge University Press, 1995)

Wall, M., 'The rise of a Catholic middle class in eighteenth-century Ireland', *Irish Historical Studies*, 11:42 (1958)

Waters, M., *The Comic Irishman* (Albany: State University of New York Press, 1984)

Whelan, K., *The Tree of Liberty: Radicalism, Catholicism and the Construction of Irish Identity 1760–1830* (Cork: Cork University Press, 1996)

White, B., 'The criminal confessions of Newgate's Irishmen', *Irish Studies Review*, 14:3 (2006)

Whitman, J.Q., *The Origins of Reasonable Doubt: Theological Roots of the Criminal Trial* (New Haven: Yale University Press, 2008)

Wiener, M., *Men of Blood: Violence, Manliness and Criminal Justice in Victorian England* (Cambridge: Cambridge University Press, 2004)

Wiener, M., 'Judges v. jurors: Courtroom tensions in murder trials and the law of criminal responsibility in nineteenth-century England', *Law and History Review*, 17:1 (1999)

Wiener, M., *Reconstructing the Criminal: Culture, Law and Policy in England, 1830–1914* (Cambridge: Cambridge University Press, 1990)

Wolf, N., *An Irish-Speaking Island: State, Religion, Community, and the Linguistic Landscape in Ireland, 1770–1870* (Madison: University of Wisconsin Press, 2014)

# Index

Lightning Source UK Ltd.
Milton Keynes UK
UKHW010235241120
373986UK00001B/53

9 781526 132925